ROUTLEDGE LIBRARY EDITIONS: ACCOUNTING HISTORY

Volume 17

EDUCATION FOR THE MERCANTILE COUNTING HOUSE

T0384410

EDUCATION FOR THE MERCANTILE COUNTING HOUSE

Critical and Constructive Essays by Nine British Writers, 1716–1794

Edited by
TERRY K. SHELDAHL

Routledge
Taylor & Francis Group

LONDON AND NEW YORK

First published in 1989 by Garland Publishing, Inc.

This edition first published in 2021
by Routledge
2 Park Square, Milton Park, Abingdon, Oxon OX14 4RN

and by Routledge
52 Vanderbilt Avenue, New York, NY 10017

Routledge is an imprint of the Taylor & Francis Group, an informa business

© 1989 Terry K. Sheldahl

British Library Cataloguing in Publication Data
A catalogue record for this book is available from the British Library

ISBN: 978-0-367-33564-9 (Set)
ISBN: 978-1-00-304636-3 (Set) (ebk)
ISBN: 978-0-367-51873-8 (Volume 17) (hbk)
ISBN: 978-0-367-51875-2 (Volume 17) (pbk)
ISBN: 978-1-00-305556-3 (Volume 17) (ebk)

Publisher's Note
The publisher has gone to great lengths to ensure the quality of this reprint but points out that some imperfections in the original copies may be apparent.

Disclaimer
The publisher has made every effort to trace copyright holders and would welcome correspondence from those they have been unable to trace.

Education for the Mercantile Counting House

■■■■■■■■■■■■■■■■■■■■■■■■■■

Critical and Constructive Essays by
Nine British Writers, 1716-1794

Edited with an introduction by
TERRY K. SHELDAHL

GARLAND PUBLISHING, INC.

NEW YORK & LONDON 1989

For a list of Garland's publications in accounting,
see the final pages of this volume.

Library of Congress Cataloging-in-Publication Data

■ ■

Education for the mercantile counting house : critical and
constructive essays by nine British writers, 1716–1794 /
edited with an introduction by Terry K. Sheldahl
p. cm. -- (Foundations of accounting)
Bibliography: p.
ISBN 0-8240-6132-2 (alk. paper)
1. Merchants—Education—England—History—18th century.
2. Business education—England—History—18th century.
I. Sheldahl, Terry K. II. Series.
HF1142.E54E38 1989
371'.00942--dc 19   88-29172

Design by Renata Gomes

The volumes in this series are printed on
acid-free, 250-year-life paper.

Printed in the United States of America

*To Mary Jane and Christopher, and
our faithful cats Dusty
and Bow-Tie*

Acknowledgments
■■■■■■■■■■■■■■■■■■■■■■■■■■■■■■■■■

This book may be traced to a projected collaboration with my friend and teacher Gary John Previts.* In 1983 we made preliminary plans to develop a two-volume history of accounting education in America that, before both of us became otherwise committed, supplied my principal scholarly focus for more than a year. Indirectly as a result of a five-day visit to Philadelphia in April 1983 spent mainly in local libraries, I became acquainted with the Early American Imprints microform series, 1639–1800 (Shipton 1955–83). That collection would most appropriately provide a number of sources for coverage in chapter 10 of the English-American author Milns, and indeed my first access to his educational essay reprinted there.

In the fall of 1983 I unsuccessfully sought external funding for the collaborative project. Graciously serving as one of my references was the distinguished accounting historian Paul Garner, who sent me a copy of a newly published article by Louis Dow (1983) of the University of Alabama in Birmingham that introduced me to three educational pamphlets by the Rev. William Thom (1762a,c,d), including the one (a) that appears in chapter 7. That article

---

*In light of the reference within its title to the "countinghouse," as the seat of mercantile operations, the origins of the book might through Professor Previts be pushed back another seven years, to a classroom project of 1976 that led to a coauthored article by happenstance not cited in the text. Gary John Previts and Terry K. Sheldahl, "Accounting and 'Countinghouses': An Analysis and Commentary," *Abacus* 13 (June 1977): 52–59.

led me belatedly in 1986 to the publication by Redlich (1970) on *The accomplish'd merchant* ([Postlethwayt c. 1730]), reprinted in chapter 5 following a rejection of his revisionist account of its authorship. Professor Dow was kind enough at that time to send me copies of the three items by Thom, providing the very useful advice (as reflected in the source library credits given below) that he had obtained the material at the University of Edinburgh.

In the spring of 1984 I spent twelve days in Chicago and Baltimore, working particularly at the Joseph Regenstein Library at the University of Chicago and the Langsdale Library at the University of Baltimore, with Special Collections and the Herwood Library of Accountancy, respectively. During that time I found in one or more editions the writings by Watts, Webster, and Gordon that appear in chapters 2, 4, and 8, as well as four other sources cited in the reference list. Ironically, the several pages that I reproduced from the copy of Clare's text that would later be the source of the reprint found in chapter 3 did not include the brief preface on education. The visit to Baltimore also led indirectly to my acquisition some months later, from the Milton S. Eisenhower Library at Johns Hopkins University, of a photocopy of the principal material reprinted in chapter 6 from Postlethwayt's *Dictionary* (1751–55).

At the University of Baltimore I was assisted generously by Geraldine (Watkins) Yeager, who in her capacity as archivist and head of Special Collections, including the Herwood Library, has more recently made further valuable contributions to my work on this volume.

By serendipity, then, I had by early 1985 become acquainted with several of the essays reprinted below. Immersed, however, in work on a book for the 1986

Garland accounting series and, later in the year, a paper on accounting education in eighteenth-century America for presentation to an Academy of Accounting Historians seminar, I as yet had no time to consider how I might make significant use of them. That opportunity would arise in the fall of 1986, when editor Richard Brief invited me to submit one or more anthology proposals for his 1988 Garland series. Along with a collection of early American accounting literature (Sheldahl 1988), I suggested a compilation of the British educational writings that I had gathered or become (at least partially) aware of. Subject to my making appropriate reprint arrangements, Professor Brief generously approved both ideas.

By late August of last year I had made (or, in one case, was in the final stage of making) such provisions for six educational essays, having modestly supplemented Postlethwayt's entry "The British Mercantile College" with related *Dictionary* material and selected a single pamphlet by Thom. At last I was ready to study English educational history. The first major source consulted was Hans's book (1951) on the eighteenth century. From it I learned of the writings by Clare and by Henry and W. Augustus Clarke found in chapters 3 and 9, and references made to Milns as a London schoolmaster led me to inspect his *Plan of instruction by private classes*, appearing in chapter 10.

In September I made reprint arrangements for the essays by Clare and Milns. Unable to locate an American library source for it, I excluded the Clarkes' 1793 school announcement from the summary and table of contents submitted on the book at the end of the month. When it was finally obtained from England in March of this year, Professor Brief consented to its addition to the anthology. Both general (chapter 1) and individual (chapters 2–10)

introductions had by then been incorporated within the summary announcement for the book. In the interim, with assistance from Kenneth Craven, a research associate at the Harry Ransom Humanities Research Center at the University of Texas at Austin who also supplied an archival item cited in chapter 5, the title page had been obtained from a New York source.

Finally, in May I happened to reread a reference by Butts (1973) to an educational essay by Priestley that I had not adequately followed up on when first noting it in the prevoius September. A copy was obtained in early June, and, with the kind consent of Garland's associate editor Brian Cook, was incorporated as appendix 1.

My greatest debt concerning this study is to Richard Brief. Without his approval there would of course have been no project to start with. He has supported my efforts throughout, despite my falling hopelessly behind schedule (delaying the other anthology in turn) as the work took on the dimensions of a monograph as well as anthology. He was also instrumental in securing for me a very beneficial grant from Garland Publishing to cover reprint fees and associated costs. I am very grateful in this connection also to former Garland vice president Ralph Carlson, who approved such funding, and to his successor Leo Balk.

I wish to thank Dean Leo Parrish, Jr., of our School of Business at Savannah State College for providing me a working environment that is ideally suited to undertaking scholarly activities of this scale. Our librarians Evelyn Richardson and Linda Holmes have been consistently helpful in arranging for interlibrary loans and identifying potential source libraries. In the latter regard, and likewise concerning the acquisition of certain bibliographical data, Ben Lee of the library at Armstrong State College has ably

assisted me on a number of occasions. Throughout the course of the work I have used the resources of both libraries.

I am immensely indebted to Susan Morris of the Reference Department of the central library at the University of Georgia. Over the past eighteen months she has provided outstanding help on a wide variety of bibliographical and other reference matters, assisting me in regard specifically to the coverage of Watts, Webster, Postlethwayt (first chapter), and Milns. She has often gone beyond my particular questions to provide detailed information that, as in the bibliographical discussion in chapter 4, would contribute materially to the study.

Special gratitude is expressed also to my fellow accounting historian Patti Mills of Indiana State University. Her excellent help regarding the translations from French and Latin presented in appendices 2 and 3 is cited in prefatory notes to those supplements. Also at Indiana State, Rare Books and Special Collections librarian David Vancil has assisted me in relation to Postlethwayt, whose *Dictionary* (1751–55) is in one of his collections.

Charles Aston, Jr., and Margaret Howell, respective heads of Special Collections departments at the University of Pittsburgh (Hillman Library) and the University of Missouri-Columbia (Elmer Ellis Library), have supplied useful source material concerning Webster and Thom in turn. I owe a similar debt to A. Ronald Tonks, Assistant Executive Director of the Historical Commission of the Southern Baptist Convention, in regard to W. A. Clarke.

Linda Haynie of Savannah has served as my typist, preparing chapters 1–10, aside from the reprint material, in camera-ready form. I thank her for providing excellent and timely work from the beginning, as I have presented the

material in numerous installments, moving back and forth between the general and individual introductions.

Family references may sometimes be regarded as ritualistic formalities. I can only say that I feel genuinely grateful to my wife Mary Jane and our son Christopher for their patience as I have spent most of the past year working on this book, not to mention the months of preliminary activity. Also, without Mary Jane's income from her job as a social services caseworker I could ill afford to devote so much of my time to writing.

The library at the University of Mississippi has made a unique contribution to the coverage in chapter 10 of William Milns by providing, generally, the various titles cited from the Early American Imprints microform series (Shipton 1955–83). Indeed, I first saw Milns's essay by courtesy of an interlibrary loan made of the microprinted edition by that institution. The nearest library holding the collection is located some 170 miles away.

Recognition is due also to Edward R. Hamilton, Bookseller, from Falls Village, Conn., from whom I purchase discount books by mail each month. A number of these acquisitions are cited in the reference list, including two books that arrived only this month.

Also contained in that listing are various instances of correspondence, telephone communication, and office visitation. I wish to thank the contributing individuals, and unnamed other parties who have provided comparable assistance.

Finally, it is a genuine pleasure to cite source libraries or publishers and their representatives for supplying reprint material and/or granting rights for publication.

1. Watts: Reprinted courtesy of Baker Library (publisher), Harvard Business School; Ruth R. Rogers,

Curator of Kress Library of Business and Economics. Source copy provided with approval of Bonnie J. Clemens, Acting Director of Libraries, University of Georgia.

2. Clare: Langsdale Library, University of Baltimore; Geraldine Yeager, Head of Special Collections, inclusive of Herwood Library of Accountancy.

3. Webster: William Andrews Clark Memorial Library, University of California, Los Angeles; John Bidwell, Reference/Acquisitions Librarian.

4. Postlethwayt [c. 1730]: Reprinted from original in Kress Library of Business and Economics, Baker Library, Harvard Business School; Ruth R. Rogers, Curator, and Martha H. Gallagher, staff.

5. Postlethwayt 1751–55: Vol. 1, Georgetown University Library, Joseph E. Jeffs, Librarian, and G.M. Barringer, Special Collections. Vol. 2, Alderman Library, University of Virginia; George Riser, Rare Book Dept. Photographs made from microfilms by Damar Photo Supplies, Savannah, Ga.

6. Thom: New College (Divinity), University of Edinburgh; John V. Howard, Librarian, Special Collections, Edinburgh University Library.

7. Gordon: Bancroft Library, University of California, Berkeley; Anthony S. Bliss, Rare Book Librarian.

8. H. and W. A. Clarke: The British Library, Jane Carr, Head of Marketing and Publishing. Title page, New York Public Library; Research Libraries, Donald Anderle, Associate Director for Special Collections, and Francis 0. Mattson, Curator of Rare Books.

9. Milns: William L. Clements Library, University of Michigan; John C. Dann, Director, and Richard Ryan, Curator of Books.

10. Priestly: Dartmouth College Library; Stanley W. Brown, Curator of Rare Books.

11. Postlethwayt 1751, opposite title page: Reprinted, page 235. Hutzler Collection of Economic Classics, Special Collections Division, The Milton S. Eisenhower Library, The Johns Hopkins University; Carolyn Smith, Rare Books Librarian.

12. Nicholas Hans 1951, 67 (*New trends in education in the eighteenth century*): Reprinted, page 112, courtesy of Routledge & Kegan Paul, Associated Book Publishers (U.K.) Ltd.; Caroline Marsden, staff. Source copy provided with approval of David Cohen, Director of Libraries, College of Charleston.

I was able to obtain for reprint every item that I wished, and was on no occasion denied copy or consent by a pertinent library or publisher. Such cooperation speaks for itself.

Terry K. Sheldahl

School of Business
Savannah State College
July 29, 1988.

Contents
■■■■■■■■■■■■■■

ACKNOWLEDGMENTS   vii
PREFACE   xxi

1. GENERAL INTRODUCTION: THE DEVELOPMENT
OF ENGLISH SCHOOLING, FROM ANGLO-SAXON
TIMES THROUGH 1800   1

Schooling in Anglo-Saxon England, 597–1066   2

The Later Middle Ages: From the Norman Conquest to
the English Reformation, 1066–1529   9

   Rationale for this Periodization   9
   Less Direct Ecclesiastical Control of "Grammar
   Schools" in an Era of Diversified Sponsorship   10
      Later Monastery Roles   10
      New Sponsors   13
      Ecclesiastical Teacher Licensing   15

   A Pre-Modern "Renaissance," French Language
   and Culture, and Medieval "Scholasticism"   17

   Oxford and Cambridge, and Other
   Higher Education   23

   Emergence of "Humanism": The Two Universities,
   and

Three Related Grammar School Foundations   29

Clientele of Medieval Grammar Schools, and Opportunities for Elementary Education   33
  Reasonably Wide Access   33

  Exclusion of Females   37

  Elementary Schooling   40

The Early Modern Period: From the Reformation
to the Restoration, 1529–1660   43

  Educational Reorganization During the
  Reformation   43

    Positive Response to Dissolution of Monasteries and
    Other Institutional Sponsors or Patrons   43

    Clerics, Merchants, and Other Leading School
    Sponsors or Patrons   48

  Trends in Grammar School Instruction   51

  Dominant Religious Influence in an Era of
  Expanding Clientele   57

  New Educational Initiatives: Designs for Academies,
  and Early Commercial Schools   63

    Educating a Privileged (or Meritorious) Elite   63

    Early Commercial Schooling   67

Later Modern Schooling: From the Restoration through
the Eighteenth Century, 1660–1800   71

Religious Restoration and the Schools: Legislated
Anglican Monopoly, Active Dissent, and Evolving
Toleration   71

   The "Clarendon Code": Parliament versus King on
   Religious Toleration   71

   Relaxation of Repression, Beginning with the Tol
   eration Act of 1689   78

The Dissenting Academies   81

Oxford and Cambridge   91

   Early Scientific Leadership: Oxford Scientists, the
   Royal Society, and Newton at Cambridge   91

   Less Decline in the Eighteenth Century than Tradi
   tionally Assumed   94

The Elite "Public Schools," Especially Eton   98

Other Grammar Schools, and Related
Institutions   104

   Grammar Schooling in General   104

   Other Classical Schools   109

Private Academies   110

2.PIONEER EDUCATION WRITER
THOMAS WATTS   117

Essay 1, Watt's *Essay*, 1716 (1946 reprint ed.)[1]   121

3.GENERAL TEXTBOOK AUTHOR
MARTIN CLARE   139

Essay 2, Clare's "Preface," 1719   143

4.WILLIAM WEBSTER, WRITING MASTER AND
ACCOUNTANT   147

Essay 3, Webster's "Attempt," 1726   155

5. MALACHY POSTLETHWAYT, AND A POSSIBLE AL-
TERNATE, OR SECOND, AUTHOR FOR *The accomplish'd
merchant*   173

Essay 4, Postlethwayt's *Accomplish'd merchant*,
[c. 1730]   177

6.MALACHY POSTLETHWAYT: ENTRIES
FROM HIS *Dictionary*   201

---

[1]The entries given for essays 1–9 are not formal titles of chapter sections, as each introductory writeup is followed directly by the reprint material. Title pages are included for source works of essays drawn from larger publications.

Essay 5, Postlethwayt's "British Mercantile College" and Related Entries, 1751–55   209

7. THE REV. WILLIAM THOM: ANONYMOUS SCOTS POLEMICIST AGAINST THE UNIVERSITIES   235

Essay 6, Thom's *Defects*, [1762]   239

8. GLASGOW SCHOOLMASTER
WILLIAM GORDON   295

Essay 7, Gordon's "Essay," 1763   299

9. THE LITERARY, MATHEMATICAL, AND COMMERCIAL SCHOOL OF THE BROTHERS CLARKE: MATHEMATICIAN HENRY AND BAPTIST CLERIC W(ILLIAM) AUGUSTUS   319

Essay 8, the Clarkes' "Plan," 1793   331

10. "WELL-BRED" BRITISH AND AMERICAN SCHOLAR WILLIAM MILNS   339

Essay 9, Milns' *Plan*, 1794   349

Appendix

1. AN ESSAY FROM THE DISSENTING ACADEMY AT WARRINGTON: PRIESTLEY'S TRACT, ORIGINATING IN 1765, ON "Liberal Education for Civil and Active Life"   365

2. TRANSLATIONS OF THE FRENCH (OR LATIN) PAS-
SAGES IN POSTLETHWAYT'S ENTRY, FROM CHAPTER
6, "The British Mercantile College"   391

3.TRANSLATIONS OF THE LATIN PASSAGES FROM
GORDON'S TITLE PAGE AND ESSAY   397

REFERENCE LIST   399

Preface
■■■■■■■■■■■■

In the United States, higher education in preparation for business careers is mainly a twentieth-century development. Within even that limited time frame, general acceptance of a need within business studies for a strong "liberal arts" component is rather recent. It is particularly interesting, then, that basically throughout the *eighteenth* century there was in Britain significant advocacy, and even practice, of liberal education for the businessman, who remained preeminently the merchant trader even as an industrial revolution developed after 1750.

In English education the eighteenth century was a period of major reform, generally forgotten until the appearance in 1951 of an authoritative study by Nicholas Hans. Religious, intellectual, and utilitarian motives converged to broaden curricula well beyond the classical tradition of the "grammar schools" and universities, in part by giving rise to or nurturing new institutional forms. Pioneering commercial educators, forming "academies" that often represented alternatives to the grammar schools, stood in the forefront of such progress.

Following a broad survey in chapter 1 of the evolution of English schooling from Anglo-Saxon times through 1800, this collection presents the educational views of six such teachers (including authorities from several disciplines), a noted economic "scribbler" linked to a wine merchant, and respective Scots and "Dissenting" clerics.* All of these men championed studies designed for prospective merchants. The often polemical essays differ on the utility of studying Latin, proper attention to fundamental mathematics, the merits of offering a complete course within a single school, and perhaps other matters. The authors were agreed, however, that a British merchant needed strong verbal and compositional skills, rooted in intensive study of English; that he should be fluent in French, and know substantial history, geography, and (with a partial dissent from William Webster) applied math beyond arithmetic; that facility in accounts, penmanship, and mercantile calculation was vital; and that even the latter areas, in which several of these men themselves wrote prominently, were not suited to on-the-job training. William Milns' closing essay was a prospectus for an innovational school conducted in New York, in part for young ladies, by the learned former London schoolmaster.

This material should be of interest to accounting, broader business, and educational historians alike. Although the first essay is drawn from a reprint volume, and at least isolated references may be found in reasonably accessible secondary sources to several of the others, it is thought that few of the items, or writers, would routinely be known to historians of eighteenth-century Britain from any of the three categories. Taken as a group, they provide a striking rebuttal to the premise that liberal education for business, in the English-speaking world, is fundamentally an idea of the present century.

---

*The "Dissenter" was Baptist minister William Clarke, listed with his brother Henry as coauthor of the writeup on their Liverpool academy that appears in chapter 9. Not included in this tabulation is Joseph Priestley, whose essay reprinted as appendix 1 emanated from a "Dissenting Academy."

The survey of English schooling developed in chapter 1 will of course be more informative to accounting and business historians than to their educational counterparts. Through its breadth, however, this historical synthesis by a newcomer to the field may attract the latter group as well, even specialists in English education. Their comments would be most welcome.

As recently as last fall, this book was projected as a conventional anthology with a reasonably short introduction. It was evident, however, that background information needed to be supplied on English education of the period covered by the essays, and on the authors themselves. It was soon clear that the educational context pointed back a number of centuries, to medieval development of "grammar" schools. The Latin schools that would represent or dominate English secondary education well into modern times could indeed be traced to the arrival at Canterbury in 597 (J. Blair 1984, 67) of a Christian mission sent by Pope Gregory "the Great." The decision to start at that point, and to try to refer meaningfully if less systematically to other levels of schooling as well, made a "long" introduction assured, even with only brief coverage of events prior to 1066.

In referring to "British" writers, the subtitle provides for coverage of Scottish as well as English sources, specifically the essays by William Gordon and the Rev. William Thom. In light, however, of the additional time and space that would have been required, it did not seem feasible to include Scotland, politically united with England as of 1708, more than incidentally within the scope of chapter 1.

As for the individuals covered, only theologian and scientist Joseph Priestley, included by way of appendix 1, is a widely known historical figure, and only mathematician Henry Clarke and economic writer Malachy Postlethwayt are also listed in the *Dictionary of National Biography* (1917). Students of British accounting history of the day will be familiar, at least by name, with Webster, Gordon, and possibly Martin Clare as authors of bookkeeping texts or essays. It seemed appropriate to supply some measure of detail about the writers, granting that the chapter introductions differ widely among themselves in length. The principal scholarly controversy addressed is that of authorship and approximate dating of *The accomplish'd merchant*, credited in chapter 5 to Postlethwayt, circa 1730.

Even before it began to take on a life of its own, the general introduction was intended to be a self-contained chapter. To have tried to tailor it specifically to the literature reprinted would only have jeopardized the breadth of perspective that was sought, particularly since business-oriented schooling had meager roots in earlier times. If the consequence, in part, is to supply distinctly more information and interpretation than are essential to appreciation of the anthology material, it should only broaden the potential value of the study.

In parenthetical reference citations, quotation is attributed directly after the page number(s), so that "1, 2, quoted" signifies quotation from page 2; "title" stands for title *page*; "entry n" refers to the nth separate listing of the term in the reference work; and "def. n" refers to the nth definition given within the given entry.

CHAPTER 1

GENERAL INTRODUCTION: THE DEVELOPMENT OF ENGLISH

SCHOOLING, FROM ANGLO-SAXON TIMES THROUGH 1800

The essays in chapters 2-10 generally reflect secular and utilitarian currents that, after eleven centuries of dominant religious control or influence and classical subject-matter, were rising within English education during the 1700s. Traditional "grammar" schooling criticized by several writers had originated in Anglo-Saxon cathedrals and monasteries in vital support of the Christian religion brought by Benedictine missionaries in 597.

Broadened institutional sponsorship of schools after 1066 did not impair religious dominance. Building on Latin study at the grammar school, the "higher" education at Oxford and Cambridge stressed logic and theology with an infusion, in its time, of Renaissance humanism. Access to the grammar schools, by male youth, and royal patronage of schooling continued to expand as the English Reformation of the sixteenth century lodged basic educational authority in the Church of England, headed by the crown.

When the church fell with the monarchy in the mid-1600s, a number of Protestant sects gained a following that would not yield to respressive legislation of the '60s that reasserted an educational monopoly for the restored church. "Dissenting" academies joined grammar schools (though not those of highest prestige) and "private" academies in providing scientific and, particularly identified with the new secular institutions of main concern in this book, vocational education. At the same time classical instruction itself was reformed, in part within a second new kind of private school.

1

Schooling in Anglo-Saxon England, 597-1066

Formal schooling emerged in Anglo-Saxon England as during some ninety years starting in 597 the "Seven Kingdoms of the Heptarchy" (Grun 1979, s.v. "686 C," "828 A," in quoted form)[1] accepted Christianity.[2] The creation of a centralized episcopal system and of national synods fostered religious and political unity over the latter third of the seventh century (P. Blair 1962, 134-38; and Langer 1972, 179, s.v. "669-690").

Three bishoprics were formed during the first seven years of the original missions (J. Blair 1984, 67), and by 737 there were seventeen episcopal sees (P. Blair 1962, 143). Upwards of fifty major monasteries were established over this period (P. Blair 1962, 146-47), beginning with Canterbury in 597 (Grun 1979, s.v. "597 C"), and a far higher number of smaller "'minsters'" emerged, representing in substance the start of an English parochial system (J. Blair 1984, [70]). Beginning perhaps with Folkestone in 616 (Grun 1979, s.v. "616 C"), there were several "double houses" for men and women, in addition to separate nunneries (P. Blair 1962, 147).

---

[1] Following Bede (731), the Heptarchy is divided among three principal Germanic population groups: the Angles of East Anglia, Mercia, and Northumbria; the Saxons of Essex, Wessex (having also a Jutish element), and Sussex; and the Jutes of Kent. Frisians were probably often mixed with Saxons (J. Blair 1984, 54; and Langer 1972, 179, s.v. "410-442").

As of the early seventh century, these kingdoms may have been only "gradually emerging from a state of flux" (J. Blair 1984, 59, 61). In addition, four other "independent states" have been identified (P. Blair 1962, 27, quoted, 28), and there were "smaller peoples, lying between the big kingdoms or absorbed within them." Among the principal states of the seventh, eighth, and (prior to Viking invasion) ninth centuries, there was a shifting balance of power, as certain kings achieved relative dominance in their times (J. Blair 1984, 61, quoted; P. Blair 1962, 49; and Gilbert 1968, 8).

[2] Bede (731) is the principal source for the early Christian period, and for overall English history of the seventh and early eighth centuries (J. Blair 1984, 52). References made to the Colgrave and Mynors edition (1969) are to the English translation juxtaposed page-by-page with the Latin.

For basic reasons noted in part by Cremin (1970, 168), early cathedrals and (much less commonly, beyond novitiate instruction) monasteries introduced formal schooling:

> [T]he new religion clearly required a native clergy fluent in the Latin language, steeped in Christian literature, and thoroughly grounded in the Roman Catholic liturgy; but there were simply no means at hand for educating such a clergy [or teaching Latin to worshipers (Leach 1915, 3)].

Probably opened by the original missionaries soon after their arrival (Leach 1911, xi; 1915, 3; Grun 1979, s.v. "598 C"; and Watson 1916, 27), a school at Canterbury was a model for a cathedral school started in Dunwich around 631 by the East Anglian king (Bede 731, 267, 269; Colgrave and Mynors 1969, 266n, 354n; and Leach 1911, xi). Three schools of the seventh and eighth centuries achieved especial eminence. At Canterbury, under Archbishop Theodore, 669-90 (Bede 731, 333; and Colgrave and Mynors 1969, 333n), both youth and more mature scholars (P. Blair 1962, 140, 326; and Leach 1911, 9, 11[3]) studied Greek as well as Latin. There was instruction "not only in the books of holy Scripture but also in the art of metre, astronomy, and ecclesiastical computation," focused in the latter case on the dating of Easter (Bede 731, 333 and 335, quoted, 539-47, odd nos.).

Patterned after Canterbury (Colgrave and Mynors 1969, 334n) were two great schools of the eighth century. Monasteries formed in Theodore's day at Wearmouth and nearby Jarrow functioned for at least half a century as in substance parts of a joint Benedictine house (Colgrave and Mynors 1969, xx). Gracing Jarrow during this period, first as a novitiate (who had entered Wearmouth at seven) and later as a schoolmaster, was the father of English history, the Venerable Bede. His own voluminous writings on

---

[3] The reference made to Leach (1911) is to an English translation of the selection juxtaposed to the Latin text, a pattern that applies (as relevant) throughout the collection.

Scripture, metre, chronology, and other teaching subjects, and a superb

library more generally, lent preeminence to Bede's school (Bede 731, 567,

569, 571 P. Blair 1962, 139-40; and Colgrave and Mynors 1969, xix-xxi,

xxv-xxvi).[4]

The passage of the educational torch from Jarrow to the cathedral

school founded seventy-one years earlier at York was foreshadowed in 735 by

the death of Bede, the birth at York of the educator Alcuin, and the estab-

lishment there of an archbishopric (P. Blair 1962, 142; and Grun 1979, s.v.

"664 C," "735 C"). As a York schoolboy Alcuin (c. 786; and Leach 1911,

xiv) studied the trivium[5] and quadrivium as defined below, along with law,

the theory of the calendar, zoology, architecture, and theology. He stayed

on to teach at the cathedral school, becoming its master before Charlemagne

called him to the Frankish court to conduct a palace school and serve as

his educational advisor. In the latter role Alcuin oversaw the remarkable

educational expansion associated with the "Carolingian Renaissance" (Butts

1973, 150, 151, quoted; and The dictionary of national biography (D.n.b.)

1917, s.v. "Alcuin").

In an era of severe scarcity of written material, Alcuin wrote useful

textbooks in several fields (D.n.b. 1917, s.v. "Alcuin"). Cathedral

and monastic schooling were centered on preparation for religious vocations

---

[4]Conventional reference, as above, to Bede as master of a noted school
at Jarrow is strongly challenged by Leach (1915, 51-52), arguing that the
scholarly monk, born in 672 or '73 (Colgrave and Mynors 1969, xix), probably
did not teach after becoming a priest at age thirty. According to Colgrave
and Mynors (1969, 334n), "many" of Bede's writings were intended as school-
books, rather than "perhaps" two as supposed by Leach (1915, 51).

[5]Although Alcuin (c. 786) did not in his poetic tribute to his teacher
Albert (usually known (Leach 1915, 57) as Ethelbert) mention logic, it seems
likely that his youthful studies included that field, one in which he later
wrote an important text.

through study of Latin "grammar," understood in terms more of literature and practical use than of structural form (Abelson 1906, 11-12; Leach 1911, x; and Watson 1916, 6). Literature from the "patristic" authors (Leclercq 1961, 41) or "Church Fathers" (Young 1969, 41n) was sometimes combined as at York, with earlier pagan "classical" works (Alcuin c. 786, 17; and Leach 1911, xxiv, quoted). Resourceful masters teaching Latin as a foreign tongue built upon elementary experience in singing verse and reciting psalms in the language (Abelson 1906, 12-14).

Latin education in Anglo-Saxon England was not confined to males. An eighth-century source indicates that "high-born abbesses and nuns" would routinely have been so schooled, along with princesses (Leach 1911, xi, xvii, quoted); and exercises presented in a noted grammar text from around the year 1000 referred to Latin study by women and girls (P. Blair 1962, 357-58; and Leach 1911, xvii, 51).

Rhetoric and logic were the other two subjects in the classical "trivium." The first field was tied to Latin grammar through ecclesiastical need for skills in letter writing and document preparation (Abelson 1906, 60; and Southern 1961, 26). A text by Alcuin may have been the most influential source of instruction in logic (Abelson 1906, 79-80).

It is sometimes stated (as in Butts 1973, 154) that early medieval schools largely ignored the mathematically oriented "quadrivium" of arithmetic, geometry, astronomy, and, approached in terms of theory rather than performance (Abelson 1906, 128), music. In keeping, however, with the significant religious applications or bearings of such fields, geometry possibly excepted (Abelson 1906, 90-91), there is ample evidence that they were pursued to the very limited extent of knowledge of the day (Abelson 1906, 90-93).

5

Worthy of note in this regard is correspondence between two eleventh-century scholars from leading cathedral and commercial cities Cologne, northern Europe's largest city, and Liège, capital of a large "prince-bishopric" of the same name (The Columbia encyclopedia 3d, s.v. "Liège," entry 2, quoted; and Garraty and Gay 1972, 383-84). The same series of letters that included the first known mention in the West of an important scientific invention, the astrolabe, also revealed that the two churchmen had no idea what was meant by a famous theorem's reference to the interior angles of a triangle (Southern 1961, 31-32).

Several Roman Catholic councils of the eighth and ninth centuries asserted that cathedrals and monasteries must offer free instruction to all young men who sought it (Southern 1961, 26), as with an 826 mandate (Canonical duty of bishops to maintain schools, 21) that bishops supply "masters and teachers who shall assiduously teach . . . the principles of the liberal arts" (the trivium and quadrivium). Such injunctions were not enforceable, however (Southern 1961, 26), and but for rare exception made for sons of distinguished neighbors (Charlton 1965, 14-15), monasteries after the eighth century restricted schooling to "their own younger brethren" (Leach 1911, xiii).

Reasserting principles dating from 692 (Leach 1911, xxv), late tenth-century church canons (Council of 994 (?)) asserted that priests "shall keep schools in the villages and teach small boys freely," sending their own kinsmen to cathedral schools on the same terms. It seems that parish priests were expected to provide elementary instruction for youth of under seven years (Leach 1911, xxv), sometimes preparatory to cathedral schooling. "Song" schools emphasizing the learning of religious chants were associated with at least three major cathedral schools of the seventh century (Bede 731,

6

207, 335, 337; and Leach, 1911, 7). After retiring from Charlemagne's court Alcuin (796) recommended formal division at York among studies for "those who read books, [those] who serve singing, [and those] who are assigned to the writing school" (teaching the vernacular?).

The distinction between priests and monks was sufficiently ill-defined over the first two or three centuries of English Christianity that pastoral responsibility accrued to "monastic or quasi-monastic bodies." Early "mynster[s]" (emphasis deleted) or "'minsters'" ranged from "true Benedictine houses to small, loose-knit communities of priests" (J. Blair 1984, [70]), and "priests" were called upon even later "to keep schoolmasters in their own houses" (Council of 994 (?)). By 750 there were hundreds of small minsters with pastoral roles (J. Blair 1984, [70]). Parish churches were later usually founded by "lay notables" who appointed the priests, and derived income from the properties (P. Blair 1962, 157). Manorial lords often formed churches for their households and tenants (J. Blair 1984, 98).

English schooling declined dramatically during the ninth century, as Danish invaders destroyed three kingdoms, disrupted episcopal sees, and plundered "innumerable" monasteries (J. Blair 1984, 84, quoted; and P. Blair 1962, 329). King Alfred ([c. 893], 23, quoted, 25), known to history (J. Blair 1984, [81]) as "the Great," wrote late in the century that competence in Latin had nearly disappeared in the English clergy. He had joined an assembled circle of court intellectuals in translating into English, for his subjects' benefit, many books deemed "most useful for all men to know."

To provide trained administrators, Alfred set up schools for the sons of nobles and thegns (or thanes), freemen holding lands in return for military service to king or lord (Langer 1972, 180, 182; and The Random House dictionary of the English language 1966, s.v. "thane," "thegn"). He

7

also devised "far-reaching plans for lay education" in England, prominently involving the cathedrals (Southern 1961, 26), under which every freeman's son would learn to read English, some of them proceeding to Latin in preparation for religious life (Leach 1911, xv).

Under royal patronage there was during the tenth century a strong monastic revival, leading to uniform Benedictine rules and a predominantly monkish episcopacy (J. Blair 1984, 88, 90-91; and P. Blair 1962, 173-78, 181-82). It was intended not only to repair ravages brought by the Viking invaders, but also to correct perceived widespread corruption within surviving monasteries and secular cathedral chapters (J. Blair 1984, 88, 90; and Southern 1961, 25-26). These developments revitalized English education while maintaining the contrast between cathedral and monastic schooling, as instruction at monastic cathedrals remained under episcopal authority (Leach 1911, xxi).

Destined to be highly influential, a further educational setting must be noted before leaving the Anglo-Saxon period. England's first "collegiate" churches appeared well before 1066 (Watson 1916, 4). Maintaining an assembly or "chapter" of clerics or "canons" not subject to monastic rules, these churches differ from secular cathedrals only in that they do not represent bishoprics (Random House dictionary 1966, s.v. "canon[2]," "collegiate church"). Medieval collegiate churches were commonly endowed in part for an educational function (Watson 1916, 4), as in the case of the church of the Holy Cross at Waltham. It was founded in 1060 by an earl who as King Harold, the last Anglo-Saxon ruler, would die six years later at the Battle of Hastings (J. Blair 1984, 103-5; and Leach 1911, xviii, 55, 57).

The Norman Conquest is the logical dividing point between the "early" and "later" English medieval world, whose endpoint is less clearcut. During

8

the later centuries religious authorities generally exercised less direct control over "grammar" schooling than before, as various new sponsors emerged. Culturally, a pre-modern "renaissance" was followed by long domination of logical and theological studies at the "universities" formed at Oxford and Cambridge, where curricular reform associated with the "English Renaissance" began to appear shortly before or after 1500. For male youth, the grammar schools of the era provided reasonably broad opportunity for secondary schooling.

The Later Middle Ages: From the Norman Conquest to the English Reformation, 1066-1529

Rationale for this Periodization

The political division at 1066 between "early" and "later" medieval England[6] has educational warrant. The Normans arrived from France during the early stages of a remarkable revival of European learning, the "Renaissance of the Twelfth Century," to which the French were leading contributors; and brought with them a foreign language and culture that would enjoy immense influence within England for more than three centuries.

The transition to "modern" times has no unique focal point. The start of the Tudor dynasty in 1485 (Morgan 1984, [618]) is educationally meaningful in coming not long after Gutenberg had introduced the printing press (Grun 1979, s.v. "1450 C"), and on the eve (Charlton 1965, 41) of the sprouting of an English humanistic renaissance long in the making (Charlton 1965, 41-85). Before printing, manuscripts were in such short supply that

---

[6]Morgan (1984, [xi] all capitals) reserves the term "Middle Ages" for the four centuries between the Conquest and the Tudors, distinguishing between "Early" and "Later" segments of the period 1066-1485, and referring separately to an "Anglo-Saxon" era commencing around 440. The present usage broadly conforms with Garraty and Gay's (1972, 363) dating of the Middle Ages from "the decline of Rome," granting that Roman rule continued in Britain through more than a century of such decline (Morgan 1984, 602, s.v. "409").

the educational process was "almost entirely oral" (Butts 1973, 154; and Charlton 1965, 15, quoted). Afterwards, numerous new Latin grammars were issued in quantity from the University of Oxford during roughly the first half century of Tudor rule (Charlton 1965, 106).

Later, the scientific revolution of the sixteenth and seventeenth centuries would over the long run have profound educational impact. Selected as the transition point for this survey, however, is the onset of the Englis "Reformation," a movement that would fundamentally alter prevailing school sponsorship and organization. It may conveniently be dated from Cardinal Wolsey's ouster as Lord Chancellor (Guy 1984, 238, 246) in 1529.

With their traditional emphasis on Latin grammar, schools of the kind originating in early cathedrals and monasteries became known in time as "grammar" schools. Use in England of the Latin term "'Scola grammatice'" has been traced to roughly the beginning of the Norman period, and became more common in the thirteenth century, serving to distinguish traditional schools from units of the new "universities" (Watson 1916, 2). After the Conquest, several other institutions joined, mainly, cathedrals and collegiate churches as sponsors of grammar schools. Significant ecclesiastical authority was asserted over the teaching field even as English churches declined more than relatively in educational terms, and monasteries continu to play only a limited role.

Less Direct Ecclesiastical Control of "Grammar
Schools" in an Era of Diversified Sponsorship

Later Monastery Roles

According to one authority (Charlton 1965, 90), cathedrals and collegiate churches were by 1400 "but a shadow of their former selves as educational and cultural centers." Among centers of early medieval schooling, however, it is the later contributions of monasteries that are apt to be obscured. Monastic predominance within the English church continued beyond 1066. During the reign of William the Conqueror, 1066-87 (Gillingham 1984, 111), Canterbury's archbishop Lanfranc, a master teacher of grammar, dialectic, and theology at the abbey of Bec in Normany (Hoyt 1966, 322), rebuffed "a determined effort" to reinstate secular control in many cathedrals (Leach 1915, 98).[7] By one count (Gillingham 1984, 154), over the period 1066-1216 the number of religious houses (male and female) rose from 50 to 700, clearly excluding monastic sees and "minsters" best classified (Leach 1915, 57) as small churches; and membership in religious orders grew from 1,000 to 13,000.

One of a number of new orders, the Cistercians led the way in a new practice of excluding from their brethren youths of under sixteen years (Gillingham 1984, 154). They conducted no schools of any kind (Leclercq 1961, 45), and Leach insists (1915, 28-29, 320) that throughout the middle ages monasteries rarely provided general schooling. Yet documents taken not to be isolated reveal the transfer of control of eight schools from bishops to abbots, 1100-1160 (Leach 1911, xxii); and reference is found (Charlton 1965, 91, quoted, 92) to sixteenth-century dissolution of abbeys that had been "patrons of the local grammar school[s]."

A school common to the listings or examples given in the two sources just cited combines with the description quoted to resolve any apparent conflict. The "'monastic'" school of St. Albans was not part of the nearby monastery, but instead operated within its sphere of influence, or was reliant on its "patronage." It was one of many grammar schools arising in

---

[7]According to Leach (1915, 98), Benedictine control at Canterbury harmed the cathedral school. "[I]nstead of being . . . taught and governed by a resident member of the Chapter," it "was left to the care, necessarily intermittent, of the generally non-resident and roving archbishop."

the neighborhood of monasteries or cathedrals, beginning in the eleventh
century, that enjoyed an informal dependency upon the nearby religious
community (Charlton 1965, 15). Each of the aforementioned transfers of
"control" (Leach 1911, xxii) from bishops to abbots may have involved a
school that strictly speaking was not part of the cathedral.

Later medieval monastic houses, finally, made a special contribution
to education in the form of the "almonry" school. As worship of the Virgin
Mary expanded dramatically at the beginning of the fourteenth century, a
movement began to develop "choristers" to sing in chapels of monastic
churches. Most monasteries maintained an "Almoner," an almsgiver or elee-
mosynary officer. The practice arose of lodging and boarding choristers
at his house by the outer gate, the "almonry," despite the violation of
strict monastic rules. In due course provision was usually made for schooling, either through hiring a master or a tutor for the almonry boys, or
sending them to outside schools (Leach 1915, 213-29).

By rough estimate (Leach 1915, 229, 230, quoted), a thousand or more
boys "of the lower classes" were housed in almonries during the final century of the English monasteries. Most of them learned to read and sing,
and some of them obtained "a more or less good grammatical or general
education." Almonry schools may have been unique to monastic houses only
in name, however, as by 1200 or earlier "great secular churches" had begun
a practice of housing and boarding choristers that apparently in time gave
rise to schooling (Leach 1915, 213).

Almonry schooling was related also to instruction that arose from
"chantry" endowments. Other new institutional sponsors for grammar schools
included "guilds" of three kinds, hospitals, and even public authorities.

New Sponsors

Chantry schools arose from endowed provision for the singing of masses
for donors after their deaths. Some endowments called for schools, but
schooling probably more often arose out of youths' participation in the
chanting (Butts 1973, 164; Leach 1911, xxxv-xxxvi; and Watson 1916, 3). As
suggested by the latter reference, chantry schools were sometimes "song,"
or elementary, schools. In some cases a priest was allotted for each kind
of school (Watson 1916, 4).

Local commercial or charitable associations, or "g(u)ilds," sponsored
many schools. The "merchant" variety, or "gild merchant," was a society of
townsmen engaged in selling that secured members a near monopoly over local
trade by imposing "tolls" and other restraints on potential rivals from outside (Lunt 1957, 179, quoted, 180). Merchant guilds were in their heyday
in the twelfth and thirteenth century, a time of lagging industrial and
commercial development in England (Gillingham 1984, 158, 160) when their
members enjoyed little protection from the central government against oppres-
sive local authorities. They were later eclipsed by "craft" associations
formed principally to regulate local manufacture and sale of the members'
particular kind of product (Lunt 1957, 180, 181-82, quoted). Finally,
"religious" or (Charlton 1965, 92) "social" guilds were formed solely for
charitable, religious, and social purposes (Lunt 1957, 180). The commercial organizations themselves ordinarily included fraternal and charitable
elements (Lunt 1957, 180, 187), perhaps not conspicuously in display when in
1267 the London goldsmiths' and tailors' guilds engaged in "fierce street
battles" (Grun 1979, s.v. "1267 G").

Through appointment of a priest to teach the children of members,
normally covering most families in the town (Lunt 1957, 179), merchant

13

guilds were more identified with grammar schooling than were craft societies (Butts 1973, 164). Craft guilds are most important educationally for establishing systems of "apprenticeship" for entry into their industries (Lunt 1957, 181). London's organized "mercers," or textile dealers (Random House dictionary 1966, s.v. "mercer"), accepted control in 1443 of a new grammar school founded by a member (Leach 1915, 244), however, foreshadowing their leadership of the celebrated St. Paul's, discussed below. Similarly, the Goldsmiths' Company[8] was designated in 1488 (in a will) and 1505 by members who had been lord mayors of London to govern schools in respective towns a hundred or more miles from the capital, one of them a major source of export shipping. In the second case, the guild more than three centuries later still paid the master of the '"free gramer scole"' the original salary of ten pounds per year (Gilbert 1968, 34, 75; and Leach 1915, 245, 246, quoted).

Religious guilds frequently sponsored schooling, sometimes as a defining purpose (Leach 1915, 202, 211, 267-68, 288, 292). In some cases it was closely associated with a chantry endowment (Leach 1915, 197, 292, 325). A grammar school at Stratford-on-Avon that Shakespeare entered at age seven in 1571 was descended from one formed, by 1295, by a religious guild (Leach 1915, 241; and Watson 1916, 4). Two local societies formed Corpus Christi College at the University of Cambridge in 1352 (Hall and Frankl 1982, 32).

In the sense that appears most relevant, a "hospital" is "an institution supported by charity or taxes for the care of the needy, as an orphanage, old people's home, etc." (Random House dictionary 1966, s.v. "hospital," def. 3). In 1277 Queen Eleanor, wife of Henry III, endowed a school for "poor scholars" at St. Katherine's Hospital in London within a broader

---

[8]The patronage of the "Worshipful Company of Goldsmiths" ([Postlethwayt c. 1730], outer cover) gave rise to the famed Goldsmiths' Library of Economic Literature at the University of London.

14

expansion of charitable provisions made 130 years before by an earlier queen (Leach 1915, 136). Two centuries later a grammar school was founded at Oxford in association with a "college" that had hospital roots, as did Cambridge colleges founded in 1280 (as the university's first such community) and 1511 (Hall and Frankl 1982, [56, 63], and 1983, 50).

Perhaps the foremost center of hospital schooling prior to the Reformation was St. Anthony's in London, where early Renaissance humanists Thomas More and John Colet (Charlton 1965, 41) are said to have studied (Leach 1915, 261-63). John Stanbridge was recognized nationally for his Latin instruction at an Oxford grammar school and, beginning in 1501, the school of the Hospital of St. John in Banbury. Statutes adopted at four schools, at least for Merchant Taylors', London, in 1560, after the origin of an official national grammar associated in part with Colet, called for the use of the Stanbridge grammar (Charlton 1965, 106-8; and Watson 1916, 40-42).

A few medieval schools were publicly supported. The master at Hull in the early 1300s was paid from town funds and subjected to public oversight (Charlton 1965, 15). Inviting some resistance, independent teachers occasionally set up their own schools (Butts 1973, 164). Finally, as illustrated by later reference to three particularly distinguished institutions, clerical and royal patrons of learning were included among individual founders of grammar schools.

The development of extensive schooling outside religious institutions was presumably a key factor in the emergence of ecclesiastical licensing of teachers.

Ecclesiastical Teacher Licensing

By the time of the Norman Conquest, European bishops often delegated management of their cathedral schools to a "chancellor," authorized to issue licenses to qualified pupils that would permit them to teach within the diocese (Butts 1973, 177). In twelfth-century England, the licensing of teachers by bishops, or their designates, became a regular requirement (Cremin 1970, 172; and Leach 1911, xx). The Roman Catholic Church expressly forbade any charge for teaching permits (Leach 1911, xxv).

St. Paul's (London) and Winchester cathedrals made notable efforts early on to enforce licensing by threat of excommunication, and one case was referred to the pope (Leach 1911, xx). Enforcement zeal ebbed and flowed over subsequent centuries, reaching its peak (Cremin 1970, 172) during periods of "Lollard" challenge to orthodoxy associated with fourteenth-century Oxford theologian John Wycliffe, who produced the first English translation of the Bible (Griffiths 1984, 212, 214; and Hall and Frankl 1983, 10, 32, 68).

In an important common law case of 1410, it was decided that the state should not intrude upon punishment assessed under canon law against unlicensed schoolmasters. In the same year, however, the Gloucester Grammar School case established that no civil action could be taken against such teachers. It was submitted that "'to teach youth is a virtuous and charitable thing to do and helpful to the people'" (Watson 1916, 70-71).

Licensure was never intended (Leach 1911, xx; and Watson 1916, 70) to restrict teaching to priests. A clear signal that by late medieval times teaching was becoming a profession in its own right was the founding at the University of Cambridge of the first recorded teachers' college. Having observed on one personal journey that seventy grammar schools previously flourishing had closed, London parish priest William Bingham in 1439 founded "God's House" for schoolmaster training (Leach 1911, xl, xli, quoted). It became Christ's College in 1505, when major expansion was begun of facilities

16

and endowments. Under new statutes probably drawn up by St. John Fisher, later martyred as a victim of Henry VIII's personal battles with Rome, the college taught theology, philosophy, and the arts. Matriculating in 1825 at the onetime teachers' seminary was one Charles Darwin (Columbia encyclopedia 3d, s.v. "Fisher, John"; and Hall and Frankl 1982, 27-28).

Bingham's initiative took place within the new educational environment of higher, or university, education, the center of the "Scholastic" movement that dominated later medieval intellectual life. Scholasticism had followed a great revival of learning in which the language and culture brought by the Normans in 1066 had played a leading role.

A Pre-Modern "Renaissance," French Language and Culture, and Medieval "Scholasticism"

Around the middle of the eleventh century, a remarkable cultural reawakening began that in one expression or another would highlight European intellectual life for the better part of two centuries (Haskins 1927, 8-10). The period was one of flourishing literature, in Latin and vernacular languages alike; art, science, mathematics, historical writing, and legal thought; and, at the root of much of this vitality, study of Greek and Latin classics (for example, Haskins 1927, 6-8; Hoyt 1966, 327-33; and Munro 1908. Also, Haskins 1927 and Young 1969, general sources).

Particularly definitive (Heer 1962, 17-18) of the "Renaissance of the Twelfth Century" (Haskins 1927, title of work) was a European recovery of ancient learning centered on Greek philosophy, mathematics, and science. Greek learning had been virtually unknown in the West since early Roman times, while within the Byzantine empire Greek was "the language of law and government . . ., of the Orthodox church, of learning, and of literature" (Haskins 1927, [278]-79, 280, quoted). Greek scholarship had spread from

Constantinople eastward with translation of writings of Aristotle and other
ancients into Semitic languages (Haskins 1927, 281). Arabs had in turn
carried the classics to Sicily and Spain, while adding valuable commentaries
and making scientific and mathematical advances vastly eclipsing any contemporary Western contributions (Butts 1973, 173; Haskins 1927, 281-85; and
Hoyt 1966, 328-29).

These ancient and medieval intellectual treasures finally (re)entered
Western culture in the twelfth century. Europeans flocked to Toledo and
other Spanish towns, in particular, to translate them from Arabic into
Latin, often by way of trilingual Jewish interpreters (Haskins 1927, 284-90;
and Hoyt 1966, 329). Scholars based in Sicily or southern Italy were translating many of the same works, as well as writings of Plato, directly from
the Greek (Haskins 1927, 291-93, 298-99). Although history and literature
were conspicuously absent from Greek studies of the period (Haskins 1927,
300), the twelfth century was a time also of vigorous study of classical
and patristic Latin literature, and of "historical writing" that "reflect[ed]
the variety and amplitude of a richer age" (Haskins 1927, 7, quoted; and
Hoyt 1966, 327).

The medieval renaissance was profoundly significant educationally.
Earlier schooling had been limited largely to the "bare outlines" of the
seven liberal arts (Haskins 1927, 6), especially the quadrivium. Afterwards, Aristotle's complete logic was available to be "welcomed into the
university curriculum" (Abelson 1906, 86, 87, quoted; and Hoyt 1966, 316,
333); grammar and rhetoric had been the focal studies in the revival of
Latin literature that represented "the high point of medieval humanism"
(Hoyt 1966, 327); arithmetic, geometry, and astronomy had been "transformed
from rudimentary studies . . . into the basic mathematical disciplines that

are necessary for advanced scientific work" (Hoyt 1966, 329); and the gradual development since the tenth century of a "distinctive medieval musical theory" had continued on course (Abelson 1906, 134). Revival of science in the twelfth century included the (re)acquisition of the principal literature (Greek and Arab) of medicine (Haskins 1927, 322-26), while comparable developments in the field of learned law are cited later.

John of Salisbury, c. 1115-1180 (Columbia encyclopedia 3d, s.v. "John of Salisbury"), was England's most versatile scholar of the day (Hoyt 1966, 328). He knew the Greek classics only in translation (Haskins 1927, 280), but his cultivation of Latin literature was unmatched in his time and beyond (Munro 1908, 6). John had attended the remarkable cathedral school (Heer 1962, 22; Hoyt 1966, 327-28; and Southern 1961, 28-32) at Chartres, and would close his "long and varied career" as bishop of the French city (Hoyt 1966, 328). There had been a strong philosophical thrust in the teaching of grammar and rhetoric at Chartres in the eleventh century (Southern 1961, 28-29), and in John's day the school was a great center of Latin studies (Butts 1973, 174; and Southern 1961, 36). John of Salisbury also studied in Paris with the famous logician Abelard (Butts 1973, 174-75; and Columbia encyclopedia 3d, s.v. "John of Salisbury"), who may himself have once been a pupil at Chartres (Heer 1962, 22).

For all the scholarship, there was strong emphasis in the twelfth century on the "practicality," or "practical" application, of knowledge (Haskins 1927, 300; 2d term; and Munro 1908, 9, 1st term). John was critical of this mentality in a manner that stamped him to a degree as a prophet (disapproving) of the "Scholasticism" that was to follow. Referring to the "Cornificians," who stressed a utilitarian approach to education (Munro 1908, 9, quoted; and Young 1969, 9n), he lamented a tendency already present to reduce logic and philosophy to "pedantic and technical" subjects "cut off from the totality of human experience," and to neglect literature, in streamlining educational preparation for careers in the schools or in church or secular government (Hoyt 1966, 328).

John of Salisbury was at the same time himself a successful professional bureaucrat. He was secretary to two archbishops of Canterbury, including Thomas Becket (Columbia encyclopedia 3d, s.v. "John of Salisbury"). Along with other clerics and men of letters, he also served briefly as a clerk within the administrative departments of Henry II (Young 1969, 38n). Henry, the first Plantagenet king, 1154-89, is best remembered for his "dubious part" in the contrary Becket's murder (Gillingham 1984, 107, 124, quoted, 125-26; and Morgan 1984, [616]).

To administer an empire that by 1189 included as possessions or dependencies a number of major French provinces besides Normandy (Gilbert 1968, 22), Henry's government became "increasingly complex and bureaucratic" (Gillingham 1984, 124, 126, quoted). It was an ideal environment for applying intellect and learning to the world of affairs (Southern 1961, 36-37). Patrons of learning and literature (Young 1969, 55n), Henry and wife Eleanor of Acquitaine set up palace schools of art, literature, and science (Butts 1973, 166).

Henry's reign only reinforced the French cultural influence brought to England by a Normans a century earlier (Gillingham 1984, 107). Although no one country dominated the medieval renaissance, contributions made to theology, philosophy, poetry, and art gave France special eminence (Haskins 1927, 11), as French became "a language spoken--and written-- by anyone who wanted to consider himself civilized" (Gillingham 1984, 107). The Italian archbishop Lanfranc had been one of a "persistent trickle" of scholars to journey from Italy to northern France for their studies, as he moved from law to grammar and logic (Southern 1961, 27).

Displacing English as the translation vernacular, French after 1066 was long the language of the English church and schools (Gillingham 1984, 156; and Leach 1911, xix); it was the language of estate management and, as a legal profession developed, of law (Gillingham 1984, 107, 152); and even into the fifteenth century remained the language of "the court, the gently born, and officialdom" (Richardson 1941, 271). During the second half of the fourteenth century, however, English had become once again the vernacular of the grammar schools (Leach 1911, xxxvi), and by 1450 educated Englishmen rarely corresponded in French (Richardson 1941, 274). The sharp decline in the use of French occurred during the "Hundred Years" Anglo-French war, 1337-1453 (Griffiths 1984, 171, quoted, 173-74), which ended with the loss of all English territorial possessions in France but one following an earlier restoration of extensive holdings (Gilbert 1968, 37; and Griffiths 1984, 200-[2], 203, quoted).

The recovery of ancient learning continued into the thirteenth century, as a "flood" of new Latin translations of Aristotle and his Islamic commentators appeared in the early 1200s. This profusion of scientific literature reopened theological issues that had seemingly yielded to close linguistic and grammatical analysis of sacred texts (Southern 1987, 138). Theology assumed new rank as a field of study, and in the next century the papacy, temporarily in Avignon, assembled a coterie of scholars to try to forge acceptable solutions to the problems raised (Southern 1987, 139-40).

New theological disputation was a central feature of the rise in the thirteenth century of "Scholasticism," an intellectual movement destined to dominate the remaining medieval period. Mainly philosophers and theologians, the Schoolmen approached all areas of thought in terms of precise definition, logical rigor, and very subtle (or even merely verbal) distinctions. The relationship of this tradition to the classical "humanism" of the twelfth century remains a subject of intense scholarly debate (Young 1969, 3-4, 77-102). Unquestionably, however, educational emphasis shifted from literature to logic (Charlton 1965, 10); rhetoric, perhaps a partial victim of elaborate rules for letter writing developed by twelfth-century scholars (Southern 1961, 39), was scarecely studied at all (Charlton 1965, 10), at least as an independent subject; and grammar was reduced to an elementary study geared to argumentative use that in the words of one author (Watson 1916, 6) "belonged more to metaphysics [or logic] than to linguistics."

In the latter regard, Heer (1962, 20-21) has contrasted the "living, flexible" Latin language of the twelfth century with the "precise scholars' tongue" of the Schoolmen, who demanded rigorous, unambiguous definition for every word. Such an approach would be strongly attacked by the humanist writers and educators of the "modern" Renaissance, whose viewpoint is ably captured, and evidently shared, by two twentieth-century commentators:

> [The schools] were clerkish and pedantic in character; they had managed to trivialize or lose much that was essential in the very classical wisdom they attempted to convey (Cremin 1970, 169).

> Latin studies [of the late Middle Ages] . . . were . . . anti-humanistic and illiberal, and Greek studies had almost dropped out of sight (Watson 1916, 9).

Yet these critics concede significant utilitarian virtues to late medieval schooling. Cremin (1970, 169) acknowledges that it contributed immensely to a substantial spread in literacy, in Latin and English alike (Griffiths 1984, 214-15), during the period. Watson notes (1916, 9-10) that

Latin was needed by doctors, lawyers, clergymen, clerks and record-keepers, ambassadors, travelers, secretaries, and (not least) international traders. Even if the language as learned was "decadent and 'barbarous'" (Watson 1916, 7-8), it nonetheless served its purposes.

The centers of Scholasticism in general, and of theological studies in particular, were the two universities, representing the major new educational institution of later medieval times. Oxford and Cambridge also provided a range of professional education, and, at least in the first case, rudimentary business studies.

Oxford and Cambridge, and Other Higher Education

The town of Oxford, with a collegiate church and, nearby, two important monasteries and a new royal palace, became the major center of study in twelfth-century England. Scholarly lecturing may have begun there as early as the 1090s; is in any case documented by 1117; and became increasingly widespread as new religious houses, the palace, and migrations from other scholarly communities brought increasing numbers of teachers and learners to Oxford (Charlton 1965, 12; and Hall and Frankl 1983, [5]). A kind of "[e]xtension" education began to thrive in the 1130s and '40s as clerics lectured on divinity, law, medicine, and arts to growing congregations of students. By late century masters were organized into several distinct faculties, and the University of Oxford was "in full bloom" (Charlton 1965, 12; and Leach 1911, xxiii-xxiv, quoted).

Beginning with the arrival in 1209 of a dissident group from Oxford, a second university took root at Cambridge during the first third of the thirteenth century. Both institutions were in the predominant early mold of a university as "a guild of teachers with the power to award degrees" (Hall and Frankl 1982, [7]) that originated as licenses to teach, and soon

23

became titles of academic honor (Butts 1973, 179; Charlton 1965, 12; Hall and Frankl 1982, 6; and Leach 1911, xxiii, xxv).

Students normally entered a university at age 14 or 15 (Charlton 1965, 131, referring to sixteenth century; and Hall and Frankl 1982, 7). A full course in the liberal arts, not completed by most students, required (at Cambridge) seven years of study. The Bachelor of Arts degree was centered on the trivium, with logic taking center stage as preparation for organized public "disputations," although some reading in medicine and Aristotelian science was included (Hall and Frankl 1982, 7, quoted; Oxford curriculum in 1267; and Poynter 1970, 236). In theory, the mathematical quadrivium was the focus of study for the Master of Arts degree; and Oxford already enjoyed a European reputation in mathematics and natural science by the 1220s (Hall and Frankl 1982, 7, 1983, [6]). The prevailing scope of mathematical and scientific studies during the long Scholastic period has been assessed both favorably (Abelson 1906, 108, 112, 116-18, 124-27, 129-30) and unfavorably (Charlton 1965, 14) by prominent commentators, in the substantially more detailed first case referring to European universities generally.

The medieval university curricula imply that the grammar schools were expected to do little more than teach basic Latin. Cambridge engaged a "Master of Glomery" to superintend the local schools, and Oxford had two such officials (Leach 1915, 180). The Cambridge master supervised the teaching of simple Latin to entry-level pupils, "'glomerals'", intending to become schoolmasters (Hall and Frankl 1982, 7). A 1276 document (The jurisdiction of the grammer-schoolmaster, . . . defined) suggests that this official was contested by the university chancellor and an archdeacon for jurisdiction over students of certain kinds (Leach 1911, xxix). One of his counterparts at Oxford was a resident of one of the "colleges" who seems to have worked with students and scholars at various levels, including school-children residing in the house as charitable wards (Statutes of Merton College in the University of Oxford 1274, 183, 185).

Oxford also maintained a kind of adjunct faculty, normally not university graduates (Richardson 1941, 259), who taught languages, at a beginning level, and very practical subjects not included in regular studies. Over the second half of the fourteenth century, for example, Thomas Sampson taught Latin and French grammar; composition in both languages, with particular reference to correspondence and the drawing up of a variety of legal instruments; and the keeping of accounts (Richardson 1941). Although basic language instruction served remedial purposes for regular university students (Richardson 1941, 271), the primary demand was probably for short-term "intensive cramming in business methods" (Richardson 1941, 260) to allow young men to manage an agricultural estate. Such management was inseparable from the personal affairs of the landowning family (Richardson 1941, 269).

After completing a liberal arts education, or in the third case (Poynter 1970, 236) a bachelor's degree, a student could prepare at Oxford or Cambridge for a socially beneficial and well paid career in theology, law, or medicine (Hall and Frankl 1982, 7, and 1983, [6]). These fields required many years of schooling, however, respective totals of 16 and 13 years in the case of Oxford doctorates in theology and medicine (Hall and Frankl 1983, [6]); and Poynter 1970, 236). The early "colleges" were endowed, beginning in the latter half of the thirteenth century, to support small groups of resident scholars seeking advanced degrees (Charlton 1965, 13; and Hall and Frankl 1982, 7, 1983, [6], 9). The collegiate system of resident undergraduate instruction did not take hold until the sixteenth century, although Oxford colleges had begun before 1400 to house a few undergraduates (Hall and Frankl 1982, 7-8, and 1983, 9).

In medicine, most of the early students were clerics. As time progressed, however, laymen increasingly pursued the field, particularly after monks and clergy were barred by the church from practicing surgery, recognized (with the apothecary's craft) as a secondary medical art (Lobban 1976, 22-23). It was possible to obtain a university license to practice medicine based on a bachelor of arts degree, and thence to work toward bachelor and doctor of medicine degrees, through advanced textual study of medical classics, while obtaining professional experience (Poynter 1970, 236-37). Neither English university had a distinguished medical program, however (O'Malley 1970a, 89-90), and indeed as late as the seventeenth century neither medical school provided for clinical instruction or experience at a hospital or with practicing physicians (Poynter 1970, 236). Many English students preferred to study medicine abroad, especially in Italy (O'Malley 1970a, 89).

Italy was educationally preeminent also in the field of law. Learned Roman law as codified in the sixth century (Grun 1979, s.v. "529 C," "534 C") under Byzantine emperor Justinian I was largely unknown or neglected in the West for several centuries, but a somewhat degenerate popularized form that emphasized local custom and carried forth certain formal practices prevailed in parts of Italy and in southern France (Haskins 1927, 194-98). Full recovery of the Justinian texts during the late eleventh and early twelfth centuries led to a remarkable profusion of legal scholarship centered at the University of Bologna that included Gratian's definitive codification of church ("canon") law (Butts 1973, 172; and Haskins 1927, 198-208). Spurred in part by contemporary political consolidation and

26

commercial expansion, these developments of the 1100s, "[o]f all centuries the most legal," were a vital element of the medieval renaissance (Haskins 1927, 193, 194, quoted, 207).

From the twelfth through the sixteenth centuries, Italy was the central source from which Roman law was diffused across Europe, a process that was centered at the early universities (Haskins 1927, 208-10). At Oxford, for example, a visiting scholar from (probably) Bologna lectured on the learned "civil" law in 1149 (Leach 1911, xxiii, quoted, xxiv), and from early on bachelor and doctoral degrees were awarded in civil and canon law alike (Richardson 1941, 260, 266-67; and Southern 1987, 134, 143). Advanced studies were likewise offered in both fields at Cambridge (Hall and Frankl 1982, 7). Many English clerics studied canon law at Bologna, with some coverage of civil authorities, and John of Salisbury was highly learned in the Roman tradition (Haskins 1927, 211).

Even as legal scholars were forming a faculty at Oxford and ecclesiastics such as John were serving in the king's government, however, the English crown was rejecting Roman jurisprudence. Henry II seems to have officially forbade the teaching of the learned civil law, perhaps because of its close relationship to a newly defined canon law that (as his bitter struggle with Thomas Becket (Gillingham 1984, 124-26) only illustrated) could well conflict with state authority (Haskins 1927, 210, 212). Yet even under Henry the crown employed university graduates as royal justices (Brand 1987, 162), and in the centuries that followed his successors increasingly "found that Roman lawyers had the concepts and arguments which met their needs" in conducting international diplomacy and maintaining domestic sovereignty (Southern 1987, 142). Correspondingly, between 1300 and 1460 the percent of Oxford men studying law rose from 15 to 25; by

1500, by which time a brief decline had been reversed, there were more than twice as many law as theological students; and by and large the increases were accounted for by civil law, rather than ecclesiastical (Southern 1987, 143-44).

The major impact of Roman law in England was indirect. Over the centuries it materially influenced the development of the great legal system of the king's court (Haskins 1927, 195), the "common law" that took root in particular under Henry II as the national government became very complex and bureaucratic (Gillingham 1984, 126). By 1300 the common law was a "sophisticated and highly technical" system supporting an established pleading profession (Brand 1987, 150). For pertinent instruction, however, young Englishmen were forced to look beyond the universities, because Oxford and Cambridge did not teach the common law (Haskins 1927, 220).

There is clear evidence of formal education prior to 1300 in the law of the royal court. Detailed manuscripts from the 1270s bear the mark of lecture notes, and a variety of legal treatises from the thirteenth and fourteenth centuries appear to be compilations of formal lectures. Although some of the teaching, most of which took place in or around London, may have been of a free-lance nature, it seems that by 1300 senior "chancery clerks" conducted an organized course for the benefit, in particular, of junior colleagues. There may have been some provision also for more advanced instruction for apprentices in the king's courts. All the while, attendance at court was itself an important element of legal training (Brand 1987, 151-59, quoting 155).

After 1400, formal instruction in the common law became associated with the ten "inns of chancery," and the four more advanced "inns of court," located in London. These institutions, which had grown out of residential communities of lawyers established during the fourteenth century, provided a rich combination of academic and practical training in the law (Brand 1987, 147-49; and Charlton 1965, 169-95).

The universities naturally stood in the forefront of the break with Scholasticism known as the English Renaissance, a topic that invites very closely related reference to three renowned grammar schools founded in the latter part of the era.

Emergence of "Humanism": The Two Universities, and Three Related Grammar School Foundations

England's leading patron of literary and humanistic studies during the first half of the fifteenth century was Duke Humphrey of Gloucester, brother of Henry V, king (Morgan 1984, [617]) from 1413 to 1422. Humphrey donated 263 books to Oxford, 1439-44, including many important new translations of, or commentaries on, Greek and Latin classics that he had obtained from Italy. He also commissioned new translations by Italian scholars and funded study in Italy by young Englishmen (Charlton 1965, 44-45). The duke helped finance the construction of Oxford's earliest designated faculty building, the divinity school. A room built above the structure in 1488 (Gilbert 1968, 34) to house his excellent library colection was the forerunner of the modern-day Bodleian Library reading room known as "'Duke Humphrey'" (Hall and Frankl 1983, 17).

A decisive turn toward humanism was forged by the presence at Oxford late in the fifteenth century of, in particular, William Grocyn, Thomas Linacre, John Colet, and (above all) Thomas More and Erasmus of Rotterdam. They were perhaps the leading exponents of a new learning that included in particular the study of Greek (Charlton 1965, 41; Guy 1984, 242-44; and

29

Hall and Frankl 1983, 10).[9] The presence of Erasmus during the years
1511-14 helped launch at Cambridge (also a site of increasing work in mathematics) the study of Greek, the reading of classical authors beyond Aristotle, and biblical scholarship (Hall and Frankl 1982, 10). Greek instruction may have developed rather slowly, however. It is said that Grocyn,
on becoming in 1491 (Leach 1915, 247) the first Englishman to teach the
language at Oxford, lectured without pay; and Greek study at Cambridge of
nearly a century later is known to have begun with the basic elements
(Eliot 1884, 26-27).

These references to fundamental intellectual change at the universities
relate to three celebrated grammar schools founded during the 150 years
preceding the Reformation. Leading prelate William of Wykeham founded Winchester as the preparatory school for his New College at Oxford, the university's first college to accommodate undergraduates, and its early (if not
prolonged) center of humanistic study (Hall and Frankl 1983, 59-60, [63]);
Leach 1911, xxxiv-xxxv; and Watson 1916, 30-33). His endowment provided
full scholarships for seventy "poor and needy" or "poor and indigent" youth
([William of Wykeham] 1382, 323, 325). Winchester boys subsequently elected
to New College scholarships would two years after admission become fellows
of the college, an appointment that they could hold (barring an inheritance)
until, ordinarily, acquiring an ecclesiastical living or entering a monastic order (Ollard 1982, 18).

---

[9] Leach (1915, 248, quoted, 249) rightly cautions against identifying
"Humanism" with the introduction of Greek studies, or simply the elevation
of grammar or literature over logic as the primary field of study. Fundamentally, "[i]t was the substitution . . . of this world for the next, as
the object of living, and therefore of education, that differentiated the
humanists from their predecessors." Similarly, certain schools "took to
Greek" because they already were "scholarly and literary" institutions.

A nephew of Duke Humphrey's (Griffiths 1984, 200), founder Henry VI
later established the same relationship between Eton and King's College,
Cambridge (Hall and Frankl 1982, 44-[45]; Ollard 1982, 18; and Watson 1916,
33-34). Henry (1440, 407) provided originally for 25 "poor and needy"
scholars gathered "to learn grammar," along with a provost,[10] 10 priests as
(Ollard 1982, 17) "fellows," 4 "clerks," 6 "chorister[s]," 25 "poor and
weakly men" devoted to prayer, and a schoolmaster. "The almshouse element
was scrapped" a few years later, however, as the number of scholarships was
increased to seventy (Ollard 1982, 17, quoted, 18, 20). Besides the resident scholars, or "Collegers," Eton's student body included a lesser number,
evidently, of "Commensals" (the original name) or "Oppidans." Although in
keeping with Henry VI's plan (1440, 407) and early statutes they paid no
tuition or fees, and dined with the Collegers, the Oppidans lodged in the
town or "oppidum" at their own expense. Except for twenty boys of noble
birth who ate at their own "higher tables," they were not materially different in social background from the scholars themselves (Ollard 1982,
19-20, emphasis in original).

Winchester and Eton almost certainly were pioneers in the teaching of
Greek in England, having evidently through a Winchester graduate who served
as headmaster at both schools introduced the language before 1500 (Leach
1915, 247). Their influence was felt in the founding of at least three
new grammar schools in the sixteenth century with substantial linkage to
Oxford or Cambridge colleges (Charlton 1965, 131), not counting an ill-fated

---

[10] The provost headed (and still heads) the governing body of the school,
consisting also of the fellows. Evolving over time into a kind of "constitutional monarch," the provost prior to nineteenth-century reforms (Ollard
1982, 18-19, 54, 57) was paid more than the headmaster (Ollard 1982, 28n).

effort of Cardinal Wolsey's related below. On balance, however, the exclusive relationships maintained between Winchester and New College and Eton and King's College had serious "cramping, confining" effects at each institution (Ollard 1982, 18, 19, quoted).

After its early leadership in humanistic studies at Oxford, which included lectures on Greek by a foreign scholar (Leach 1915, 247), New College "lapsed into three centuries of idleness and introspection" (Hall and Frankl 1983, [63]). At Cambridge, King's "became a kind of club to which the fortunate members [fellows] were elected for life, excused from duties and comfortably accommodated" (Ollard 1982, 19). It was not until after 1850 that scholarships and fellowships at the colleges were opened to men not schooled at Winchester or Eton. Amidst further reform, both colleges soon markedly enhanced their academic stature (Hall and Frankl 1982, 48, and 1983, 63, 65). King's College was "noted for intellectual brilliance" by 1900, around the time that Eton graduate John Maynard Keynes matriculated there (Hall and Frankl 1982, 48; and Landreth 1976, 442-43).

Early in the sixteenth century, finally, Dean John Colet founded a new St. Paul's school at the London cathedral, fully eclipsing if not, contrary to statutes, strictly displacing a school that could reasonably be traced to the beginnings of the bishopric in 604 (Charlton 1965, 92; and Leach 1915, 6, 279). Colet's statutes (c. 1518b, 154-55) for the affluent new school attracted the praise of Erasmus in calling for enriched grammatical instruction that would include Greek literature as well as Latin, although ancient classics, as contrasted with patristic writings, were not included. St. Paul's first headmaster and assistant master were both proficient in Greek, but there is circumstantial evidence that the language may have been offered only in the early years (Leach 1915, 247, 277-81; and Watson 1916, 12-13).

32

Dean Colet (c. 1518b, 151-52) placed his school under the control of the Mercers' Company of London, to which he himself on some basis belonged. St. Paul's provided free tuition for 153 boys, fully six times as many as were accommodated at the school the same guild had conducted since the 1440s (Leach 1915, 278, 280-81). An entry fee was assessed to benefit "the poor scholar . . . that swepeth the scole and keepeth the seats cleane" (Colet c. 1518b, 153).

The reference made to scholars' poverty directs attention to the clientele of medieval grammar schools, and in turn to opportunities that existed for elementary study. Between the extremes of the social spectrum there was reasonably wide access to grammar schooling, subject to a severe exclusion based on gender.

Clientele of Medieval Grammar Schools, and Opportunities for Elementary Education

Reasonably Wide Access

William of Wykeham's foundation deed (1382, 321, quoted, 322) reserved Winchester scholarships for youth whose "means barely suffice[d] . . . to allow them to continue and profit in [the study of] the . . . art of grammar." Eligibility was confined to boys with no more than five '"marks"' to dispose of annually (Leach 1915, 207). Stated in terms of a unit of account worth two thirds of a pound (Random House dictionary 1966, s.v. "mark[2]," def. 4), that amount exceeded the yearly "livings" of sixty-seven priesthoods in the Winchester diocese, and was more than twice the maximum income level for a skilled artisan of the day. Winchester was clearly not intended for "the sons of serfs or the gutter poor" (Leach 1915, 207).

Leach states (1915, 207, 208, quoted) that William sought to assist families headed by "the younger sons of lords and squires, the landed gentry and farmers in the country, the burgesses and traders in the towns." Perhaps biased upward, disregarding 'young "noblemen" who [suggestive of nonscholarship Eton students] came [to Winchester] as commoners' (Leach 1915, 207), this statement glides too lightly over a rather complex social hierarchy.[11] It is useful, however, in declining to take at face value the reference to "poor and needy" pupils, and secondarily as a reminder that younger sons of "gentlemen" (Morrill 1984, 297) did not retain their status.

Certainly neither Winchester nor (Ollard 1982, 20) Eton admitted the children of serfs. Matters are complicated somewhat, however, by the distinction drawn traditionally between "free" and "unfree" peasantry (whose unclarity led to classification of land as "free" or "servile"). Disregarding the "wide diversity" of gradations that existed (Columbia encyclopedia 3d,

---

[11] A "Model Feudal System" (emphasis deleted) included "strict division into social classes," including "nobility, clergy, peasantry, and, in the later Middle Ages, burgesses" (Columbia encyclopedia 3d, s.v. "feudalism"). In the last case, and regarding Leach's (1915, 208) use of the term as well, the intended reference is probably to town or borough freemen not otherwise classified, rather than to Parliamentary representatives (Random House dictionary 1966, s.v. "burgess," defs. 1, 2) or other officeholders. A major basis for class distinction was the "manorial system" that regulated "peasant land tenure and production" and administered "local justice and taxation" (Columbia encyclopedia 3d, s.v. "feudalism," "manorial system," quoted).

The beginning of widespread "inclosure" of estates in the fifteenth century (Griffiths 1984, 189, "enclosure") only hastened the passing of a manorial system already long in decline (Columbia encyclopedia 3d, s.v. "inclosure or enclosure," emphasis added, "manorial system"). Referring to a later time, circa 1580-1640, Sheldon Cohen (1974, 13) distinguishes among five social classes: (1) landed aristocrats with roots traceable to the Conquest; (2) landed gentry "recently elevated," and wealthy merchants, artisans, and bankers; (3) lawyers, physicians, clerics, teachers, and yeomen farmers, the major "middle-class" groups; (4) poor workingmen, tenant farmers, and tradesmen; and (5) beggars, squatters, and other indigents, Leach's "gutter poor" (1915, 206). Another commentator (Morrill 1984, 296-97) on the early modern period refers somewhat similarly to the hereditary "peerage" and the "gentry" as the "noblemen" of the day, but states that country "gentlemen" clearly outranked prosperous city dwellers socially.

s.v. "manorial system"), a "serf" was no more than a laborer "attached to the lord's land," while a "villein" enjoyed a freeman's status except in relation to the lord (Random House dictionary 1966, s.v. "serf," "villein").

In any event, it seems that the peasantry were long subject to heavy fines for sending their youth to school without their lords' consent, as a barrier to an escape from villeinage or serfdom through education (Leach 1915, 206). A parliamentary petition that would simply have excluded their children from the schools was denied in 1391 by the ill-fated (Griffiths 1983, 198) Richard II in one of a series of otherwise legislative or judicial actions that established a principle of wide access to schooling (Butts 1973, 166). In particular, the Statute of Labourers and Apprentices adopted fifteen years later softened the exclusion of youth of landless families from trade or manufacturing apprenticeships with a remarkably inclusive statement (Leach 1911, 387):

> '[E]very man or woman, of what estate or condition that he be, shall be free to set their son or daughter to take learning at any manner school that pleaseth them within the Realm'.

Although that case may have been rather isolated, this statement did not prevent Eton from later barring, evidently (Ollard 1982, 20) by statute, the sons of serfs and (perhaps) villeins. The striking implication that "daughter[s]" were free to attend grammar schools is considered below. Otherwise, the principle expressed in 1406 is meaningful only to the extent that schools were affordable by the general population, and were sufficiently numerous and dispersed to serve the country, factors related by the inability of poor families to send their children to distant schools.

In keeping with the mandate of a twelfth-century church council (Lateran Council . . . 1179) that cathedrals provide free schooling for "poor scholars," the schools of cathedrals and collegiate churches were "open to all boys, [were] ordinarily free of cost to poor boys, and never requir[ed] heavy fees" (Watson 1916, 2). Virtually opened with the declaraation of free access cited above, the fifteenth century was a time of substantial growth in number of "free" schools (Leach 1911, xxxvii-xxxix). Educational endowments derived from various sources presumably permitted extensive free or low-cost schooling.

By the 1540s, on one estimate (Leach 1915, 330), there were on average at least 100 grammar schools per county, or some 400 in total. In Herefordshire on the Welsh border, famous for cattle (Columbia encyclopedia 3d, s.v. "Herefordshire or Hereford," emphasis added), 17 such schools served a population of around thirty thousand people; and overall no more than one of the forty-two towns appearing in poll tax returns lacked such an institution (Leach 1915, 329-30). Estimated total population (1541) was 2.77 million people (Guy 1984, 224), or (1545) 3.0 million including Wales (Wilson 1977, 116). Although these data or estimates are impressive, and some schools reckoned enrollment "not by units but by scores" (Leach 1915, 330, quoted, 331), chantry schools in particular were usually very small (Watson 1916, 5), and the general population would have been youthful by present-day standards.

A conspicuous exception regarding grammar school enrollment was found at the top of the social spectrum. The medieval "ruling class" of noblemen and knights educated their sons in a chivalric tradition that placed more emphasis on cultivating practical skills and virtues of various kinds than on book learning (Butts 1973, 166-67; Charlton 1965, 16, quoted, 17-20; and Columbia encyclopedia 3d, s.v. "feudalism," "knighthood and chivalry," general source). Girls from such families enjoyed somewhat comparable opportunity that usually included training at home or in a convent and later in the court of a manorial overlord (Butts 1973, 167).

With chivalry already in decline by 1350, private tutoring had at least by the sixteenth century become the fundamental mode of upper-class education (Charlton 1965, 20, 213). The brief reference made to chivalric education points up, however, a biological exclusion from grammar schooling that eclipsed any and all social exceptions, notwithstanding the 1406 statute of Apprentices.

Exclusion of Females

During the middle ages women were often pressed into duty for running their husbands' estates, and at a lower level were sometimes included among manorial tenants or town merchants. Girls were generally assumed, even so, to have no need for grammar schooling (Charlton 1965, 205-8), a cultural assumption reflected in the practice between the Conquest and Reformation of addressing nuns in the vernacular, French or (later) English, rather than in Latin (Leach 1911, xviii). Based on the Latin word "childra," school statutes in English often referred simply to "children." On a long-standing usage that became associated especially with Winchester, however, the Latin term was understood to apply to male youth alone (Leach 1915, 88-89, emphasis in original).

An exceptional viewpoint was expressed by Thomas More, whose own household was a remarkable center of study, family-wide, in writing his daughters' tutor that '"learning by which the reason is cultivated is equally suited to both"' sexes (Charlton 1965, 204, 207, quoted). Protestant clergyman Thomas Becon, who had been exposed to advanced educational doctrines while exiled abroad during a brief Catholic restoration, quoted More in demanding in 1564 the establishment of girls' schools "'in letters and manners'" (Charlton 1965, 207, 207n; and Watson 1916, 52-54, 65, 66, quoted). A breakthrough of sorts was finally achieved thirty years later when a new school from the Manchester and Liverpool vicinity of western England (Columbia encyclopedia 3d, s.v. "Cheshire," entry 1; and Gilbert 1968, 75) allowed a limited number of girls to study reading in English through, at most, age nine (Watson 1916, 116).

Teaching reading and needlework, possibly the first school endowed for girls was established in 1655 along with a coordinate boys' school that seems also to have been of rather elementary level (Leach 1911, xlviii). One source (Sheldon Cohen 1974, 25) states that by then private-venture finishing schools of urban areas offered 'such "refined" subjects as French, sewing, dancing, and singing'. In any event, more than rudimentary schooling was confined in late medieval and early modern times to girls of social privilege enjoying private tutoring at home or as a guest of a cultured family, or (ideally) a position at the royal court (Charlton 1965, 209-10). Particularly learned women of the sixteenth century included Queens Mary and Elizabeth and Lady Jane Gray, who ruled (Guy 1984, 261) for nine days before her ouster by Mary. All three were "accomplished linguists" (Charlton 1965, 208, quoted, 209).

However strong their academic preparation might be, females were excluded from the universities not only during the later middle ages, but even well beyond the endpoint of this educational survey, 1800. Cambridge and Oxford were just beginning or about to begin to make a place for female students when in the late 1870s (Hall and Frankl 1982, [78], and 1983, 89) the University of London, founded (Butts 1973, 347; and Gilbert 1968, 114) in 1836, first awarded degrees to women. Although women became eligible for university examinations at Cambridge in 1881 and at Oxford thirteen years later, they were not awarded degrees by the two ancient institutions until 1948 and 1920, respectively (Hall and Frankl 1982, 87, 89, and 1983, 76, [78]-79).

The irony is that women had long served both universities as founders of men's colleges. During the era leading up to the Reformation, two women had important supporting roles in the founding of colleges at Oxford. Exising as a group of scholars by 1266, Balliol College was finally endowed and granted statutes sixteen years later by the widow of John of Balliol. The Queen's college was formed in 1340 by the chaplain to Edward III's wife (Griffiths 1984, 178, quoted, 180) Phillipa of Hainault, "a paragon among queens," who had consented to official recognition as its foundress (Hall and Frankl 1983, 32, 68).

At Cambridge, Pembroke College was founded in the mid-fourteenth century by the Countess of Pembroke, and three colleges formed before the Reformation had women cofounders. After Henry VI endowed King's College, his wife Margaret of Anjou began in 1447 to reestablish St. Bernard, set up only the prior year with "a small and poor endowment," as Queen Margaret's College. This endeavor on behalf of "'laud and honneure of sexe femnine'" was continued by new queen Elizabeth after Henry was deposed in 1461 (Morgan 1984, 606) by Edward IV. As the plural form indicated, "Queens'" College recognizes both women as founders (Hall and Frankl 1982, 53, 59, quoted).

The foremost female educational patron was Margaret Beaufort, mother of the first Tudor king (Morgan 1984, [618]), Henry VII. It was Lady Margaret who in 1505 refounded God's House as Christ's College, to which she would make frequent visits over her remaining four years as she commenced the founding of St. John's. That project was completed in 1511 by Bishop John Fisher, the (Cremin 1970, 87) Cambridge chancellor, who had probably

39

drawn up his friend's very strict statutes governing college life at Christ's (Hall and Frankl 1982, 27, [63]).

The founding of St. John's coincided with the arrival at Cambridge of Erasmus. Although he resided at Queens', his influence as Lady Margaret Reader in Greek and Professor of Divinity may have helped the new college "establish itself as an important cent[er] of learning" (Hall and Frankl 1982, 61, 65, quoted). Margaret, whose patronage included "many religious houses" and two early English printers, endowed a divinity professorship at Oxford as well (Columbia encyclopedia 3d, s.v. "Beaufort, Margaret . . .," "Caxton, William"). The first English university eventually honored her with the naming of one of its two original women's colleges, founded (The Columbia-Viking desk encyclopedia 2d, s.v. "Columbia University") in 1878 and '79, as Lady Margaret Hall. The case for so remembering Margaret Beaufort, a widow of 13 or 14 on the birth in 1457 of the future Henry VII (Columbia encyclopedia 3d, s.v. "Beaufort, Margaret," "Henry VII, 1457-1509"), was stated by the "Hall's" first principal (Hall and Frankl 1983, 87):

'[S]he was a gentlewoman, a scholar, and a saint, and after having been three times married she took a vow of celibacy. What more cound be expected of any woman?'.

In general, any opportunity that girls might enjoy for formal instruction was limited to very elementary study. Provision made for such learning is of interest in view further of grammar school statutes and of fundamental schooling objectives.

Elementary Schooling

Statutes adopted by Eton and St. Paul's provided an example often followed or expanded upon during the Reformation era. Eton stipulated that entering pupils possess "'a competent knowledge of reading and the [Latin] grammar of Donatus and of plain song'" (Charlton 1965, 98). Dean Colet required (c. 1518a, 155) that youth entering St. Paul's be able to "rede & wryte Latyn & englisshe sufficiently" for lesson purposes.

Children not headed for grammar school still needed literacy in the vernacular for general commercial purposes or in preparation for religious observances of certain kinds. Learning elements of arithmetic or religious Latin would meet similar needs (Charlton 1965, 100-1; and Cremin 1970, 169).

Where was such instruction to be found, beyond an occasional parental home or, for example, the rare almonry school? It probably remained largely the responsibility of parish and chantry priests (Charlton 1965, 15, 98; and Guy 1984, 243, by photo). In 1200 the Council of Westminster (Schools of the Council . . ., 139) had called on priests to "keep schools in their towns and teach little boys gratis." Women who taught the alphabet in '"dame"' schools in their homes (Sheldon Cohen 1974, 20) may sometimes, as later in New England (Cremin 1970, 129), have proceeded to teach children to read.

An important avenue to literacy in the late middle ages was apprentice-ship. Childhood apprenticeship with a skilled master, followed by training as a "journeyman," was the traditional route to membership as a "master craftsman" in a craft guild (Butts 1973, 165). As this institution came under increasing guild oversight, there arose in the fifteenth century a general expectation that the master would supply instruction in "the three R's" to his apprentice, who in a number of cases was female. A 1498 agree-ment by a young man to serve an extra year if his master would support him at a "writing school" suggests that independent writing teachers had arrived on the scene. During the century that followed, however, "the educative function" of apprenticeship "declined in significance" (Charlton 1965, 54-55).

Grammar schools of the 1500s increasingly assumed responsibility for remedial instruction of boys entering with insufficient basic skills. Small rural schools would necessarily rely mainly on their brighter older students to assist such boys as "'pupil teachers"', a practice that was also commended in the statutes for the (Leach 1915, 296-97) refoundation of Manchester Grammar School in 1525. As the century progressed there developed a trend of appointing, where possible, an assistant master or "usher" whose responsibilities would include teaching elementary subjects as needed, and by 1600 "most grammar schools of any size" would have engaged such a person (Charlton 1965, 198, 99-100, quoted). By around this time, too, privately sponsored elementary or "petty" schools that often included girls were beginning to emerge in large numbers, in rural and urban areas alike (Sheldon Cohen 1974, 20). Cremin's supposition (1970, 169) that under the auspices of towns, guilds, or individual teachers such schooling was already prevalent by late medieval times appears to be an isolated opinion.

It has been estimated that by 1640 male literacy in the vernacular exceeded 50% in London, and the rate outside the capital was approximately one third (Sheldon Cohen 1974, 17). It appears (Guy 1984, 293; and Wilson 1977, 116-17) that London then had roughly an eighth of the population of England and, with less than 10% of the total in 1603 (Guy 1984, 224), Wales. Although the estimates for 1640 fall short of Thomas More's "enthusiastic" conjecture of some 140 years earlier that more than half of his (male?) countrymen were literate (Guy 1984, 293), they do imply substantial access to elementary schooling from one source or another.

Six schools destined to form with Winchester, Eton, and St. Paul's a celebrated group of "Public Schools" were among the numerous new educational foundations between the onset of the English Reformation in, on one reckoning,

1529 and the "Restoration" of the monarchy in 1660. They illustrated the diversity of school sponsorship within the fundamentally new environment created by the dissolution of religious institutions that had carried much of the educational load. Grammar shcooling of a day of expanding clientele and enhanced provision for elementary study reflected in some part the broadened learning and intellectual vitality of the Renaissance. Religious influences permeated the schools, with the leadership and full support of the state, and important educational initiatives and proposals provided a backdrop to subsequent advances in commercial education.

The Early Modern Period: From the Reformation to the Restoration, 1529-1660

Educational Reorganization During the Reformation

Positive Response to Dissolution of Monasteries and Other Institutional Sponsors or Patrons

As lord chancellor and highest religious authority in the land, Thomas Cardinal Wolsey stood through the deference of Henry VIII as England's dominant figure from 1515 to 1529 (Guy 1984, 238, 240; and Hall and Frankl 1983, 36). Educationally, in 1525 he established "Cardinal" College, destined to become "Oxford's grandest college" after its two-phase refounding by Henry as "Christ Church" (Hall and Frankl 1983, 36). He turned then toward developing at Ipswich a feeder grammar school, absorbing the publicly controlled school already there that he himself (Charlton 1965, 97) had attended, in the tradition of Winchester and Eton. The setting was an eastern seaport "of great [contemporary] ecclesiastical and commercial importance" (Columbia encyclopedia 3d, s.v. "Ipswich," entry 2).

Wolsey erected a handsome red-brick building at Ipswich in 1528, laid out an advanced classical curriculum, and proposed specific teaching methods

(Charlton 1965, 91; Leach 1915, 298; and Watson 1916, 16-19). The next year he was ousted from government, however, due to the bitter "divorce crisis" with the papacy that threatened Henry's plans to marry Anne Boleyn (Guy 1984, 245, 246, quoted). Wolsey's school '"fell with him"', as lamented in Shakespeare's Henry VIII, as in a partial preview, only, of later policies the crown soon seized the property and endowment. The building was destroyed (leaving a gateway), but local authorities received a fraction of the endowment, and schooling continued at Ipswich under, in time, a refoundation by the incorporated town (Charlton 1965, 91; Leach 1915, 298; and Watson 1916, 16, quoted).

Cardinal Wolsey's removal in 1529 marks the start of a train of official events that yielded, in a nation in which anti-clerical sentiment had been growing for a generation (Guy 1984, 240), the break with Rome known as the English Reformation. Over the years 1532-36 Parliament adopted six key acts. They included the 1534 "Act of Supremacy," foreshadowed (Gilbert 1968, 44; and Grun 1979, s.v. "1531 A") three years earlier, by which the king was recognized as "Supreme head" of an English church (Guy 1984, 246, quoted, 247) thus clearly "severed . . . from Rome" (Gilbert 1968, 44). By way of the companion "Treasons Act," it led to the execution in 1535 of Wolsey's successor as lord chancellor, Sir Thomas More (Guy 1984, 246-47).[12]

Educationally, the major early development was the dissolution of the monasteries and convents, beginning in 1536 (Guy 1984, 249; and Watson 1916,

_____

[12]More's thousand days as lord chancellor were filled with irony. He opposed the king on the divorce issue that had been Wolsey's undoing and would lead to the assertion of "royal supremacy"; and he betrayed his own brilliant humanist past in a pursuit of "repression and extermination of [religious] heresy." More's martyrdom, in the company of St. John Fisher and the Carthusian monks of London, was based on his steadfast belief in "papal primacy" over the church (Columbia encyclopedia 3d, s.v. "Carthusians"; and Guy 1984, 244-46, quoted, 247).

26). Within less than four years, 560 of them had been suppressed. Henry VIII was compelled to dissolve the religious houses by their almost invariable allegiance to "parent institutions" outside England and Wales; his own desperate need for additional sources of revenue; and his need for "massive injections of new patronage" to secure support for the Reformation from the lay nobility and gentry (Guy 1984, 248, 249, quoted). Educationally, the issue was not the loss of scattered almonry schooling, but the fate of nearby schools governed or supported by monasteries, and of cathedral schools from episcopal sees that had remained monastic.

Instruction was rarely discontinued, however. Anticipating developments under the next king's broader dissolution policies, schooling was ordinarily maintained in the first case through cooperative arrangements of one kind or another between state and locality. The grammar school operated by the abbey at Reading in "a decayed hospital for widows" provides an interesting example in that (Gilbert 1968, 44) the abbot was one of at least sixteen heads of monasteries to be executed by Henry. Upon dissolving the religious house, the king assumed patronage of the school, appointing the prior teacher (an Eton graduate responsible for the first English text on rhetoric) as its master at an annual salary of ten pounds charged to a royal manor. In 1562 control was passed to the town of Reading. Earlier, Parliament had granted a petition brought by the citizens of St. Albans, led by the former local abbot, to reconstitute their grammar school under borough control (Charlton 1965, 90-92; and Leach 1915, 311, quoted).

Formerly monastic cathedrals were reorganized as "Cathedrals of the New Foundation" (Guy 1984, 249), with canons replacing monks. The king "enriched and expanded" existing instruction. At least seven cathedral schools were reorganized,[13] on a much enhanced basis, while an exception was made at Winchester in support of the distinguished local school discussed above (Leach 1911, xliii, quoted, and 1915, 311-12). In the six new bishoprics established (Guy 1984, 249) at former monastic sites, perhaps excepting Oxford, excellent provision was made for cathedral schools, with a well-paid master and assistant, to replace local grammar schools having a variety of origins and sponsorships (Leach 1915, 312). Sound educational arrangements were made also in the three recorded cases in which monasteries were replaced by collegiate churches, although for different reasons two of the schools were short-lived. The third one was reportedly in 1915 (Leach, 317, 318, quoted) "still one of the chief schools of Wales."

Collegiate churches were themselves among the targets of a second dissolution campaign launched by Henry. Although barely underway when it expired with the king, it anticipated a major initiative of his successor's. As closure of the monasteries had proceeded, many feudal lords had begun to "dissolve the hospitals, colleges [collegiate churches], and chantries, of which . . . they were patrons," or to sell or convert to personal gain properties whose charitable purposes (leprosy treatment in particular) were no longer relevant (Leach 1915, 319, quoted, 320). In light especially (Guy 1984, 249, quoted, 256) of "colossal" expenditures for war with France and Scotland, and high demands by laity for sharing the Reformation "spoils,"

---

[13] Secondary sources employed are less than clear on this point. Leach writes (1915, 311) that twelve grammar schools were refounded 'as part of the cathedrals "of the new foundation"', and then specifically lists (312) six previously existing bishoprics and five of the six new ones. Watson states (1916, 25) that Henry VIII "arranged for [only] six new Cathedral Foundations," and proceeds (28) to cite the York Grammar School as one of them. Although not listing it among the refounded schools, Leach (1915, 279) had identified York as a cathedral school of the fifteenth century. Earlier (Leach 1911, xliii), he had referred to the (re)foundation of thirteen grammar schools, perhaps intending to include York plus Oxford (not cited in 1915) and the five other new episcopal sees.

46

Parliament late in 1545 authorized the king (Leach 1915, 320) to seize the

"colleges, fre chappelles, chantries, hospitalles, fraternities, brotherhoods, guilds and stipendarie prestes [priesthoods] having per-
petuitye for ever" which had been illegally dissolved before Christmas
[of that year].

Although the king was granted still further discretionary authority
in the area, his early death (January 1547) and time-consuming due process
seem to have limited seizures under the act to four colleges, one hospital,
and three chantry endowments. At least five of the institutions had evidently conducted schools (Leach 1915, 320-21). Injunctions issued in 1547
in the name of Edward VI, Henry's nine-year-old son (Guy 1984, 258), directed
all chantry priests to teach youth (Leach 1911, xliii). The Chantries Act
of the following year, however, dissolved all chantries, collegiate churches,
social and religious guilds or brotherhoods, charitable hospitals, and free
chapels, and thereby formally terminated the schools associated with them
(Leach 1911, xliii-xliv; and Watson 1916, 26-27).

On balance, although Leach's negative opinion (1911, xliv) was for some
time "widely accepted" (Charlton 1965, 89), this development seems to have
been favorable to education. Granting (Guy 1984, 258) that shorter-range
political applications may have taken priority, an express objective was to
free endowments and revenues for educational usage. Even where this intent
was not directly achieved, as was often the case (Charlton 1965, 92; and
Leach 1911, xliv), individuals and localities found numerous ways to reestablish schools, often on a more secure basis than before.

By purchase or gift, the property or rents of a former endowment were
frequently (re)acquired for schooling purposes by towns or local inhabitants.
Incorporated towns or reconstituted societies themselves often reorganized
schools founded by religious guilds, while merchant or craft guilds that
had supported education through chantries or similar endowments could take

on direct supervision. In many cases schools were continued with "a reorganized curriculum set out in statutes." In addition, purely lay-sponsored education, which had expanded considerably (Leach 1915, 281-300) under Henry VIII, "continued [to grow] with added strength throughout the sixteenth century" (Charlton 1965, 90, 91-92, quoted). Many prominent clerics and <u>merchants</u> were patrons of new or reconstituted schools.

Clerics, Merchants, and Other Leading School Founders or Patrons

Archbishop of Canterbury Thomas Cranmer, the leading prelate in the early development of English Protestantism, exercised major influence over at least the teaching in "a considerable group" of new or refounded schools. A champion of education for the poor, based on ability, he proposed that his cathedral at Canterbury conduct secondary education in grammar <u>and</u> logic in three ancient tongues, and higher studies in those languages, divinity, medicine and law, scientific learning, and French. Noncurricular innovations would have included payment of stipends to scholars at each level and major educational employment of resident canons (Watson 1916, 20, quoted, 21-22). An obscure document of King Henry's not published until 1838 (Watson 1916, 23n) laid out a much expanded scheme calling, for example, for twenty-one or more academically enriched cathedral grammar schools (Watson 1916, 22-25). Cranmer wrote the first two editions of the Book of Common Prayer for the new church, under Edward VI, and secured their enforcement by parliamentary Acts of Supremacy jeopardizing the doctrine of supreme royal authority (Guy 1984, 258-60).

Archbishop Cranmer had been educated at Cambridge early in the sixteenth century, along with two bishops who would join him as "the chief propagators of the new religion," and eventual martyrs on its behalf

(Hall and Frankl 1983, 10). His university quickly became the leading center for Protestant thought, or the "'new learning',", while Oxford remained more orthodox or traditional in outlook despite the teaching of visiting Cambridge scholars (Guy 1984, 245, quoted; and Hall and Frankl, 1982, 10, and 1983, 10). During the brief Catholic restoration under Queen Mary, Thomas Cranmer was burned at the stake just outside one Oxford college in 1556 following a trial at another one. Bishops Ridley and Latimer had met the same fate a year earlier (Gilbert 1968, 44; Guy 1984, 261; and Hall and Frankl 1983, 10).

Mary burned at least 274 English Protestants during her reign of 1553-58, but permitted some 800 others to emigrate to Frankfurt, Zurich, Geneva, Strasbourg, Basel, and other cities of continental Europe (Cheney [1904], 132-33; Guy 1984, 263, source of numerical data, citing only first three cities listed; and Watson 1916, 51). Making firsthand acquaintance with many Reformation leaders, including major educational reformers, "these exiles launch[ed] a relentless crusade of anti-Catholic propaganda and subversive literature against England." Upon their return to England with the accession of Queen Elizabeth in 1558, many of these men were appointed bishops (Guy 1984, 262, quoted; and Watson 1916, 52-54).

Among the many Marian exiles who founded Elizabethan grammar schools were future archbishops Edmund Grindal and Edwin Sandys, both of whom had been in Strasbourg. Alexander Nowell, who had exiled in Frankfurt after serving as headmaster at Westminster (discussed below), had profound influence on education as dean at St. Paul's for forty-two years, benefactor of the grammar school and Oxford (Hall and Frankl 1983, 34-36) college of his youth, author of school statutes and of an authorized school Catechism, and respected "consultant-educationist" (Watson 1916, 55-68, especially 55-59, quoting 58).

Another major class of founders and supporters of grammar schools in the Reformation era were great <u>merchants</u> of the day. With the passing of traditional chantry practices, successful men were often disposed to endow or augment the endowment of schools in their native towns or cities (Watson 1916, 46). A long list published in 1603 of London citizens who had endowed schools was dominated by members of the commercial class. For example, textile merchant John Gresham willed his mansion to the county of Holt as the quarters for a school that was said in its first two centuries, through around 1750, to have sent more than eighty boys to a single college at one of the universities. Other schools were founded by country gentlemen, yeomen, and lawyers (Charlton 1965, 92-93; and Watson 1916, 46-49).

An excellent picture of the diverse sponsorship of new schools is provided by the six grammar schools that along with Winchester, Eton, and St. Paul's would become England's most elite secondary institutions long before their official designation in 1864 as the nine "Public Schools" (Hans 1951, 17, quoted, 19). Rugby and Harrow were founded respectively by a grocer and a yeoman farmer (Watson 1916, 47-48). Merchant Taylors' bore the name of the sponsoring craft guild, one of whose leading members reserved for graduates thirty-seven places in the Oxford college he had founded in honor of patron saint of tailors John the Baptist. Established during Mary's reign as a divinity school "to combat Protestant heresy," St. John's was known to "harbo[r] Catholic Sympathi[z]ers" during the remainder of the sixteenth century (Charlton 1965, 131; and Hall and Frankl 1983, 72, 73, quoted).

On the initiative of town officials and citizens, Shrewsbury was financed from revenues obtained from two dissolved collegiate churches (Charlton 1965, 91). Charterhouse, the only school of the group not founded before 1600 (Hans 1951, 17), grew out of a charitable hospital "for old men" endowed in London in 1611 on the site of a Carthusian monastery established 240 years earlier (Columbia encyclopedia 3d, quoted, and Random House dictionary 1966, s.v. "Charterhouse").

Westminster, finally, has roots in an almonry school dating from 1367 or thereabouts (Leach 1915, 219-20). The monastery was replaced by Henry VIII with a cathedral that included a school; the bishopric was abandoned under Edward VI, leaving a collegiate church; and there was a brief monastic restoration under Mary after the queen had appointed "a fashionable Protestant intellectual" as headmaster (Guy 1984, 249; Leach 1915, 321; and Ollard 1982, 27, quoted). Modern-day Westminster dates from 1560, when Queen Elizabeth refounded the cathedral church, including the grammar school as an integral element (Leach 1915, 321; and Statutes of the Westminster School 1560).

Studies at early modern grammer schools reflected in limited measure broader cultural currents of a day in which, increasingly, traditional practices came under critical scrutiny and the native language invited serious respect.

Trends in Grammar School Instruction

School statutes, books by schoolmasters, and incidental sources of the day provide considerable information about studies of the era (Charlton 1965, 100, 104; and Watson 1916, 99). The rise of Protestantism augmented support for the teaching of Greek as well as Latin, due to its significance as a scriptural language, a consideration that likewise commended the study of Hebrew. Influential proponents of Greek as a grammar school subject

included Colet, Erasmus, Cranmer, and the author of the first major Latin-

English dictionary of the period, Sir Thoms Elyot (Charlton 1965, 116-17).

It was frequently cited in school statutes, as within a detailed classical

curriculum laid out for Westminster in 1560 that also called in more general

terms for the teaching of Hebrew (Charlton 1965, 117-18; and Statutes of

Westminster School, 499, 509, 511). Early seventeenth-century schoolmaster

John Brinsley (1627, xv-xvii) included both Greek and Hebrew in the model

curriculum he laid out in an important primary source.

Charlton (1965, 117, quoted, 118) questions, however, whether "any-

thing more than lip service" was paid to either biblical language in "the

general run" of grammar schools, citing Westminster and Merchant Taylors'

as among the few schools that seem to have offered Hebrew. A school at York,

probably (Leach 1915, 328) a "free" institution founded in 1547 distinct

from the early modern descendant (Watson 1916, 28) of Alcuin's cathedral

school, was another one of the "very few Elizabethan grammar schools" teach-

ing Hebrew (Sol Cohen 1974 , v). As for Greek, an 1884 commentator (Eliot,

27) found it "altogether probable that" it "had no real hold in the . . .

schools until the end of the sixteenth century," noting that Cambridge

undergraduates of 1578 began with the rudiments of the language.

A major limiting factor was a severe shortage of qualified school-

masters in a day of transition to a lay teaching profession (Watson 1916,

111-12) in which prevailing salaries were "miserably small" (Charlton 1965,

124). One author (Charlton 1965, 124-25) estimates that during the six-

teenth century nominal base salaries of schoolmasters and their assistants

doubled, on the average. Between 1510 and 1610, however, the price of a

"composite unit of consumables" nearly quintupled (Guy 1984, 227), and relative price stability, destined to endure for a century and a half, was not achieved until around 1640 (Wilson 1977, 138). According to one source (Sheldon Cohen 1974, 21) referring specifically to elementary schooling, teacher salaries had improved prior to that date.

The principal school subject remained Latin grammar. Rhetoric and logic were generally taught during the period by way of "traditional expositions of . . . Aristotelian-Ciceronian analyses." The former field was approached through imitation of classical forms or styles (Charlton 1965, 112, quoted, 113).

Despite the broader intellectual rebellion against scholastic pedantry, and the contributions to classical education made by selected teachers and schools, it appears that most Latin instruction of the period still emphasized mechanical repetition or rote learning of the sort decried by John Milton as "'gerund grinding'" (Charlton 1965, 125-26, 127, quoted). Writing in 1644, the great poet (Milton, 183) stated that pupils were still "spend[ing] seven or eight years meerly in scraping together so much miserable Latine and Greek, as might be learnt otherwise easily and delightfully in one year."

Earlier strong critics of such practices included Roger Ascham, a Cambridge scholar who tutored Princess Elizabeth and was later Latin secretary to Queens Mary and Elizabeth (Ryan 1963, 4-5); and clergyman John Brinsley, an outstanding classics master who was in 1619 or '20 banished from the classroom '"by the bishop's officers"' due to uncompromising Puritanism (Pollock 1943, iii, iv, quoted). Having himself encountered Latin as a small boy by rote methods that impeded genuine understanding, evidently including a hasty emphasis on speech, Ascham recommended instead an approach used very successfully with Elizabeth. Under "double translation," a pupil knowing the rudiments of formal grammar would write an English translation of a Latin passage selected by his teacher, and then after the lapse of an hour or more translate that rendition back into Latin. The instructor would "gently" and constructively evaluate the work throughout (Ryan 1963, 11, 254-55, quoted). The method of "Grammaticall translations" was explained, illustrated, and defended in detail by Brinsley (1627, xxv-xxvii, 89-125), who (1622, 32, and 1627, xxv) readily acknowledged his indebtedness to Ascham for an approach that (Ryan 1963, 254) goes back to Cicero.

The availability of printed Latin texts was of course a major advantage over prior times. Related materials produced by Erasmus, Colet, Cardinal Wolsey (Axtell 1968, 268), and charter master William Lily for use at St. Paul's gave rise, following authoritative approval on the eye of the Reformation by Wolsey and a Church convocation, to a "Royal Grammar" whose use throughout the realm was mandated by the crown. "Lily's Grammar" was officially prescribed by Henry VIII, and its status was reaffirmed by Edward VI, Elizabeth I, and ecclesiastical canons of 1571 and 1604. As revised in the eighteenth century, it remained Britain's principal text until 1867 (Charlton 1965, 107, 108, quoted; Leach 1915, 309-10; and Watson 1916, 41-42, 72-73).

The emphasis placed on Latin is underscored by several contemporary school statutes that, taken at face value, required boys to converse in the language throughout the schoolday (Charlton 1965, 119-20). A new constitution for the oldest school, at Canterbury, stated that "whatever they are doing in earnest or in play" the boys "shall never use any language but Latin or Greek" (The re-foundation of Canterbury Cathedral and Grammar School 1541, 469). The Statutes of Westminster (1560, 517) declared that a pupil would "be made custos [evidently, be cited and caned by a schoolmate assigned to monitor speech, in a "usuall custome" opposed on behavioral grounds by Brinsley (1627, 219, quoted, 220)] in each class who ha[d] spoken in English." Brinsley stressed (1627, 212, 215, 219-20) the difficulty of maintaining such requirements in practice.

Furthermore, serious effort to prohibit the use of English in the classroom would have defied its appearance in texts since the early 1400s; the publication of a number of books on English instruction; the translation of the Bible into the vernacular, leading to the magnificant King James version; and the growing literary importance of the language in the age of Edmund Spenser, Christopher Marlowe, Ben Jonson, and above all William Shakespeare (Charlton 1965, 102-3, 120-23; and Guy 1984, 281-84). Spanning the eras separated at 1660 were the active literary lives of renowned poets Andrew Marvell, Abraham Cowley, and the "[t]owering" John Milton (Morrah 1979, 82, quoted, 83-90).

It seems reasonable to conclude that at least in practice the prohibition of English speaking concerned those hours of school life reserved specifically for recitation in Latin. Indeed, attention to English grammar, and insistence on writing in the vernacular as well as Latin, evidently increased in the schools as the sixteenth century progressed, even if "English as a separate subject never appeared on a [grammar] school timetable" (Charlton 1965, 120, quoted, 121-23).

An outstanding teacher of Latin, Greek, and Hebrew, Spenser's schoolmaster at Merchant Taylors' was also a strong advocate of English instruction. Richard Mulcaster, headmaster for the school's first twenty-five years, asserted that boys who began their studies with English reading and writing, along with drawing and vocal and instrumental music, would learn more Latin from ages 12 to 16 than they would in ten years (7-17) otherwise.

He was remarkably early in urging his fellow learned Englishmen to write
in their native tongue, following (Mulcaster 1581, 2) his own example, in
preference to Latin (Quick 1888, 300, 303-8). Mulcaster (1581, 166-82), who
like his Eton master regarding Queen Mary and earlier Anne Boleyn produced a
number of school plays for Queen Elizabeth (Ollard 1982, 27; and Quick 1888,
303), devoted a chapter to education for girls. He insisted upon elementary instruction, either at home or within an outside school; welcomed study
of the trivium, plus additional languages, by "greater borne Ladyes and
gentlewymen" especially; and wished females generally the "most successe in
learning," all the while supporting their exclusion from grammar schools
(Mulcaster 1581, 167, 176-81, 182 and 297, quoted).

The Richard Mulcaster was headmaster of St. Paul's for a dozen years beginning in 1596 (Quick 1888, 302), the year that Edmund Coote published a
primer of English spelling and writing that would over the next 141 years
(Coote 1596; and Note 1968) appear in fifty-three more editions. Coote
(1596, title (original)) was master of the "Freeschoole" at Bury St.
Edmunds, located east and a bit north of Cambridge (Black 1966, [xiv]). It
was probably the local grammar school (Charlton 1965, 104) nationally known
for studies that required Greek as well as Latin and included elective work
in three Romance languages (Black 1966, 14).[14]

The 1596 manual (Coote, title, 1) was intended for elementary pupils
preparing for grammar school, their teachers, and tradesmen or artisans

---

[14]The Bury St. Edmunds school had grown up beside the ruins of an abbey
church for "simple grandeur . . . unsurpassed in Western Christianity" that
had been destroyed by the townspeople as "a hated symbol" in 1539. In
attendance some eighty years after that date was John Winthrop, Jr., the
dominant figure in the early history of Connecticut and, based on his scientific interests and attainments, an early member of London's Royal Society,
discussed below. The description given for the school relates to Winthrop's
day (Black 1966, 1, 13-14, 217-18).

(male or female) still responsible for teaching apprentices to read and write (Butts 1973, 273; and Note 1968). It included "the first attempt at an English dictionary" (Coote 1596, 72-94; and Note 1968, quoted), and substantial religious content (Charlton 1965, 105) extending to an introductory coverage (Coote 1596, 65-72) of numeration. John Brinsley likewise (1627, 12-27) stressed preparatory training in English, expressing concern that "in most Schooles there hath bene litle care, to teach Scholars to expresse their mindes" properly in the language, and commending the text provided by "that honest and painfull Maister Coote" (Brinsley 1622, 59 (2d passage, emphasis in original), 76).

Even amidst expanding lay sponsorship and instruction, religious influence over grammar school education was fully as strong after the English Reformation as before, as the church and state jointly took responsibility for the schooling of a broad cross-section of the population, or at least the male segment of it.

Dominant Religious Influence in an Era of an Expanding Clientele

Beyond coverage of the break with Rome itself, Watson (1916, 49-92) devotes three and a half chapters to religious influences over schooling of the period. Reference has been made to the Marian exiles, described (Watson 1916, 50) as "[t]he real directors of the polity and doctrine of the Elizabethan Church." The summary that follows is based largely on Watson's (1916, 68-92) chapters 6 and 7 (68, 83, in capitals), "Church control of the grammar schools" and "The church and the grammar schools: religious observances and instruction."

In essence, the new church "inherited the system and the school traditions of the medieval church" (Hans 1958, 130), within a new theological

57

environment in which personal reading and interpretation of the scriptures were emphasized. Whereas Wolsey's successor More had strongly supported the Catholic bishops' opposition to the authorization of an English bible, based on a fear of heresy, Henry VIII was enlightened enough to permit the publication of such a translation in 1536 (Guy 1984, 242), a development vital to the Reformation (Charlton 1965, 120).

Henry required all schoolmasters to take an Oath of Supremacy acknowleging the crown's supreme authority over the church. The first Act of Uniformity, requiring teachers to be active members of the Church of England, was adopted under Queen Elizabeth. Although the act seems to have been enforced primarily against Catholics, no such restriction was expressed in a 1580 statement calling for a penalty of ten pounds on employers of masters "not resorting to Church," and "Disability and Imprisonment" for such teachers themselves (Leach 1911, 526).

The Tudor monarchy taxed clergy to finance schooling, and required them to contribute toward scholarships at both grammar schools and universities. Injections issued by Edward VI and Elizabeth I in 1547 and '59 to require well-beneficed priests to provide elementary schooling within their parishes were widely ignored, however (Hans 1958, 131; and Leach 1911, xlv, 472, 494).

In 1559, also, Elizabeth reaffirmed the old rule of teacher licensing by bishops or their representatives. A later act of her reign forbade the employment of a teacher not church approved or churchgoing. Soon after the beginning of the Stuart dynasty, a penalty of forty shillings (two pounds) per day was imposed in 1604 for teaching without a license (Leach 1911, 528), representing fully a tenth or a fifth of the estimated average annual salary of a schoolmaster or assistant master (Charlton 1965, 124-25). In addition (Sheldon Cohen 1974, 21),

> a concerned Parliament requested bishops to examine the personal and professional qualifications of all schoolmasters within their diocese and to remove all those found unfit.

Extensive provision made for priestly visitation at schools permitted more active enforcement of licensing requirements than had existed before, even as the common-law concept of a general right to teach retained considerable authority.

Besides pronouncements of church and state, educational statutes of the period strongly promoted religion in the schools. They generally required prayers and religious observances in the grammar schools; religious instruction in Catechism and the content of Christian faith; and church attendance, at least on Sundays, by the schoolboys. Such requirements, found in the case of lay-sponsored schools as well as church institutions, were enforced vigorously as truly "a matter of life and death" (Watson 1916, 87) following the martyrdom of many Protestants under Queen Mary. Schoolmasters were expected to examine their pupils on the Sunday service; and it is speculated (Watson 1916, 91) that shorthand arose originally as a means of taking notes on the worship services.

The pupils of these religiously oriented schools represented considerable breadth within society. The grammar schools, many of them free of charge, "afforded ample opportunity for the middle classes to enter learned professions" (Hans 1958, 130). With chivalric education outmoded, the sons of peers were usually taught by home tutors, a group who taken overall "often left much to be desired," a point "bitterly" noted by Roger Ascham (Charlton 1965, 97, 213, quoted, 214; and Sheldon Cohen 1974, 24, reference to "landed aristocracy"). Increasingly, however, the sons of gentlemen (newly known (Morrill 1984, 297) as the '"squirearchy"'), lawyers, and

merchants were filling the grammar schools. Furthermore, admissions books
of two Cambridge colleges reveal that many students were drawn from the sons
of yeomen, husbandmen, and tradesmen, suggesting that the infusion of boys
with gentle or mercantile roots did not displace traditional needy youth
(Charlton 1965, 97). Overall, however, during most of this period the
position of the English middle classes was enhanced at the expense of the
poor and, to some extent, the rich (Morrill 1984, 297). Of course need
among schoolboys seldom implied "uncertainty as to where the next meal was
coming from" (Ollard 1982, 164, reference to Eton).

The era under discussion closed with the "Commonwealth" period of the
1640s and '50s in which three civil wars were fought; Charles I was executed
and the monarchy was abolished; the country was run in turn by Parliament
and a military protectorate; and the Church of England was officially dissolved (Morrill 1984, 312-29). The struggle between King and Parliament
was in large measure a conflict between Anglicans and "Puritan" religious
groups opposing an episcopal ecclesiastical structure recognized by James I
during (Hans 1958, 156) an earlier Presbyterian challenge as vital to royal
supremacy. His statement "'No Bishop, no King'" only acknowledged the
degree to which religion dominated English life (Morrah 1979, 163, 166,
quoted).

In 1641 the House of Commons lent support to a Presbyterian plan to
establish a national system of education by resolving to abolish deans,
chapters, canons, and other church institutions and apply the revenues
obtained to '"the advancement of learning and piety"'. Although some action
was subsequently taken, the bulk of the funding was used in financing the
first civil war (Hans 1958, 158). A few years later the national church was
officially disbanded in favor of a Presbyterian system in a "Puritan

experiment" that in actual fact was "stillborn" (Morrill 1984, 320, 321,
quoted). That failure reflected the rise within the parliamentary army of
the religious "Independents," poet John Dryden's "'numerous host of dreaming
sects'"[15] that were "united only in hostility to Anglicanism, Presbyterian-
ism, and the Church of Rome." Out of those military ranks came Lord Protector Oliver Cromwell, "the accepted leader of the Independents," who
practiced general religious toleration, Catholics excepted, during his five
years (1653-58) in power. The outlawed Church of England, since 1645 without an Archbishop of Canterbury, was not "actively persecuted" under the
protectorate (Morrah 1979, 2, 168, 169, quoted, 171).

Educationally, the Commonwealth period was one of enhanced government
patronage even without the completion of a grand design. Subsidies were
granted to many schools and schoolmasters, especially under an act adopted
in 1649. The vigor of educational progress during the fifties is suggested
by a nineteenth-century report that identified seventy-three schools created
during that decade as still existing (Hans 1958, 158-59). One of the new
schools offering studies in writing and arithmetic was England's first
recorded maritime institution (Leach 1911, xlvii).

The Commonwealth years, although as discussed below bringing high scientific vitality to Oxford, were a trying time for the universities. Both
were identified primarily with the monarchy in opposition to prevailing town
sentiment, in keeping with policies pursued by Archbishop William Laud (note
16) and a broader episcopal influence that had from early in the century
required formal assent by undergraduates to approved doctrine (Black 1966,

---

[15]These groups included "Separatists" or (in later terms) Congregationalists (Columbia encyclopedia 3d, s.v. "Congregationalism," quoted, all capitals; and Hans 1958, 157, quoted, 158), Anabaptists, Quakers, Seventh Day
Adventists, Deists, "Fifth Monarchy Men," and "Socinians," or early Unitarians, along with "many other" (final 's' deleted) sects "whose names have
faded into oblivion" (Morrah 1979, 169, quoted, 177).

18, reference to Cambridge). During the original civil war, 1642-46 (Morrill 1984, 317), Charles I and his queen held court at respective Oxford colleges, as instruction almost ceased at a university where studies in fields such as geography, archaeology, mathematics, and astrology, besides divinty, had "flourished" since Elizabethan times (Hall and Frankl 1983, 10). The "Rump Parliament" that governed England from 1649 to '53 (Morrill 1984, 326) appointed a nonresident "board of Visitors" that with a "heavy hand" swiftly imposed desired discipline at Oxford (Axtell 1968, 27, quoted, 28).

The town of Cambridge was represented in Parliament by Oliver Cromwell, who as lord protector later took reprisals against the university he had briefly attended by placing the presidents of three colleges in the Tower of London (Hall and Frankl 1982, 10). His own college at the university (Sidney Sussex) had been conspicuously royalist (Hall and Frankl 1982, 68), despite earlier leanings toward Puritan theology (Cremin 1970, 614), but another one founded on the site of a suppressed monastery (Hall and Frankl 1982, 35) may have opposed prevailing university attitudes (Cremin 1970, 614). Formed at a low ebb of theological studies at Cambridge, Emmanuel had in any case lent support to Puritan viewpoints while becoming the institution's "principal cent[er]" of Protestant thought. Another Protestant/Puritan theological stronghold was Gonville and Caius ("'keys'") College, while during Elizabeth's reign or (Ryan 1963, 5) even earlier St. John's (Charlton 1965, 146) had been known for "Protestant dissension and faction." The thirty-five Emmanuel men emigrating to America for, in some part, religious reasons had included John Harvard, educational benefactor in the Cambridge of New England (Hall and Frankl 1983, 35, quoted, 36, 39, quoted in parens.).[16]

---

[16]Oxford was a logical royal capital largely due to policies pursued by Archbishop of Canterbury William Laud as since 1629 evidently more than

62

In regard, finally, to the major theme of the anthology, the period between the onset of the Reformation and the Restoration was most important for the origin of various plans for broadened educational "academies," a few of them implemented to some degree; and the rise of private-venture commercial schooling supplemental to the grammar schools.

New Educational Initiatives: Designs for Academies, and Early Commercial Schools

Educating a Privileged (or Meritorious) Elite

A marked increase in the entry of the sons of (nontitled) gentlemen into the grammar schools, and of peers' sons as well into the universities, reflects steadily increasing need for a well-educated professional bureaucracy to govern the country (Lee 1970, 274). University matriculation by youth from titled or gentle families, as yet England's only classes having "'social'" status as distinguished from "'economic'" standing (Morrill 1984, 296), expanded in particular under Queen Elizabeth (Hall and Frankl 1983, 10). With many younger sons of landed aristocrats serving in the lower house, along with other men representing the interests of "rural nobility" (Morrah 1979, 51, referring specifically to the Restoration period beginning

---

in name head (Sheldon Cohen 1974, 24; and Hall and Frankl 1983, 93) of the university, as chancellor, and as earlier for ten years president of his own undergraduate college, St. John's (Columbia encyclopedia 3d, s.v. "Laud, William"; and Hall and Frankl 1983, 75). One of the king's "most devoted adherents" (Hall and Frankl 1983, 10), Laud enjoyed the support of Charles as he "sought to revolutionize the church" in ways that offended "almost every vested secular interest in the State," and were particularly anathema to Puritan elements (Morrill 1984, 302 and 312, quoted, 310-11). Particularly critical of the relatively informal chapel services held at Emmanuel, Cambridge (Hall and Frankl 1982, 35), Laud relied on "carefully planted dons" to spread his ideas at both universities (Morrill 1984, 302). He was executed in 1645 following conviction by Parliament on a charge of high treason (Hall and Frankl 1983, 75), preceding his king in martyrdom by four years (Morrill 1984, [324]).

in 1660), it is pertinent that whereas only one fourth of the members of the House of Commons in 1563 had been to a university or an inn of court, thirty years later more than twice that share had undertaken higher education (Lee 1970, 274).

Throughout the period between Henry VIII and Oliver Cromwell, however, there were serious proposals to establish for the sons of English nobility inclusive, sometimes, of gentry a new form of institution, an "academy" separate from the grammar schools and universities that would train them above all for public service. There was ample precedent for a courtly academy among the Italian, German, and French nobility (Butts 1973, 275; and Lee 1970, 274), as well as within the medieval courts of Alfred the Great and Henry II. The concept never got "a real foothold" in England (Lee 1970, 275), however, as the peerage (some 120 in number by 1640) and, (more fully) the gentry or squirearchy (20,000 by that date) (Morrill 1984, 297) joined the established educational system. Although this development may have weakened the nobility prior to Commonwealth days, it contributed in the longer run to their survival as a "ruling elite" (Butts 1973, 275).

Charlton (1965, 82-85, 154-57) and Lee (1970, 276-82) summarize the positions and, as pertinent, practical initiatives taken by a number of academy proponents from the reign of Henry VIII to the abolition of the monarchy more than a century later. Notable contributions of very different kinds were made by Sirs Thomas Elyot (1531) and Humphrey Gilbert (c. 1570), and John Milton (1644). In "probably the first major treatise on the human-ist point of view in education to appear in . . . English" (Sol Cohen 1974, v), Elyot called for strong emphasis on classical learning focused on the cultivation of a variety of civic and personal virtues, under the guidance of a private tutor. Queen Elizabeth's "premiere councilor" Sir William

Cecil (Guy 1984, 265), who largely embodied Elyot's ideals of public responsibility (Charlton 1965, 83), created a small academy of royal wards and
other select youth in his own household, combining academic learning, training in social graces, and preparation for public leadership (Lee 1970, 277).

Gilbert (c. 1570) optimistically proposed creation in London of "Queen
Elizabeth's Academy," conbining grammar school and university functions.
One group of masters and assistants would teach the trivium, Greek, and
Hebrew; mathematics and moral philosophy would be taught with special reference to practical applications; there would be lectures on several modern
languages, and strong emphasis on English speech; and instruction in civil
law, divinity, and (with an empirical or clinical element) natural philosophy and medicine. A variety of graces or skills such as music, dancing,
riding, and weaponry were to be offered (Lee 1970, 277, quoted, 278).

Although Gilbert's expensive plan was not implemented, a less elaborate
version was started in the court of James I by Prince Henry. The five hundred members of this '"courtly college"' in 1610 included many youth of birth
and wealth pursuing a combination of civil and military training. It was
disbanded upon the death of the young prince from (Morrill 1984, 308) small-
pox two years later (Lee 1970, 278, 279, quoted), the year (Pollock 1943, iv)
that John Brinsley (1627, iii) dedicated his principal work to Henry and his
ill-fated brother, the future Charles I. Henry was a key contributor to the
royal library donated in 1757 to the British Museum (Fletcher 1902, 2-8).

During the first civil war, finally, "fanatical . . . Puritan" and
staunch antiroyalist (Morrah 1979, 82, quoted, 83) Milton proposed (1644)
the creation of an academy for (Lee 1970, 282) an educational "elite"
defined in terms of "worth and . . . godliness" rather than birth and means.
The headmaster would assemble some 150 puils and 20 teachers in "a spatious
house" for study whose ultimate end was "to know God aright, and out of that

knowledge to love him, to imitate him, to be like him, as we may the neerest by possessing our souls of true vertue" (Milton 1644, 183-84). At a more practical level, Milton (1644, 184) sought to define a program of education for youth between 12 and 21 years that would fit graduates "to perform justly, skillfully, and magnanimously all the offices both private and publick of Peace and War." Amidst strong criticism of conventional nonliterary methods of teaching languages, an extraordinary range of studies covering almost every known subject, including learned law and medicine, were laid out in sequence (Milton 1644, 184-86).

An important initiative associated by Charlton (1965, 155) with academy ideas, and related in part to business schooling as next discussed, was a landmark venture in adult education. Sir Thomas Gresham, perhaps best remembered for an economic "law" that he neither originated nor (even) formulated, was a wealthy banker, mercer, merchant, and royal financial agent and diplomat who principally founded one of England's foremost financial institutions (Wilson 1977, 132), the Royal Exchange (Columbia encyclopedia 3d, s.v. "Gresham, Sir Thomas," quoted word in boldface). In accordance with a large bequest of nineteen years earlier, "Gresham College" was set up in London in 1598 with the appointment of seven professors to give public lectures in as may fields. Coverage included both geometry and astronomy, approached in terms beneficial to navigators and other practical mathematicians, and Gresham professors made important contributions as lecturers and writers, and (anticipating further Oxford coverage below) discussants in their fields (Charlton 1965, 283-87, quoting 285), even if they did not adhere to the original provision for daily lecturing.

The Gresham lectures were suspended in 1666 as the rooms for a time were "given up to business purposes" with the loss of the Royal Exchange and related buildings in the Great Fire of London. Salaries lapsed three

66

years later, and the lectures were not resumed for an extended period, at least, until 1706, The new program lasted sixty-two years (D.n.b. 1917, s.v. "Goddard, Jonathan," 25, quoted; and Hans 1951, 136).

If the various academy designs laid out during the era did not find wide support, the ideals of broad and well-rounded study were carried forward in the last period to be reviewed in a number of non-elitist "academies" of the eighteenth century. Their studies often included commercial subjects that had gained prior standing through the work of private teachers.

Early Commercial Schooling

A conjecture by Arthur Cole (1946, 5) that professional teachers of writing and arithmetic may have begun to appear in England, as in continental Europe, by 1400 or earlier draws support from the reference made earlier to adjunct lecturing in commercial subjects at medieval Oxford. A reference of a century later to a "writing school" has also been noted. Commercial education of the later middle ages seems to have been largely confined, however, to apprenticeship programs of the craft guilds (Charlton 1965, 253-255, quoting 254). During the reign of Queen Elizabeth, 1558-1603, the governance of apprenticeship was shifted substantially from guilds to civil authorities, and the institution was coordinated with public welfare "poor laws" (Butts 1973, 272, 273, quoted).

By this time, there was definite need for a much higher level of business instruction, suited specifically to preparation for a "merchant" career as an international wholesaler, "the highest class of business man from at least the thirteenth to the early nineteenth century." The merchant frequently was also engaged to one degree or another in retail selling, banking, warehousing, shipping (as a common carrier), and land speculation (Gras 1928, 1, quoted, 2). The English mercantilists formed numerous "trading companies" in the eixteenth and seventeenth centuries to promote trade in Europe, Russia, India, the Near East, Africa, and the New World (Cheney [1904], 86-88; and Gilbert 1968, 40). Prominent economic developments at home included continuation in the 1500s of extensive land enclosure, which had started to become widespread in the latter years of the prior century (Gilbert 1968, 40; and Griffiths 1984, 189); continuing development in the seventeenth century of small-scale industry, especially in the textile field, conducted in cottages or outbuildings; and movement during the 1600s toward an integrated national economy from a series of more or less independent regional ones (Morrill 1984, 289, 292).

Early commercial writers provided a natural nucleus in England for the rise of a class of private-venture commercial teachers offering instruction supplemental to grammar schooling. The first English accounting book is thought to have been published in 1543 by one Hugh Oldcastle, reputedly a London teacher of arithmetic and, and from his own text, bookkeeping. He and his book are known only through an adaptation of the work produced forty-five years later by John Mellis (Yamey 1963, 155-56). Both Mellis and an intervening writer on accounts on whose work he also drew (Yamey 963, 156), James Peele, were themselves teachers (Cole 1946, 5; and Murray 1930, 221, 226). Although as observed below Peele combined several occupations, such references lead Cole to state (1946, 5) that during the second half of the sixteenth century or, at least, by the early 1600s "instruction in bookkeeping . . . became a sufficient specialty to take up men's full time."

Later, Richard Dafforne included in an accounting text originating in 1635 a special preface asking his '"Fellowe-Teachers"' of bookkeeping to help him combat widespread ignorance of their '"Noble Art"' (Reigner [1958],

10, 11, quoted). By the time his second text appeared, in 1640, the long-time Amsterdam resident was teaching arithmetic and accounts in both English and Dutch at his home on Abchurch Lane (Murray 1930, 245-47; and Reigner [1958], 11), the London street on which Thomas Watts (1716a, title, and b, [13]) was teaching when he wrote the lead essay collected in this volume. Dafforne, whose two accounting books went through at least eight editions between them (Murray 1930, 245-46; and Thomson 1963, 204-5),[17] probably used rhyming devices in his teaching, as in the following directions for posting (Murray 1930, 245):

> 'The owner, or the owing thing, Or what so-ever comes to thee;
> Upon the LEFT hand see thou bring; For there the same must placed be.
> But
> They unto whom thou dost owe, Upon the RIGHT let them be set:
> Or what-so-e'er doth from thee go[,] To place them there do not forget'.

Toward the end of the sixteenth century, "a growing number of writing masters" had begun to form schools of penmanship. Independent teachers of navigation, surveying, and (likewise commercially useful) modern languages were also coming to the fore (Charlton 1965, 267, quoted, 269-71, 292-95). Certain early commercial texts were well suited, however, to self instruction. Appearing in six editions between 1589 and 1640, John Browne's Marchants avizo was a seventy-page general mercantile handbook "designed expressly for factors and apprentices by a merchant with long experience" (Charlton 1965, 266, quoted; and Thomson 1963, 203). Brinsley (1627, 26) recommended Robert Recorde's "classic arithmetic" of the sixteenth century (Charlton 1965, 265) for self-study by youth having difficulty with basic

---

[17] The merchants mirrour appeared in four editions, 1634-84 (Thomson 1963, 204). Murray (1930, 245-46) lists four editions for The apprentices time-entertainer accomptantly through 1670, whereas Thomson (1963, 204-5) identifies the 1670 book as a third edition while citing a 1700 publication, with a related title, as a fourth. It is of course possible that one numbered edition of the work went through separate printings.

concepts of numeration. A more advanced work was The ancient law-merchant by experienced merchant and economist Gerard Malynes (Murray 1930, 240), a full legal analysis of selling and trading first issued in 1622 (Reigner n.d., 12; and Thomson 1963, 204) that included ten folio pages on double-entry bookkeeping (Malynes 1656, 241-50).

Probably the foremost center of commercial schooling of the era was Christ's Hospital, founded at a former London monastery in 1553 by Edward VI (Columbia encyclopedia 3d, s.v. "Christ's Hospital"; and Watson 1916, 5) as a home for foundlings or orphans and children of the truly poor (Butts 1973, 272; and Leach 1915, 208).[18] Appointed in 1562 (McMickle and Vangermeersch 1987, 12, '"Clercke"') as "Clerk," the chief financial officer (McConnell 1985, 85) in the present day, was James Peele, a salter and '"practizer and teacher"' of accounts whose first of two bookkeeping texts had appeared in the founding year. Peele, the father of a dramatist, also wrote verse (Murray 1930, 221, quoted, 221n, 226).

A remarkable educational program was conducted at Christ's Hospital that besides regular grammar schooling (Butts 1973, 272) included two teachers at the elementary level, a writing master (Charlton 1965, 99), and (Butts 1973, 272)

> instruction in . . . arithmetic, commercial accounts, and other subjects that would enable the boys to enter the world of trade and commerce with some educational skills.

The institution supplied a number of merchants' apprentices to the British East India Company in the formative years of that organization founded (Gilbert 1968, 40) in 1600 (Butts 1973, 272, referring through a printing error to the "sixteenth" century rather than the "seventeenth").

---

[18] In referring to poor children from "free" families, Butts (1973, 272) invokes a somewhat unclear concept from a largely defunct manorial system (note 11). Along with McConnell (1985, 86, 93), he (Butts 1973, 272) gives the founding date as 1552.

At the grammar school level, Christ's Hospital would make pioneering

contributions in the era that began with the "Restoration" of the monarchy

in May 1660, ending (Morrah 1979, 4-8) twenty months of political crisis

that had followed the death of Lord Protector Cromwell. Charles II, elder

son of the martyred king (Morrah 1979, 10-11), was a popular and reasonably

effective leader over the next quarter century. He was unable, however, to

prevent Parliament from imposing a highly repressive religious settlement

that would profoundly affect education.

In particular, the formation throughout England of illegal "Dissenting"

schools of different levels launched a movement that thrived after modest

relief was granted in 1689, in part because religious tests largely barred

nonconformists from Oxford and Cambridge, neither of which flourished over

the next century. The most elite grammar schools remained bastions of

classical instruction through 1800 even while new studies were rising in

many other secondary schools, including private "academies" offering commer-

cial subjects.

Later Modern Schooling: From the Restoration through the Eighteenth Century, 1660-1800

Religious Restoration and the Schools: Legislated Anglican Monopoly, Active Dissent, and Evolving Toleration

The "Clarendon Code": Parliament versus King on Religious Toleration

The restoration of the crown brought with it the restoration of the

Church of England. The major issue raised was "how far toleration should

go" (Morrah 1979, 170) regarding Presbyterians, Independents of one stripe

or another, and Catholics. Puritanism had begun as a nonseparatist Anglican

movement, but by 1660 there was probably no question of accommodating more than the Presbyterian variety within the restored church (Morrah 1983, 166, 170; and Morrill 1984, 344). The "highly disciplined" Presbyterians had led the way in restoring the monarchy; were far removed from "lawless excesses" associated with some Puritans; and had if anything surpassed Anglicans in offending Independents through authoritarian intolerance (Hans 1958, 157; and Morrah 1979, 168, 174, quoted).

Fanned by generations of economic beneficiaries of the break with Rome, there was throughout England intense prejudice against Catholics, based on association with foreign rivals and with the Marian persecutions as well as "sheer ignorance" (Morrah 1979, 175, quoted, 176). Finally, in an "almost exclusively Christian" land where ordinary life was dominated by religion "to an extent difficult to realize today," few people favored toleration for non-Christian religions, much less "the heathen or the atheist" (Morrah 1979, [162]-63).

King Charles II was himself, however, vigorously committed to religious toleration, continuing and extending a tradition forged by James I and even Charles I, "as convinced an Anglican as ever lived." He was a well-traveled former exile who had observed and made friends within a variety of Christian persuasions; been at great risk befriended and protected by Catholic priests on his escape from England in 1651; and become convinced of the "absurdity and futility" of trying to impose belief (Morrah 1979, 19-20, 167 and 173, quoted, 172). Though not a religious man (Morrah 1979, 172), Charles may himself have long before a deathbed conversion been "strongly drawn to Roman Catholicism." His mother, wife, brother (and successor), favorite sister, and admired cousin Louis XIV were all Catholics, as with many of his father's most "conspicuously loyal" subjects (Morrill 1984, 333).

Prior to departing for England in 1660, Charles had in a written "manifesto" promised "'a liberty to tender consciences'" (Morrah 1979, 8, 173). Only months later as king he reaffirmed the principle in a declaration making a qualified commitment to Catholics. He also pledged freedom of worship to Quakers, whose deliberately offensive exhibitionism had incited much violence and been used to discredit Puritanism (Morrah 1979, 174-75).

As a first step toward a religious settlement, King Charles offered Anglican bishoprics to four Presbyterian leaders. One of them accepted and another was appointed royal chaplain with a conditional license to preach within the London diocese. Three of the four clergymen gathered late in 1660 with the king, his lord chancellor and another longtime political advisor, and a number of Anglican bishops in an effort to develop a detailed policy. The Presbyterians were partially satisfied with concessions offered by the Anglicans concerning (Morrill 1984, 330) episcopal authority and autonomy and controversial ceremonies and Prayer Book language, and it was agreed that unresolved matters could be left to a national synod. To his keen disappointment, however, the religious leaders opposed Charles on broader toleration, specifically condemning "the dreaded papists" and radical Protestant groups (Morrah 1979, 20, 174-76, 177, quoted).

Even a declaration confined to the accommodations agreed upon was rejected by the House of Commons in an action that probably doomed the synod of early 1661. Both Anglicans and Presbyterians took very hard lines at the ten-week meeting, and consequently no progress toward a settlement was made (Morrah 1979, 177-78; and Morrill 1984, [331], mentioning only Presbyterian obstinacy). At that point the king finally passed the initiative to Parliament, where a "rigorist Anglican majority" (Morrill 1984, 330) that was only enhanced by the working of the earliest act itself adopted a series of highly repressive measures in the next four years that "made the established church narrowly Anglican and ended toleration" (Lunt 1957, 447, quoted, 448). The resultant "Clarendon Code" expressed the viewpoint of Lord Chancellor Edward Hyde, the Earl of Clarendon, "an uncompromising High Churchman" as defined in terms of formality of ritual and sacrament (Morrah 1979, 170).

The thrust of the code was that ministry, teaching, or public worship outside the domain or authority of the Church of England was illegal and would be penalized, often (Lusk 1957, 448; and Morrah 1979, 181-82) harshly. Educationally, there were two principal measures. A new Act of Uniformity of 1662 that disallowed non-Anglican ordination also required exclusive use of the Prayer Book in public worship; clerical assent to all its doctrines and provisions; and church licensing of all teachers based on sworn doctrinal conformity and loyalty to the state (Butts 1973, 188; Hans 1958, 130-31; and McLachlan 1931, 1, principal source).

Rather than stifling nonconformity, the 1662 law forced Presbyterians and moderate Puritans generally to line up with separatist Independents, defiantly, as "Dissenters" (Hans 1958, 159; and Morrill 1984, 345-46). A subsequent act forebade non-Anglican worship starting at slightly more than a household level before "the most crippling measure yet" was adopted in 1665. The Five Mile Act prohibited Dissenting ministers not pledged to acquiesce in the government of church and state from approaching within five miles of any "city or corporate town" (Morrah 1979, 182), or of any "parish" (an ecclesiastical/civil administrative unit) in which they had taught or preached (Lusk 1957, 383, 448). Prison terms and fines were also specified for teaching without a license conferred by church officials (Stephens and Roderick 1977, 48-49).

74

The Act of Uniformity drove out of the established church from one (Morrah 1979, 179) to two (McLachlan 1931, 1; and Morrill 1984, 345) thousand ordained ministers, including (Hans 1951, 42) many university dons. On the higher estimate, about a fifth of the clergy were expelled (Morrill 1984, [331]). Combined with institutional statutes, the act also severely limited Dissenters from matriculation at Cambridge and, particularly, Oxford, and basically excluded them from English degrees (Hans 1951, 42, 57-58, 97; and McLachlan 1931, 1).

During this time, and beyond, King Charles continued to champion toleration. At Christmas of 1662, he made a new declaration on behalf of "tender consciences," only to be rebuffed in both houses of Parliament as his lord chancellor spoke against the bill (Morrah 1979, 179, quoted, 180). Ten years later Charles issued an "immensely unpopular" Declaration of Indulgence that would have suspended penal laws against Dissenters and Catholics, but, several years before a "trade boom" markedly enhanced royal revenues (Morrill 1984, 337), backed down in order to obtain parliamentary funding needed for a military campaign. In 1672, also, Parliament passed a "Test Act" requiring officeholders under royal appointment to take Anglican communion and reject the (Catholic) doctrine of transubstantiation (Lunt 1957, 451).

An historian of early Restoration England (Morrah 1979, 182) states that the Clarendon Code was "rigorously enforced" by justices of the peace spurred on by a clergy with a "persecuting fervo[r]." He amplifies (while technically contradicting) the remark by saying that people were often jailed arbitrarily under pertinent acts and imprisoned after unfair trials. Another authority (Langford 1984, 358) asserts that limited concessions

75

granted in 1689 were welcome to "Dissenters who had [as a class] been vigorously persecuted as recently as the early 1680s." Certainly "oppression
was real," as in the case of the great writer John Bunyan, whose first
imprisonment (twelve years, for unlicensed Baptist preaching) began a year
before the first statute of the code was enacted (Columbia encyclopedia 3d,
s.v. "Bunyan, John"; and Morrah 1979, 183, quoted).

Educational developments show, however, that vigorous enforcement
was sporadic, as dissenting ministers formed many schools, and a number of
them prospered. The Five Mile Act, which by implication forbade Dissenters
from teaching, was often not enforced against the founder of a school (Hans
1958, 131, 159). Masters were often able to avoid or evade persecution by
moving their schools frequently (McLachlan 1931, 2). Perhaps, as in the
political sphere, they could also escape trouble by "resort[ing] to occasional conformity" in taking the Anglican sacraments once a year (Morrill
1984, 360).

The presence of many moderates on both sides, Anglican and Dissenter,
assured a measure of accommodation (Hans 1951, 57-58). Presumably so did
the persistent tolerant attitude of a king whose "iron nerve, pragmatism,
and easy goodwill to all" (Morrill 1984, 337) secured his place as "the
undisputed master of the nation" in the final years of his quarter-century
reign (Morrah 1979, 215). Further, as one of the few lasting political
reforms of the Commonwealth period courts that were especially subject to
national control, such as Star Chamber, had been abolished. As a result,
local "gentry magistrates" who were often sympathetic in some degree to the
Dissenters were left primarily in charge of enforcing the Clarendon Code
(Morrill 1984, 332, 341, 342, quoted). Finally, from early on Dissenting
schools of higher education served pupils from Anglican families

attracted by their low costs, academic quality, or both (Hans 1951, 57-58, and 1958, 160; and McLachlan 1931, 24-25).

On his death in 168 Charles was succeeded by his brother James. Two years later King James II issued a new Declaration of Indulgence, and he reissued it in 1688. After an intense legal battle on the matter with Anglican bishops ended in defeat for the king (Lunt 1957, 457-58), he resorted to desperate measures that included replacing most justices of the peace, among other officials, and in an indirect effort to "'pack'" Parliament turned over control of most incorporated towns to Dissenters. Yet the latter elements only united with the Anglicans in forcing James from the throne later in the year in favor of his (Protestant) daughter Mary and her husband William, ruler of the Netherlands (Lunt 1957, 457-61; and Morrill 1984, 337, quoted, 338-41).

The basic reason for the unlikely alliance that ushered in the "Glorious Revolution" of 1688 is that James was a committed Catholic who intended to reestablish Catholicism in England on an equal footing with the Anglican church. He had converted twenty years earlier; become involved in the 1670s in certain "intrigues with the Catholics and the French"; and as for two years royal commissioner there severely persecuted Dissenting (that is, non-Presbyterian) Protestants in Scotland, which (Morgan 1984, 609) would finally unite with England in 1708. In addition, the birth of a son in June 1688 to James and his "staunchly Catholic" second wife raised realistic fears of a Catholic dynasty (Columbia encyclopedia 3d, s.v. "James II, 1633-1701," quoted; Columbia-Viking desk encyclopedia 2d, s.v. "Scotland, Church of"; and Morrill 1984, 337-38).

The political realities of the Glorious Revolution assured a prompt easing of repression against Protestant dissent, foreshadowing developments that a generation later would further weaken the Clarendon Code even though it would substantially remain on the books of English law for many more years to come.

Relaxation of Repression, Beginning with the Toleration Act of 1689

Dissenters were rewarded in 1689 with "the least that could be offered," a limited Toleration Act granting freedom of worship subject to affirmation of most Anglican articles (Langford 1984, 358, quoted; Lunt 1957, 462; and McLachlan 1931, 2, 39). Excluded were Catholics, Unitarians, and perhaps (Hans 1958, 131) Quakers (Lunt 1957, 462; and McLachlan 1931, 2). This act opened the way to a "tolerant, pluralist society" (Langford 1984, 359), even as it may have revealed the Anglicans as "a spent spiritual force" (Morrill 1984, 346), at substantial cost to its support from the middle classes (Hans 1958, 131).

Educationally, the Toleration Act removed legal barriers only to elementary schooling by Dissenters. Together, however, with an influential court decision of 1700 (Stephens and Roderick 1977, 49) that denied relief only at the grammar school level, it meant in practical terms that such elements "could openly endow their institutions and were not compelled to change the place" periodically to escape persecution (Hans 1958, 131). Societies were thus formed to raise and dispense funds for dissenter schools and pupils. Presbyterians and Congregationalists created a '"United Brethren"' fund, later divided, that contributed to forming a variety of new academies for higher education. Also, many students were supported at such schools or at Scottish or Dutch universities (Hans 1958, 158, 160, quoted). Since 1410 universities had been founded in Scotland at St. Andrews, Glasgow, Aberdeen, and Edinburgh (Gilbert 1968, 114). At least seven other major funds were established before 1800, three of them by Baptist (two) or "Calvinistic" elements (McLachlan 1931, 3).

Three years after the adoption of another Toleration Act (Hans 1958, 131), a reverse step was taken in 1714. The Schism Act of that year, "aimed directly at nonconformist tutors and schoolmasters," withdrew prior educational concessions (Hans 1951, 58; and McLachlan 1931, 39, quoted). It may have represented a political reaction to the impeachment of an Anglican minister (for preaching a discarded doctrine) known as a bitter opponent of dissenter schooling (Hans 1951, 58; and Langford 1984, 361).

The Schism Act was quickly repealed, however, due to political factors surrounding the accession in England of a new dynasty (Hans 1951, 58). Queen Anne was succeeded in 1714 by George I, a German prince, as "Elector of Hanover," who was a great-grandson of King James I (Langford 1984, 362, quoted; and Morgan 1984, [619]). The House of Hanover was at once threatened by armed uprisings by the "Jacobites," a militant group that had emerged after the ouster of James II to champion his claim to the throne, and since his death been dedicated to the crowning of his son as James III.

Although the Jacobites had substantial support from "high churchmen," Catholics, and other elements, their rebellion of 1715 was crushed by loyalist forces that among other Dissenters included three ministers and members of their congregations. When the Jacobites undertook another insurrection thirty years later, on behalf of James II's grandson Charles ("Bonnie Prince Charlie"), nonconformist Protestants stood once again solidly with the House of Hanover. Having on both occasions seen their schools and meeting houses attacked by Jacobite mobs, they recognized that a second Stuart restoration would hardly serve their interests (Columbia encyclopedia 3d, s.v. "Jacobites," quoted; Langford 1984, 362; and McLachlan 1931, 39).

According to Hans (1951, 58, 59, quoted), after 1715 the Clarendon
Code was in keeping with their vital dependence on one another "disregarded
both by the Government and by the Dissenters." A 1773 statement by a dissenting tutor that teachers were still '"put to no small trouble"' by the
seventeenth-century legislation (McLachlan 1931, 39) implies that some
risk remained, however, if only because local officials need not always
follow the preference of the crown. It is striking in the latter connection
that early Hanover kings from time to time "grant[ed] subsidies to the
Dissenters out of their own purse" (emphasis added). In 1727 an alliance
of Presbyterian, Congregationalist, and Baptist clerics obtained express
authority to petition on behalf of their constitutional rights (Hans 1958,
158, 160, quoted). A critical gesture made by George II in support of a
prominent dissenting master is related below.

The Clarendon Code was not fully dismantled until the 1840s or even
later. Ninety years after passing the original Toleration Act, however,
Parliament had finally in 1779 granted further legal relief to Dissenting
schoolmasters, around the time of making an initial opening to Catholics
to be broadened a dozen years later in an extension in coverage of the 1779
act (Hans 1958, 116; McLachlan 1931, 39; and Watson 1916, 82-83, principal
source).

Catholics had since early Elizabethan times been largely prevented from
keeping schools in England, even as preparatory institutions for English
"colleges" set up to educate their youth abroad. A few Catholic schools
were formed at home during the reign of James II, but only one of them,
located near Winchester, survived that brief period. A number of new
schools were formed during the eighteenth century, prior to the 1790s, but
generally they "exist[ed] precariously for short periods" only (Hans 1951,
21, quoted passage, and 1958, 115-16).

Just after Parliament finally extended meaningful educational freedom to Catholics, English colleges in France and Belgium were closed as a result of the French Revolution. On returning to their homeland Catholic students and teachers benefited from the popular "Cisalpine" movement within the laity that stressed loyal citizenry focused on public service rather than Jacobite disaffection. English Catholics proceeded to form between 1793 and 1800 half a dozen schools that "could rival the great public schools of the Anglicans" (Hans 1958, 116). Ampleforth College, one of England's leading secondary schools of the present day, was founded in 1802 at a Benedictine house established eighteen miles north of York following the monks' return from France. Its lineage dates back, however, to the rebuilt Westminster Abbey of the eleventh century (J. Blair 1984, 100-1; and McConnell 1985, 189, 198).

While the Clarendon Code was still under development, Dissenters began defiantly, if by compulsion, to found their own schools. Some of the "Dissenting Academies" formed during the period would achieve high distinction as institutions of university grade.

The Dissenting Academies

Hans estimates (1958, 159) that some 150 men who were "ejected" from their livings or posts consequent to the 1662 Act of Uniformity opened schools at one level or another, counting those who became "private tutors in rich Dissenting families." With 160 boys in 1668, one of the largest institutions was a free school kept in (Webster's geographical dictionary 1977, s.v. "Ashby la Zouch," "Leicester," def. 4) central England by Stephen Shaw. The academically progressive Manchester Grammar School retained dissenting mathematics master Adam Martindale. Despite the

Clarendon Code, Presbyterians, Quakers, and other sects even endowed schools during the generation prior to the Toleration Act of 1689 (Hans 1958, 159).

Of particular interest is the formation in this early period of at least twenty "academies" of higher learning, in some cases by former Oxford or Cambridge dons, serving young men excluded from the universities by unwillingness to affirm religious conformity (Hans 1958, 159-60; McLachlar 1931, 2; and Stephens and Roderick 1977, 49). "[T]he most flourishing of the early academies," overall, was opened in Rathmall in northern England in 1670. Ironically, the first student of rather rigid Calvinist Richard Frankland, M.A., a product of Christ's College, Cambridge, was "the son of an Episcopalian [Anglican] baronet" (McLachlan 1931, 62 and 64, quoted in turn, 63).

Frankland moved his school in 1674 upon accepting a pastorate in another town, and six members of his class of '76 obtained Scottish university degrees. The school was relocated three times in 1683-84, to escape prosecution based on the Five Mile Act, and there was yet another move in '86. Surviving very lean enrollments over this period, the school prospered after finally returning to Rathmall in 1689 as the master and his assistant taught as many as 80 pupils in a year, and 26 Presbyterian Fund scholars matriculated, an unmatched total of the time. Even with the Toleration Act and a good personal relationship with the archbishop of Canterbury, however, Richard Frankland could not escape "petty persecution" in his otherwise very successful final years; and the academy closed shortly after his death in 1698 (McLachlan 1931, 63, quoted, 64-66, 69).

Frankland's academy was intended primarily for future physicians, lawyers, and, especially, clergymen. More than a third (Stephens and Roderick 1977, 51) of a sampling of 308 of his students became Congregational or Presbyterian ministers. Although the academy studies were themselves of university grade, about one in seven men from the sampling proceeded to earn university arts degrees, nearly half of them from Edinburgh, which required only a year's residence from Rathmall graduates. Eleven members of the sample group earned medical degrees, seven of them from the distinguished Dutch university at Leyden that (Agnew 1970, 257; and Poynter 1970, 238-39) would train Edinburgh's original medical faculty. The academy's five-year course emphasized logic as well as divinity, and included metaphysics, natural philosophy, jurisprudence, and probably Greek and Hebrew, among other fields (McLachlan 1931, 63-64, 66-70).

In general, early dissenting academies conducted a traditional classical, and even "scholastic," course of studies (McLachlan 1931, 19). With theology a leading field, it is noteworthy that Presbyterians and Congregationalists insisted on a learned ministry, while Baptists and Quakers emphasized qualification for the pulpit through an "Inner Light" of spiritual inspiration. There were fifteen Quaker schools in 1671, for boys and girls alike, but there is no indication that any of them was of academy grade (Hans 1958, 158, quoted, 159). A 1695 bequest by a private individual endowed in Bristol a Baptist academy of classical orientation having slightly earlier roots, but aside from a very small school founded in 1794 by a nonorthodox element there were no further Baptist institutions of that level through 1800. Many members of the faith attended the Bristol school or other Independent academies (McLachlan 1931, 91-92, 102-3).

A very broad curriculum including both classical and modern subjects was offered at an academy at Newington Green, near London, opened around 1675 by a mathematically gifted graduate of Wadham College, Oxford. Charles Morton had been a particular favorite of Wadham's distinguished midcentury head cited below, and would become vice president of Harvard College after sailing to America in '86 to escape religious persecution.

One of Morton's first academy students was the remarkably versatile writer (D.n.b. 1917, s.v. "Defoe, Daniel," especially 741-43) Daniel Defoe, the creator of Robinson Crusoe. In five years at Newington Green he '"went through a complete course of theology"' and studied '"five languages, . . . mathematics, natural philosophy, logic, geography and history . . .[,] and politics as a science"', or at least nearly all those subjects. Even more innovative than the curricular breadth, through no doubt contributing to it, was the master's practice of lecturing (exclusively) in English, and requiring his students to recite oratories and write theses in the vernacular. The academy was still further a pioneer in supplying pupils with an excellent variety of scientific and mathematical instruments (McLachlan 1931, 76-80, quoting 79).[19]

Daniel Defoe's work included several books on commerce (D.n.b. 1917, s.v. "Defoe, Daniel," 742; and in reference to bookkeeping, Murray 1930, 256-59). Although evidently highly skilled in Latin, French, and Italian, he had only praise for the use of English in his boyhood academy. Defoe was a very early champion of utilitarian education that need not always include foreign languages, noting that seamen rarely knew Latin, but could be good navigators without it. More heretically, he asserted that a person who wished to read only in English could still "'be a gentleman of learning'" (McLachlan 1931, 78-79; and Watson 1916, 128, 129, quoted, emphasis added).

---

[19]Another early pupil at Warrington Green later recalled that his classmates had included '"not a few"' sons of noblemen (McLachlan 1931, 77, 78, quoted). Samuel Wesley's son John founded the Methodist religion after leaving Oxford in 1735. The university's "leisured and worldly dons" of the day had scorned the "Holy Club" religious society founded by John and brother Charles Wesley (Hall and Frankl 1983, 48, 50, quoted).

New funding societies, usually exercising substantial control, founded many new academies in the distinctly freer period after 1689 (McLachlan 1931, 3). Two of the strongest new schools, however, represented the older personalized pattern. Although after only eight years it died in 1723 with its master, Congregational minister John Jennings, Kibworth Academy in the "East Midlands" was one of the day's leading schools. Its four-year course included eight separate units that embraced ancient langauges, several branches of mathematics, divinity, and several areas of natural philosophy or physical science (Stephens and Roderick 1977, 50, quoted, [53], caption).

Late in 1729 Philip Doddridge, a student of his whom Jennings had identified as a possible successor, moved to Northampton, sixty miles north-northwest of London, a recently founded academy that became "in many ways the most famous of nonconformist seminaries" (McLachlan 1931, 143, quoted, 144; and Webster's geographical dictionary 1977, s.v. "Northampton," def. 4). More than half a century after Charles Morton had opened his school, Doddridge was still one of the first masters to lecture in English, a prac-tice that accommodated in four years a broad range of mathematical, scien-tific, theological, and historical studies. Ancient languages were taught in evening tutorials, and French was an optional subject. Doddridge pioneered the use of shorthand in dissenting academies, requiring his pupils to learn a system that he himself improved and routinely used.

Only a 1734 intervention on his behalf by King George II quelled a local effort to require the Northampton master to obtain an ecclesiastical license for his academy. Doddridge was in later years, however, highly respected and frequently consulted by Anglican clergymen, as well as dis-senting clerics and leading laymen. His school was closed a year after his death in 1751 after having educated some two hendred men, 60 percent of whom became ordained ministers (McLachlan 1931, 144-52).

85

Around midcentury a more "modern" kind of divinity college emerged within "institutional" academies having their own trustees and subscribers (McLachlan 1931, 2 and 4, quoted in turn, 3) from organized religious bodies (Hans 1958, 161). The best known of the later schools was formed in 1757 at Warrington, located in northwest England between Liverpool and Manchester (Gilbert 1968, 75; and Webster's geographical dictionary 1977, s.v. "Liverpool," def. 4, "Manchester," def. 11, "Warrington," def. 2).

At academies offering dual programs, the students in the usually five-year theological course had already completed at least a substantial part of the usually three-year secular course as an entry requirement (McLachlan 1931, 25), so that "even their graduate clergymen" were "sent out . . . with a grounding in mathematics, chemistry and physics" (Stephens and Roderick 1977, 54). Lay pupils themselves were required to attend religiously oriented lectures that at Warrington included the topic "Evidences of Natural Religion" (McLachlan 1931, 25).

Warrington's secular program was intended in particular for students planning careers in business and commerce, but was scarcely narrow in coverage (Stephens and Roderick 1977, 51, emphasis added):

> The first year offered Arithmetic, Algebra and Geometry, French and Universal Grammar and Rhetoric. This was followed by more Mathematics (notably Trigonometry, but with Navigation as an optional extra), Natural Philosophy and Astronomy, and French in the second year. The third year consisted of Natural Philosophy, Chemistry, and 'A short system of Morality'. Book-keeping was stressed throughout, and short-hand would be taught if requested. A broad-ranging course of Geography was held with one or two lectures each week.

The most famous tutor an an academy founded on a platform of open-minded pursuit of knowledge and full freedom of judgment and conscience asserted '"the same liberty of thinking, debating and publishing"' for all persons, '"whether Christians, Papists, Protestants, Dissenters, Heretics

86

or Deists"' (Hans 1958, 161). Before his 1761-67 tenure, famous scientist, cleric and theologian, and teacher Joseph Priestley had learned a number of languages from grammar school, a private tutor, and self-study; attended the new dissenting academy founded at Daventry as (McLachlan 1931, 152; and Webster's geographical dictionary 1977, s.v. "Daventry," "Northampton," def. 4) nearby Northampton's successor; preached for several years; and kept his own "flourishing school" (D.n.b. 1917, s.v. "Priestley, Joseph," 357-58, 359, quoted). Already a freethinker as a teenager, Priestley had vetoed family plans that he enroll at a London academy kept (in not an isolated case (Hans 1951, 55-56)) by a doctrinnaire cleric requiring his pupils to affirm monthly "'ten printed articles of the strictest Calvinistic faith'." He was much more at home in Daventry's remarkable climate of free inquiry and disputation. The headmaster lamented only of his "'bad name, Priestley; those who give him it I hope were no prophets'" (D.n.b. 1917, s.v. "Priestley, Joseph," 357-58, quoted, 359).

With the preferred chair of natural philosophy already taken, Priestley was appointed tutor in languages and belles-lettres at Warrington Academy, where he taught ancient and modern languages, logic, philosophy, oratory, and (briefly) anatomy. He also lectured on "the theory of language and universal law" and offered three courses of historical lectures (D.n.b. 1917, s.v. "Priestley, Joseph," 359; Huxley 1874, 11, quoted; and McLachlan 1931, 214-15). The latter lectures (Priestley [1803], 25-438) concerned "the STUDY OF HISTORY in general," the "HISTORY OF ENGLAND," and Britain's "PRESENT CONSTITUTION AND LAWS," and were designed to fill a void in the training of young men planning careers in "active" or "civil life" (Priest-ley [1803, 7]-8, 12-13, shown as in text). Priestley ([1803], 10-11) defines

such vocations to include merchant business in the essay, originating ([7])
in 1765, that is presented as appendix 1.

Joseph Priestley went on to a remarkable if highly controversial
career, warranting a twenty-page D.n.b. entry (1917, s.v. "Priestley,
Joseph"), as in particular a Dissenting minister and founder of the society
that formalized the English Unitarian movement traced (Columbia encyclopedia
3d, s.v. "Biddle, John") to the 1640s; and a scientist accorded both membership in the Royal Society and the highest award made by that renowned
group discussed relative to Oxford below. Lacking the theoretical acuity
of distinguished English, French, and Scots contemporaries Cavendish,
Lavoisier, and Black, he nonetheless ranks high as a chemist for discovering
(besides carbonated water) a number of gases including oxygen, as his field
finally discarded air, water, and fire as fundamental elements (Huxley
1874, 13-14, 16-27). Along the way, Priestley served for more than seven
years as a well-paid librarian and tutor on a lord's estate (Hans 1951,
182; and Huxley 1874, 15-16), and lectured (gratis) at an academy of metro-
politan London patterned after Warrington (McLachlan 1931, 246, 250-51; and
Webster's geographical dictionary 1977, s.v. "Hackney").

In keeping with Priestley's historical coverage ([1803], 12) of the
field, Warrington Academy provided lectures on commerce. Political philos-
ophy and economics were taught for a time, and a '"Writing and Drawing
Master" was [intermittently] engaged . . . "to teach book-keeping, mer-
chants' accounts,and occasionally surveying"' (McLachlan 1931, 222).
Finally, Warrington students could train for both medicine and the law.
In the former regard, one of the three tutors who collectively replaced
Priestley on the faculty in 1767 taught anatomy, which in combination

with physiology was alternated with chemistry beginning in '72 (Hans 1951, 162; and McLachlan 1931, 215, 219, principal source).

Beset by financial problems and socially disruptive student conduct, traced in part to overzealous support of the rebellious American colonies, Warrington Academy closed in 1783. Half the proceeds from the sale of the buildings three years later went to newly established Manchester Academy,[20] along with the school library (McLachlan 1931, 216, 224, 226, 229). Associated primarily with training for the Unitarian ministry although most of the early students were preparing for commercial careers, that school moved three times, once back to its native town (McLachlan 1931, 262, 268-69), before finally settling in Oxford in 1888. Over the past century Manchester College has been one of the numerous "'permanent private halls'" whose members may take university examinations in training for holy orders, in its case Unitarian (Hall and Frankl 1983, 85).

In the principal source used in the above coverage, McLachlan in 1931 (6-15) identified 71 principal dissenting academies, of which 33 were formed before 1701 and 3 after 1800.[21] Thirteen pre-1801 institutions still existed as of his writing, two of them, including Bristol Academy, dating from the 1600s. Otherwise, based on uncertain dating in some instances and omitting the two cases for which a termination date could not be estimated, longevity

---

[20]The other half went to Hackney College, likewise founded in 1786, the site of aforementioned nonpaid lecturing (in chemistry and history, 1792-94) by Joseph Priestley (D.n.b. 1917, s.v. "Priestley, Joseph," 364-65; and McLachlan 1931, 226, 250-51).

[21]McLachlan's list (1931, 11) includes Manchester College, 1786-1803, and Manchester "New" College, 1803-, as two separate institutions. As in directly prior coverage, the numeration above recognizes the school established in York in 1803 as in substance a continuation of Manchester College. McLachlan (1931, 262) himself supports this interpretation in writing that in 1803 "the academy . . . migrated to York."

of the 17th-century foundations ranged from 4 years to 88, with an average of 27.0 years; and 18th-century academies ranged in life from 6 years to 84, with an average of 22.6 years (McLachlan 1931, 6-15). According to Hans (1951, 163), in the 19th century dissenting schools became "purely theological institutions."

The dissenting academies educated many leading figures of the day (McLachlan 1931, 43-44). A survey conducted by Hans (1951, 16-[18]) of 3,500 men born between 1685 and 1785 who are listed in the Dictionary of national biography (1917) shows that 265 of them attended dissenting schools, academies in 80% of the cases. Comprising about one tenth of the D.n.b. group excluding Scotch and Irish entries, this total is "far above" a proportionate level of representation for such schooling within English society. The academies at Daventry, Northampton, Bristol (Baptist), and Warrington alone accounted for 64 members of the select group (Hans 1951, 20).

A close linkage existed between dissenters and Scottish higher education. Thirty-six of the sixty-two men from dissenting schools in Hans's sampling who went on to universities attended Scots institutions, primarily Edinburgh or Glasgow. Fifty-six English dissenting teachers or authors, including Doddridge, Priestley, and (from a secular school, as covered in chapter 9) Henry Clarke, were awarded doctor's degrees, often or usually of an honorary nature, by universities of Scotland (Hans 1951, [18, 247]).

By all accounts dissenting schools made a major contribution to English education in the eighteenth and latter seventeenth centuries. In contending that "Anglican . . . and secular bodies and institutions played an equally important role" in the movement toward modernized curricula, Hans (1951, 54, quoted, 55) intends only to correct an influential viewpoint

90

that the dissenting academies alone were significant agents of reform. An

important element of the latter position is a widespread belief that,

following earlier scientific leadership tied in one case to the formation

of an illustrious learned society, the two English universities were parti-

cularly in academic decline in the eighteenth century.

Oxford and Cambridge

Early Scientific Leadership: Oxford Scientists, the Royal Society, and Newton at Cambridge

Professorships or chairs were established at Oxford during the second

decade of the seventeenth century in natural philosophy, astronomy, and

geometry (Hans 1951, 47). Due in part to worthy appointments made by Puri-

tan authorities (Hans 1958, 159, somewhat overstating the factor in light

of D.n.b. entries), taken together the university and town were home in the

1650s to an extraordinary group of scientists and mathematicians (D.n.b.

1917, s.v. "Ward, Seth," 794, "Wilkins, John," 265; and Poynter 1970,

238). They included anatomy professor Sir William Petty, better known as

a pioneering statistical economist (Landreth 1976, 369) and compiler of

"vital statistics" who was an important predecessor (Johnson 1937, 93-116)

of Adam Smith's; geometry professor John Wallis, who in anticipating the

development of both differential and integral calculus stood as England's

foremost mathematician prior to Sir Isaac Newton; and Wadham College head

John Wilkins, a scientifically gifted cleric noted for his breadth of learn-

ing (D.n.b. 1917, s.v. "Petty, Sir William," 999, 1002, quoted, 1003,

"Wallis, John (1616-1703)," 599, 601, "Ward, Seth," 794, "Wilkins, John,"

264-65).

Brilliant Oxford students of the day included (Sir) Christopher Wren

of Wadham, appointed professor of astronomy at Gresham College, London in

1657 and at Oxford four years later prior to becoming probably England's greatest architect (Morrah 1979, 121-22); and Robert Hooke of Christ Church, one of her most distinguished physicists and inventors. While achieving a remarkable scientific reputation as an undergraduate, Hooke became the chemical assistant to a notable laboratory scientist working independently in Oxford. In that role he helped Robert Boyle, "'the founder of modern chemistry'" (Morrah 1979, 118), develop the first practical air pump (D.n.b. 1917, s.v. "Boyle, Hon. Robert," 1027, "Hooke, Robert"; and Hall and Frankl 1983, 13).

Apparently excluding Hooke, the men just cited and at least five other individuals included in the D.n.b. (1917, s.v. "Bathurst, Ralph," "Goddard, Jonathan, M.D.," "Rooke, Lawrence," "Ward, Seth," "Willis, Thomas, M.D.") actively participated in weekly scientific discussions at Oxford (D.n.b. 1917, s.v. "Ward, Seth," 794, giving incorrect dates for Wallis, "Wilkins, John," 265). Those meetings carried on the tradition begun at Gresham College in the 1640s by some of the same people, as did the gatherings of the residual group in London, with whom the Oxford men kept in touch. John Wilkins, John Wallis, and (while still in his teens) Robert Boyle had been leaders of the original London group. After moving to Oxford in 1654 Boyle joined Wilkins, the central figure overall, and William Petty as a frequent host of the meetings (D.n.b. 1917, s.v. "Boyle, Hon. Robert," 1027, "Petty, Sir William," 999, "Wallis, John," 599, "Wilkins, John," 265).

By the fall of 1660, six of the ten members identified from the Oxford group had for one reason or another moved to London, three of them (although Christopher Wren was about to return to Oxford) as Gresham professors. Petty had been ousted a year earlier by anti-Cromwell factions in the polit- ical aftermath of an historic land survey he had supervised in Ireland,

but had at once become a favorite of the new king's, and would be knighted
in '62. To a degree future bishop John Wilkins had also, after a year's
mastership at Cambridge, become a brief casualty of the times (D.n.b. 1917,
s.v. "Goddard, Jonathan," "Petty, Sir William," 999-1001, "Rooke, Lawrence,"
"Ward, Seth," "Wilkins, John," 265-66; and Morrah 1979, 4, reference to
Cromwell's son and, briefly, successor). At the end of the year, the two
discussion groups were united as the "Royal Society for Promoting Natural
Knowledge" (D.n.b. 1917, s.v. "Wilkins, John," 265; and Morrah 1979, 119,
quoted).

Chartered in 1662 by King Charles, a genuinely interested patron, the
Royal Society searched in its weekly meetings at Gresham College for "no
less than the interpretation of all natural phenomena in the light of human
reason" (Morrah 1979, 119, quoted, 120). Although Robert Boyle remained
in Oxford until six years later, his assistant Hooke moved to London in
1662 to become "curator of experiments" for the society, a position he
later combined with a Gresham professorship and an appointment as city surveyor (D.n.b. 1917, s.v. "Boyle, Hon. Robert," 1028, "Hooke, Robert,"
1178, quoted).

The university at Cambridge may never in the 1600s have matched the
wealth of scientific talent found at Oxford at midcentury. Its consolation
lay in the presence for many years of the greatest natural philosopher of
the age. Sir Isaac Newton was appointed a fellow of Trinity College in
1667 at age twenty-five, following two years of stupendous intellectual
achievement that took place largely outside plague-ridden Cambridge. Two
years later he bacome the second Lucasian Professor of Mathematics, and in
1687 his monumental three-volume Principia appeared (D.n.b. 1917, s.v.
"Newton, Sir Isaac," 371-73, 381). A series of disputations on the two

men's contributions to optics and celestial mechanics led over the years to a "bitter and burning hatred" between Newton and Hooke (Koyre 1965, 221-60, especially 221-32, 253, quoting 222).

The presence of celebrated men of science at Oxford and Cambridge during the seventeenth century does not refute Charlton's assessment (1965, 152) that if scholasticism was in decline in the 1600s, "it took an unconscionable time in dying." More importantly, the expulsion of Dissenting lecturers and tutors, the exclusion of dissenters from degrees, and changing enrollment patterns otherwise are generally thought (Hans 1951, 42) to have brought serious and prolonged decline to Oxford and Cambridge in the eighteenth century. Not challenged in popular short histories of the universities (Hall and Frankl 1982, 10, and 1983, 13) used for general reference, this view has as intended been partially rebutted by Hans (1951, 41-54).[22]

Less Decline in the Eighteenth Century than Traditionally Assumed

By conventional opinion, Oxford and Cambridge were principally in the 1700s playgrounds for the rich, idle and undisciplined, where professors rarely lectured and, beyond isolated advances that included (Hall and Frankl 1983, 13) the commencement of Anglo-Saxon studies at Oxford, intellectual life as it existed was dominated by scholastic rather than scientific or humanist values. A number of famous contemporary students and observers contributed damaging appraisals (Hans 1951, 41-42; and McLachlan

---

[22] In an historical work with a later copyright, Hans himself (1958, 132) takes a more traditional position in referring briefly to the two universities. That book represents, however, a minimal revision of a work first published in 1949 (Hans 1958, [iv], x).

1931, 17). At Oxford, for example, economist Adam Smith recalled his
Balliol years, 1740-46, with distaste (Hall and Frankl 1983, 32; and Hans
1951, 53); historian Edward Gibbon found his fourteen months at Magdalen
("maudlin"), 1752-53, as "'the most idle and unprofitable of [his] whole
life'" (Hall and Frankl 1983, 50 and 55, quoted in turn, 52); and philosopher Jeremy Bentham, who had entered Queen's College at age twelve in 1760,
remarked later that he had "'learnt nothing'" there as a student of tutors
who were "'all either stupid or dissipated'" (Hall and Frankl 1983, [71]).
At a more general level, debaucheries and offensive pranks of wealthy students were widely reported in newspapers of the day (Hans 1951, 46).

Substantial enrollment declines of the era are cited (Stephens and
Roderick 1977, 47) as a quantitative index of educational trends. Over the
century that followed the Restoration, as the population of England and
Wales rose from 5.8 million people to 6.6 million (Wilson 1977, 116,
1670-1761 figures), there was marked reduction (Hans 1951, 44) from respective student levels of some 3,000 and 2,500 undergraduates at Oxford and
Cambridge (Morrah 1979, 69). Whether or not combined freshman matriculation ever fell to 317 boys (Stephens and Roderick 1977, 47, citing 1750),
enrollment moved still lower during the years 1761-80, only to rebound
considerably thereafter. By 1796 Cambridge, with more than 2,100 students,
had recovered to the levels found at the beginning of the century (Hans
1951, 44).

The favorable trend after 1780 might be attributed in part to an
expanding general population, as the total number of Englishmen and Welsh-
men increased by 1.7 million, to 9.2 million people, over the years 1781-
1801 (Wilson 1977, 116). More importantly, earlier declines were consistent
with the religious restriction on degrees, the rise of popular and

95

inexpensive Dissenting Academies, and changes noted below in student social composition. Furthermore, evidence to be cited that scientific instruction declined mainly after 1760 challenges the use of enrollment trends as a reflection of academic qulaity.

The proportion of sons of the gentry within the student bodies rose only moderately during the 1700s. On one estimate, it rose at Cambridge from about 25 percent to around 35 percent, and at Oxford to a somewhat higher level still under one half. Representation of the lower classes declined somewhat, but students from "intermediate [social] groups increased in percentages continually" despite (Hans 1958, 131) the Toleration Act's loosening of the Anglican hold thereon. Poorer students, graduating with impressive regularity, were also far more likely than young men from the upper classes to stay on to complete degrees (Hans 1951, 44, quoted, 45-46).

At both universities, new professorial chairs were added in the natural sciences, and until about 1760 outstanding scientists regularly lectured on their subjects, including leaders in new experimental methods (Hans 1951, 47-51). New Cambridge chairs of the early eighteenth century in anatomy and botany "made little impression," but the university's distinguished reputation in physiology dates to the unofficial establishment in that period of England's first physiological laboratory by a student of Newton's (Poynter 1970, 238).

Around 1760, both institutions made unfortunate appointments to science professorships, based on seniority rather than specific competence, and for some years to come assistants did much of the lecturing. Yet even unqualified chairholders lectured in nonscientific fields in which they were authorities, and a Cambridge chemistry appointee untrained in the field became by dint of outstanding effort a capable scientist after assuming his chair. Also, Cambridge University Press issued "a constant supply of scientific books" throughout the eighteenth century (Hans 1951, 51-52, 53, quoted).

Hans (1951, 31-32 and 34, 41, quoted in reverse order) supplies a further item of evidence from the science area that Oxford and Cambridge were less "moribund" in the 1700s than is generally supposed. About 30 percent of a select group of nearly five hundred English "scientists" of the day attended the two universities, down from 53 percent of a smaller sampling from the preceding century, but still most impressive in light of a significant negative bias in classification. The total sampling of 680 scientists (of whom 44 were archaeologists, historians, or political economists) included 300 men from subclasses (Hans 1951, 53) often or commonly not university-trained in that time. Specifically, there were 240 physicians and surgeons and 60 technicians, such as surveyors or navigators.

Two centuries after Henry VIII had endowed Regius professorships of medicine at each institution (O'Malley 1970a, 90), and a century after the Oxford incumbent of 1611-47 had "infused new life" into his medical school as a worthy predecessor of the Royal Society founders, Oxford and Cambridge remained only secondary centers of medical training. They lagged well behind study under physicians and surgeons of London hospitals, which tripled in number during the 1700s, or the medical faculty at the University of Edinburgh (Poynter 1970, 238, quoted, 239), which soon after its formal organization in 1726 became preeminent in Europe (Agnew 1970, 257-58). The long tradition by which Oxford and Cambridge did not train surgeons (Talbot 1970, 81) indeed persisted into the nineteenth century (Hans 1951, 53-54). Significant advances were made, however, with the foundation in each university town, 1766-70, of a hospital that could be used for clinical instruction; the formation of a lasting connection between Cambridge and

St. Thomas's Hospital of London; and a belated streamlining of the medical program at Oxford that finally reduced the study commitment to a reasonable number of years (Poynter 1970, 238-39).

A very visible area of eighteenth-century decline, finally was the opening of new colleges. Until Downing was formed at Cambridge in 1800, the only new foundation was that of Worcester College, as a successor to an academic hall itself rooted in a monastic school, at Oxford in 1714. To draw broader negative conclusions is also, however, to condemn the universities of the 17th century, when Wadham at Oxford was the only college founded, and Oxford of the 19th century up to 1870, when the first post-Worcester foundation took place (Hall and Frankl 1982, 68, and 1983, 82, 86, 31-85, references to founding dates). Also, the 1700s were "the most glorious period of Oxford architecture," as (among other developments) one college was "completely rebuilt" and almost all the others "acquired new and beautiful extensions" (Hall and Frankl 1983, 13).

Evidently until Oxford introduced (partially) its "modern" system in 1801, neither institution was conducting a significant program of examination for bachelor's degrees, in particular, a deficiency that invited unfavorable comparison with dissenting academies (Hall and Frankl 1983, 13, quoted; and McLachlan 1931, 41-42). As blemished as they may have been, however, the universities had strong appeal for graduates of the most elite grammar schools of the day, which despite undoubted intellectual merits were probably the least progressive element in contemporary English education.

The Elite "Public Schools," Especially Eton

An authority on the educational thought of English philosopher John Locke writes (Axtell, 1968, 21, emphasis added) that "the large public schools" supplied "the most prestigious," and usually "best," grammar schooling of the seventeenth century. The reference is to endowed grammar schools that had begun "to attract pupils from all over the country and become in a sense national institutions" (McConnell 1985, 7, emphasis added).

Locke, Robert Hooke (D.n.b. 1917, s.v. "Hooke, Robert"), Christopher Wren, poet and diplomat (Columbia-Viking desk encyclopedia 2d, s.v. "Prior, Matthew") Matthew Prior, and remarkably versatile "pre-eminent" man of letters John Dryden were among the most illustrious contemporary products of Westminster (Morrah 1979, 68-69, 96-100, quoting 98),[23] "by most standards the finest" such institution of the day (Axtell 1968, 21). They were there during the fifty-seven-year mastership of Dr. Richard Busby, a severe disciplinarian but revered scholar and teacher whose authority was never questioned (Morrah 1979, 68):

> When Charles II visited the school he [Busby] asked (and was given) the King's permission to keep his hat on in the royal presence, lest his pupils should think that there was any person more important than himself.

Westminster was favored more permanently by its location in the borough of the same name in which both Buckingham Palace and the Houses of Parliament were located. A similar advantage accrued to Eton, founded by Henry VI, as its proximity to Windsor Castle only buttressed its tradition of royal patronage (Morrah 1979, 68; and Webster's geographical dictionary 1977, s.v. "Eton," "Westminster," and 683). Even during Commonwealth times Eton was accommodated by the national authorities, as there were no threats to

---

[23] Dryden was a member, or "fellow," of the Royal Society, reflecting the breadth both of his own interests and of the society's appeal to "the leading intellectuals of the day" (Morrah 1979, 120). Locke, who earned a bachelor's degree in medicine from Oxford and served intermittently as private physican to a titled aristocratic family, was also elected to the Royal Society (D.n.b. 1917, s.v. "Locke, John," 1028-29).

confiscate its endowments, and fellows (welcomed back in 1660) were turned
out only after refusing to swear loyalty to the antiroyalist government
(Ollard 1982, 33-34).

As illustrated below regarding Eton, the period 1660 to 1800 was distinguished neither by educational reform (Hans 1951, 38, quoted) nor by
genteel conduct (McConnell 1985, 51) at the famous nine "Public Schools"
ranging in date of origin from Winchester to Charterhouse. Yet the service
of several exceptional headmasters (Watson 1916, 136-39) and, in some cases,
unique associations with the universities and thence favored careers brought
enhanced social prestige to these schools. In "cater[ing] for the titled
aristocracy and squiarearchy," they trained "most of the ruling members in
State and Church" of the era (Hans 1951, 38). A recent historian of Eton
confirms (Ollard 1982, 40) in that instance that the hereditary peerage had
begun to send their sons to such institutions, making several references
of a more general kind to the affluence of many eighteenth-century Etonians·
(38, 40, 42-44).

Of Hans's large sampling of eighteenth-century men listed in the D.n.b.
(1917), 22 percent attended one of the "famous nine Public Schools," inclusive of Scotch and Irish entries. Thirteen percent of the notables matriculated at either Westminster or Eton. At the other end of the scale, Rugby
and Shrewsbury enrolled just 31 of the 3,500 men between them (Hans 1951,
16-19, quoting 17), as total enrollment at the latter school had fallen by
1798 to fewer than twenty boys (McConnell 1985, 43).

A record of living conditions and discipline or deportment that only
conformed to a "savage" pattern found at the elite schools (McConnell 1985,
51) would hardly have recommended Eton. Especially among resident "Collegians" on scholarship, but also among "Oppidans" living in private homes,

there was an extraordinary amount of rowdiness, fighting, and hooliganism. Fighting was "the great test of social acceptability and an approved form of physical recreation." A few sports were played, though not in organized games, including "the most brutish and least elegant mutation of football to have survived into the present day" (Ollard 1982, 40-41). Rules adopted at Rugby in 1845 finally produced a reasonably controlled game of football (McConnell 1985, 52).

Thus if indeed the Battle of Waterloo was "won on the playing fields of Eton," it was perhaps because they were mainly "area[s] in which the boys fought each other" (Ollard 1982, 42). The reputation of Dr. Edward Barnard, Eton's foremost eighteenth-century leader (Ollard 1982, 38), as "'the Pitt of masters'" (Watson 1916, 138) calls to mind the standing of his contemporary "the elder" William Pitt as "the most gloriously successful war minister in British history" (Langford 1984, 399, [400], quoted in turn).

Various factors contributed to the "harshness" and "violence" of life at Eton in the 1700s. Granting that the boys could have learned ably to defend themselves in a more peaceful environment, the period itself was by later standards a violent one, "for all its veneer of social grace and intellectual enlightenment" (Ollard 1982, 41). A faculty ranging in size from 4 or 5 men to 8 or 9 was consistently too small to hope to exercise control outside the classroom as enrollment fluctuated widely based on headmaster reputations, for example falling to 246 pupils in 1775 just ten years after Barnard's mastership had ended with an historic high of 552. Also, the headmaster and his assistants often had to contend with boys having a well-developed "consciousness of rank" who surpassed them in social status. Moreover, enforcement of stringent disciplinary rules among resident

101

pupils ranging in age from 8 to nearly 20 was left almost entirely to senior boys; assistant masters were generally not permitted to board students; and off-campus housing for Oppidans was only loosely supervised by school authorities (Ollard 1982, 38-39, 40, quoted).

As reflected in the formation of a great library for the provost and fellows (Ollard 1982, 43), the life of the mind was not ignored at eighteeth-century Eton. Boys receiving "a grounding in Latin and Greek grammar that made slovenliness of language and cloudiness of thought uneasy to them" often acquired a lifelong love of classical literature (Ollard 1982, 42, quoted, 43). The general picture is one, however, of stagnation under "a long succession of comfortable divines" as provosts who seemed to be invigorated only by opportunities for personal or family advancement (Ollard 1982, 43). The major kind of initiative found at the headmaster level was an often unseemly interest in finding new ways to exact fees from the young men. The practice by which departing students were for some time expected to make a cash payment to the master attracted a recent comment (Ollard 1982, 44) that a "Head Master ought to be distinguishable from a headwaiter."

Academically, Eton "was not merely stable: it was static" (Ollard 1982, 37), a place where (43)

> learning may have been sound, but it had become mechanical[, though n]ot, indeed, in the literal sense of that word. The curriculum did not alter in the slightest degree from the beginning of the century to the end. Wars were fought: an empire was won in India and another was lost in America: the French Revolution engulfed the states and societies of Europe. But Eton took no cognizance of these transformations.

A small opening occurred in the 1780s, as Eton and comparable institutions, which likewise had not modernized their curricula, began to invite scientists from outside to offer lectures on experimental philosophy (Hans 1951, 38). Also, the proprietors (including landladies) of boarding houses in which the Oppidans lived "were often teachers of extra-curricular subjects, writing masters, music masters, drawing masters, teachers of fencing and dancing" (Ollard 1982, 38).

Against this background of rough and violent behavior and stagnant classroom studies, what commended Eton and similar schools to "the well-to-do, and even peers," as well as "tradesmen and artisans" (Ollard 1982, 40)? For one thing, the behavioral environment was defended as an antidote to "the evils of softness, of effeminacy, of degeneration," and (for resident pupils) as a side effect of a valuable opportunity for self-governance (Ollard 1982, 39, 41, quoted).

More persuasively, the political world that was "born in the struggles of the seventeenth century," which was (Morrah 1979, 50-51) dominated by the upper classes, lent to classical studies "a new aptness and point" in light of the "saturat[ion]" of the Greek and Roman literature "with political ideas" (Ollard 1982, 36). One of the headmaster's favorite scholarship students at Eton in the 1690s was Sir Robert Walpole (Ollard 1982, 35-36), the statesman whose skill in handling the 1720 "South Sea Bubble" financial scandal and crash would lead to twenty years' service, 1721-41 (Morgan 1984, [621]), as Britain's first prime minister (Langford 1984, 363, quoted, 364-66).

Most importantly, however, Eton, Winchester, and to a lesser extent at least two other schools attracted students through distinctly favored connections with the English universities. Even aristocrats were sometimes willing to subject their sons "to th[e] ordeal" of life as a Collegian at Eton "for the chance of seeing them permanently settled in life with at the very least a Fellowship at King's," Cambridge, a most comfortable and undemanding post (Ollard 1982, 19, 40, quoted). The same attraction existed at Winchester regarding placement at New College, Oxford, and in part at Merchant Taylors' with the reservation of numerous places in each class at St. John's, Cambridge. Furthermore, with strictly limited campus boarding capacity Westminster held annual competitions in grammar and classical literature, among advanced students, for King's Scholarships that provided free lodging and eligibility to compete later for a university award. In 1652 a dozen King's scholars were elected in turn to scholarships of 20 pound at Christ Church, Oxford or 10 pounds at Trinity College, Cambridge. The sixth and final selection for the larger award was John Locke (Axtell 1968, 23, 25-27).

If the connection with King's College was Eton's greatest attraction, it likewise contributed much to the insular and stagnant academic environment that prevailed. "The closed circuit . . ., the easy circumstances awaiting the privileged entrants" were too appealing to allow anything to "be done that might disturb th[e] felicitous arrangement" (Ollard 1982, 43, 44, quoted).

The nine institutions just discussed were only an unusually affluent, exteemed, and, in curricular terms, rigid group from among several hundred Latin grammar schools of the day. Also, many other "classical" schools were kept by private masters, mainly ordained Anglicans with English degrees.

Other Grammar Schools, and Related Institutions

Grammar Schooling in General

Hans estimates (1951, 38, 119, quoted) that in eighteenth-century England around five hundred "endowed grammar schools" existed at one point or another, about a fifth of which predated 1601 and a like number of which

104

were formed after 1700.[24] In a more recent study Tompson (1971, 32-35)

raises the estimated total to seven hundred schools, and for a sampling of

nearly half that size attributes more than 50% of the foundings to years

prior to 1600 and barely more than 10% of them to 1700 or later. Dating

discrepancies might conceivably reflect (in part) different accountings

for schools representing a refoundation, or a less formal successor

relationship.

Other inconsistencies between the two accounts raise the possibility

that the authors have used different classification criteria. In particu-

lar, it is respectively stated that in the eighteenth century one county,

Norfolk, had only one grammar school (Hans 1951, 121), and that it instead

had seventeen such institutions, a dozen of them formed before 1700 (Tompson

1971, 32-35). In light, however, of Tompson's examination (1971, 33,

quoted, 34-35) of "foundation documents (deeds, wills, and Letters Patent)"

for 307 of the 334 cases sampled, intensive primary research that lends

strong credibility to his coverage, it appears that he has addressed the

same category of schooling as Hans.

The two writers are in any case agreed (Hans 1951, 38; and Tompson

1971, 34-36) that by the eighteenth century, or earlier, many grammar

schools had begun to offer an expanded curriculum, adding modern subjects

to the classics. The later study addresses directly the statutory restric-

tion (no doubt accommodating classical rhetoric) to Latin or Latin and

Greek, cited by Watson (1916, 131) as evidence of prevailing "decadence"

among such institutions during the period.

---

[24]The two dates cited are based on strict interpretation, as covering
the years 1601-1700, of Hans's reference (1951, 119) to the "seventeenth
century." Tompson (1971, 33-35) explicitly defines his spans of coverage
as pre-1600, 1600-99, and 1700-99.

Tompson makes two major points. First (1971, 33-35), there was vast change through time in the curricular provisions made for grammar schools. Founding statutes preceding 1600 almost invariably restricted studies to classical languages and literature; a clear, but much reduced, majority from the 1600s did likewise; and the original pattern was reversed thereafter, as 29 of the 33 foundations reviewed from the period 1700-99 specified subjects besides Latin and Greek.

Second, various means were found to modernize curricula in the face of statutory restriction to the classics. Curricula could be revised "by schoolmasters or trustees, or at a higher level, by visitors, by the Court of Chancery, or by Parliament." Although direct documentation of action by schoolmasters or trustees is "scanty," indirect evidence indicates that the two "local agents of change were most often used" (Tompson 1971, 35). In one case, the master at the "fashionable resort of Tonbridge," in (Webster's geographical dictionary 1977, s.v. "Tonbridge") southeast England, engaged a resident assistant and two outside teachers, including a weekly visitor from London, to add instruction in French, penmanship, and dancing. Trustees would most often enlarge curricula through their powers to appoint schoolmasters or assistants or, sometimes by express provision of founding statutes, to regulate school operations (Tompson 1971, 36, quoted, 37-38).

Local trustees wishing against schoolmaster objection to introduce writing, accounts, geography, geometry, and natural philocophy at Heath Grammar School appealed successfully to their distinguished visitation officer, the archbishop of York. Appeals for curricular change were not often made to courts of chancery, administering (Lunt 1957, 234-35) principles of equity, or to Parliament, empowered to enact private legislation.

106

Both approaches were costly, and the courts were rarely supportive (Tompson 1971, 38-39).

The most common supplements to school curricula were the three Rs, "Reading, writing and arithmetic," sometimes with explicit coverage of English grammar. Other fields listed in Tompson's (1971, 36) tabulation of 146 curricular additions from the eighteenth century include mathematics, French, geography, history, and, in two instances, bookkeeping.

In his D.n.b. survey, Hans (1951, 20) identified some 220 grammar schools besides the "Great Nine" as contributors to the education of listed eighteenth-century notables, about 50 of which were preparatory for larger schools. In cumulatively enrolling nearly 600 of the 3,500 persons in the survey, they stood slightly behind the four schools Eton, Westminster, Winchester, and Merchant Taylors'. Even so, Christ's Hospital in London and town grammar schools at Manchester and Exeter actually produced more "selected men" than either Rugby or Shrewsbury.

Exeter, an ancient city of southwest England (J. Blair 1983, 58; and Webster's geographical dictionary 1977, s.v. "Exeter," def. 6), was one of the nation's "[m]ajor provincial cent[er]s" (Langford 1984, [375]). When the local bishop founded Exeter College at Oxford in 1314, the prominent eighteenth-century grammar school (or at least a direct forerunner) was already in existence. Soon afterwards the cathedral in cooperation with a hospital that boarded the boys began to supply a few select pupils (Leach 1915, 193-94). Also predating the Reformation, Manchester Grammar School is discussed in chapter 9 in relation to its outstanding alumnus Henry Clarke. Hans (1951, 38) cites Manchester and Newcastle as representative "commercial communities" whose schools "took the lead" in adding modern fields of study.

Discussed above as a notable pre-Restoration school, Christ's Hospital lost half its (former monastery) buildings to London's "Great Fire" of 1666, a year after an eighth of the 260 pupils had fallen to the "Great Plague" of the day. Rebuilt with architectural assistance from Christopher Wren, the institution founded by Edward VI was rechartered by Charles II in 1673. With the patronage of famous diarist (Columbia-Viking desk encyclopedia 2d, s.v. "Pepys ['peeps'], Samuel") Samuel Pepys, the Royal Mathematical School was founded there the same year (McConnell 1985, 86), teaching all areas of math and navigation. A Dissenter recommended by Newton conducted a second mathematical school at Christ's Hospital for nine years in the early 1700s (Hans 1951, 38).

The vigor of the continuing mathematics school was evident throughout the eighteenth century as ten shipmaster assistants were provided yearly for the Royal Navy (Hans 1951, 38-39). Its master in the years 1755-57 was James Dodson, a mathematician, insurance pioneer (founding the Equitable Assurance Society), and cost accounting authority (Hans 1951, 214; Murray 1930, 19; Wells 1978, 45-46; and Yamey 1963, 171n). Many mathematicians and naval officers were educated at Christ's Hospital as its example spread to other grammar schools (Hans 1951, 39).

After 350 years in London, Christ's Hospital moved in 1902 to the countryside, near Horsham in Sussex, a southern county on the English Channel. As associated girls' school was by then thriving in Hertford, twenty-two miles north of London, and would finally be incorporated within the larger school at Horsham in 1985. "[T]he needy" continue at newly coeducational Christ's Hospital to "form the main body" of students (McConnell 1985, 85, quoted, 87, 93; and Webster's geographical dictionary 1977, s.v. "Hertford," entry 2, "Sussex," def. 6).

Endowed grammar schools were joined in the eighteenth century by many other schools offering classical instruction.

Other Classical Schools

There were hundreds of less formalized "private classical schools," identified more fully with their masters (Hans 1951, 119). The distinction was not precise, since "[m]any" grammar schools (Hans 1951, 119)

> were as small as the majority of private schools, had the same inter-mittent existence and [like the other class] depended on the local clergy as their masters.

Also, private classical schools not only were usually kept by their founders for same years, but occasionally endured much longer. One founded at Cheam, fourteen miles from London, completed its third century in 1947. Perhaps uncommonly among such schools, Cheam under the masterships of the Rev. William Gilpin, Sr. and his namesake son offered over the latter half of the eighteenth century an expanded curriculum that included French, writing, arithmetic, dancing, drawing, religion (as a separate course), and perhaps botany (Hans 1951, 117, 119, 121, 123-125).

The private schools were generally small boarding houses in which the schoolmaster himself housed the resident pupils. Already popular in the seventeenth century, this approach attracted the sons of "[m]any aristo-cratic families, country squires and members of the clergy," while farmers and craftsmen often found a local institution of this kind cheaper and more accessible than the nearest grammar school. Socially, there was a reaction against "the customs of bullying and the atmosphere of corruption" found at many endowed schools. Academically, the alternative classical schools generally did not favor rote memorization of Latin and Greek grammar, felt to impede cultural understanding even if it were otherwise successful (Hans 1951, 117).

The private classical schools were kept mainly by Anglican priests intending to prepare students for Cambridge and Oxford, where they had themselves been trained. A study of 260 schoolmasters revealed that 240 of them were Church of England clerics. The same number were university men, nearly all of them from the two English institutions, generally representing middle or lower social classes within that context. Because there was "a constant interchange" with the endowed Latin schools, it is reasonable to infer a similar profile for the masters of eighteenth-century grammar schools (Hans 1951, 117, 119, quoted, 120, also, 121-35, 221-42).

The overwhelming preponderance of priestly schoolmasters obscures an important internal division. Many of the men were fundamentally professional teachers who had taken holy orders as a matter of scholarly tradition. Others were "resident rectors and vicars, who started a boarding-school sometimes to educate their own sons and sometimes to add to their very limited incomes." The schools of the former group were ordinarily larger and longer-lived. Even this distinction was not hard and fast, as some individuals moved from one class to the other in the course of their careers (Hans 1951, 118).

A further kind of "private" schooling is an especially appropriate topic in concluding this educational survey, as it represents the prevailing academic context of the essays that follow.

Private Academies

In his 1951 study of eighteenth-century English schooling, Hans (63-116) through fifty-four pages comprising three chapters devotes more attention to "private academies" than to any other category. Although they were not always sharply divided from private classical schools or (more likely to have modernized curricula) grammar schools, these institutions in general stressed mathematics and technical or vocational subjects; were called "Academies"; and were headed by laymen without university degrees (Hans 1951, 63). Decidedly secular in nature, they were pioneers in many cases in introducing scientific studies (Hans 1951, 54), and, expanding on the tradition of early arithmetic and writing schools (Watson 1916, 131), were the principal centers of business instruction.

Private academies were an immensely varied species, as a group offering "all branches of contemporary knowledge and art" (Hans 1951, 64). Hans (1951, 65) distinguishes among five "streams of schooling" that were provided for career (or academic) preparation of as many kinds. They included the grammar school for university matriculation; the naval school for the navy or mercantile marine; the military school for the army; the commercial school for business or legal clerkship; and the technical school for serveying, guaging, architecture, shipbuilding, and similar vocations. Fields that tended to be common to the five divisions, besides English, arithmetic, and (as available) sporting activity, included geography, geometry, French, and drawing. To the more limited extent that it was taught, history also cut across the several programs of study (Hans 1951, 65-[67]).

Since they might offer any selection of "streams of schooling" from one alone to all five, private academies were often in whole or part supplemental or complementary to schools of other kinds. Hans's tabulation (1951, [67]) of programs at twenty-eight academies, shown as exhibit 1, indicates the number of streams provided, and subjects offered from a selection of fields grouped under four headings. One of the two schools listed that at one time or another offered all five programs was the Little Tower-Street Academy founded in London by Thomas Watts, author of the first

111

EXHIBIT 1

HANS'S SURVEY OF CURRICULA AT TWENTY-EIGHT PRIVATE ACADEMIES

TABLE VI. Subjects taught in Private Academies

Academies	Streams	English and Writing	Latin	Greek	French	Other Languages	History	Geography	Arithmetic	Mathematics	Astronomy	Natural Philosophy	Navigation	Military Subjects	Merchants' Accounts, etc.	Surveying, Gauging, etc.	Dancing	Drawing	Music	Fencing and Sports	Logics, Philosophy, Morals
Hackney	3	+	+	+	+	+	?	?	+	+	?	+	+	+	+	+	+	+	+	+	+
Soho	4	+	+	+	+	+	?	+	+	+	+	+	+	+	+	+	+	+	+	
Tower Street	5	+	+	+	+		?	+	+	+	+	+	+		+	+	+	+	+	+	
Naval, Chelsea	1	+	+		+		+	+	+	+	+	+	+	+		+	+	+		+	+
Military, Little Chelsea	-	+			+		+	+	+			+		+			+			+	
Bridgewater Square	2	+	+		+		+	+	+	+				+	+			+			
Islington	5	+	+		+		+	+	+	+		+			+			+			
Kensington	2	+	+		+			+	+	+				+	+			+			
Ewell	3	+	+	+	+	+	+		+	+		+	+		+	+	+	+	+	+	+
York	4	+	+	+	+	+			+	+	+				+		+	+	+		+
Lancashire	4	+	+	+	+	+			+	+	+				+		+				+
Bristol	4	+	+		+				+	+					+		+	+	+		+
Bath	3	+			+				+	+		+	+	+		+					
Lambeth	2	+	+						+	+		+	+	+		+					
Mathematical, Chelsea	3	+						+	+	+	+	+	+	+	+	+		+			
Wapping (Kelly)	4	+						+	+	+	+	+	+		+			+			
Wapping (Haselden)	3	+						+	+	+	+	+	+		+			+			
Southwark	1	+						+	+	+	+	+	+	+	+	+		+			
Naval, Gosport	-	+							+	+	+	+	+		+	+					
Mathematical, Newcastle	4	+			+	+			+	+	+	+		+	+	+	+	+	+	+	
Manchester	2	+							+	+	+		+	+	+		+	+			
Chesthunt	2	+							+	+	+	+	+		+		+	+			
Sloane Street	3	+	+	+	+		+	+	+	+	+		+		+	+	+	+		+	
Quesnay's (London)	1	+	+	+	+				+	+	+			+	+						
Deptford	-	+	+	+	+		+		+	+											
Auten Corner	2	+							+	+	+					+	+	+	+	+	
Plymouth	1	+	+		+				+	+	+			+			+	+		+	
Stroud	2	+							+	+	+	+	+	+		+	+	+		+	

Only those subjects are marked by + which are definitely mentioned in advertisements.

Reprinted, with the consent of the publisher, from Hans 1951, 67.

112

essay in this collection.. Among the five academies providing four streams

of career preparation was the Soho Academy organized by Martin Clare, the

subject of chapter 3. The majority of the schools offered three courses

of study. Even the purely naval and military schools respectively at

Chelsea and Little Chelsea were not narrowly vocational in nature. Also,

as illustrated in several of the essays, the commercial and technical pro-

grams "in larger Academies included [a variety of] general subjects" (Hans

1951, 65, 66, quoted).

Both Clare and William Milns, covered in chapter 10 regarding his

American career, are specifically cited (Hans 1951, 66) among advocates of

"liberal" education for business and technical men. The quarrel of academy

people with the grammar schools was by and large not with the continued

teaching of classical languages, but with the rigidity of approach by which,

for example, all pupils were forced to pass through the same laborious

sequence of "'forms'" or instructional units.

Most academies were boarding schools, although day students, including

adults, were welcome. It appears that the headmaster often boarded a few

resident pupils while the others were scattered among several houses (Hans

1951, 68). The masters were "a heterogeneous crowd" who as a group were

"able and efficient teachers who must be considered as pioneers of modern

education" (Hans 1951, 68):

> A few were University graduates and even ordained priests . . .. Some
> were well-known scientists and Fellows of the Royal Society . . .. The
> great majority were 'Teachers of Mathematics' with no University
> training, mostly self-made men who acquired their knowledge and exper-
> ience by attending courses in privatate Academies or [through] private
> reading, and often started their careers by giving private lessons.

These statements are supported by an analysis made (Hans 1951, 68) of

144 headmasters or assistants. Fully two thirds of them were "Teachers of

Mathematics," an official professional designation used by free-lance teachers whose classes would sometimes develop into full-scale academies. Such a progression was evidently less common for "Writing Masters and Accountants," concentrated in London, who taught penmanship, arithmetic, and mercantile accounting, sometimes combining the three fields in their student exercise material (Hans 1951, 185, quoted, 186). In this usage an accountant was a teacher of arithmetic "and the art of keeping accounts" (Murray 1930, 17). As covered in chapter 4, William Webster (1722 and 1735, frontispiece) was a conventional writing master and accountant.

The business or mercantile orientation of many private academies, with double-entry accounts a staple of coverage, invites particular reference to professional accounting practice of the day. A person skilled in accounts would be "found on the staff of most large mercantile concerns and public offices." The South Sea (trading) Company and the York Buildings Company, for example, each had its own accountant, as did, in Scotland, the city of Edinburgh (Murray 1930, 20, quoted, 21).

The South Sea "Bubble" (Langford 1984, 363-65) provided ample occasion for the auditing of accounts, a task undertaken in 1720-21 for two interested firms by London teacher Charles Snell (Murray 1930, 64-65). From at least the beginning of the seventeenth century there had been demand for expert help in stating, adjusting, or settling complex or disputed accounts. Such an assignment was made to order for early bookkeeping teacher/authors such as Richard Dafforne; John Collins, whose practice included serving the courts as a consultant and expert witness; and Thomas Browne, who advertised his services in 1670 for '"the Auditing, Stating or Drawing up [of] any Reports of Accompts"'. James Dodson of Christ's Hospital, among others, continued this tradition in the eighteenth century (Murray 1930, 59-66,

66n, quoting 64). Skilled accountants were also sometimes engaged in the settlement of estates and bankruptcies, including service as creditor trustees (Murray 1930, 66-95, principally in reference to Scotland).

All but one of the essays presented in chapters 2-10 is concerned with private academies, actual or projected, in Hans's terms, three of them within a Scottish (two) or American environment. The exception is itself only partial, as Webster agrees with the other writers that schooling for a business career should be broadly based. The same point is underscored by Joseph Priestley in the appended contribution from the "dissenting" academy environment.

In concluding his study of eighteenth-century education, Hans notes (1951, 210, 212) that the private academies would gradually disappear before 1850, along with the union of classical and scientific subjects achieved in many schools of the 1700s. Industrialization had created a sharp social cleavage between the "new . . . middle class" of factory owners and the workers they employed (Hans 1951, 211). It was reflected educationally in a "differentiation of social prestige" between theology and the classics, studied as "a sign of social privilege," and science, "narrowed down to technical skill" deemed unworthy of pursuit "by cultured families" (Hans 1951, 212). More generally, in the movement from a mercantile economy to an industrial one the educational "achievements and pioneering ideas of the eighteenth century were forgotten" (Hans 1951, 210), evidently including the principal advances in academic preparation for business careers that are recorded or reflected in the essays that follow.

CHAPTER 2

PIONEER EDUCATION WRITER THOMAS WATTS

Thomas Watts of London may well in 1716 have been the first English author of a booklet devoted specifically to commercial education (Cole 1946, 1). Watts (1716a, 30, b, 23) quotes a passage from John Locke's influential treatise (1705, sec. 21a) on proper tutorial instruction for the young gentleman, extolling the utility of "Merchants' Accompts" (as shown by Locke (Axtell 1968, 337, s.v. "319," "320")) to the property holder. Twenty years before Locke's first edition appeared (Axtell 1968, 98), activist Catholic printer and bookseller (Martin 1854, xv) Obadiah Walker had in 1673 (252-64) included in a precursor of that work (Axtell 1968, 61, 65, 67) thirteen pages on attitudes, habits, and practices to be cultivated by businessmen.

A year before his essay originated (Hans 1951, 82), Watts (1716a, [44], b, 28) had opened a school on Abchurch-Lane in London to qualify young men for "Trades, Merchandize, the Public Offices, Clerkships, Stewardships, or any other Parts of Business." The advertisement went on to emphasize instruction in double-entry bookkeeping and "the several Parts of the Mathematicks."

Watts soon took on Cambridge graduate Benjamin Worster as a partner (Hans 1951, 82). By 1722 their '"Academy"' at Little Tower-Street drew boarding students from wealthy families as well as day pupils of more humble origns (Cole 1946, 7, quoted; and Hans 1951, 85-86). With a usual entry age of 13 or 14, or older, the school was designed for graduates of grammar schools (broadly defined), particularly youth wanting immediate preparation for merchant business at established quarters or at sea, clerkships in merchant or legal offices, skilled trades, or other business employment. Also welcomed were university men on vacation wishing to study accounts and mathematics or take work in '"Experimental Philosophy"' (Cole 1946, 9), or physical science, a then controversial field in which Watts and Worster were conducting adult education lectures off campus (Hans 1951, 141-42).

Teaching subjects at the academy around 1722 included writing and arithmetic, merchants accounts, geography, navigation, algebra and geometry, mensuration, and surveying, costing from two to six guineas (valued at 21 shillings (Junge 1984, s.v. "Guinea")) each (Cole 1946, 9-10). Additionally, a resident master taught French (the original language of a mechanics text that Watts had translated); famous miniature artist Bernard Lens gave drawing lessons three days weekly, and dancing instruction was likewise available; and another person gave private lectures in Latin and Greek (Cole 1946, 7, 10; and Hans 1951, 82-83, 85). A year's room and board cost twenty-six pounds (at 20 shillings per unit) (Cole 1946, 9; and Random House dictionary 166, s.v. "shilling," def. 2).

Reprinted below, as edited by Arthur H. Cole, is the first of five editions of Watts's Essay (1716b) that appeared between 1716 and '22, the last one as a revised fourth edition (Cole 1946, 7). Ellipses indicate the deletion of five passages (Watts 1716b, 16-18), which concern the "virtues of giving attention to the variant characters of individual students" (Cole 1946, 8n). In the omitted material, representing slightly under 4 pages of an original text of 43 pages, Watts (1716a) elaborated on the teaching of comparatively slow (6-7) and fast (8-9) learners; discussed the effects on student attitudes of subtle teacher mannerisms (10-11); and explained the need for rigid discipline to ward off temptation (12-13) and underscored the hazards of taking vacation breaks during the course of study (14).

Changes made in later editions were "quite limited in number and diversity" (Cole 1946, 9). As illustrated by the curriculum cited above, coverage of "liberal arts" fields was somewhat expanded (Cole 1946, 10). Along with the original one (Watts 1716a), the final two editions, the earlier one of which was the same as the third edition, are available within a renowned microfilm series (Goldsmiths'-Kress Library of Economic Literature . . . 1976-87, s.v. "6095," "5515.3" ("Supplement" vol.)).

By 1727, a year after poet James Thomson had served as a resident tutor, at least five new instructors had joined the academy staff. They included the founder's son William Watts; internationally known mathematician James Stirling (Fellow of the Royal Society), having evidently been recommended by Isaac Newton, who had helped him with publications; noted penman John Bland, trained by Charles Snell, who wrote that the school's mix of instruction in writing, featuring business examples, and accounts turned out qualified bookkeepers; and William Vream, a talented craftsman of scientific instruments (Cole 1946, 6; and Hans 1951, 82-85).

Stirling had evidently replaced Bernard Worster in 1725, and the latter teacher was listed as deceased in a source of 1730, by which time Thomas Watts was no longer listed on the faculty at Little Tower-Street (Hans 1951, 82-84). Although Watts himself may have died by '30 (Hans 1951, 84-85), it is noteworthy that a London directory of ten years later listed one Thomas Watts '"Esq."', at the address of the Bank of England (Cole 1946, 8).

By 1740, at any rate, the academy was under the sole ownership of William Watts, who moved it to a new address a few years later. Around that time the school seems to have reverted to mainly vocational training, with emphasis on preparation for army, navy, and business. A 1750 proposal by William Foot of Bristol that he turn his boarding school into a preparatory

119

school for Watts's academy suggests that it retained a distinguished reputation (Hans 1951, 86-87).

The academy founded by Thomas Watts in 1715 survived into the nineteenth century (Hans 1951, 87). Cole (1946, 8) credits the founder with a strong emphasis on teaching arithmetic by reference to realistic business examples; and on "simplicity and directness" in penmanship and expression.[1]

---

[1]An earlier writer on vocational education was William Petty, cited in chapter 1 as a contributor in the 1650s to flourishing scientific activity at Oxford, where he had taken a medical degree. In (Charlton 1965, 297n) 1648, at age twenty-five, Petty had issued a "'Tractate on Education'" (D.n.b. 1917, s.v. "Petty, Sir William," 999) that proposed that a "College of Tradesmen" be created to train men in numerous skilled trades, "the mechanical arts and manufactures." Besides much enhancing (Charlton 1965, 297) production in the fields taught, such an institution would according to the author draw away from divinity, law, medicine, and teaching many individuals not suited to those professions (Butts 1973, 216, 217, quoted).

Petty's treatise was presented as a letter to Samuel Hartlib (Charlton 1965, 297n), a noted writer on education and farming, in particular, to whom his friend John Milton had earlier (1644) addressed his own educational tract (D.n.b. 1917, s.v. "Hartlib, Samuel"). Petty built upon Hartlib's proposal that residential '"literary workhouses"' be set up in London to train poor children in domestic arts and teach them to read and write, the boys as a base for apprenticeship or, '"if quickwitted"', pursuit of careers as '"scholars or accountants"' (Butts 1973, 216).

AN ESSAY ON THE PROPER METHOD FOR FORMING THE MAN OF BUSINESS
1716

WITH AN INTRODUCTION BY
ARTHUR H. COLE
Professor of Business Economics and Librarian
Harvard University Graduate School of Business Administration

BAKER LIBRARY

HARVARD UNIVERSITY GRADUATE SCHOOL OF
BUSINESS ADMINISTRATION

SOLDIERS FIELD, BOSTON, MASSACHUSETTS

Publication Number 4 of
The Kress Library of Business and Economics

PRINTED AT THE
HARVARD UNIVERSITY PRINTING OFFICE
CAMBRIDGE, MASSACHUSETTS, U.S.A.

A N
E S S A Y
ON THE
Proper Method
For FORMING the
Man of *Business*:

IN A
LETTER, *&c.*

By THOMAS WATTS, of the ACCOUNTANT's OFFICE
for Qualifying Young Gentlemen for *Business*,
in *Abchurch-Lane*.

L O N D O N:
Printed for *George Strahan* over-against the *Royal-Exchange, William Taylor* in
Pater-Noster-Row, Henry Clements in *S. Paul's Church-yard, Edward Nutt* at
the *Middle-Temple Gate*, and *John Morphew* near *Stationers-Hall.* 1716.

Price. 6 *d.*

S I R,

'TIS but Just, that he who undertakes so difficult and important a Concern as any Part of Education is, ought to give some Satisfaction, how capable he is of the Performance; especially if he proposes to do it in a Method out of the common Way, and in which others have not trod. In Consequence of this Reflection, I here present you with those *Sentiments* on the *Subject* of *Forming* the *Man* of *Business* and *Employment*, which the other Day you were pleas'd to be so Indulgent to, as to wish 'em committed to Paper. There is no Inclination, I assure you, Sir, wanting in me to serve the Publick; and I must confess, the Success I have had with the hopeful Young *Gentlemen* you have done me the Honour to place under my Care, is an Encouragement to me to pursue its Advantage in what I can: But still, if it should receive any Benefit from my Service, 'twill be oblig'd to the Deference due to a Judgment founded upon so large an Experience of Men and Business, and so accomplish'd as Yours, Sir; and to which, if I did not submit, I should forfeit my Own.

Sir, I need not observe, that *Education* in general is of such vast Importance, and of such singular Use in the *Scene* of *Life*, that it visibly carries its own Recommendation along with it: *For*, on it in great Measure depends *all* that we hope to be, every Perfection that a generous and well-dispos'd Mind would gladly arrive at. 'Tis *this* that stamps the Distinction of Mankind, and renders one Man preferable to another; is almost the very Capacity of doing well, and remarkably adorns every Point of Life. This is what no body will dispute; and therefore 'twould be impertinent to insist on it. The Misfortune is, that, like a stately Mistress, 'tis difficult of Access; 'twill not condescend to shew itself at the first Visit, but will be sought for as Silver, and search'd for as for hid Treasure, or 'twill not be seen, much less won. Hence it comes, that some have not Resolution enough to make Court to it; and many that have, are discouraged, and forc'd to give over the Pursuit, and sit down under that unconceivable Loss that is always inseparable from the Want of it. Wherefore, an

Attempt to make the Way to it more easy, may hope to be receiv'd with Indulgence, whatever the Success may prove. And since the same Difficulty, in Proportion, that attends the Pursuit of *Education* in general, affects the particular Branch I am concern'd for, if I can assist its Growth, and make it thrive and flourish with the greater Vigour, as 'twill yield me no small Pleasure, so will it justify the Undertaking to all that understand their own Interest, and desire, what's but natural for them to do, the Promotion of it.

The superiour Advantage of this Part of *Education* will easily be confessed by all who shall but turn their Eyes upon this great and magnificent CITY, and consider that immense Wealth and extensive Commerce which makes this Nation known to, and honour'd in the most distant Places of the habitable World. *Hence,* as from the Heart to the Body, flow such continual Streams, that diffuse Life and Spirit, Trade and Riches, through the whole; *here* the best Returns are made of a Ripen'd Capacity, and an improvable Fortune; *here* your Men of *Years* treasure up abundance, and your young Men are best qualify'd to tread in their Industrious and Successful Steps: The Man of *Commerce* is the Man of *Business;* 'tis his Element, and to manage it well and successfully, his Care and Labour.

But to set out well, is to have his Business half done; and 'tis the Design of what I *here* offer, to prevent his Miscarrying; which in great Measure depends on his *first* Appearance in the World, as that does upon the Qualifications he is Master of when he makes it. But I trust he'll be secure in this Point, if manag'd in the Method I advance. But,

Sir, I must premise, and 'twill be own'd, that tho' He that undertakes to teach an ART must be Master of it, yet 'tis not every one that is Master of an Art, that is equally qualify'd to teach it; since many times it is much more difficult to communicate an Art to another, than it is to attain it ourselves: And the Reason is visible; because the *Capacities* and *Tempers* he has to do with, may be as various as the Number of his Pupils; so that his first Care must be to make a right Judgment of their several *Capacities and Tempers*, which he must always have in his Eye, when he sets them Rules, and deals out Instruction to them. 'Tis in vain, as 'tis unmerciful, to lash on the Horse that has no Heels; but the Master's Skill, and the Scholar's Industry, in time will improve and brighten the less promising and more cloudy Parts; and the narrow Genius will widen and enlarge under the Art of infusing Instruction into it leisurely and by degrees. . . .

Secondly, On the other hand, tho', where Nature has been more generous of her Gifts, and the Scholar's more ready Apprehension and Felicity of Parts save the Instructor much Time and Labour; Yet *there* the Exercise of his Skill and Judgment is rarely less, but generally more indispensably required. For, as in the *former* Instance, he can't have too much Patience and Diligence, so in *this* he can hardly be enough on the Guard and Watch; but must still have his Eye on his CHARGE, and narrowly observe his Motions; which if he does not find very various and inconstant, 'tis more than he ought to expect; both Reason and Experience forbid it. And therefore, tho' he be at less Trouble to point out to him the Path he is to tread in, and the End it leads him to; yet to prevent his breaking out of it, and to confine him to it, often proves a sufficient Trial of his Skill. . . .

But farther, as the different *Capacities* of Youth require a different Management for the Improvement of their Understandings; so a distinct and proper Regard must be had to their different natural Tempers and Dispositions, which commonly are the more or less gentle and tractable, as their Parts are the less or more brisk and *Prominent*. A mild *Temper* generally attends upon the less lively Parts, and succeeds best under the Influence of Kindness and Tenderness. . . .

And, tho' the *Confidence* that is generally observ'd to attend on the more forward and sprightly Parts may in order to reduce it to a modest and becoming Assurance, demand a Check; yet I must confess, I can't fall in with the Notion of the Necessity of *Severity* even in this Case. A *generous* Spirit will regard Reason, and conclude it more Fitting his Nature, to be lead like a *Man*, than to be drove like a *Brute*. An over *severe* Usage has, I am satisfy'd, been the Ruine of Abundance of Youth, which an *engaging* Temper, and a discreet Conduct might have made eminently useful in their Generations. By saying so, I do not design to be understood to recommend a senseless Indulgence of *Youth* in misemploying their Time or Thoughts; *all* I mean is, that a *great* and active Spirit should only be regulated, and kept within just Bounds, but not broken, or subdu'd to an *Indolence*, or *Stupidity*; which is the fatal Effect generally of too *rigid a Discipline*. . . .

What I have hitherto offer'd in a Manner *indifferently* affects the *Education* of the greener as well as of the riper Years. But *those* that come more *immediately* under my *Management*, are generally of *Stature* fit for *Business*, and in an *Age* when the Love of Idleness is too often strong and predominant, and the Tide of Passion runs high, and carries all before it; and drove on by the Vanity of *unthinking Youth*, impatiently brooks every necessary Restraint. But this is a *Crisis* of Life that often determines the whole *Course*; and therefore cannot be too narrowly observ'd, or too carefully provided for: *Business* and full Employment is the only Barrier to keep out the Enemy, and secure the Man: Vacant Hours move on heavily, and drag Rust and Filth along with 'em: A Breaking-up, or three or four Weeks *Vacation* in *this* time of Life, has often destroy'd the *Labour of Years*; . . .

Children may play by the *Almanack*, but he that is taking on him the Countenance of a *Man*, and intends for *Business*, should rather let the *Exchange* be his Oracle for *Vacations*; especially when he considers that Time insensibly glides on to the farthest Distances; that *He* and his *Friends* are impatient till he lives for *himself*; and is settled to Satisfaction: And then what vast Hindrances and Interruptions must idle Days, Weeks and Months, needs be to him that perhaps has not above three or four Months to employ in Qualifying himself for *one* great *Business* of his *Life.*

'Twas these last Reflections mov'd me to dissent from the *Common Practice* in *this* Respect, among many others, by breaking through the ancient *Custom* of being *Idle* on all *Holy Days*, and in one Regard or other losing one Fourth of the Year in Vacations; which however pleasing to the over Indulgent Mother, and Darling Child, must needs be of the most untoward Consequence, as I have observ'd, in *our* Case. And I am the more confirm'd in *this* and every other *Method* I have taken to promote the speedy and perfect accomplishing of *those* plac'd under my *Inspection*, in that, Sir, they entirely fall in with your *Sentiments*, and have likewise had the Approbation of most of those Gentlemen I have had the Honour for some Years to be employ'd by. (And now, Sir, give me Leave, as short as possible, *particularly* to touch on those *Qualifications* necessary to *Form* the *Man* of *Business*. And,

First, Whoever would be a *Man* of *Business*, must be a Man of *Correspondence*; and Correspondence can never be so commodiously, or at all to the Purpose maintain'd, as by the Use of the Pen: So that WRITING is the *First* Step, and *Essential* in furnishing out the *Man* of *Business*. And this *Qualification* is more excellent as 'tis more useful in *Business*, and beautiful to the Eye, and may not improperly be consider'd in two Respects, as it proceeds from the *Eye* and the *Hand*; from the one, we have *Size* and *Proportion*, from the other *Boldness* and *Freedom*. For as the Exactness of the *Eye* fixes the *Heights* and *Distances*; so the *Motion* of the *Joints*, and *Position* of the *Hand*, determine the *Black* and *Fine*

Strokes, and give the same *Inclination* and *Likeness* in the *Standing* and *Turn* of the LETTERS. But, in order to write *well*, there must be just Rules given, and much Practice to put 'em in Execution. Plain, Strong, and Neat *Writing*, as it best answers the Design for Use and Beauty; so it has most obtain'd among Men of *Business*; with whom all *affected* Flourishes, and quaint Devices of Birds and Bull-Beggars, are as much avoided, as Capering and Cutting in ordinary Walking. A full free open *Letter* struck at once, as it discovers more of Nature, so it gives a Masterly Beauty to the Writing; to which may be added such Ornamental *Turns* of the *Pen*, as seem rather design'd to fill up Vacancies on the Paper, than studiously compos'd to adorn the Piece. In Flourishing, the *Fancy* would be so *Luxuriant*, was it not corrected by the *Judgment*, as almost to destroy the *End* of *Writing*; as *Airs* in *Musick*, when too often repeated, or too long or too variously perform'd, disorder the Harmony of a just Composure. But those who are Excellent this Way, and display Art and Nature by the gentle Turns of a well-guided Pen, do certainly deserve their Commendations for their *Curiosity* and *Ingenuity*; if not for performing any thing much tending to the *Use* and *Benefit* of *Mankind*. But, as above, if Usefulness and Beauty are the Excellencies of WRITING; that which will with the greatest Facility contribute to these, is the *best* Method of *Teaching*. Supposing, therefore, the Make and Proportion of the Letters and Joinings to be once well fixed and understood, single Line Copies will cease to be of Service: For they are apt to create a *Stiffness* in the *Operation*, and a Formality more like painted than native Beauty; whereas, if the Learner is us'd to Copy the common Forms of *Business*, Letters, Long Accounts, and Estimates, &c. his Hand will grow confirm'd in an Aptitude and Readiness which will insensibly arrive at Perfection and Dispatch; and give in *Writing*, what we admire in *Fine* Gentlemen, an *Easiness* of *Gesture*, and *disengag'd* Air, not to be attained by *Art*, but insensibly caught from frequently conversing with the Polite and Well-bred.

Secondly, The mutual Intercourse and Dependence of Mankind upon each other, from whence arises a *Variety* of Affairs for Computation, makes ARITHMETICK the next necessary *Qualification* for the *Man* of *Business*: And *this* is more valuable, as 'tis the more exact, easy, and short. If the Rules and Principles are once well fix'd and understood, frequent *Application* will make the *Practice* easy, and wonderfully reduce the *Operations*: The Art lies in giving as *few* Rules as possible, and clearly explaining them. Confounding Principles together, and Diversifying them into several Rules, when they are built on the same Reason, is what has made ARITHMETICK seem so Difficult; and the Learning all by *Rote* has spoil'd many an Accountant. In Teaching ARITHMETICK, I shall have a special Regard, Sir, to your Advice, that the Questions the Learner is exercis'd in, be such as generally occurr in *real* Business; which will not only be what he may most commonly meet with, but as they are about such Things as are generally within his Hearing and Notice; so he will the more readily conceive the Reason of his *Operations*, and take the greater Delight in Working them: For there is Nothing sooner perfects a Man in any Study, than the *Secret* of engaging him to find Something pleasant and delightful in it; then the Labour goes down easily, and a little Confusion or Perplexity only quickens, and gives a fresh Relish to the Satisfaction.

Thirdly, MERCHANTS ACCOUNTS is the third *Qualification*. The Un-skill'd often confound this and Arithmetick together; insomuch that 'tis sometimes taken for *Arithmetick*; and so, he that is a good *Arithmetician* is erroneously judg'd a good *Book-Keeper*: But *Book-Keeping* is a distinct Art; and is the Business of *Reason* to determine the just and proper *Debitors* and *Creditors*; of *Art* to methodize our Results, and of *Arith-metick*, only to answer the several Questions of Computation arising. The *Italian* Method of Book-Keeping by *Double Entry*, as now practis'd by you *Gentlemen* of Commerce, may truly be allow'd to comprehend all Excellencies in Accounting: For as the Judicious Author of the GENTLE-MAN ACCOUNTANT observes, "All other Methods, which particular Persons have occasionally instituted for their own private Concerns, are found in this; and all those Methods, whatsoever they are, were, or can be invented, for the Use of any Accounts, are Parts of, and as it were taken out of the *Debitor* and *Creditor*; and so much as they want of that, however in private Concerns serviceable enough, just so much they want of desirable Perfection. For the *Debitor* and *Creditor* is pure and perfect right Reason, and contains the whole Material Truth and Justice of all the Dealing, and nothing else; and this not only between the Accounter and his Traffickers, but also between all the several Traffickers one with another; so far as they have intermix'd in the Subject Matter of the Accounts: And not only so, but also of the Incidents, Circumstances, and Consequences of the *Traffick*, such as Estimates, Losses, or Advantages thereby. And all this in a perpetual State; so as every Question that can be propos'd, concerning any Dealing, is answer'd almost as readily as demanded: And no Person can be injur'd, who takes his Account upon the Stating of the Books, so far as it runs; and in all Times, even in After-Ages, the Transactions will be understood as well as if the same had been inquisited at the very Instant of the Writing." And in another Place the *same* excellent *Author* says, "That 'tis a Method so Comprehensive and Perfect, as makes it worthy to be put among the Sciences, and to be understood by all *Virtuosi*, whether they ever intend to make use of it or no, but even for pure Speculation, Curiosity, or rather Admiration; as happens, when with some Pains we have attain'd the Knowledge of some Art or Skill, tho' less complex than this; which thro' the Invention of Past Ages, Universal Practice, and in Matters of Interest (the fiercest Engagement of Humane Wit and Stratagem) is reduc'd, as this is, to the strictest Compendium, and (respecting the Intention, or Use of it) to a consummate Perfection, and in Rule and Method is so contracted and circumscrib'd, that, without a Fault, nothing can be rescinded from, or added to it." From all which 'tis abundantly evident, how ridiculous that common Error is, which many are apt to fall into, that BOOK-KEEPING is so different among Merchants and Men of Business, that hardly two make use of the same Method; and consequently, that he who keeps Books well in one *Compting-House*, is not Qualify'd to do the like in another: But this false Objection can proceed only from not understanding the Art. A Just and Proper *Debitor* and *Creditor* is founded on Reason and Demonstration; and that which is so in itself, must be so to every one that understands it, and therefore the Method must be in Effect the same; there being only *Double* Entry and *Single* Entry, that is indeed Method and no Method. By the first we have such a Relation and mutual Dependence of Accounts, and a perpetual Balance of all, that Nothing can be afterwards plac'd in the Books with dishonest or unfair Design; nor any Error made in the Progress left uncorrected. By the Latter, the Way lies open to Fraud and Deceit, Confusion certainly attends it; and there's no Possibility of ascertaining Truth and Exactness: To all which every Method is liable, except the *Debitor* and *Creditor* by *Double* Entry. So that this Dispute can be only between those that do, and those that do not understand Book-Keeping. And 'tis certainly true, that he who comes from a *Compting-House* of Confusion, or at best only recording Facts and Things *Simply*, as they occurr (as in common Shop-Books, *&c.* where they so speciously mimick the true *Debitor* and *Creditor*, that the Ignorant really think it so; whereas Nothing of that Art, Truth, and Justice, is found in it) can never be qualify'd to succeed him who has digested his Affairs into a most exact Order, and concise Method, according to Reason and Art. 'Tis true indeed, as Men are of different Complections and Constitutions, and have different Ideas of Things, so every Man may have some Peculiarity in his Method; but then this Difference cannot be in Essentials, not in the general Reason and Manner of Book-Keeping, but only in Particulars indifferently, that are as soon known as seen. But I have Reason, Sir, to ask Pardon, for so long insisting on the Excellency and Usefulness of that, which you practise with so much Exactness and Delight, and so happily recommend: But 'tis, as you call it, my *Darling Science*; as such, I can't help dwelling on the Subject, and being zealous in Propagating of it: To do which successfully, that is, to complete a Book-Keeper, there's much more requir'd than is generally taught. 'Tis not *Copying* a Sett of Books, or even being able to make a proper *Debitor* and *Creditor*, is all that's necessary: For almost in every Case, besides the *Debitor* and *Creditor*, there are many Incidents, and seemingly small Circumstances, that will often puzzle a tolerable Theoretick Accountant; and as 'tis allow'd in all Affairs, that generally the Circumstances of an Action should be as much consider'd as the Action itself: Therefore the *Learner* should not only be instructed how to Enter, Post, and Close an Account; but also in the previous and consequent Incidents, as Terms of Agreement, and general Customs observ'd among Merchants and Men of Business, with the Forms of common Use in the Variety of Affairs, as Invoyces, Bills of several Sorts, Bonds, &c. as also the Duties of Merchandize, and shortest Ways of computing them, and the Nature of Remittances as to Bills of Exchange, or the Course, Rise, Fall, &c. of the Exchange, and all other intervening Circumstances that can be imagin'd to happen; and this not only as to the bare Form and Manner; but the Learner should trace every of these as incident in each particular *imaginary* Case, as if he was transacting *real* Affairs. And, Sir, I have referr'd to this Place (where the Use will appear most evident) the humble Thanks I owe for those Books of *real Business* you were pleas'd to send me the other Day, so justly kept, and consisting of such Variety of Transactions: I know not any thing will more promote my Design for the Advancement of this Art; and therefore have made some Progress in digesting a proper *Waste-Book* of Cases for the Uses above, and shall find no small Improvement from Stating them as my Copy directs; only, as you have advis'd me, I shall continually add such Cases to them as may be drawn from any new Manner, or Place of Trading I shall be inform'd of, or can possibly get light into. And I'm persuaded, if this Method was follow'd, and each *Professor* qualify'd to perform it, we should not find so many Youths on their first Entrance on Business so much Strangers to it; but the Instructing *Compting-House* might produce as accomplish'd Clerks as the Merchants or Publick Offices, provided the same Application was made use of.

But that which is call'd *Merchants Accounts* is not only absolutely necessary for every Merchant or Trader, but is what no Man of Business should be Ignorant of, and is the best Method for Men of all Professions and Estates to keep their own Accounts in; with this Difference, that as the Incidents alter with the Variety of Affairs, so they should be accordingly apply'd and consider'd; and the Knowledge of this Art (tho' not made use of in every ones private Concerns) yet creates an excellent Capacity for Business in general, with Ease unriddles the most confus'd Accounts, and renders a Gentleman capable, with the greatest Readiness, to overlook his Affairs when manag'd by others; and I cannot better conclude my Thoughts on this Subject, than in Mr. *Lock's* Words. "Merchants Accounts, tho' not likely to help a Gentleman to get an Estate, yet possibly there is not any thing of more Use and Efficacy to make him preserve the Estate he has. 'Tis seldom observ'd, that he who keeps an Account of his Income and Expences, and thereby has constantly under View the Course of his Domestick Affairs, lets them run to Ruin. And I doubt not but many a Man gets behind-hand before he is aware, or runs farther on when he is once in, for want of this Care, or the Skill to do it. I would therefore advise all Gentlemen to learn perfectly Merchants Accounts, and not to think it is a Skill belongs not to them, because it has receiv'd its Name, and has been chiefly practis'd by Men of Traffick."

Fourthly, The several Parts of the MATHEMATICKS are of that extensive Use and Benefit to Mankind, that hardly any thing is to be done without them; Consequently the *Man* of *Business* can have no small Share in these Sciences: For he that has a thorough Knowledge in them, must have the best Foundation laid, and a Mind exquisitely furnish'd for the undertaking of any Business. From *this* Fountain all *Arts* and *Sciences* flow; it enlarges the Mind, extends our Ideas, and strengthens the Judgment. By *this* we even soar into other Worlds, and as it were pry into the very Secrets of Nature. And tho' the Knowledge of this vast useful and extensive Learning is not absolutely necessary for *every* Man, yet he that attains any Part thereof, will never repent his Labour. But there are *Some* Employments of Life that cannot be carry'd on without them. All concern'd in Weight or Measure should learn *Geometry* and *Mechanicks*: Every *Artificer* will *here* find the Foundation and Demonstration of his *Art:* And indeed *Geometry* is the *Ground* Work of all the other Parts of the *Mathematicks*, by which all *Operations* are perform'd and demonstrated. Monsieur *Fontenelle*, in his Preface of the Usefulness of *Mathematical* Learning, says, "That *Geometry* and *Algebra* are the *Keys* of all the Enquiries that can be made concerning *Magnitude*." Besides, a thorough Knowledge herein greatly cultivates the Art of Reasoning, and may even supply the Want of Logick itself.

Country Gentlemen, Stewards of Estates, and all concern'd in Land, Building, or Farming, should by all Means understand *Surveying* and *Measuring*; and indeed, for the Nobleman, or Gentleman's *Steward*, these Parts of the Mathematicks seem to be Essential Qualifications. For tho' his *Chief* Business be to receive Rents, let Leases, keep Courts, *&c.* and also to keep a just and clear Account of all, yet 'tis also a Pleasure and Satisfaction to the Owner of the Estate to view his Lands in his Closet, that is, to have 'em *Survey'd*, and every Mannour, or particular Tenants Farm neatly *Map'd*, the Timber he Sells, Builds, or Repairs with; as also Walling, Paling, Tiling, Cieling, or Painting, to be exactly measur'd: And who so Proper to do this, or so fit to be trusted in an *Affair* of this Nature (where often is great Deceit and Damage by trusting to others) as the Chief Manager, the *Land Steward*, or *Rent-Gatherer?* But to instance in all the Concerns and Employments where some Parts or other of the Mathematicks are useful and necessary, would be as tedious as that Knowledge is extensive: Therefore, Sir, I shall only just mention the peculiar Excellency of two Parts more, as Accomplishments worthy the prime Man of Business, the Merchant; that is, GEOGRAPHY and NAVIGATION.

GEOGRAPHY not only teaches the *Situation* and *Distance* of Places and Countries, the *Knowledge* of the *Earth* in general and particular, but is one of the greatest Accomplishments in Conversation, and the very Inlet to *History*, which informs us of the *Laws, Manners*, and *Customs* of *Nations*, their Advantages and Disadvantages; from whence we may be enabled to form a right Judgment to promote the Interest of our own Country, and to lay down such Rules as may be useful in our *private* Concerns.

NAVIGATION is the ART by which our Ships are conducted through the wide extended OCEAN, which carries off our Superfluities, and brings us home our Conveniences, and makes the Pleasures, Riches, and good Things of the whole World, common to all Mankind. To *us* of *this* Nation, 'tis our *Wealth* and *Defence*, and the Envy and Terror of our *Enemies*. And tho' this *Science* more immediately concerns the *Mariner* to be Master of it, yet the *Merchant* will scarce think it belongs not to him to have a Taste thereof: For, from it he may draw great Advantages in Trade. For Instance, a Knowledge of the Length, Distance, and Safety of *Voyages*, will furnish him with good Reasons to conjecture the Rise and Fall, and may point to him the most probable Markets to vend his Commodities.

Fifthly, To accomplish the *Man* of *Business*, 'tis requisite he should be Master of the *Propriety* of *Expression*. He that delivers his Sense in *improper* Terms, converses to his Disadvantage; and his other Acquisitions, be they what they will, often suffer for this *Imperfection*. He that absurdly, or darkly, or dubiously, or with Difficulty, expresses his own Mind, will be thought not very ready in apprehending the Mind of others; or what is still a greater Misfortune, brings his *Ingenuity* or *Integrity* under Suspicion; whereas his *Judgment* alone is in the Fault. And yet, according to the *common* Method of fitting *Young Gentlemen* for *Business*, a *Style* in Writing is what they seldom or never hear of; and the *Masters* generally take themselves to be no farther concern'd, than that their Scholars should write a fair *Hand*, without considering how monstrous and ridiculous their Conceptions may appear. But surely, to speak and write with *Propriety* and *Elegance*, has too great an *Influence* on *Business* to be neglected. I need not here in so plain a Case produce Reasons of the Importance of this *Qualification*; Common Experience is an undeniable Proof of it. Who undertakes *Business* to most Advantage, or succeeds best in it? but he who shews he understands the Nature of it, by the Manner of his Address, and who expresses himself without Ambiguity or Affectation. Subjects of different Natures will be treated of indeed in different Kinds of *Style:* One is peculiar to the Pulpit, another to the Bar, and a third to common Conversation. 'Tis this *last* that can alone suit Commerce; which, tho' like other *Arts* and *Sciences*, it has proper *Rules* and *Terms* belonging to it, yet delights in a *Short* and *Familiar*, but withal a *Neat* and *Significant* Way of Expression. So that the *Merchant* must converse with his *distant* Correspondent with no more *Stiffness*, than if he met him on the *Exchange*. He must not detain him an Hour for the Business of a Minute, nor put him to Pains to understand him, nor express himself to be understood to his Damage. This would render a Correspondence less agreeable to his Friend, and consequently less beneficial to himself. *Majesty* and *Grandeur* are a Stop to *Dispatch*, whereby *Business* lives, and thrives, and flourishes. So that the Style for Commerce must be Concise, Perspicuous and Natural; not lin'd with swelling impertinent Epithets, but purely *Epistolary*, and Expressing the Thoughts with the same *Facility*, as if the Correspondent were Face to Face.

And now I am shewing how necessary for the carrying on *Business* happily, a proper *Style* is; let me not part with my CHARGE, till I recommend to him the Knowledge of the *Modern Languages*. He that deals or trafficks with such whose Language he's a Stranger to, will soon be sensible not only of the Conveniency, but also of the Necessity of this *Accomplishment*. There's no Man but must needs reap greater Satisfaction, and generally greater Advantage, from transacting his Affairs himself: That's the way for him to be sure of the Condition they are in, and what he has to trust to, and what Foot he is to proceed upon: Whereas to leave 'em to the Management of other Hands, which it may chance have not Skill enough to see and pursue his Interest; or if they have, may not have Integrity enough to do him Justice, is running the Hazard of being *undone:* Or if he should have the Fortune to escape, yet it must be a continual Uneasiness to him to think he's all the while at the Mercy of such as might, if they would, have ruin'd him. But, to shorten my *Young Gentleman's* Pains, 'twill be sufficient for him to make himself Master of the FRENCH TONGUE; which will answer in a great Measure for the rest. For, at present, it seems to be the *Universal* Language. 'Tis so far Universal, that the Place is scarce known where 'tis not spoken; and we hardly find the *Foreigner*, of whatsoever Country he claims his Birth, but is able to transact his Affairs, or hold a Correspondence in it. In short, he must needs be much at a Loss, and very unequal to *Business*, that has not attain'd to a competent Skill in this Language.

But, Sir, I forget that there's nothing requir'd to Form the *Man* of *Business*, but what may be learnt with greater Advantage from your Practice, than from any thing I can offer. And I should think it as great Indecency in me to address peremptorily to so complete a Judge of this Subject, as 'twas in *Phormio* to talk of the Rules of War before *Hannibal*. Only pardon me, Sir, whilst I observe, that tho' my *Young Gentleman* should be furnish'd with all these Qualifications I have instanc'd in, he's still deficient in the main Article, if he has not imbib'd the Knowledge of RELIGION and GOOD MANNERS along with 'em. And, therefore, it must be his chief Care, constantly to attend the Stated Times of God's Publick Worship, as well as to pay him his Devotions in Private. He must be possess'd with a Sense of the Necessity of God's Blessing upon his Endeavours, if he would hope to succeed; nor can he expect the Divine

Blessing, without living in Obedience to the Divine Will. Besides, *Religion* obliges a Man to be just and conscientious in his Dealing, punctual to his Word, and open, and fair, and honourable in all his Actions. A Man of this Character will be valu'd by all Men; and his Correspondence coveted and courted; especially if Humility, and a thankful Heart, accompany his Success and Prosperity, and discover themselves in Compassion and Charity. If Patience and Temper, if Resignation, and Chearfulness of Mind, attend him in Misfortunes and Adversity, (for the wisest and greatest Men are subject to some of these) such a Man is in the likeliest Way to repair his Fortunes; which, if he should fail in, yet he will sit down with the Support of a good Conscience, which is worth all the Comforts in the World besides whilst he lives, and will be remember'd when dead with lasting Honour. When I am thus marking for the Youths design'd for Business, the Steps they are to take, if ever they'd arrive at the End propos'd, and become Men of Consideration and Importance; methinks I feel the Weight of that *Trust* that lies on *us* who have the *Care* of them. What Vigilance, what Prudence, what Management, is not necessary for the successful Discharge of our Duty! But equal Improvement must not be hop'd for in such as we are concern'd with but at *certain Hours*, and instruct *only* in *Arts* and *Sciences*, but who are at *Liberty*, because out of the reach of our *Observance*, to spend the rest of their Time as they please; as may reasonably be expected, and is generally found in such as are *constantly* under our more immediate *Inspection*, confin'd to our *Walls*, and within the Cast of our *Eye*. If these do not better answer the Expectations of their Friends, with Regard both to their *Knowledge* and *Manners*, I do not see how we shall be able to acquit ourselves from Want of Ingenuity, or due Application in our Undertaking.

Thus, Sir, I have in as little Compass as possible trac'd out what I take to be requisite to *build up* the *Man* of *Business*, and touch'd on the properest Manner of *Communicating* and *Enforcing* his *Qualifications*. The Copiousness of the *Subject* has drawn out this *Letter* to a greater Length than I at first design'd; but I hope for your usual Candour and Pardon to,

Sir,

December 12-
1715.

Your very Obedient, and
much Oblig'd Humble Servant,

THO. WATTS.

P. S. My Thoughts agree with Yours, Sir, in the Name I shall affix to my House in *Abchurch-Lane*, viz.

The A<small>CCOUNTANT</small>'s O<small>FFICE</small> for Qualifying Young Gentlemen for *Business.* Which I hope may be justify'd from the *Peculiarity* of my *Method* in this Part of *Education.*

F I N I S.

Obverse of final page

Advertisement.

A<small>T</small> the Accountant's Office in *Abchurch-Lane*, Young Gentlemen are taught the several Parts of the Mathematicks, and Qualify'd for Trades, Merchandize, the Publick Offices, Clerkships, Stewardships, or any other Parts of Business. To all which the *Italian* Method of Book-Keeping, according to the Modern Practice, is peculiarly apply'd and adapted, after a New, Expeditious, and Approv'd Manner of Instruction, free from the Interruptions, or Loss of Time, in Common Schools. By *Thomas Watts* of the Accountant's Office for Qualifying Young Gentlemen for Business, in *Abchurch-Lane*, Author of *The Essay on the proper Method for Forming the Man of Business.*

N. B. There are all Conveniences for Boarders, and such Gentlemen as desire to be instructed in Private.

CHAPTER 3

GENERAL TEXTBOOK AUTHOR MARTIN CLARE

An important general commercial text of the eighteenth century was
Youth's introduction to trade and business by M(artin) Clare, published in
eight editions between 1720 (Hans 1951, 87) and 1758. Reprinted below from
the eighth edition is the original preface, laying out the author's case for
a broad education for merchants. Clare was able to carry out his ideas in
practice, as from 1717 or '18 until his death in 1751 he was master of the
Academy in Soho Square, London (Hans 1951, 87, 89; and Murray 1930, 336n).

This school may have descended from one kept by one Mr. Meure at Soho
Square for some fifteen years beginning in or slightly before 1690, representing possibly the first designated "Academ[y]" (Hans 1951, 69, quoted,
114). In 1704 two sons of the governor of the Indian state Madras were
pupils at Meure's academy, "'esteemed the best in England'" according to a
third son, taking "'Latin, French and accounts, fencing, dancing and
drawing'" (Hans 1951, 115). Whether or not a formal linkage existed, the
studies mentioned foreshadowed the breadth of Clare's later school.

Besides writing on business subjects, Martin Clare published in 1735
a major text on the motion of fluids. The following year he became a fellow
of the Royal Society, but declined to use the "F.R.S." title publicly due
to objection that he had sought it for personal and professional prestige.
In the physics book Clare had acknowledged scientific indebtedness to his
friend Dr. Th. Desaguliers, a pioneering adult educator and world leader of

freemasonry (the subject of a later Clare book) who had also been associated with Thomas Watts and his school (Hans 1951, 84-85, 88, quoted, 137-42).

In 1744 the Rev. Cuthbert Barwis, an Oxford graduate, became codirector at Soho Square, gradually taking over school administration as Clare in his last years served as Justice of the Peace. By this point the academy conducted one of the broadest programs recorded, including auxiliary French, dancing, and fencing schools. Offered to resident students for thirty pounds, plus a small entry fee, was a basic curriculum of writing, arithmetic, grammar (Latin, Greek, and English), geography, and French, along with public lectures on morality, religion, and (using "'a large apparatus of machines and instruments'") natural philosophy. Mathematics, merchants accounts, drawing, dancing, fencing, and music were "extra" subjects carrying additional fees (Hans 1951, 89).

Barwis continued the school after Martin Clare died in 1751. He was probably joined as a partner in the '60s by prominent mathematics textbook writer John Barrow, evidently the father of the schoolmaster of the last two decades of the century, Dr. William Barrow. The younger Barrow was in turn succeeded by fellow Oxford man William Whitelock, who served at Soho Square until around 1822, a few years after the academy centennial (Hans 1951, 90-91).

Unlike the one founded by Watts, the academy established by Clare was a full-scale secondary school. Many graduates proceeded directly to higher education, while boys sometimes took only a brief course preparatory to entering one of the elite "Public Schools." From its early days Soho Square hosted amateur theatrical productions, and in later years a number of actors and painters studied there, suggesting the development of a special fine arts program. Some of the artists had gone on to study at the school of

140

design sponsored by the Royal Academy, the famous society formed by George III in 1768. Students at Soho square during the 1770s included a son of political philosopher Edmund Burke (Hans 1951, 89-91, 92, quoted; Langford 1984, 398; and Random House dictionary 1966, s.v. "Royal Academy").

Martin Clare's text Youth's introduction contained six regular sections, covering (1758, title):

1. Tables of contractions of words, suited to business usage, along with rules for formal address of dignitaries and officials
2. Acquittances and promissory notes, adapted to realistic business cases
3. Bills of parcels and bills on book debts, with emphasis on computation
4. Bills of exchange, orders for goods, letters of credit, invoices, and similar instruments of trade
5. Selected commercial laws ("Authentic Forms of such Law-Precedents, as are most frequently met within the Course of Traffic," emphasis deleted)
6. Diversified arithmetical exercises, applied to business.

In an appendix, Clare (1758, [163-83]) provided "A short and Familiar Sketch of Book-Keeping per Double Entry . . .," based on the supposed activities of a young gentleman living at home and receiving an allowance for "Pocket Expenses" (177), but raising livestock, poultry, and pet birds for commercial purposes. Twelve pages ([165]-77) illustrating the recording of transactions by the young man are followed by four pages (177-81) instructing a prospective accountant on proper "adjust[ment] and settle[ment]" (177) of the accounts at a particular date. The sketch generally follows the conventional mercantile bookkeeping system of the day (Sheldahl 1985, 15-19), including the closure of all accounts at each reckoning (Clare 1758, 179-80). Points of special interest include the recording in the animal accounts of the cost of food (169), accessories (169), and services (170) needed for animal care; the crediting of those accounts, on sale, at retail values (170); and periodic revaluation of holdings "at a discretionary Price, according to the present State and Condition thereof" (178, emphasis in original).

141

YOUTH'S
INTRODUCTION
TO
TRADE and BUSINESS.

CONTAINING

I. Tables of the moft ufual *Clerk-like* Contractions of Words; with proper Directions how to addrefs Perfons of *Elevated Rank*, and thofe in *Office*.

II. *Acquittances* and *Promiffory Notes* diverfified, and adapted to fuch Circumftances as occur in *Real Bufinefs*.

III. Variety of Bills of *Parcels*, and Bills on *Book-Debts*, to enter the *Learner* in the Manner and Methods of *Commerce*, and to make him ready at Computation.

IV. Bills of *Exchange*, with neceffary Directions for the right Underftanding and

Management of *Remittances*, with various *Orders* for Goods, *Letters* of Credit, *Invoyces*, and other *Merchant-like* Examples.

V. Authentic Forms of fuch *Law-Precedents*, as are *moft* frequently met with in the Courfe of *Traffic*.

VI. Great Variety of *Queftions* interfperfed, to excercife the *Learner* in the Common Rules of *Arithmetic*, to ufe him to *Calculation*, and to bring him acquainted with .he *Ufe*, the *Properties* and *Excellency* of *Numbers*, by Way of *Recreation*.

The EIGHTH EDITION, Corrected, Augmented, New-modelled, and confiderably Improved.

To which is added, by Way of APPENDIX,
A Short Sketch of BOOK-KEEPING by Double Entry, in the Italian Manner.

By *M. CLARE*, late Mafter of the ACADEMY in *Soho-Square*, LONDON.

LONDON:
Printed for J. FULLER, B. DOD, J. WARD, R. BALDWIN, S. CROWDER, P. DAVEY and B. LAW, and H. WOODGATE.
M DCC LVIII.

143

THE

PREFACE.

IN the Commerce of the World, Difpatch in Bufinefs is no ordinary Accomplifhment; which being the Refult of a well-directed Education, it cannot be amifs in a Treatife of this Nature, to touch on thofe Parts of it, which are more immediately neceffary for forming the Man of Bufinefs.

AFTER the Youth's firft Years have been employed in READING his native Language, and proper Care has been taken to explain and inform him of the Meaning and Force of Words as they prefent; the next Step is to initiate him in the Rudiments of GRAMMAR: In which, at firft, nothing is more material, than to be very particular in the regular Divifion and Formation of Syllables. While this is doing, it is neceffary for him to learn to WRITE; in which, the Teacher will find fufficient Reafon to exercife his Vigilance, and to guard againft the ill Habits his Charge will be apt to contract, both in Pofture and Performance.

IT is not my Defign to defcribe at large what Part of Grammar-learning is moft neceffary for this End, nor to trace out the Methods by which it is to be effected; thofe muft be left to the Skill and Difcretion of his Inftructor · I fhall, there-fore, only recommend two Things, not generally made ufe of.

I. IF the Scholar be enjoined to copy all his Exercifes, after Correction, into a fair Book, it will not only point out to him his Miftakes, and inform him how to mend them, but will even infenfibly improve his Hand, and fix it in a bold and manly Character.

II. As the principal End of inftructing a Youth, defigned for Bufinefs, in the Latin Tongue, is to make him a greater Mafter of his own; the Way to apply, and render it moft effectual to that End, is to ufe him frequently to Englifh Tranflations. The Meaning and Senfe of his Authors will thereby be impreffed on his Mind, with greater Advantage, and in Time, he will acquire a clear, juft and natural Man-ner of expreffing his Thoughts, on all Occafions; to which,

if

144

if the Reading of good Authors in our own Language be added, a due Proficiency may be expected, not only in Spelling and Propriety of Stile, but alſo in that Elegance and good Senſe, which diſtinguiſh one Man from another, and are abſolutely requiſite for all, that hope to be conſiderable in the World.

As the FRENCH TONGUE is, at preſent, the general Language of Europe, and conſequently moſt proper for Correſpondence, it ought to be recommended to the Learner, among his Grammar Studies, when his Parts will admit of ſo great a Variety; but not before he is ſufficiently grounded in the Latin, from whence the French is chiefly derived.

WRITING muſt always be regarded as an eſſential Part of every Day's Employment; becauſe the free and Clerk-like Manner of Writing, fit for the dextrous Diſpatch of Buſineſs, is not attainable by ſpeculative Notions, or on a ſudden, but by Practice gradually, under the Direction of an able Maſter; nor can any other Means be depended on, to make the Hand eaſy, bold, and maſterly.

ARITHMETIC now muſt be entered on; in teaching which Art, the enſuing Treatiſe will be of ſome Advantage: The Bills of Parcels, and thoſe on Book-Debts, are ſuch Examples of Computation, as daily occur in Commerce, and which are of uſe to illuſtrate the practical Rules, and apply them to Buſineſs. The Variety of Promiſſory Notes, Acquittances, Bills of Exchange, with Directions relating to them, and Things of like Nature, are all intended to give the young Clerk a Taſte and Idea of the Cuſtoms and Uſages of Dealers, and to obviate the Difficulties he would otherwiſe meet with, through his not being acquainted with Things of that general Concern in Traffic.

TRANSCRIBING and computing the Invoyces and other mercantile Precedents, will yield him a no leſs profitable Exerciſe, and conduce in ſome Meaſure, to the Underſtanding the Practice of BOOK-KEEPING; a Science ſo univerſally uſeful, that, without keeping regular Accompts, the Trader riſks the ſacrificing an improvable Fortune, to Negligence and Chance; the Man of Eſtate is thereby made ſubject to frequent Impoſitions, always to Uncertainties; and the Man in Office is likewiſe expoſed to numberleſs Perplexities; and, indeed, none can properly be ſaid to be a Judge of Buſineſs, whoſe Abilities, how conſiderable ſoever, are not aſſiſted by ſome Inſight and Skill therein.

THE

145

T H E Collections of Queſtions interſperſed, all of them ſolvable by the Rules of common Arithmetic, are ſubjoined, to exerciſe the Pupil in Numbers, to accuſtom him to Calculation, and with a Deſign to excite his Curioſity to look farther into their Properties and Uſe, not only as they regard themſelves, but alſo as they reſpect Lines, Surfaces, and ſolid Bodies.

D R A W I N G is an Attainment worth every Man's Purſuit ; but it is indiſpenſibly neceſſary for the Mechanic : Since, among its many other Advantages, he is thereby able to convey his Deſigns to the Apprehenſions of others, by a Sketch off-hand, with much Clearneſs and Certainty.

G E O G R A P H Y, as it informs us of the Situation of the ſeveral Parts of the Earth, the Diſtance and Bearing of Places, the Extent, Language, Religion, and Products of different Countries ; as it is the Key to Hiſtory and the public News, and needful to the forming a right Judgment of our Country, its Intereſt and Concerns ; is of too great Importance to be neglected.

To theſe more neceſſary Qualifications of the Man of Buſineſs, the practical Parts of the Mathematics, as M E A S U R I N G, G A U G I N G, S U R V E Y I N G, N A V I G A T I O N, are to be conſidered as very advantageous and uſeful Additions : The more ſpeculative Parts, as G E O M E T R Y, A S T R O N O M Y, with E X P E R I M E N T A L and N A T U R A L P H I L O S O P H Y, and A L G E B R A, are alſo Informations that give a ſublime and noble Turn of Thought ; and which, though they may not ſeem Occurrences in immediate Buſineſs or Commerce, yet do they frequently conduce to the Improvement of both, and are always Amuſements highly proper for the virtuous and intelligent Mind.

I H A V E ſuppoſed the Learner of a promiſing Genius, and teachable Diſpoſition ; happy in Parents able and willing to allow him an handſome and proper Education ; and happy in Teachers, who want neither Capacity nor Integrity in their Calling. Where all thoſe do not concur, the Misfortune is not eaſily retrieved. When once the Time of Youth is loſt, the Cares of Life are ſo great and many, that few or none are ever able to recover themſelves from the low Condition always attending the Want of a proper and early Education.

Soho - Square,
Dec. 30, 1719.   M. C L A R E.

CHAPTER 4

WILLIAM WEBSTER, WRITING MASTER AND ACCOUNTANT

At his death in 1744 at or around age sixty (The national union catalog, pre-1956 imprints (N.u.c.) 1968-81, s.v. "Webster, William, ca. 1684-
1744," heading subsequently assumed), William Webster of "Castle-Street,
near Leicesterfields" (emphasis deleted) in London was remembered as '"a
noted writing master and accomptant"' (Murray 1930, 19n, quoted from Gentlemen's Quarterly obituary). He had for some years kept a boarding school
at (presumably) his home, teaching arithmetic, writing, and bookkeeping
(Bidwell to Sheldahl, 1988, concerning 1735 reference; and Webster 1722 and
1735, frontispiece). Webster (1719 and 1726, title, 1722 and 1735, frontispiece) had evidently maintained the same address for a quarter century or
more, as references between 1719 and '35 to "Orange Street" or "Court,"
near Leicester Fields or "Square," include one that places the school at the
Orange Court corner "in" Castle-Street.

The eighth numbered edition of Webster's text An essay on book-keeping
. . . appeared the year he died, and through 1772 seven more of them were
published, in London like their predecessors. Just as successive editions
through '44 had been set forth as "corrected and improv'd," posthumous
volumes were presented as having been "carefully corrected" by Ellis Webster, likewise a "writing-master and accomptant." The text of each edition
was in fact seventy-two pages in length (N.u.c. 1968-81, numbered editions
of Essay; and Thomson 1963, 211), however, and apparently represented one

147

of two slightly different formats covering the "waste-book" of original entry, journal, and "leidger." The original coverage of 1719 was moderately rearranged by no later than the 1726 third edition (Bidwell to Sheldahl, covering 1726 and '35 editions; Sjoblom, and Yntema, to Sheldahl 1988; and Webster 1719, 1734).

Webster's Essay is of present interest because of a pamphlet that was appended to it from the beginning, namely, the author's treatise on business education reprinted below in (Webster 1726, [73]-88) its third edition. "An attempt towards rendering the education of youth more easy and effectual" had originated in 1718 (Webster) as a free-standing publication (N.u.c. 1968-81, entry 4) that was added to the bookkeeping text (Webster 1719) the next year without altering pagination. At least by 1726 (Webster, [73]-88), however, the "Attempt" was consecutively numbered in its pages with the accounting material, even though it carried a distinct title page and table of contents that until some point between 1735 and '65 (Bidwell, and Yntema, to Sheldahl 1988) did not carry page numbers.

Just as with the bookkeeping text, there was a change in the educational essay between 1719 and '26 that would apparently (Bidwell, and Yntema, to Sheldahl 1988; and N.u.c. 1968-81, numbered Essay eds.) be permanent. Page length, disregarding front and (in 1718) rear matter, declined from 17 pages to 12, although with a substantial increase in page length the third edition was actually a bit longer than the first one (Webster 1718, 5-21, and 1726, 77-88). Beyond minor refinement in expression and the introduction of numbered paragraphs, there were several changes in text between versions 1 and 3 of the "Attempt." The later edition, in paragraphs 1-3, had a longer introductory passage; expanded the sixth paragraph to explain the need to teach English grammar even in training "scholars"; and added

148

paragraphs 17 and 18 to deal with additional objections and explain the utility of studying French. These changes were not substantial, especially as Webster had from the first (1718, 10) deemed it necessary for aspiring "clerks" to learn French.

Between 1719 and '79, Webster's Essay on book-keeping appeared in unnumbered editions three times in Dublin, twice in Glasgow, and once in Newcastle (N.u.c. 1968-81, last four entries and prior entry on 1741 Irish ed.; and Webster 1734, title). Introduced in 1758 as the first accounting text published in Glasgow,[1] the Scots version edited by an anonymous '"Teacher of Book-Keeping"' added 144 pages of his own on various special-ized accounts relating to Britain or her colonies (Murray 1930, 39, quoted, 337). The editor of the 1779 Newcastle edition (N.u.c. 1968-81, 4th entry from end) had added a section on "housekeeper's accompts," besides having at least ostensibly "revised and corrected" the accounting text. In what most likely was an error, his title page supplies the only evidence found that the Essay had first appeared in 1718, as with the educational pamphlet that was omitted from the Glasgow and Newcastle volumes.

Used for the Goldsmiths'-Kress microfilm series (Morris to Sheldahl 1987; and University of London Library 1970-83, s.v. "5599"), the 1719 Dublin edition of the bookkeeping text also excluded the "Attempt." The original book-keeping format was retained in the Irish edition of 1734 (Webster, 1-72; and Yntema to Sheldahl 1988), but the revised version of the educa-tional document appeared in small print, without front matter, as a nine-page

---

[1] Pryce-Jones and Parker (1976, 3, no. 9, 6, no. 22) list Glasgow books of 1715 and '49 in their historical bibliography, but they are respectively a "ready reckoner" and an arithmetic text. Although the name may not have emerged until after 1750, ready reckoners providing completed calculations of various kinds regarding moneys (for example, interest tables) and weights and measures had long been valuable aids to commerce (Murray 1930, 296-302).

appendix (Webster 1726, 77-88, and 1734, 73-81, identical but for minimal differences in punctuation, capitalization, or use of italics). The same format was clearly retained in the 1741 Irish edition (N.u.c. 1968-81).

A further edition, of sorts, of William Webster's educational pamphlet appeared without attribution as a two-part American newspaper article in January 1735. It is of particular interest in light of the ready transplantation of Latin grammar schooling that had occurred in at least the New England American colonies (Cremin 1970, 182-87; and Watson 1916, 124-26). The American Weekly Mercury had been introduced in 1719 by Philadelphia printer Andrew Bradford as the third continuing colonial newspaper (Kobre 1944, 28, 37). In the two issues dated 12/31/34 through 1/7/35 and 1/7/35 through 1/14/35, Bradford[2] presented a selective version of Webster's essay under the title '"Some thoughts of education"' (Seybolt 1925, 103-7, all capitals in title, 103). Deleting the numbers, the newspaper item (Seybolt 1925, 103-7) omitted paragraphs 7-9, 12, 18-20, and 23 from the revised version of Webster's "Attempt" (1726, 77-88, 1734, 73-81); substantially reduced numbers 13-14 and 22, and made modest stylistic changes; and added a concluding paragraph discussed below. The effect in part was to reduce the coverage of arithmetic and writing and drop reference to instruction in French.

More importantly, the American article expressed an attitude on the teaching of Latin far different from the one taken by the (principal)

_____

[2] Seybolt (1925, 103n) lists the dates as "Dec. 31-Jan. 7, Jan. 7-14, 1735," prompting the question of whether they were actually dates of (after December 31) 1736 as stated in an "Old Style" calendar by which the new year began on March 25 (Columbia encyclopedia 3d, s.v. "Calendar, Old Style, New Style," emphasis in heading). Such an interpretation was ruled out through correspondence (Park to Sheldahl 1988) that also revealed that each installment of the article appeared on the first two pages of the weekly paper; and that although he was "off and on" during the years 1721-39 in partnership with his father (Kobre 1944, 38), Andrew Bradford was at the time listed alone as publisher (warranting editorial attribution).

English source author. Whereas Webster (1726 and 1734, paragraphs 7, 9, quoted, emphasis in original) had assumed that even "Clerks" should study the ancient language, although only (pars. 4-6) after first mastering English grammar, Andrew Bradford added a concluding paragraph (Seybolt 1925, 106-7) that roundly condemned any such suggestion. The following sentence (106-7) is illustrative:

'Can there by anything more Rediculous, than that a Father should waste his own Money and his Sons Time, in setting him to learn the Roman Language, when at the same Time he designs him for a Trade, wherein he having no use for Latin, fails not to forget that little which he brought from School, when 'tis Ten to one he abhors for the ill usage it procured him'.

Neither this sentence nor the broader passage was original with the 1735 editor. As acknowledged unsatisfactorily at best (Seybolt 1925, 106), the closing paragraph was drawn instead from LOCKE's Some thoughts concerning education (1705, sec. 164). At the beginning of the section, however, Locke had declared that Latin was "absolutely necessary to a Gentleman," and he had followed the paragraph otherwise appended to Webster's edited essay with ten sections (165-74) on the teaching of the language, strongly criticizing (170-74), as would Webster (1726 and 1734, par. 4), conventional grammar schools. Also, Locke (1705, sec. 162) had not restricted the classes of youth who should learn the "living" language French.

As an accounting author, William Webster (1719, [v-vi]) offered his "short and concise" text as an alternative to the "voluminous, and consequently tedious" books otherwise found. Thomas Dilworth (1768, [iv]), a noted English textbook author of the eighteenth century whose works were widely reprinted in America (Sheldahl 1985, 7, 17; and Shipton and Mooney 1969, s.v. "Dilworth, Thomas"),[3] called him his own single forerunner in

---

[3]Another collection within the Foundations of Accounting series (Sheldahl 1988) includes a 1794 American edition of Dilworth's accounting text.

style of bookkeeping exposition. Murray (1930, 336, quoted, 336n) states
that Webster and Martin Clare were among the first English authors to refer
expressly to '"double entry"' accounts. Concerned with fundamental presentation rather than pedagogy or terminology, however, Yamey (1963, 173)
describes the popular Essay as "undistinguished."

Webster's other major text was Arithmetic in epitome . . ., already in
its second edition when the educational tract originated in 1718 (Webster,
title). Editions 7-10, "carefully corrected, with additions," were brought
out by Ellis Webster from 1746 through '67 (N.u.c. 1968-81, 1st three
entries, 9th ed. not cited). Webster appended to a multivolume work of
1735 (or possibly '34) an applied mathematics manual titled "The description
and use of a complete sett of pocket-instruments . . .," later issued in
three free-standing editions (N.u.c. 1968-81, entries for 1739, 1768, 1780;
and Webster 1735, 72).

The arithmetic text was also the first volume of the larger work,
A compendious course of practical mathematicks, particularly adapted to the
use of the gentlemen of the army and navy. Volumes 2 and 3 covered geometry, trigonometry, mechanics, and military, including naval, applications;
and navigation, shipworking theory, and the use of globes. The work was
"[f]or the most part" a "translat[ion] from . . . tracts publish'd in French"
by Paul Hoste, 1652-1700. Hoste had taught mathematics at the "Royal Academy" at Toulon, a Mediterranean port noted since the third century for naval
training and operations. In his writing he had appropriately concentrated
on naval science, shipbuilding, and related subjects, as in L'art des armees
navales, ou, traite des evolutions navales . . . (The art of naval forces,
or, a treatise on naval evolutions). The posthumous second edition of
William Webster's adaptation from the French writings seems in 1751(-52)

152

to have been issued in two slightly different forms, one of which was associated with Ellis Webster. A third edition of the work, "corrected and improved" in a reduction to two volumes, was brought out in '69 by mathematician Samuel Clark (N.u.c. 1968-81, s.v. "Hoste, Paul," quoting, 2d and 3d entries for A compendious course, passages other than "Royal Academy"; Webster 1735, 72, quoting "Royal Academy"; and Webster's geographical dictionary 1977, s.v. "Toulon," entry 2).

The educational essays by Thomas Watts, Martin Clare, and William Webster invite especially close comparison in having first appeared, in an earlier edition in the last case, almost simultaneously from the hands of contemporary London schoolmasters.

AN
ESSAY

ON

BOOK-KEEPING,

According to the

True Italian *Method*

O F

Debtor *and* Creditor,

By DOUBLE ENTRY.

Wherein the Theory of that excellent Art
is clearly laid down in a few plain Rules; and
the Practice made evident and eafy, by variety
of intelligible Examples.

The whole in a Method new and concife.

The THIRD EDITION, corrected and improv'd.

By WILLIAM WEBSTER, Writing-Mafter,
at the Corner of *Orange-Court*, in *Caftle-Street*,
near *Leicefter-Fields :* Author of *Arithmetick in
Epitome.*

LONDON: Printed for C. KING in *Weftminfter-
Hall*, and A. BETTESWORTH in *Pater-nofter Row*; and
fold by F. FAYRAM at the *Royal Exchange Gate* in *Corn-
hill*; and T. WORRALL at the *Judge's Head* over againft
St. *Dunftan's* Church in *Fleet-ftreet*. 1726. · Price 1 *s*. 6 *d*.

AN
ATTEMPT

Towards rendering the

Education of YOUTH

More Eafy and Effe&tual,

Efpecially with Regard to their

STUDIES

AT THE

WRITING-SCHOOL.

By WILLIAM WEBSTER, Writing-Mafter,
Author of *Arithmetick in Epitome.*

𝔗𝔥𝔢 𝔗𝔥𝔦𝔯𝔡 𝔈𝔡𝔦𝔱𝔦𝔬𝔫.

LONDON:
Printed in the Year M.DCC.XXVI.

REFERENCES

To the feveral

PARAGRAPHS.

Introduction.   Parag.

DIfferent kinds of Learning ——————   1
 Writers on each ——————————   2
Education a general Term ——————   3
Its feveral Parts applicable to feveral ⎱ ib.
  Perfons —————————————— ⎰
The prefent Method, with Objections a- ⎱
  gainſt it ——————————————— ⎰   4
A Remedy propos'd ——————————   5

The Education of Scholars.
Grammar to be taught in Englifh ———   6
Writing, when to be learnt ——————   7
Arithmetick when —————————   8

The Education of Clerks.
French neceſſary as well as Latin ———   9
Writing, &c.————————————   10

Parag.

Why many lose their hands on their first entrance on Business ; with a Caution to prevent it —————— } 11

Digreffion on unfkilful Teachers —— 12

Arithmetick ———————————— 13

Book-keeping ——————————— 14

Education of Traders

Latin *not neceffary* ————————— 15

Objections anfwer'd ——————— 16, 17

French *ufeful* ——————————— 18

Drawing, its advantage —————— 19

Mathematicks ——— —————— 20

Other proper Studies for the English *Schollar* —————————— } 21

Writing and Accompts ——————— 22

Conclufion ——————————— 23

A N

A N
ATTEMPT

Towards rendering the

Education of YOUTH

More Eafy and Effectual.

1. AS the knowledge of *Greek* and *Latin* is the foundation of that kind of Learning which ufually denominates a Man a *Schollar* ; fo a competent fkill in *Writing* and *Accompts*, is the chief of thofe accomplifhments which are generally underftood by the name of *Clerkfhip*, in the prefent acceptation of the word.

2. Several ingenious Gentlemen have communicated to the world their thoughts upon the attaining the learned Languages, and enter'd, as it were, their Protefts againft the common method of Inftruction : but the other part of Education, tho of much more general ufe in Life,

feems

2

feems to have been neglected, and the only Attempt I have hitherto feen on that fubject, is a fmall Treatife under the Title of *An Essay on the proper method for forming the man of Bufinefs.*

3. Education is indeed a word of very large extent, and implies the whole compafs of Learning, every thing a Youth may be inftructed in; but certainly, every part is not applicable to every perfon, and the *Counting-Houfe*, and the *Counter*, require Qualifications very different from thofe which fit a man for the *Pulpit*, or the *Bar*.

4. Yet notwithftanding, the prevailing method of Education at prefent, is without any regard to the Child's capacity, or diftinction, with refpect to the future Figure we intend he fhall make in the World, the prefent method I fay, is, as foon as he can ftammer over a chapter in the *Bible*, and before he has well loft the uncouth tone of pronunciation, which he has perhaps learnt of his Miftrefs, immediately to fend the Boy to the *Latin-School*; where, inftead of ftudying his own Language, and improving in the neceffary qualifications of reading it diftinctly, and with proper *Emphafis*, he is unreafonably enter'd upon a *Latin* Grammar, and not only perplex'd with abftrufe Terms of Art, but confounded with Rules wrote in a Language he is altogether a ftranger to. To learn an unknown *Science* in an unknown *Tongue*, muft certainly be acknowledg'd an hardy undertaking, even in a grown Perfon, with the utmoft application of his whole thought and reafon; how much more difficult and unreafonable muft it then be, for Children

to

to go thro' the unaccountable tafk, and whilft they labour under the load, to ftand liable to the lafh for every failure of capacity, as well as negligence of duty ! But the whole of the Objection is not againft the difficulty of the Study, it is oftentimes as fruitlefs as it is difficult ; for after, it may be, feven years pains are paft, and the Youth fomewhat advanc'd in his Learning, either difcourag'd by experienc'd hardfhips, or determin'd by his Friends inclinations, his Studies are fuddenly chang'd, and he is immediately remov'd to the *Writing-School*, to be qualify'd for Trade, or other Bufinefs ; where, entirely neglecting his former applications, the little *Latin* he had learnt, is loft ; and for all his time and labour paft, he is perhaps unable to give the fenfe of a *Motto* or *Infcription* ; nay, it may be, is ftill uncapable of reading or writing *Englifh*.

5. To remedy thefe inconveniencies, I would therefore humbly recommend it to thofe who have the care of Children, to obferve betimes their inclinations and capacities, and, as foon as poffible, to come to a refolution how they intend to place them in the World; for tho' it is not poffible fo foon to fix upon any diftinct Trade or Profeffion, yet they may, and ought early to determine, whether they intend them for *Scholars, Clerks,* or *Traders*, that they may receive their Education accordingly.

6. As for thofe who are to be brought up *Scholars*, it is out of my fphere to direct ; but leaving them to the Profeffors of that part of Education, I would

I would only take the liberty to obferve, that if, before they were perplex'd with *Latin*, they were taught the grounds of Grammar in the *Englifh* Tongue, they would make their advances in that learned Language with more eafe and fuccefs, and would give their *Latin*-Mafters lefs trouble, and more credit : To that end, for the particular ufe of my own Scholars, I have compos'd an *Englifh* Rudiment, built upon the method of the *Latin* Grammar, by which the Learner may not only come to the perfect knowledge of his Mother-Tongue, but be alfo fitly prepar'd for the ftudy of other Languages, more efpecially the *Latin*, the difficulty of which will, by that means, be in a great meafure remov'd : For *Grammar* is not, as it is too often conceiv'd to be, only an Appendix to *Latin* and *Greek*; but is of itfelf an abfolute *Science*, teaching the nature and diftinction of Words, and the juftnefs and proprieties of Speech; and confifts, like other Sciences, of feveral general Principles, applicable to all the Languages of the Univerfe: Every one, therefore, fhould firft learn *Grammar* in his own Tongue, and then he may with eafe be taught the feveral peculiarities of any other Language he fhall afterwards apply himfelf to the Study of

7. At the fame time that Children are thus learning *Englifh*, it will be proper they fhould be taught to *write*; not only as it is a delightful exercife, and eafily attained, but as it is of abfolute ufe and neceffity for their future advances, and particularly to the performing their *Latin* Exercifes.

For

8. As to *Arithmetick*, it may be beſt for ſuch to let it alone till their more advanc'd years, when it will be a proper introduction to their *Mathematical* Studies.

9. Thoſe who are intended *Clerks*, are the next under conſideration ; and for theſe, having made the ſame beginning as the others, it will be neceſſary that they as well ſtudy the *French* as the *Latin* Tongue, from both which they ought to be capable of making a good tranſlation.

10. *Writing* and *Accompts* are indeed their very profeſſion ; and therefore to be wanting in either of thoſe qualifications, is to be deficient in eſſentials, and unworthy the very name of a *Clerk*. Nor is it ſufficient barely to write a fair character ; a *Clerk* ſhould have an eaſy freedom in his Hand, a bold ſtroke with his Pen, and the ſkill and command of ſtriking a neat Capital, or proper Ornament ; by which means he will not only be able to do his Buſineſs without difficulty, but alſo make it appear to advantage.

11. 'Tis a common thing to find a young Man, who writ very tolerably at the *Writing-School*, immediately upon his entrance on Buſineſs, to loſe his Hand ; occaſion'd by his falling at once from a ſlow way of practice, to attempt diſpatch ; but if either at the time of their learning, they were brought by degrees from ſet Copies and Pieces, to write after larger Specimens, and real Preſidents of Buſineſs, (as is my conſtant method with my *Scholars*) or on their firſt entrance into Offices, *&c.* they would themſelves have the

M   prudence

prudence carefully and leisurely to copy what is given them, and leave it to time and practice to render them ready and expeditious, they would find their account in their patience, and have their diligence crown'd with perfection.

12. And here I cannot forbear lamenting the Unhappiness of our *Profession*, on account of its being, like those of Law and Physick, so crowded with ignorant Undertakers, and unskilful Pretenders. When a man has try'd all Shifts, and still fail'd, if he can but scratch out any thing like a fair *Character*, tho' never so stiff and unnatural, and has got but *Arithmetick* enough in his head to compute the minutes in a year, or the inches in a mile, he makes his last recourse to a Garret, and, with the Painter's help, sets up for a Teacher of *Writing* and *Arithmetick*; where, by the bait of low Prices, he perhaps gathers a number of Schollars; and thus imposing on the inconsiderate Parents, both robs them of their money, and the more unhappy Children of their time. Again, others there are, who, tho' better *Writers* and *Accomptants* than the former, are yet so shamefully ignorant in other respects, that they can neither write sense, nor spell *English*: And sure the Scholars of such Masters are like to prove great proficients! But to return;

13. *Arithmetick* is more the business of the head than the hand; and he that proposes himself for a *Clerk* or *Accomptant*, ought to have a particular turn of thought that way: 'Tis true, there are distinct peculiar methods, and a common road of practice in most Offices and Employments, as particularly in the *Custom-House* and

and *Excife*; by which many men of but dull genius, make fhift to rub through their bufinefs; but what fatisfaction can a man take in doing what he does not underftand ? And how much muft he be out of countenance if call'd upon for an explanation ? Whereas, he that works with knowledge, and can render a reafon for what he does, not only goes on with certainty and pleafure to himfelf, but to the fatisfaction of others : Befides, he who is a Mafter of the Theory, and whofe bufinefs puts him upon conftant Practice, can hardly fail of adding new improvements of his own, to the difcoveries of others in that inexhauftible Art : But, as fome perfons may be engag'd in Bufinefs, wherein is very little ufe of this Science, by which means they may be liable to forget what they had learn'd ; and others may be fo haftily enter'd upon what may very much require it, as not to have time to obtain a fufficient knowledge therein, I fometime ago publifh'd a little *Treatife*, in a neat pocket Volume, under the Title of *Arithmetick in Epitome*; or, *a Compendium of all its Rules, both Vulgar and Decimal.* Which Book, as it was chiefly intended, and, at firft, particularly dedicated to the ingenious *Clerks* and *Accomptants* of the feveral Offices of *Great Britain*, fo it has had the good Fortune fo far to pleafe, as to have already paft three Impreffions.

14. The next neceffary qualification of a *Clerk* or *Accomptant*, is that moft excellent Art of *Italian* Book-keeping, a *Science* beyond the praife of words, and without which a man is neither fit for the Cabinet nor the Compting-Houfe : And, indeed, the World now feems to be more

M 2　　　　than

than ever fenfible of its value, every one almoft being defirous of having thofe under their care inftructed therein. In this Art too I have endeavour'd to ferve the *Publick*, by a fmall *Treatife* call'd, *An Effay on Book-keeping, according to the true* Italian *Method of Debtor and Creditor by Double Entry*, which has likewife been fo well receiv'd, as to have been twice printed in little more than a twelvemonth's time, and is now, with this *Attempt*, come to its third Edition.

15. Having thus confider'd the proper attainments of thofe who are intended *Clerks*, &c. I now proceed to point out what I think the proper method of preparing thofe who are defign'd for *Trades*. And here I hope I fhall be excus'd if I entirely declare againft fuch Children lofing their time about *Latin*.

16. *Grammar*, which is the only thing they can propofe thereby to learn, I have already thew'd may more eafily and effectually be taught them in their own Mother-Tongue: And for the general receiv'd notion, that there is no attaining to fpell *Englifh* without learning *Latin*, it is an obfervation falfe in fact, and no better than a vulgar Error. 'Tis true, indeed, the *Latin* Scholar, by his daily reading, and conftant perufal of books, can hardly fail of improving himfelf in that refpect; but then it is not becaufe what he ftudies is *Latin*, but the fame application to *Englifh* Authors would produce a like or greater Effect; for the main difficulty of *Spelling*, is not in thofe words deriv'd of the *Latin* Tongue, which are indeed of all others moft eafily fpelt, by reafon no fuperfluous letters are therein

therein ufed, every letter having its full power, and every fyllable exactly writ as founded; whilft the chief difficulty is really found in thofe words which are merely *Englifh*, or of *Saxon* Original: if therefore we muft needs learn fome other Language to teach us to fpell *Englifh*, it ought certainly to be the old *Saxon*, not the *Latin*.

17. Another Plea for the Neceffity of learning *Latin*, is, that without it we cannot underftand the many *Englifh* words thence deriv'd; but this Argument either proves nothing, or it proves too much; for if it be neceffary to learn *Latin* for the underftanding the words borrow'd from that Language, it muft confequently be alfo neceffary to learn *Greek* for the fame reafon; and thus this neceffity of becoming Etymologifts, will lead us thro' all the *twelve Languages*, from which *Skinner* in his Dictionary deduces our Speech: but, above all, we muft again be referr'd to the old *Saxon*; from whence almoft all our Monofyllables, and the greateft number of our other primitive words, are brought.

18. I would therefore, inftead of the aforemention'd fruitlefs difficulty, earneftly recommend the ftudy of the *French* Tongue, which will both be much eafier attain'd, and prove much more ferviceable in Bufinefs, as being now almoft the common Speech of *Europe*; and, confequently, not only qualifying a man to travel abroad, and by that means to improve his Traffick beyond the Seas, but alfo of frequent ufe in their Shops at home, to their great advantage in ferving their foreign Cuftomers.

19. To

19. To this ufeful ftudy, I muft add another very neceffary qualification, of general ufe to all Mankind, but more efpecially to thofe who are to get their living by the invention of their heads, and the work of their hands ; I mean the ingenious Art of *Drawing* ; for how can he be fuppos'd capable of performing a piece of work, who is not able to give a Draught of his Defign ? Or what content is he like to give to his Employers, who cannot lay before them a reprefentation of what they are to expect ? It is to this admirable fkill that we owe both the invention and improvement of every ufeful inftrument, and every pleafing curiofity. Is it not ftrange then, that an Accomplifhment fo advantageous and neceffary, fhould be fo much flighted and neglected, as that perhaps of fifty *Britifh* Youths put out to Bufinefs abfolutely requiring it, fcarce one fhall be found therein fitly qualify'd ? Upon which account the Parents are not only oblig'd. to part with larger Sums to place them out, but the young Men too uncapable of doing their Mafter's better bufinefs, muft be content to be employ'd in Errants, and other mean fervice, 'till fuch time as they become proficients. Our neighbour-Nations have another opinion of this Art, and whatever they intend their Sons for, feldom fail of giving them this part of Education ; and I hope that being influenc'd by confideration and example, and convinc'd by experience, the fame good cuftom will in time obtain in *Great Britain* alfo.

20. With this Art of *Drawing* fome Profeffions may require a little fkill in *Mathematicks* ; but as
this

this is not fo generally needful, I fhall content myfelf with having only mention'd it.

21. And now if it fhould be objected that thefe Attainments will not take up all the time a youth has for learning before he is put out Apprentice ; without urging that I am afraid few go abroad fo well furnifh'd, I may anfwer, that there are other things an *Englifh* Schollar may be inftructed in, as *Geography, Chronology,* and *Hiftory,* and, above all, a good *narative Style,* or a facility of expreffing himfelf handfomely by Letter; and thefe fure are parts of knowledge which will turn to much more account than all *Lilly*'s Rules and Exceptions; and will make him more capable of Converfation, as well as Bufinefs, than if his head were furnifh'd with a few *Latin* Words and Phrafes, which he would foon forget, or never be able to make a right ufe of. As for the fabulous Hiftory of the Gods and Heroes of the Poets, if that knowledge is to be infifted on, it may as well be learn'd in *Englifh :* For the *Pantheon,* or Dr. *King*'s Hiftory of the Heathen Gods, will give fufficient light into the whole *Pagan* Theology ; and *Dryden, Pope,* and other *Englifh* Poets, have fung all the Fables of Antiquity in our native Language.

22. If whilft young Men are learning thefe feveral Accomplifhments they are remov'd from the *Writing-School,* (tho' they may very well be carrying on their Improvements there at the fame time, and indeed if there was proper Encouragement given, all thefe things might be there taught) it will be neceffary, before they go out to Bufinefs, they fhould return again, both

to

to brighten up their *Writing*, and to finish them
in *Accompts* which laft, as it is the fooneft of
all other things forgot, without practice, fo it
fhould be always the laft Attainment; and a
young Man, having added a competent knowledge in that Art to his other Acquirements, cannot but make his entrance into the world with
advantage: When, if good Manners and Virtue
alfo join his Accomplifhments, he will hardly
fail of good ufage and encouragement from the
Mafter he ferves; the utmoft endearments of his
Friends and Relations; civility and refpect from
all about him; in himfelf an inward fatisfaction; and what will undoubtedly crown all, God's
blefling and protection.

23. I have thus thrown together a few Hints
on *Education* as they have occurr'd to my thoughts,
which I humbly fubmit to the confideration of
the Publick: I would only add, that as I have
fuccefsfully try'd what I here offer; fo I would
rather have it look'd upon as an Account of the
Practice of my *School*, than as a defign'd Treatife
on the Subject.

F I N I S.

CHAPTER 5

MALACHY POSTLETHWAYT, AND A POSSIBLE ALTERNATE,

OR SECOND, AUTHOR FOR The accomplish'd merchant

Of the two unsigned essays included in this volume, only The accom-

plish'd merchant presents any uncertainty of authorship. Printed pri-

vately without place or date by "a Merchant of London" (title, emphasis

in original), this very rare work was reported in 1970 (Redlich, [199])

to be listed in no "generally used bibliograph[y]."

Copies of this educational essay are found, however, within both the

Goldsmiths' Library of Economic Literature at the University of London, and

the Kress Library of Business and Economics at Harvard. The former copy

was used for the microfilm series based on these collections ([Postlethwayt

c. 1730], micro. ed., outer cover), while the latter one is the source of

the reprint presented below. Handwriting on Goldsmiths' outer cover tenta-

tively (via question marks) attributes the pamphlet to Malachy Postlethwayt,

who is profiled in chapter 6, and dates it at 1740, no doubt an intended

approximation.

Since the essay had in 1970 (University of London Library 1970-83,

s.v. "8561") been recorded as an anonymous work of or around 1750, these

imputations were evidently made in the course of microfilm project research

(Goldsmiths'-Kress Library 1976-87, s.v. "7769.1," citing author without

question mark). Prior use of the later date may have been based on the

appearance in 1750 of a book by Postlethwayt and "Merchant of London"

James Royston subtitled "The accomplished merchant" (Redlich 1970, opposite 202, emphasis in original).

Postlethwayt was identified as author of the unsigned pamphlet, circa 1740 (University of London Library 1970-83, 3:14, s.v. "7769.1"), based on his statement in a 1751 work (Postlethwayt, 12-13) that "before the late war" he had "printed but [beyond a private level] not published" a "sketch of a plan" of education. Well before declaring war against France in 1744, Britain had become involved in the War of the Austrian Succession, 1740-48 (Langford 1984, 373; and Lunt 1957, 515-16). From this evidence, 1740 was the logical "rounded" printing date.

A second 1751 source, however, points to an earlier origin for the writing while offering seemingly decisive evidence of authorship. In a preface to his foremost work, Postlethwayt (1751-55, 1:xiii) stated that after having "above twenty years" earlier set his sights on forming a new kind of mercantile academy, he had anonymously "draw[n] up and print[ed] a small tract, intitled the Accomplished Merchant," laying out his preliminary design. It was clearly on this basis that a 1938 commentator (Fraser, 29) dated The accomplish'd merchant at approximately 1730. Since the earlier year is consistent with the other source as well, it seems only reasonable to date the work accordingly.

There remains, however, a legitimate question of credibility of Postlethwayt's 1751 accounts, in light of a well-documented feature of his writing discussed in chapter 6, and the listing a year before of a second author for a restatement of the educational plan. The imputed source of The accomplish'd merchant is well known for having "freely plagiari[zed] other writers" (D.n.b. 1917, s.v. "Postlethwayt, Malachy"). Would it not have only been in character, then, for him to have taken credit for an essay actually

174

written, at least in part, by his 1750 collaborator? Indeed, why would Postlethwayt, clearly "not the man to hide his light under a bushel" (Redlich 1970, 204n), have printed an essay anonymously in the first place?

The other author was James Royston, a London wine merchant who died in 1759 (List of deaths for the year . . . 1759, 293), a year after '"eminent wine merchant"' James Royston, Jr. (Redlich 1970, 200n).[1] The Roystons may have been descended from "Orthodox Roystone" (Dunton 1818, 1:292), seventeenth-century royalist Richard Royston, 1599-1686, bookseller to three Stuart kings (D.n.b. 1917, s.v. "Royston, Richard"). A more pertinent conjecture (Johnson 1937, 185, 355, note 7) is that Royston, Sr. was the "eminent merchant" with whom Postlethwayt states (1751-55, 1:xiii) that he had been "in partnership [for] several years" before writing the essay printed below, by which point he had been "also engaged in pretty considerable mercantile concerns" and for "many years chiefly conversant with mercantile people."

Such a record of experience sounds most impressive for a man of twenty-three years, by inference the approximate age of Postlethwayt, 1707?-67 (D.n.b. 1917, s.v. "Postlethwayt, Malachy"), when he wrote The accomplish'd merchant. Granting that a commercial career of the day might have begun in the early teens, Postlethwayt may have in 1751 somewhat exaggerated his experience circa 1730 (or the vintage of the pamphlet). There is no reason to doubt, however, that he had been a "merchant of London" over the years leading up to the publication in 1746 of his first generally recognized book, which like the earlier pamphlet was unsigned (D.n.b. 1917, s.v. "Postlethwayt, Malachy"; and Postlethwayt 1751-55, 1:xiii-xiv).

---

[1]The basis for identifying the senior Royston as Postlethwayt's associate is the identity of the business address given in the 1759 obituary (List of deaths for the year . . . 1759, 293) with the one cited by Postlethwayt in a reference of 1751 (111).

Postlethwayt relates (1751-55, 1:xiii) that upon giving copies of the newly printed educational essay to selected acquaintances, he had been asked "to take some gentlemen's sons of fortune into his counting-house" for instruction, and actually made a year's commitment of that kind. He had evidently abandoned the project almost at once, however, due to demands of personal business, and a recognition of his own limitations as an authority on commerce. Against this background Postlethwayt (1751-55, 1:xiii-xiv) had commenced the personal study and research that would eventually produce the massive dictionary sampled in chapter 6.

Redlich in 1970 ([199], quoted, 200) attributed The accomplish'd merchant to James Royston, but it is clear from his suggestion that it was written "in the late 1740s" that he was unaware of Postlethwayt's references to the work. He makes the interesting conjecture, however, that Royston might have turned "his" plan over to Postlethwayt, after their 1750 publication, in order to forestall "difficulties with conservative colleagues . . . object[ing] to his criticism of the apprenticeship system" of business education (Redlich 1970, 200).

The same consideration might have prompted anonymity twenty years earlier for the wine merchant or the youthful Postlethwayt, either as Royston's junior partner or an independent merchant. Having so directly identified himself with the proposed plan in 1750, however, it seems unlikely that Royston would have sought at that point to deny responsibility for the original tract, were it his, or that if he had he would have signed himself as, like the original author, "a Merchant of London." It is worth noting that one source for attributing the pamphlet to Postlethwayt concludes by citing Royston as a correspondent on the plan, suggesting that the two men remained on good terms (Postlethwayt 1751, 111; and Redlich 1970, 200).

176

THE

ACCOMPLISH'D

MERCHANT.

By a MERCHANT of *London*.

THE

Accomplifh'd MERCHANT.

EVERY Man that has Money thinks himfelf fufficiently qualify'd to commence *Merchant*. 'Tis only buying and felling, paying and receiving, fays he, that
comprehends the whole Circle of Mercantile Tranfactions: And
what mighty Myftery is there in all this? When a low Idea is
thus entertain'd of the Qualifications neceffary for an Employ,
'tis rare that Accomplifhments overfhoot the Mark of current
Opinion. Whence it is that thoufands plunge into the Ocean
of Trade deftitute of Acquirements indifpenfibly requifite; ruin
themfelves and Families, and prejudice Trade in general by their
Ignorance and Incapacity to profecute it with Judgment and
Ability.

Whoever reflects on the various ways of *foreign* Commerce;
the univerfal Correfpondence and Intelligence neceffary to thofe
Ends, the perfect Knowledge of the Situation of the Trading
World; its Produce and Manufacture; what will, and what
will not anfwer to traffick in, and the critical Seafons when;
what Knowledge of the Laws and Cuftoms of foreign Countries
is requir'd for fecure Exportation and Importation; what *Duties*

A   and

and *Imposts* they lay upon foreign Commodities, (without which no previous Calculation can be made whether foreign Trade will turn to account or no ;) whoever considers the wonderful Circulation of Property among the mercantile part of the World, the nature of Paper Credit, and the exquisite Laws of Honour, Justice, and Punctuality establish'd among *Merchants* for the support of universal *Credit*; what Understanding in the *foreign Monies* of the World is required, the speedy Methods of converting those of one Country into those of any other ; the political Contrivance of real and imaginary Coins for this purpose, the Courses of *Exchange* instituted throughout *Europe* to this End ; their perpetual variation, and the Skill requisite to *arbitrate* the *Exchange* whereby to make the best Advantages of this constant Fluctuation ; whoever, I say, will attend to the numberless other Occurrences that diversify Trade, as *exporting*, *importing*, for *Proper*, *Company* and *Commission* Account ; *drawing*, *remitting* and *negotiating* Bills, and those in many Parts of the trafficable World at the same time, will soon raise his Idea of the Merchant's Employ. But when he considers what a clear Head, what great Skill in *Numbers* and *Accountantship* are requir'd to regulate and adjust such an extensive variety of Transactions, that a *Merchant* may always have a true Representation of the State of his Affairs before him ; what Judgment, Learning and Address are necessary to support a solid and engaging way of Correspondence with foreign Merchants in their own, or the most universal Languages ; whoever, I say, takes a View, even from this faint Description, of what is proper to form the intelligent and judicious Merchant, will hardly differ with me, if I should assert, that few Professions require a sounder Judgment or a greater Share of useful Learning ; and yet I may venture

to

to affirm, that none is in general more shamefully neglected in point of essential Accomplishment. But to trace this more minutely.

Are not the Generality designed for the Counting-House hurry'd thither from *School* before they are in a Capacity to derive any Advantage from it? Is not mere mechanical Writing, and a little common School Accounts the whole of their Education? For want of Ability to write Sense and Grammar, and a competent Skill in *Figures* and *Accountantship*, how few in the Course of their Apprenticeship are capable of carrying on the foreign Correspondence, keeping the Books, and making the various nice Calculations, which necessarily arise in a Counting-House of extensive Business? Is not this general Incapacity and Disqualification of young *Gentlemen* bred Merchants one Reason why they are kept in Ignorance of the prime and essential Parts of their Master's Business; chain'd to a *Coppy-Book* of Letters, *Invoyce*, or *Account of Sales* Book, or else employ'd in running o'er the Town with *Bills of Exchange*, to the *Post-Office*, &c. with all the other Drudgery of the *Counting-House*? However notably this kind of Employment may qualify a young *Gentleman* of Fortune for a *Hackney-Writer* or a *Bank-Runner*, I am at a Loss to conceive how five or seven Years thus spent will any way contribute to his becoming a good *Accountant* and a well accomplished *Merchant*.

Whatever Plea there may be for this, at the first Reception of an *Apprentice* into the *Counting-House*, there is no Reason that he should be kept to act this under Part the Whole of his Servitude. Nor is it always the Inability of a young *Gentleman* to learn and execute the superior Parts of Business, that occasions his Ignorance thereof. It is too often the great Care that is taken that he fhould be as little acquainted with the State of his Mafter's Trade, the Profits or Loffes arifing upon thofe Branches he may be engag'd in, his foreign Correfpondents, and the accurate Method of keeping his Accounts, as one who never enter'd his *Counting-Houfe.* Such who lock up their Principal Books from their Apprentices, and fcarce fuffer 'em to caft an Eye over them, left they fhould be the better for their *Clerkfhip,* and the five hundred, feven, or thoufand Guineas they may give to be qualify'd; fuch Merchants who thus injure their Apprentice, keep him only employ'd in the low Slavery, fome disjointed Appendage to the chief Books, and caft a conftant Cloud o'er his Underftanding; fuch who rather difcourage young Gentlemen of Fortune from becoming ingenious and accomplifh'd in their Profeffion, than animate them to Application and Inquifitivenefs, who rather encourage them in Levity, Neglect and Supinenefs of their *own* Intereft, left they fhould afterwards prove injurious to *theirs,* I muft take Liberty to tell them act with the greateft Difhonour and Injuftice.

Such is the nature of the Mercatorial Employ, that nothing is eafier than to keep a young Man in Ignorance, by rendring every thing myfterious and unintelligible to him. For as it requires fuch Variety of Accounts, Diverfity of Books and multitude of different Calculations, it is only tying a young *Gentleman* to fome inferior Book, fome labouring Oar, and he fhall remain as totally unacquainted for feven Years together, with the Effence of *Merchandizing* and the Arts of *Accountantfhip* and *mercantile Calculation,* as one bred to a different Employment.

'Tis

'Tis next to an Impoſſibility, that a *Merchant* ſhould ever be qualify'd to be at the head of a *Counting-Houſe,* and direct his Affairs with Judgment, unleſs in his *Clerkſhip* he has kept every Book in its *Turn,* beginning from the Inferior 'till he arriv'd at the moſt material and important. This would render the diſtinct Uſe of each Book ſo familiar to him, that he could ſcarce avoid ſeeing the Dependency and Connection of the Whole, and taking a comprehenſive View of every Scene of Buſineſs; provided the Books are kept in an *accountantlike* manner; and if they are not, it is the greateſt Misfortune that he ever enter'd into ſuch a *Counting-Houſe.*

And as it can never be ſuppos'd but the Tranſactions of a *young Merchant* will be in many reſpects widely different from thoſe of his *Maſter*; ſo if he is no better skill'd in *Accounts* than to be able to regulate and adjuſt ſome *peculiar* Occurrences, he will ſtill be very much at a Loſs to methodize his own Affairs, if in his *Apprenticeſhip* he has not the *rational Principles* of Accountantſhip plainly and intelligibly inculcated; ſo that he can apply thoſe Principles in a maſterly manner to any kind of Buſineſs, be it ever ſo diſtinct from what he had ſeen, or of ever ſo abſtruſe or complicated a nature.

To this end was he put upon keeping a *rough* ſet of Books of his Maſter's Buſineſs, all form'd by his own hand, and were thoſe daily corrected, and the Reaſons of his Miſtakes familiarly pointed out, he would ſoon be capable of taking the real Books under his Management. For when he had been inur'd to Reflection for a Time by ſtating of his foul Books, that Levity, Unſteddineſs and Inattention, natural to young Men, would wear off; and without blundering he would be able to carry on the Journal and the Ledger with Facility. At leaſt by theſe

means

means he would be enabled to infpect the Books with Advantage, fhould it be thought a Truft of too great Importance to put a young Man upon keeping the grand Books.

It is the Bufinefs of a young Gentleman of Fortune, to qualify himfelf to be at the Head of a *Counting-Houfe*, that he may be able to give Directions how Bufinefs ought to be done in the beft manner, fuitable to the nature of his Affairs, not make himfelf the Slave, the common *Sailor*, but the *Steerfman*. To fit him for this, he muft not only be bred a meer Accountant, but inftructed, regularly and rationally inftructed, in all the Niceties of the *Exchanges*, and the *private* Motives to his Mafter's Conduct in Trade fhould be *unrefervedly* communicated for his future Government. Thus fhould he be put upon reading the Letters with the utmoft Attention, (not merely to fcribble 'em over with the greateft Hurry and Confufion, for the fake of *Tranfcripts* only) and thereby ftore up a Treafure of experimental Knowledge before he engag'd for himfelf. And would a Mafter with Affability, condefcend to ask a young *Gentleman*, what he would do in fuch a Cafe, what Anfwer he would make to fuch a Correfpondent, put him upon writing, and where his Diction was low, barren and unintelligible, to correct it. Such Behaviour to young Men would attach their Inclinations, and make them delight more in the *Counting-Houfe* than the Play-houfe. When a Mafter's Bufinefs thus became a Pleafure, is it not more than probable that Numbers of young Men of confiderable Fortunes, would by fuch Treatment be reftrain'd from taking Careers in Pleafure during their *Apprenticefhip*, which ever after give them a Difrelifh for Bufinefs, and fpoil them for that great and honourable Employment for which they were intended?

Whatever

Whatever fome may object, that the Bufinefs of a Merchant will not admit of his fpending fo much Time to form his *Apprentice,* will be of little Weight with Men of Senfe and Impartiality. The large Confideration generally taken, and the additional Advantage of Servitude, very amply Recompence the Trouble neceffary to be taken for his Accomplifhment, and therefore a Neglect is unjuftifiable and unpardonable.

Trade, Figures and *Accountantfhip* are but dry things for juvenile Minds; and unlefs they are reprefented in a lively and captivating manner; unlefs young Men are encourag'd to Application and Reflection upon the prime Parts of Bufinefs, which ftrike the Mind moft powerfully, and not upon the low Drudgery; can it reafonably be expected they fhould make good *Servants* or skilful *Mafters?* Foreign Commerce, even from that imperfect Defcription juft given of it, manifeftly requires extenfive Knowledge and deep Judgment to make any Figure therein; and whatever Shifts Numbers have made under the greateft Difadvantage of Accomplifhment, I am convinc'd, experimentally convinc'd, they would otherwife have had much greater Succefs; thoufands would have been fav'd from Diftruction, and the Trade of *Great Britain* confiderably extended from the Ability and Judgment of thofe who are engag'd in it.

Should it fo happen, (as none will think impoffible) that a young Gentleman is bred to *Trade* under one who is unskill'd in Accounts, whofe Books are in Confufion, never pofted-up, never fit for a Balance; and whofe Head is as well turn'd for foreign Negoce, as a *Fox-hunter's* for Mathematical Difquifitions; fhould it be the ill fortune of a young *Gentleman* to fall into fuch Hands, what a hopeful Figure is he likely to make in Trade, when he launches into that Ocean for himfelf? If he
efcapes

efcapes Ruin will it not be matter of Admiration? Is it not as impoffible that a *Merchant* fhould be profperous in Trade without being a thorough-pac'd Accountant, and having all other Accomplifhments fuitable to the Nature of his great Employ, as that a Mariner fhould conduct a Ship to all Parts of the Globe without a Skill in Navigation?

Neither is every Man who is thoroughly acquainted with Mercantile, or any other Science capable of bringing up others in the fame.   The Talent of Communication whereby to ftamp your own Ideas on another Perfon's Mind is abfolutely neceffary to this End.   And perhaps this requires greater Abilities than may be imagin d.   Not only muft he have acquir d a happy Turn of Reafoning methodically, clearly and diftinctly, but he muft in fome degree be endowed with the Power of Eloquence to illuftrate and enforce what he delivers with Energy, that it may leave a lafting Impreffion behind it.

'Tis not the perpetual Practice of Trade only that will give this, tho it furnifhes Materials for the Purpofe. 'Tis Study and Reflection, founded on Reafon and Practice, a good general Education, and a Genius for familiar Explication that fit a Man for the well forming others.

Be it the Fate therefore of a young Merchant, either to be train'd up under the *skilful* but *difhonourable*, or the *ignorant* and injudicious, it is irretrievably injurious; not only to the immediately concern'd, but to their Country and Pofterity; for fuch incapacitate many from doing Juftice to their Apprentices, who would be inclin'd to it; and thus at length the Race of Underftanding and Experienc'd Merchants would be extinct, Foreigners by their fuperior Knowledge and Sagacity fupplant them, and *England* ftript of its *Commerce* and *Navigation*

tion from a Caule no Body fuspected. For let *Trade* afford ever fuch extraordinary Advantages, yet if *Traders* have not Knowledge to difcern them, and Qualifications to reduce their Knowledge into Practice with Credit, the *Defect* lies in them, not in *Trade*. This is the Cafe of all Profeffions the moft lucrative and honourable; They yield little Benefit to thofe who are not duly qualify'd for them. If the Lawyer, Phyfician and Divine for want of Abilities and Accomplifhments, make no Figure in their refpective Capacities, nor receive fuch Honours and Emoluments thofe do, who are Ornaments to their Profeffion, why may not this be the Cafe of the Merchant? As we are indebted to the *Lawyer*, *Phyfician* and *Philofopher* for Improvements in their peculiar Provinces, fo are we to the *Merchant* for the advancement of *Trade* and *Navigation*. For every Attempt of a State to benefit Commerce avails little without a Capacity and Induftry in the Merchant to profecute it with Advantage to himfelf as well as his Country. But what Helps are there for this Purpofe? We abound with Inftitutions for other honourable Claffes of the Community, but what well-regulated Inftitutions have we for the mercantile Order? The Point is, moft are of Opinion, that *Merchandizing* is a light eafy thing, no extraordinary Attainments are neceffary for it; and if a young Fellow is but thruft into a Counting-Houfe, this will infpire him with a Knowledge of Trade and every thing prerequifite to its Execution; and therefore no fuperior Qualifications are expected than what are acquir'd in the common way.

I would not be underftood to infinuate that this Incapacity in young Men is always the Fault of the Mafter, and that *Merchants* in general are guilty of the difhonourable Practice I

B   would

187

would explode, No; these Sheets are no more intended as a general Reproach or Satyr on the one than an Encomium on the other. Sensible I am that too many young People, as well among Merchants as other Ranks of Men of Business, make little use of the great Advantages they enjoy during their time of Servitude; the best Examples, the greatest Incitements to *Industry* and Affiduity have little Influence o'er the defultory and giddy-headed. The Figure in Trade some young *Gentlemen* make to what others do sufficiently discriminates what superior Benefits they have receiv'd. And therefore as this Design is to put the Publick upon their guard with respect to the dishonourable and incapable (for both are equally prejudicial to the Community;) so it is to extol those who are the reverse, excite young Merchants to Application and Ingenuity in their great Profession, and make them sensible what a Blessing it is to be bred under an intelligent, judicious, and conscientious Master, who consults his Reputation in bringing up his Apprentice to make a wise and expert Merchant, as much as he consults the general support of his Credit in his Profession.

And here it will be suggested, perhaps, that this publick Spirit is far from being prevalent on the side of the Majority; whence it will naturally be inferr'd, that more are injur'd than otherwise in their Apprenticeship. Should this be the Case, as indeed there is too much Reason to fear it is, the Question will then be, how is this great Evil to be remedy'd? It is to little purpose to make Discovery of a lurking and destructive Malady without being able to remove it by some sovereign Application. Many have an extraordinary Talent of laughing at the Craft and Errors of Mankind, but few have Fortitude and Prudence personally to engage in their Extirpation: The one is a

Matter

Matter of light Converfation, which many have the Knack of, the other a Work of Labour, Induftry and Refolution, which agrees with few. But to thefe few is the World indebted for the execution of all Defigns of publick Happinefs and Utility. And fuch, we may prefume to fay is the Nature of the prefent. For it is not only to expofe to publick Regard an Evil which appears to be of a very pernicious nature to this Trading Nation, but it is to propofe at the fame time a Remedy ; and fuch a one as is humbly conceiv'd to be adequate to the Diftemper. For having had very particular Occafions of knowing the Nature and Caufe of the Evil here complain'd of, and feeing its fatal Effects to fome; fo for feveral Years paft we have been privately inftrumental in preventing its de-ftructive Confequences to others. Our Knowledge therefore of this Matter under Confideration is not from Hear-fay, and ill-grounded Suggeftions ; it is experimental and practical.

I am well aware of the Antipathy of many to every new Defign, of the Envy of fome, Cenfure and Obloquy of more. But when it ftrikes at the Intereft of many, expofes the un-juftifiable Conduct and Incapacity of others, we muft natu-rally expect that every Artifice will be ufed by thofe who think themfelves affected, to depreciate fuch an Undertaking. It will hardly therefore want an Excufe with the attentive; that we have been fo explicit and diffufive in urging the Ne-ceffity of the prefent Plan; which fhall now be laid open, after having premis'd that this Defign is calculated for none but young Gentlemen of Fortune, who are propos'd to be brought up three or four, or about half a dozen at a time, in our own Counting-Houfe; or in feparate private Apart-ments by themfelves, for fuch who may rather chufe them, and for whom Privacy and Retirement may be moft fuitable.

B 2 *The*

189

The PLAN.

A Thorough Knowledge of Figures being previoufly neceffary to every thing elfe, we propofe to go thro' *methodically*
all the Courfes of *Mercantile Calculations.* And as from the whole
of this Defign we have in view the Improvement of the Reafon
and ftrengthning the Judgment in general; fo nothing, we conceive,
will be more conducive thereto, than demonftrating as we proceed
the *Reafon* and *Foundation* of all Rules given in Arithmetical Operations.   'Tis allowed by all Men of Learning and Science, that
nothing inures the Minds of Young People to clofe Thinking,
Steddinefs and Attention fo much as Mathematical Studies.   The
Rationale of Numbers being founded on thefe Principles, we fhall
be obliged to have fome Recourfe to them in our Demonftrations.
Not that we would be underftood to engrofs too large a Portion of
the Young *Merchant's* Time in Speculations of this Kind, to the
Exclufion of what is more immediately effential : All we aim at
is, to infufe the Habit of juft Reafoning, Reflection and Obfervation; which will certainly be of unfpeakable Benefit thro' the
whole of his Life.   And as the Studies we recommend abound
with Truths the moft certain, fo every other Species of Knowledge,
either of a Mercantile, or any other Nature, may receive Aid
from them.   Probabilities of every Kind, more or lefs remote from
Certainty, will fooner be difcover'd by a Mind a little feafon'd to
Truth and undeniable Reafoning.   There is a general Congruity
and Affinity in all Juft Reafoning; and this Habit happily acquir'd
in one thing, will be eafily transferr'd to any other.   From feeing
the Reafon of the Auxiliary Parts of Mercantile Science, the Mind
will infenfibly be train'd up to difcern thofe of the more grand and
cardinal

190

cardinal Parts of Commerce, and of every Thing that may conduce to Prosperity therein. 'Twould have been needless to have said any thing to justify what is so unexceptionable, were there not some Men of Business, who not only think this Science useless in the Commerce of Life, but that it rather gives the Mind a Bias to Solitude and abstruse Speculation, than a happy Turn for Trade and Business. But since we have declar'd, that our Design is not to go such Lengths as may hurt the Mercantile Life, which is a Life of Action as well as close Reflection, but so far only as may afford due Ballast to poize and keep it steddy, we apprehend no Objection can be made but by such who prefer a Rote and Parrot-like Knowledge to that of Reason and Demonstration.

A General Skill in the Rationale of Numbers, together with an Expertness and Facility in Operation being obtain'd, we next advance to their direct Application in Mercantile Uses. The Business of *Exchanges* being a Capital and Fundamental, as well as a most delicate Part of Mercantile Science, it is propofed to treat this Matter in all its various Lights, and in its full Latitude and Extent. Not only will the most practical and concise Methods of reducing the *Moneys* of any Trading Nation into *Sterling* be exemplify'd in all their Diversity of Cases, but the *Moneys* of one Trading Country into those of any other, confiftent with the Courses of Exchange establish'd throughout *Europe* for that Purpose.

And as the constant Fluctuation of the Prices of Exchange affords daily Prospect of Advantage to those who are capable of embracing them, we shall proceed to what the *Negociators* of Money term the *Arbitration* of *Exchanges*; which tho' a Matter of the greatest Nicety of Calculation, we shall treat with great Amplitude and Universality. This curious Part we shall perform by one general and unerring Rule, founded on Mathematical Principles,
and

and only practised by the ablest and most experienc'd *Negociators* in *Europe*.

Without previous Calculations 'tis certain Merchants frequently draw and remit by meer *Hazard* and *Chance*, not by *Reason* and just *Computation*. On the contrary, with a thorough Knowledge of this Kind, it shall be demonstrated, that no Prospect of Advantage can offer by the Ebbs and Flows of the *Exchange* throughout *Europe*, which will not be easily discernable. The Truth hereof is well known to the judicious and acute *Negociators*, who reap constant Benefit by their superior Skill, while others, ignorant of these Niceties of Calculation, can never hope for any Benefit thereby, which blind Chance and Accident shall not throw in their Way.

Besides the *Arbitration* of *Exchanges*, agreeable to the Variation of the Courses, there is another Branch of Exchange, with which the *English* Merchant should by no Means be unacquainted. We mean the Intrinsick Part of Exchange between *London* and the other Cities, on which Negociations in Bills are usually made. For by knowing the precise Equality between any Sum or Quantity of *English Money* exchanged into Money of a Foreign Country, Regard being had to the Fineness and Weight of both, a Merchant will always be capable of determining to the greatest Exactness the Profit that may arise upon the Exportation and Importation of Coins, *&c.* And here will be taken in the whole Business of *Bullion-Gold* and *Silver*, representing all the proper Calculations necessary to deal therein with Judgment.

Before this Topick of *Exchanges* is concluded, it may not be improper just to intimate, that, with Regard to the Customs and Usages of Merchants, as they relate to Foreign Bills, we have compiled and methodically digested an ample Collection thereof,

drawn

drawn from Practice, in Order to give our Trading Students a familiar Reprefentation of them, which may contribute to prevent Impofition from the Crafty and Ill-defigning, and being unwarily
plunged into litigious Broils; than which nothing is more incompatible with a Life of Traffick.

From Mercantile Computation of all Kinds, we proceed next
to the Art of *Book-keeping* by *Double-Entry*, as now practifed by
the moft skilful Traders in the World. So indifpenfably neceffary
to compleat the *Merchant* is a thorough Knowledge of this *Italian* Manner of adjufting Mercantile Occurrences, that all but
thofe ignorant of the Ways of Merchandizing and this admirable
Method of *Accountantfhip*, fo artfully accommodated thereto,
will judge it the utmoft Rafhnefs and Folly for any Man to prefume
to engage in Trade without a thorough Knowledge of this Art in
particular. For all other Methods of Accounts are attended with
nought but Perplexity and Confufion; whereas fuch is the Excellency of this, that it always keeps the State of a Merchant's Affairs in a Mathematical Exactnefs; and is remarkably preventive
of that Supinenefs and Negligence that unavoidably grows out of
an irregular Counting-Houfe. But all who are acquainted with
it need no Encomium to recommend it to their Regard; and fuch
who are not, can have no Idea of its invaluable Utility and Perfection.

That fuch who apply to us may be thoroughly accomplifhed
in this material Branch, a new *Syftem* of *Practical Accountantfhip*
is compofed, which confifts of fuch a Variety of Foreign and
Domeftick Tranfactions, (not only drawn from our own Practice,
but the moft extenfive and univerfal Courfe of Bufinefs of feveral
of the greateft Merchants in Europe, fome of whofe original
Books are in our Poffeffion) that whoever is capable from the rational

tional Principles of *Accountantship* of *Journalizing*, *Posting* and *Ballancing* this Sett of Books, will never be at a loss to state any Occurrence that can happen in Trade, be it ever so new or intricate. Nor will this great Diversity of real Setts of Account only ground a Gentleman to the greatest Perfection in the *Italian* Art of Accountantship, but at the same time give him an extensive Idea of *Foreign* Trade in general, and illustrate the universal Practice and Negotiation of the *Exchanges* in the most natural and intelligible manner.

But farther, Exportation and Importation leading to the *Custom-House*, a Knowledge of the Duties, Subsidies and Draw-backs, with their arithmetick Computation, naturally becomes a very useful Particular in this Undertaking. This, toge-ther with the Methods of Entring Goods, and all Forms used upon such Occasions, will fully appear thro' the Course of our Practice : There are various other Matters, the natural Conco-mitants of Commerce, as the Business of *Shipping*, Trans-actions and Accounts between *Merchants* and *Masters* of Ships, *Insurancing*, *Bottomree*, &c ; all which shall be rationally and practically represented.

But as the greatest Qualifications to manage and conduct Bu-siness without Ability to procure it, signify little, it will be Time to turn our Thoughts upon such Accomplishments as may have a Tendency thereto. Nothing perhaps will be found more con-ducive to this great End, than an happy Dexterity in maintain-ing an epistolary Correspondence. For as Trade can only be carry'd on by an Intercourse of Letters between the *Merchants* of one Country with those of another, their *Letters* will ever be the *Touchstone* of their Ability, discover who have Heads well turn'd for Business, are actuated by rational Views and Motives, and

and take wife Meafures to fupport and extend their Credit. Since therefore an engaging Faculty this Way is the great recommendatory Talent of a *Young* Merchant, and without which he can never hope to become confiderable in the Trading World, this certainly is a very important Part of his Accomplifhment: And more efpecially fo, fince the Generality is fuppofed, as before hinted, to have no great Foundation in Grammatical Learning; and therefore muft neceffarily ftand in need of Affiftance in this Particular, unlefs *Merchants* have a miraculous Advantage over other Men, by being born *Grammarians*, and writing with Judgment and Propriety by Inftinct or Infpiration. They muft have little Notion of Writing, who imagine that meer Tranfcription of other Men's Letters, and that too with the utmoft Precipitation, will qualify a young *Gentleman* to carry on a genteel and judicious Correfpondence himfelf. That this will not anfwer the End, long Experience of the Difficulties we have feen young Merchants labour under in this Refpect, has fufficiently convinced us. Nothing will effectually do this, unlefs exercifing their own Genius, having their Language corrected, and brought to a due merchantile Chaftity, Elegancy and Standard: This, and this only can make them write like Men of Senfe, and give a Luftre, Weight and Dignity to their other Endowments and Qualifications.

Nor is it propos'd that our young Merchant fhall be brought up to correfpond with Judgment in *Englifh* only, but in the Principal modern Languages alfo. Should not the bare Intimation hereof be fufficiently recommendatory, by the Benefit that may naturally be prefumed to accrue from an Ability to correfpond with *Foreigners* in their own, or the moft univerfal Languages; yet fure the Practice of the moft eminent Traders will give

C

Weight

Weight and Authority to this Branch of our Defign, it being obfervable that fuch of them, who are not able to correfpond in thofe Tongues themfelves, are fo prudent as to procure others to do it for 'em.   But to truft fo momentous a Part of a *Merchant's* Bufinefs, as that of Correfponding is, to the Ability of others, muft be judg'd the higheft Imprudence, if feeing with other Men's Eyes may ever be deem'd fo.

Nor will any one judge our young *Merchant* compleat without a thorough *Geographical* Knowledge of the World.   This, as it is allow'd a neceffary Accomplifhment in every Man, fo it is more eminently fuch in the *Merchant*; the Nature of whofe Employ intimates that he cannot have too familiar an Acquaintance with the Situation, Diftance, Trade and Navigation of all Parts of the Globe.   If *Geography* has always been deem'd one of the Eyes of antient Hiftory, it will never be look'd on as Indifferent to the Tranfactions of the modern Trading World. We propofe therefore not only to be very ample in our *Geographical* Part, but equally fo with refpect to the Part of Trade and Navigation, where we fhall defcribe the chief *Ports, Coafts, Harbours, Rivers,* &c. which our *Ships* frequent, together with the *Rifques* and *Dangers* they run; and reprefent the different *Productions* and *Manufactures,* as alfo the *Exports* and *Imports* of the whole *Trading World.*   We fhall likewife trace the Hiftory and Progrefs of Trade, and deduce the true Caufes of the Decay thereof to Particulars, which will manifeft the Neceffity of all thofe Acquirements above infifted on.

This will further appear, if we confider that *Trade* is of a fluctuating Nature.   That Branch which affords the greateft Advantage at one point of Time, is fcarce worth engaging in at another.   For the greater the Profpect of Intereft is, the greater

is

is the Conflux of *Traders* into that particular Branch. Thus Multitudes ftriking into the fame Trade, foreign Markets are glutted, the Britifh produce and Manufacture becomes a Drug, and confequently the *Profits* thereupon are reduced in Proportion as the Markets Abroad are overftock'd.

If then the moft valuable Parts of our Trade, thro' the imprudent Conduct of fome concern'd in them, are liable to Declenfion in Point of Profit to the *Merchant*, is it not requifite he fhould have a Knowledge of more Branches than one ? Should he not be able with Eafe to turn himfelf from one Branch to another, be always prepared to ftrike into the moft beneficial, and make the beft of the Harveft for the Time being?

It is one of the greateft Niceties, or Myfteries, if you pleafe, of Trade, to procure the largeft fhare of *Commiffion* Bufinefs for the leaft Portion thereof you can give in Return. And undoubtedly the Man of univerfal Knowledge in Trade will, with Regard to this important Particular, have a great Superiority over him whofe Knowledge is narrow and confin'd. Such a one will be ever capable of making rational and advantageous Propofitions to his Correfpondents; and by engaging his own Fortune in *fmall* Proportions, he will keep *large* Capitals of foreign Merchants employ'd for his own Intereft as a *Factor*, and theirs as *Principals*.

But not to enter farther into the *Arcana* of Merchandizing, we fhall only obferve, that fuch is the Nature of this great Undertaking, that the compleat Execution thereof is no way compatible with the Profecution of great and extenfive Bufinefs at the fame time. For this would fo wholly engrofs the Propofers Thoughts from an Attachment to his own Intereft in Trade, that this Defign muft naturally dwindle and degenerate

C 2 far

far below its intended Perfection. On the other hand, for no real Bufinefs to be carry'd on by the Propofer will by no Means admit of this Concern being carried to its intended Pitch of Excellency; for this would be nothing but meer *Theory*, and therefore never anfwer the important End of Practice therein aim'd at. As therefore we fhall not engage fo deeply in Trade, that the regular Courfe of Inftruction propos'd will be inconfiftent therewith; fo we fhall not carry on fuch trifling Bufinefs, which will not effectually reprefent the whole Practice of mercantile Science, and fit a young Gentleman to profecute with Judgment any Scene of Bufinefs proportionate to his own Fortune.

However, left any thing fhould be objected to our *Counting-Houfe* from a Deficiency of Practice, let it not be forgot, as before taken Notice of, that this will be moft amply fupply'd from the great Variety of extenfive and univerfal Practice of Trade we have procur'd; having in our *Counting-Houfe* the *real Books* and *original Letters* of fome of the greateft and moft skilful *Traders England* ever produced. Our young *Merchant* therefore, will not only fee our own daily Practice, have every Branch thereof familiarly and intelligibly explain'd, and act every Part therein in its due Courfe: He will not only have thefe Advantages; but likewife the Benefit of reviewing the largeft Scene of *real Bufinefs* that is to be met with perhaps in the greateft and moft eminent *Counting-Houfe* in all *Europe*. Nor will thefe Courfes of univerfal *Trade* be only explain'd in the moft natural and engaging Manner; but, that they may be thoroughly underftood, and the *Accountantfhip* thereof fully digefted, our young *Merchants* will be obliged to form with their own Hands a large and compleat Sett of Books of this real *foreign Trade*, befides that of our own Bufinefs,

draw

draw out the *Invoyces* and *Accounts* of *Sales* themſelves, and compoſe all Letters correſponding to the Tranſactions. In a Word, every young *Gentleman* will have full Employment; and ſuch only as tends to his *own* Advantage, not that of a *Maſter*. For inſtead of its being for his Intereſt to retard Accompliſhment, or act with the leaſt Diſhonour and Injuſtice, nothing will ſo much promote that as the contrary Conduct; nothing will advance our own Intereſt but promoting that of the young *Merchants* of this Kingdom: And to do that no Labour or Expence has been ſpared. Here ſhall we make the univerſal Practice of *Foreign Trade*, and its *Laws* and *Cuſtoms* both at Home and Abroad our Study: Here ſhall we read the moſt judicious Writers upon merchantile Affairs, which it muſt be allowed, are not to be met with in the *Engliſh* Tongue, unite the Theory and Practice of Commerce, cultivate the *modern Languages*, by conſtant *Reading*, *Writing* and *Converſation*: In ſhort, our Deſign will be a little Kind of *merchantile Univerſity*, where the Minds of young *Merchants* will be formed to Reaſoning and Reflection, and have the Rocks and Sands, that Numbers in Trade have ſpilt upon, familiarly pointed out.

F I N I S.

CHAPTER 6

MALACHY POSTLETHWAYT: ENTRIES FROM HIS Dictionary

The fifth "essay" is not a unified writing, but is instead a collection of related entries from a massive commercial dictionary of the 1750s
(Postlethwayt 1751-55) compiled by the noted (or notorious) English economic
"scribbler" (Redlich 1970, [199]) introduced in chapter 5, Malachy Postlethwayt. The first three items briefly discuss contemporary accounting
practice; the "countinghouse," or headquarters of merchant business; and
basic theory of "merchants' accounts." Reference is made in the second
case to an interesting apprenticeship practice ascribed to the Dutch, by
way of anticipating the author's own plan for mercantile education. The
major entry characterizes "The British Mercantile College," carrying forth
the ideas first presented in The accomplish'd merchant.

"Postlethwayt, the Publicist" (Johnson 1937, 185, chapter title) was
a prolific writer who provided "a good deal of information on eighteenth-
century English business" (Redlich 1970, [199]); and received a full
chapter (providing an excellent survey of his works) within Johnson's
Predecessors of Adam Smith (1937, 185-205). It is questioned, however
(Redlich 1970, [199]), whether a writer whose work was neither systematic,
concise, nor (more emphatically) original (D.n.b. 1917, s.v. "Postlethwayt,
Malachy") was a very "worthy" predecessor. Johnson himself (1937, 196,
205) characterized Rostlethwayt's "most important contribution to economic
literature" as "a crude moasic which lacked cohesion, completeness, and
symmetry."

Besides the dictionary, and prior sequels to The accomplish'd merchant, Postlethwayt during the years 1745-58 published at least eight books or shorter tracts on a variety of topics concerning British foreign trade, half of them relating to Africa (D.n.b. 1917, s.v. "Postlethwayt, Malachy"). That continent had commanded his attention since his appointment by 1738 as a director of the Royal African Company of England (Postlethwayt 1751-55, 1:xiii-xiv), descended from a trading company founded 150 years earlier (Cheney [1904], 86-88), and he urged that its pre-1698 commercial monopoly be restored (Johnson 1937, 356, note 32). The author championed the establishment of British colonies in Africa, in part to reduce competition from English America and, through the slave trade, increase its dependence on the crown (Johnson 1937, 188).

Other works by Postlethwayt included a pamphlet proposing a national reward for development of a workable procedure for using coal to smelt iron; an essay concerning the commerce of France, and a book elaborating a plan for financing the ongoing Seven Years' War (Langford 1984, 400-2) with that country; and a two-volume work outlining a long-term British commercial strategy. The first publication anticipated the author's later advocacy of "public assistance for all improvements in industrial technology," while the last one was his principal attempt to construct an economic theory (Johnson 1937, 189, quoted, 190, 196). Despite his severe criticism of Britain's commercial interest explained and improved, as quoted above, Johnson (1937, 196-204) devoted extended treatment to the theoretical work.

Malachy Postlethwayt's foremost work, overall, was The universal dictionary of trade and commerce . . . (1751-55), covering the commercial world in alphabetical sequence from "A" to "Zinck." The first edition (Postlethwayt 1751-55) appeared in respective volumes of 1751 and 1755 of 1,017 and

202

856 folio, or oversized, pages, not counting front matter or folded plates.

Later editions appeared in 1757, repeating those page totals ([Herwood]

1938, 76, s.v. "Savary des Bruslons"); 1766, without page numbering (Redlich

1970, 202); and 1774, as a posthumous reprint of the third edition (Johnson

1937, 355-56, note 25).   In each case the "British Mercantile College"

article directly followed the alphabetically sequenced entry on "Mercantile

Accountantship" (Redlich 1970, 202).

The full title of the dictionary (Postlethwayt 1751-55, titles) sug-

gests misleadingly that it was largely a translation of an earlier work by

a French author.   As the king's inspector general of manufactures at the

Paris customhouse, Jacques Savary des Brulons, 1657-1716, had developed a

remarkable dictionary project from a plan to prepare an alphabetical listing

of the merchandise passing through customs along with commercial and manu-

facturing terminology in general.   Savary was assisted by his brother, who

completed the Dictionnaire universel de commerce (Hollander 1953, 435n) for

publication in three volumes, 1723-30.   The French merchant Jacques Savary

quoted by Postlethwayt (1751-55, 2:218) in "The British Mercantile College"

was the father of the dictionary compilers (Johnson 1937, 356, note 27).

As a matter of record, two thirds of Postlethwayt's entry headings,

980 of 1,465, were drawn from Savary.   The connection between the two works

was nonetheless very limited.   The French author had employed almost ten

times the number of headings carried over to the English work, and in many

cases of common labeling Postlethwayt's actual entry was "either greatly

expanded [for example (Johnson 1937, 404, quoted, 404n), from one page to

sixteen for the term '"Assurance"'] or totally different" (Fraser 1938,

28).   Leading thematic differences were (Johnson 1937, 402-3):

Postelthwayt's greater interest in political problems; his more intense economic nationalism; and [especially] his exuberant belief in the economic usefulness of experimental philosophy . . . [, that is,] the nationalistic-economic functions of science."

If Postlethwayt in his title overstated his indebtedness to one Frenchman, he nowhere acknowledged any reliance on the work of another one, Richard Cantillon, c. 1680-1734. Yet the latter's Essai sur la nature du commerce en general, a "seminal" if relatively neglected contribution to economic theory that influenced both Smith and (earlier) Francois Quesnay (Landreth 1976, 7), appeared virtually in full within the dictionary, divided largely among thirteen entries (Johnson 1937, 204, 361, note 157). Indeed, partially in deference to the wishes of the murdered French financier's family the privately circulated Cantillon manuscript had evidently not previously been published (Johnson 1937, 185, 204; and Landreth 1976, 7). Apologists for Postlethwayt have accordingly suggested that he may only have been motivated by sympathetic respect in omitting reference to Cantillon in 1751 and '55 (and again in 1757, in another work borrowing substantially from his essay) (Fraser 1938, 26; and Johnson 1937, 190, 204).

The traditional view of Postlethwayt as a plagiarist (D.n.b. 1917, s.v. "Postlethwayt, Malachy) has been challenged based on extensive attribution made to other writers both in the Dictionary and other works (Johnson 1937, 405-8). Fraser concedes having noted more than five hundred attributions, many of them to "legal, scientific, historical and geographical authorities." Noting that frequent references only strengthened the work's mark of authority, however, Fraser (1938, 26) asserts that Postlethwayt was "an undoubted plagiarist" who "did his borrowing in a manner calculated to put the casual reader off the scent."

As just one example, famous author Daniel Defoe was cited as the source of two dictionary passages, but not mentioned in some seventy other items

204

reflecting substantial "verbal similarities" to his published writing. In other cases, acknowledgments were actually part of material that Postle-thwayt had lifted, without attribution, from other writers (Fraser 1938, 27, 28, quoted).

However blemished he may have been in terms of literary honesty, Postlethwayt demonstrated substantial acquaintance with literature from many fields. For example, material relating to chemistry, an area of intense interest since he and a partner had been defrauded in a "disastrous incursion into the lead industry" (Fraser 1937, 29, quoted; and Johnson 1937, 185-86), suggests familiarity with standard texts and scientific periodicals from England, France, Germany, and Sweden. The author seems to have been "an ardent experimental chemist," a deen observer of contemporary manufacturing processes, and, in a minor way, a mathematician. Knowledge of five foreign languages is reflected, with the qualification that many of the relevant books quoted had already been translated into English or French (Fraser 1938, 26, 26n, 30, quoted, 31).

In keeping with Postlethwayt's domimant interest in foreign trade, the polical articles in the dictionary emphasize the development of British economic strength. "[V]iolently nationalist," they exhibit "marked Fran-cophobia," an irony in light of the absence of anti-British rhetoric in Savary's dictionary (Fraser 1938, 32).

According to Postlethwayt (1751-55, 1:xiii-xiv), the dictionary was an outgrowth, initially unforeseen, of an intensive course of commercial study and activity that he had pursued since writing The accomplish'd mer-chant, around 1730. Evidently he was disappointed with early response to the work, 20-25 years in the making, for he rhetorically asked in 1757 (Johnson 1937, 186, quoted, 355, note 15) whether a national that had "accepted the literary services of a man's whole lifetime, and yet found for that man no patron, no vacant government post, no reward" must not "be charged with ingratitude." Bitterly contrasting his station to that of his predecessor Jacques Savary de Brulons, Postlethwayt threatened to abandon his writing unless some measure of reward or appreciation were extended him. His last known new publication appeared a year later (D.n.b. 1917, s.v. Postlethwayt, Malachy"), and he died, evidently in poverty, in 1767 (Johnson 1937, 186, quoted, 187).

The principal component of the following "essay," appearing in 1755, was (by supposition) Postlethwayt's fifth published proposal for a new form of mercantile academy. Preceding it were (1) The accomplish'd merchant, [c. 1730], 21 pages, and (Redlich 1970, 200-3):

2. The British mercantile academy: or the accomplished merchant, coauthored with James Royston, 1750, 74 pages
3. The merchant's public counting-house: or, New mercantile institution, 1750, 84 pages
4. 2d ed. of item 3, with supplement, 1751, 111 pages.

Following private printing of item 1, the subsequent volumes (by Postlethwayt, "Esq") were each published in London by John and Paul Knapton (Redlich 1970, inserts following 202). Throughout, the "teaching program" remained unchanged, with considerable emphasis on mathematics, and study of currency exchange, double-entry accounts, customhouse business, correspondence in English and foreign languages, and geography. As total length increased, the proportion devoted to the basic plan steadily declined, as more explanation and '"frills"' were added (Redlich 1970, 203). According to one commentator (Hollander 1953, 435, 435n) on the dictionary version of the proposal, Postlethwayt had in an otherwise independent entry employed Savary's "itemization of the knowledge needed by every merchant," as published in 1726. The Dictionnaire universal de commerce would in that case have influenced the educational project from the start.

Having only "humbly submitted" his plan "to the public consideration," Postlethwayt (1751-55, 2:218) was evidently not keeping a mercantile school in 1755. A few years earlier, the title pages of the two editions of The merchant's public counting-house (Postlethwayt 1751; and Redlich 1970, 2d insert following 202) had said that "[t]he PLAN" would "be carried into Execution" by the author "and Company." Facing the 1751 page, however, was an advertisement of a "New Mercantile Institution" that Postlethwayt "and Company" were conducting (Postlethwayt 1751, 111) outside London, near Hempsted. The one-page ad is reprinted as the closing selection below, directly preceding translations of the several French passages cited within "The British Mercantile College." The reference made to the adjoining (and perhaps coordinate) "New Classical Academy" is especially interesting in view of its schoolmaster's chaplainry, discussed in relation to William Gordon in chapter 8.

In a postscript to the 1751 work, Postlethwayt (111, emphasis in original, with place names in capitals) gave road directions for reaching his school:

> The direct Road to THE NEW MERCHANTILE INSTITUTION, at Waterside, in Hertfordshire, is through Edgar, and Watford, and from thence to Hempsted, and about a quarter of a Mile further is Waterside. But,
>
> The best Road at all Seasons, though it is something about, is directly through St. Alban's to Hempsted.
>
> The Berkamsted Stage goes directly to Hempsted, twice a Week, Tuesdays and Saturdays, from the Bell Inn, near Furnival's Inn, in Holborn, London.

Postlethwayt closes (1751, 111) by citing wine merchant James Royston, his recent coauthor, as the school's London correspondent.

Appendix 2 supplies translations for the French and (representing one instance only) Latin passages from "The British Mercantile College."

207

The following are the page numbers in the 1751 edition of
Postlethwayt's DICTIONARY which the reprinted entries are
taken from:

Volume I
ACCOUNTANT, or ACCOMPTANT   10
ACCOUNTANTSHIP   10-11
ACCOUNTING-HOUSE, COUNTING-HOUSE,
or COMPTING-HOUSE   11

Volume II
MERCANTILE ACCOUNTANTSHIP,
or MERCHANT'S ACCOUNTS 210-211
BRITISH MERCANTILE COLLEGE   218-236

THE

UNIVERSAL DICTIONARY

OF

TRADE and COMMERCE,

Tranflated from the French of the Celebrated

Monfieur SAVARY,

INSPECTOR-GENERAL of the MANUFACTURES for the King,
at the Cuftom-houfe of *PARIS:*

WITH LARGE

Additions and Improvements,

Incorporated throughout the Whole WORK;

Which more particularly accommodate the fame to the

TRADE and NAVIGATION

Of thefe Kingdoms,

And the LAWS, CUSTOMS, and USAGES,

To which all Traders are fubject.

By MALACHY POSTLETHWAYT, Efq;

LONDON:
Printed for JOHN and PAUL KNAPTON, in Ludgate-Street.
MDCCLI.

ACCOUNTANT, or ACCOMPTANT, one who is not only well skilled in cafting up all forts of accounts, and readily performs all arithmetical operations, but who is verfed in the art of book-keeping, by charge and difcharge, or by debtor and creditor.

This application is applicable to a perfon, or officer, appointed to keep the account of a public company, or office, as the accountant of the *South-Sea*, or *India* company, or of the *Bank*, the *Cuftom-houfe*, of *Excife*, &c.

ACCOUNTANTSHIP, comprehends not only a fkill in figures or arithmetic, and a knowledge in the art of accounts-keeping by debtor and creditor, or by the method of regular charge and difcharge, according to the nature of the several accounts; which method keeps every fort of account, if they are ever to command it, fwom what foever it springs, added at his firft rife, and be entered on the face thereof, on the debit fide from the funds, and on the credit fide, of the fum total of the fame from that of one proper.

To be fundamentally grounded in all practical operations, requires a competent acquaintance with geometry and algebra, becaufe the promoters could not know what demonftrations certain rules, and theorems, whereby to calculate numerically, in the moft correct manner, are to be properly grounded in the nature of debtor and creditor, requires a knowledge in the art of keeping accounts, according to the method of double entry, or which is commonly called by the *Italian* method of *Book-keeping*, or by the name of *Merchant's Accounts*.

From hence it may be obferved, that no perfon can be properly faid to be duly fkilled in *accountantfhip*, without being fkilled in the art of debtor and creditor, as well as in that of numbers; nor, on the other hand, does any one deferve the name of an accountant, who is only acquainted with book-keeping, and not with figures.

The art of accountantfhip is not only applicable to the regular adjuftment of the variety of tranfactions among traders of every denomination, but alfo to the private affairs of gentlemen and noblemen. And as it well becomes all perfons of the greateft diftinction to take due care of their eftates; fo nothing, perhaps, can have a happier tendency to that end, than a knowledge in the art of debtor and creditor, as well as that of numbers. For 'merchants accounts, fays Mr *Locke*, ' though a fcience not likely to help a gentleman to get an ' eftate, yet poffibly there is not any thing of more ufe and ' efficacy to make him preferve the eftate he has. 'Tis feldom ' obferved, that he who keeps an account of his income and ' expence, and thereby has conftantly under view the courfe ' of his domeftic affairs, lets them run to ruin. And I doubt ' not but many a man gets behind-hand before he is aware, or ' runs farther on, when he is once in, for want of this care, ' or the fkill to do it. I would therefore advife all gentlemen ' to learn perfectly *merchants accounts*, and not to think it a ' fkill that belongs not to them, becaufe it has received it's ' name, and has been chiefly practifed by men of traffic.'

Nor is accountantfhip lefs ufeful to the gentlemen of the law, than to private gentlemen; and not only to thofe who are intended for the bar, but to all follicitors and attornies; litigations between traders making fo confiderable a proportion of the bufinefs of our courts of law and equity. Without the perfect knowledge of debtor and creditor in particular, accounts may be fo craftily and fophiftically ftated, as to deceive the moft upright judge and jury, as well as the council, if they are not capable of unravelling them in the courfe of their pleadings.

Perfons of diftinction alfo, who are concerned in the chief pofts of the public revenue, or who act in the fenatorial capacity, cannot be too well fkilled in accountantfhip. The one will thereby be enabled to acquit himfelf with credit and reputation in whatever branch of the revenue he fhall be employed; and the other will become perfectly acquainted with the finances and money affairs of the kingdom. For fuch is the nature and excellency of the mercantile art of debtor and creditor by double entry, that it is as eafily applicable to the accounts of nations as to thofe of traders, or private gentlemen, millions being as familiarly adjufted thereby, as hundreds of pounds. When once a perfon is acquainted with the feveral funds from whence the national revenue arifes, as likewife their appropriations to the payment of interest of fuch of the national creditors; when it is duly obferved in what manner the deficiencies of fome funds are occafionally fupplied, and the furplufages of others transferred: when the general heads of fuch accounts are underftood from the ftatutes, and the accounts annually laid before the parliament are duly attended to, any gentleman, well

grounded in the art of debtor and creditor, may obtain as complete a knowledge of the money affairs of the nation, as of his own private concerns: that is, when he is a mafter of the facts relating thereunto, and the diftinct heads under which the funds are kept, he will be capable fo to ftate thefe accounts by way of charge and difcharge, or debit and credit, as always to have a fatisfactory view before him of the ftate of the national debts and funds, and of the feveral variations they fhall from time to time undergo. See MERCHANTS ACCOUNTS, or the nature of debtor and creditor, according to the method of double entry.

ACCOUNTING-HOUSE, COUNTING-HOUSE, or COMPTING-HOUSE, is a place fet apart by merchants, and other traders, wherein to tranfact their bufinefs, and to keep their books of accounts and vouchers relating thereunto.

'Tis the cuftom of the *Dutch* merchants in *Holland* to keep a kind of *Public Counting-houfes*, for the reception of a number of gentlemen's fons of fortune, more particularly of the *Englifh*, *Scots*, and *Irifh*, who pay them at the rate of one hundred pounds fterling per ann. and continue with them upon that footing from year to year, as long as they pleafe. 'Tis common to fee ten, or a dozen, or more of thefe young people in a *Dutch* counting-houfe; fome being weak enough to imagine, that a foreign country is the beft place to be bred in, in order to underftand the *Britifh* commerce, and that there are none elfe who refide in *England*, are able to qualify thefe fons fo well as foreigners who refide abroad.

An humble attempt, however, was lately made to introduce fomething of the like kind of practice, of keeping of a *Public Counting-houfe* in our own country; and accordingly, a tract was publifhed for that intent, entitled *The Merchant's Public Counting-houfe*, or the *New Mercantile Inftitution*: wherein is fhewn the neceffity of young merchants being bred to trade with greater advantages than they ufually are: with a practicable plan for that purpofe.

In this plan is difcuffed, in miniature, the various qualifications, which are ever juftly neceffary to form the accomplifhed *Britifh* merchant. And, however low an idea fome may entertain of the abilities of fuch a trader, 'tis prefumed that, upon the perufal of the before-mentioned tract, they will be of a different opinion Perfons of candor and impartiality, it is imagined, will therein fee, that it is not thrufting a young fpark into any counting-houfe, either at home, or abroad, that is likely to qualify him to fave, much lefs to improve, an handfome fortune by merchandifing. Thofe who are defirous of perufing this tract, may meet with it at Meff. *John* and *Paul Knapton's*, bookfellers in *Ludgate-ftreet*, by afking for *Poftlethwayt's Merchant's Public Counting-houfe, or New Mercantile Inftitution*, &c.

THE

UNIVERSAL DICTIONARY
OF
TRADE and COMMERCE,

Translated from the French of the Celebrated

Monfieur SAVARY,

INSPECTOR-GENERAL of the MANUFACTURES for the King,
at the Cuftom-Houfe of *PARIS:*

WITH LARGE

Additions and Improvements,
Incorporated throughout the Whole WORK;

Which more particularly accommodate the fame to the

TRADE and NAVIGATION
Of thefe Kingdoms,

And the LAWS, CUSTOMS, and USAGES,
To which all Traders are fubject.

By MALACHY POSTLETHWAYT, Efq;

Prodeffe quàm Confpici.

Je crois avoir rendu fervice au commerce, de l'avoir fait connoître comme fcience dans une nation qui n'y avoit
attaché pendant long-tems qu'une idée méchanique, & chez laquelle l'idée du noble n'eft pas toujours jointe à
celle de l'utile bien reconnu. La politique & l'humanité affigneront au commerce une place honorable parmi les
autres fciences ; & la profeffion du commerce fera noble, lorfque ceux que leur range ou leur génie diftinguent
des autres hommes, parleront en fa faveur. ELEMENS DU COMMERCE.

VOL. II.

LONDON:
Printed for JOHN and PAUL KNAPTON, in Ludgate-Street.
MDCCLV.

MERCANTILE ACCOUNTANTSHIP, or what is usually called MERCHANTS ACCOUNTS, according to the method of double entry, as practised by the most eminent merchants throughout the world.

Before the reader enters upon what follows, he is desired to consult the following articles, viz. ACCOUNTANTSHIP, ACCOUNTING-HOUSE, ANONYMOUS, BANKING, BOOK-KEEPING, DEBTOR and CREDITOR, and LEDGER; which, considered together, in the various lights there represented, will render what we have further to say very easy and intelligible, and make him a complete accountant in any kind of business whatsoever.

INTRODUCTION.

In keeping of mercantile accounts there are three principal books, the waste-book, the journal, and the ledger.

I. In the waste-book are entered, in the plainest manner, as bought, sold, received, paid, &c. all transactions of commerce, with their date, sums, conditions, and every particular circumstance relating thereto.

II. The journal is, for substance, the same as the waste-book; but, as this must be more fairly written, so it must be expressed in a very different manner, more merchant-like, as it is a preparatory for the ledger. In this book the debit and credit are rationally fixed and settled, according to the principles of accountantship; and, therefore, this requires the book-keeper's hand: and, because in journalizing the waste-book lies all the difficulty of account-keeping, we have exhibited the nature and reason thereof upon a single sheet, for the use of immediate inspection. Suppose, for example, that you have entered, in your waste-book, Received of A. B. in full 50 l. To post this into your journal, look for the article money received for a bond, or, otherwise, cash is made debtor to the person that owed it you: therefore in the journal, after the date, say, Cash debtor to A. B. received in full 50 l.

III. The ledger is the grand and principal book of accounts, which, when duly posted, regulates and adjusts all your concerns with respect to men, money, and merchandize, and brings all things under their proper heads, and to their respective accounts. And, as this book gives you a comprehensive view of all your negociations, so it does a complete balance of the whole year's traffic.

As the waste-book is posted into the journal, so the journal is into the ledger; and, if the waste-book be judiciously posted into the journal, with respect to it's debtors and creditors, in the proper journal-phrase, as follows, under the letter (J) it will be very easy to post the journal into the ledger, if you remember the following

Directions to post journal entries into the ledger.

1. In every account there is a debit and a credit part; and, though the journal doth not express the credit part, yet it is understood, for the person or thing that follows the word (To) in the creditor, or, instead of the word (To) read creditor. Take the instance above; cash debtor to A. B. received in full 50 l.—Or thus, debtor cash 50 l. creditor A. B. 50 l. Turn, therefore, to ledger to cash account, as suppose folio (1) and, in debtor side, write, Date Jan. (1) To A. B. received in full (fol. 9.) 50 l. then turn to A. B's account (fol. 9.) and in credit thereof write, Jan. (1) By cash received of him in full (fol. 1.) 50 l. From hence observe, besides the date in ledger-margin, that, after the word (To) in debit, follows immediately A. B. viz. he that must be made creditor; and, after the date and word (By) in the credit-entry, follows cash, the name of the account that is made debtor; and that debtor and creditor counter-parts refer to each other, and stand in journal as before margin thus:

(1) Debtor,
(9) Creditor.

2. Observe, once for all, whatsoever you debit in one place in your ledger, must have an equivalent credit in another. And notwithstanding in sundry accounts there is one article debtor, and several creditors, as in letter (V) or several debtors and one creditor, as in letter (L) be that as it happens; yet debit and credit are always equal, or as much value as you debit you must credit, before your journal-entry is duly posted in the ledger.

3. Besides a reference column, another inside column must be kept for the quantity of goods, as hogsheads, pipes, bales, &c. On the debtor side must contain the quantity bought in, and on the credit the quantity sold out, by which you know at any time how much of each you have unsold, &c.

Note, Although we have described the nature and use of these three essential books, wherein a merchant's dealings might be all kept, yet, by many classes of traders, the waste-book may be omitted, and the journal and ledger be sufficient; for the book-keeper might journalize at once every occurrence, without entering them at all in a waste-book. But, he not being always in the way, nay, sometimes obliged to make entries in a hurry, it is proper, in general, to keep a waste-book, from which he may at more leisure correctly and fairly form his journal.

But, to prevent those books filling up, merchants, by experience, find it necessary to keep other books subservient to them, as a cash-book, book of charges of merchandise, book of household expences, factory or invoice-book, the sale's-book; the nature and use of which are as follow:

IV. The

IV. The cash-book. This book is folioed, as the ledger, and kept to cast the account of cash there, and prevent receipts and payments being entered at all in the journal. On the left-hand side you make cash debtor to all you receive, and on the right-hand side cash creditor by all you pay.— And, at the end of the month, you may post it directly to the ledger, or, as usual, make two journal entrances, viz. cash debtor to sundries for all the receipts, and sundries debtor to cash for all the payments of the month: so, by the help of this book, you will have but 12 lines in the cash-account in the ledger on the debit, and 12 on the credit, for the 12 months. But some chuse to post their cash weekly, that they may more easily recollect any omission or mistake. Note, A book is said to be folioed, when, on opening, the right-hand side and left (though two pages) are but one folio.

V. The book of charges of merchandise is only paged, in which are entered down promiscuously the charges attending each sort of goods or voyage daily as they occur, whether belonging to yourself or others, or for company account. And the respective goods or voyages are made debtors for their proper share of charges to account of charges of merchandize. And, at the end of each month, your cash must have credit for the whole charges of the month.

VI. The book of household expences falls under the care of the housekeeper, who might put down the disbursements for family provisions, &c. house-rent, servant's wages, schooling, &c. perishing goods, as earthen-ware (but durable goods, as beds, chests of drawers, &c. do more properly belong to account of household furniture) this may be cast up once a month, or otherwise; and, having paid your housekeeper the month's disbursements, credit your cash as before; then add up your month's payments in the cash-book, which journalized, sundries (and among the rest these accounts, charges of merchandize, and house expences) will be debtors to cash their respective sums.

VII. The factory or invoice-book, is paged and used to copy out verbatim the invoice of goods you send abroad, whether for your own or others, or company account.

VIII. The book of sales is folioed as the ledger, into which is copied an exact account of sales which you send your employer; the credit side whereof contains the sales when, to whom, what quantity and price, whether for cash, barter, or to bd. and &. on time. On the debit the particular charges, abatements, commissions, and nett proceeds. But we are far from thinking it necessary that a learner should have copies of these five last subservient books: such a multiplicity of books would serve to amuse, rather than to instruct; when a specimen of all these might be given him in one single sheet of paper. To these books might be added, the book for copying letters, the book for copying bills, a remembrancer or pocket-book, and the receipt-book; but, as these are generally known, so their names carry in them a sufficient description.

Note, To save the labour of opening an account in the ledger for every person, the merchant erects a general account, the debit whereof takes in those several small dealers that owe, their respective names, to what account, and sum. And, as they pay, he discharges each, mentioning his name on the credit side also; where the merchant likewise (in posting his journal) carries those little debts he owes, and, as he pays, debits the persons.

In like manner, the merchant opens an account of merchandise general, into the debit whereof he posts all those little parcels and sorts of goods he buys in, and not like to deal much in, and for which already he has no particular account opened in the ledger; and, as they are sold, he gives the said

212

account credit, expreſſing the name of goods and quantity, in every entry, whether in debit or credit: by which, with a little trouble, he knows how much of any ſort of theſe petty wares are left, as effectually, as though he had kept a particular account for each.

If at any time you make a wrong entry in the ledger, in debit or credit ſide, make a croſs in the margin thus X, and write, in the oppoſite ſide, To or By an error committed in credit or debit of this account, wrote off the ſum, &c.

The BRITISH MERCANTILE COLLEGE, humbly ſubmitted to public conſideration.

Novimus novitios quoſdam, qui cum ſe mercaturae vix dederunt, in magnis mercimoniis ſe implicantes, rem ſuam male geſſiſſe. Et profecto imperitos mercatores multis captionibus ſuppoſitos, multorumque inſidiis expoſitos experientia videmus. Mercatores actus ſui rationem conficiant, & calamo non parcant.

Stracch. de mercatura, par. 2. p. 357.

L'ignorance des negocians vient, de ce que dans leur commencement ils manquent d'inſtruction, n'ayans pas fait leur apprentiſſage chez d'habiles marchands, qui avent toutes les qualites requiſes pour bien montrer le commerce. Il eſt impoſſible qu'un negociant reuſſiſe dans ſes entrepriſes, s'il ne ſçait parfaitement ſa profeſſion.

Parfait Negociant de Savary.

Of the neceſſity of the eſtabliſhment of a MERCANTILE COLLEGE in Great-Britain, for the education of BRITISH MERCHANTS, with greater advantages than they uſually have.

In order to animate the French nation in general to the vigorous purſuit and cultivation of it's trading intereſt, that celebrated ſtateſman Monſ. Colbert prevailed on the late biſhop of Avranches, a gentleman well read in antiquity, to write the hiſtory of the commerce and navigation of the ancients[*]; which had ſuch happy effect in the kingdom, when communicated to the moſt diſtinguiſhed perſons in it, that, from being lukewarm in regard to the national intereſts of trade, they became it's ſtrenuous advocates and zealous promoters.

[*] Hiſtoire du Commerce, & de la Navigation des Anciens. Par M. Huet, ancien eveque d'Avranches.

And, indeed, it appears from the writings of that learned and judicious prelate, that commerce, when wiſely cheriſhed and encouraged, was the firmeſt ſupport of the power of moſt of the illuſtrious ſtates and empires in ancient ſtory.

The Phœnicians, the Carthaginians, the Athenians, and Rhodians, acquired immenſe treaſure and power by the induſtry and ingenuity of their merchants, in extending their traffic. Nor did the Romans, though chiefly addicted to arms, neglect to carry on an extenſive trade to Sicily, Spain, Egypt, Barbary, and the Euxine Sea; but their perpetual victories, and the rapidity of their conqueſts, made them loſe ſight of their commercial intereſts; which, if properly cultivated, might have maintained their power, even to the end of time.

Where the people of any ſtate or empire depend altogether upon agriculture, and there are few or no traders in a nation, unleſs of the retailing and mechanic ſort; and where the farmer and the planter are the moſt uſeful members of the community; the higheſt regard will always be paid to theſe orders of men. Accordingly we find, that in the inland provinces of Aſia, they were formerly held in the moſt honourable eſtimation; and the nobles of theſe countries treated all traders with contempt; whilſt in ancient Egypt, a country naturally formed for commerce and navigation, the ſhepherd and the farmer were looked on as a deſpicable rank of men, and traders maintained their principal dignity and ſuperiority in the ſtate. Among the Tyrians, they had ſo great a ſhare of honour and power, that an inſpired writer has told us, THEIR MERCHANTS WERE PRINCES.

In free ſtates, ſuch are the natural and happy effects of commerce, that it contributes at the ſame time to aggrandize the prince, and to preſerve and extend the liberty of the ſubject: and arbitrary governments are ſo ſenſible of the benefit of traffic, that we ſee them earneſtly bent on it's advancement, whenever their wiſeſt and beſt miniſters have had the management of their affairs. Inſomuch that I believe I may venture to ſay, that it is by a rivalſhip in trade, that our neareſt and moſt potent enemy carries on a kind of warfare againſt us, more certainly deſtructive than their arms[*].

[*] This is demonſtrated in various parts of our Dictionary of Commerce.

The peculiar importance of a well regulated and extenſive commerce to the proſperity, or rather to the very being of theſe kingdoms, is ſo well underſtood, that it is now needleſs to carry theſe reflections home to ourſelves. Trade, it is to be hoped, will ever be the chief object of our public care. But the wiſeſt laws, and the beſt concerted encouragements, are not alone ſufficient to carry our commerce to it's utmoſt extent, or to ſupport it in a ſtate of health and vigour: ſomething will ſtill be wanting, which lies beyond the reach of laws, and which private perſons muſt acquire to themſelves; I mean a proper mercantile education: for, unleſs merchants are ſkilful and judicious in improving and cultivating the practical arts of trade, the beſt laws will prove little better than a dead letter; it is the intelligent trader who muſt give them ſpirit, and render them operative and beneficial.

For erudition in almoſt every other branch of ſcience, it muſt be acknowledged, we abound with the beſt regulated inſtitutions. I wiſh we could ſay the like in relation to the mercantile profeſſion. But, what well eſtabliſhed ſeminaries have we for the accompliſhment of that moſt conſiderable part of the Britiſh community? Certain I am that we have none, which are properly adapted to the peculiar nature of their province, and it's ſupreme utility to the ſtate in general. The cauſe to which this may be chiefly attributed, is not difficult to be diſcovered. Too many, who fit out in the capacity of merchants, are apt to flatter themſelves that they ſtand in need of little other qualification, than a round capital, and an adventurous diſpoſition. Buying and ſelling, paying and receiving, exporting and importing, as they think, comprehend the whole circle and myſtery of mercantile tranſactions.

When a low idea is thus entertained of the accompliſhments neceſſary for this employment, it is no wonder that ſo little regard, in general, is had to the education of thoſe who are intended for it. The conſequences hereof are fatal to numbers, who ruſh headlong into commerce, deſtitute almoſt of every one of thoſe accompliſhments indiſpenſably neceſſary, and become a ſacrifice to their folly and temerity[*].

[*] I knew a conſiderable trader in the city of London, who could neither write nor read; he made ſhift, however, to keep his head above water for many years, though he ſwam with bladders, prepared by thoſe who intended his drowning at laſt; and it is not to be admired, that bankruptcy was his fate. And numbers of bankrupts, I have known, are ſhamefully deficient in the ordinary accompliſhments requiſite for the merchant; but, if every one who pretumes to take upon him this reſpectable character, was obliged to paſs an examination by a board of ſkilful merchants, before he was admitted to practice; I am perſuaded, it would have as good an effect in regard to the intereſt of trade and traders in general, as the ſuffering no one to adminiſter medicine in any ſhape whatever would have upon the lives of his majeſty's ſubjects, till they had paſſed a due examination by the Royal College of phyſicians.

We daily ſee many, by their ſuperior qualifications, from very ſlender beginnings, accumulate great riches by merchandizing; while others, from commencing with plentiful fortunes, have, in the ſame courſe, been reduced to the loweſt penury. This ſeems ſtrange to the undiſcerning, but is eaſily accounted for; ſince they muſt have very little knowledge of the trading world, and leſs acquaintance with the practical arts of commerce, who can form a contemptible opinion of the qualifications neceſſary to the foreign trader. Without acquaintance in the produce and manufactures of the commercial world, and in the laws of our own and foreign countries relative to general trade; without abilities to obtain the beſt intelligence, in order to ſtrike the critical time when and where, exportation or importation from nation to nation, drawing, remitting, and negociating foreign bills, invite to the beſt advantage: without knowledge of the duties, impoſts, ſubſidies, drawbacks, bounties, and all other charges and allowances at home and abroad, to which trade is ſubject, is it impoſſible that any previous calculation can be made, whether an adventure will turn to account or not. If the merchant be not thoroughly ſkilled in foreign monies and exchanges, as alſo in foreign weights and meaſures, and the methods of reducing thoſe of one nation reciprocally into thoſe of others, how ſhall he be able to judge of foreign INVOICES and ACCOUNTS of SALES[*]? And, if he be not

213

perfectly acquainted with the arts of arbitrating the foreign exchanges with accuracy, he cannot embrace those daily benefits by the negociation of them, which their perpetual fluctuation affords. Nor is a knowledge of the intrinsic value of foreign specie less necessary than of the extrinsic par of exchange, in order to deal occasionally between country and country, in the export or import of foreign coins, and bullion gold and silver to the best advantage: in fine, the merchant destitute of this series of information, and talents to apply it to the most beneficial purposes in every shape, can never hope to reap any considerable profit from his profession, or sustain the character he bears with any sort of dignity. He must owe his success, if he has any, to fortunate hits, and unexpected advantages; things which no prudent man will chuse to depend upon, for the whole prosperity of his life.

* See the articles INVOICE, and ACCOUNT of SALES.

To the ignorant in these matters, commerce is but a game of chance, where the odds are against the player. But to the accomplished merchant it is a science, where still can scarce fail of it's reward: and, while the one is wandering about on a pathless ocean without a compass, and depends on the winds and tides to carry him into his port, the other goes steadily forward, in a beaten track, which leads him directly, if no extraordinary accident intervenes, to wealth and honour.

Whoever turns his thoughts on the stupendous circulation of paper-property throughout the world, by inland and foreign bills; on the various customs and usages established among traders in their money-negociations, for the support of universal credit; on the numberless different transactions, which diversify the business of the merchant; as buying and selling, exporting and importing, for proper, company, or commission account; drawing on, remitting to, and freighting, or hiring out ships for various parts of the world at the same time: whoever duly considers the skill in figures and accountantship *, requisite so to adjust and methodise this great variety of transactions, whereby such trader may always have the true representation of his affairs before him; together with the judgment to conduct such a complication of occurrences, and address to maintain a general correspondence in our own, or the more universal languages, cannot but see the extent of a course of education proper to form so distinguished a character.

* See the following PLAN of mercantile erudition.

Notwithstanding this, nothing is more certain, than that no gentlemen in the general labour under greater disadvantages in point of erudition.— To trace this matter more minutely. Few, very few, have more than a smattering of Latin and Greek, and a very superficial knowledge of figures and accounts. With this very small stock of useful literature, our tyro is turned into the practical counting-house; and, when he is there, the eager pursuit of interest in the master, who has not leisure to attend to his instruction, will not admit of his making a greater proficiency in mercantile knowledge, than what self-application shall lead him to. Here the flower of youth, we find, is oftener ripe for pleasurable impressions; and the generality of young people of plentiful fortunes are so far from spontaneously applying to the severity of business, that they rather look upon it in the light of hackney-drudgery ?.*

* This has been, and I am afraid daily is, the cause of the ruin of many gentlemen's sons of fortune.

Such indeed is the strength of natural discernment in some, and such sometimes the uncommon attention to business in others, that they make little difficulty in breaking through every obstacle to knowledge, if they obtain but a glimmering light: the case of the generality is far different. But should a merchant, or his principal clerks on whom he depends, have both leisure and inclination to instruct a young gentleman, they may neither of them always have ability suitable. It is one thing to be capable of carrying on a proportion of business in a narrow branch, a very different, to qualify others for any, much less the most extensive. Besides, it is not every one who is acquainted with mercantile, or any other branch of knowledge, is capable of training up others therein, and giving proper instructions. It is not the practice of trade that will enable a merchant to teach his apprentice his art, though it furnishes material for that purpose. It is a good general education, a course of regular study, and a genius for familiar explication, that fit

men for the office of instructors. And to these qualifications must be added still other arts. During the fire and sprightliness of youth, there is no fixing the attention, but by wisely amusing it. This age is always upon it's guard against bondage in every shape; and therefore, to give a true relish for knowledge, the arts of communicating it should be disguised under the form of pleasure.

Should it so fall out, as none will think impossible, that our young trader is bred under those, who themselves are unskilful; whose books are never duly stated, posted up, or fit for a ballance: should it be the fortune of a young gentleman to be thus situated, and to receive the first impressions from so goodly an example, is he not likely rather to take an eternal disrelish to the profession, than successfully to pursue what has been rendered so odious and disagreeable? Or, if he happens to be of an adventurous and self-sufficient turn, he may be rash enough to hazard his disgrace and ruin, by engaging in an employment he is no way qualified for.

Nor is want of leisure and ability the only cause of a youth being bred to merchandizing under every disadvantage. Interest may frequently prove the greatest motive to his obstruction. For, if a young gentleman of considerable fortune is let into the whole mystery of the business of the counting-house where it may happen to be bred, it is sometimes, I am afraid, surmised, that such a one might hereafter prove highly detrimental thereto? And, where there is any interesting inducement to keep him in ignorance, nothing is easier than to spread the veil of concealment. It is only chaining our novice to some appendage to the principal books, some labouring oar; or artfully shifting him from one auxiliary book to another, the more effectually to bewilder; and giving him an unwarrantable loose to his pleasures; and our young merchant shall turn out as completely qualified to be at the head of a counting-house, as a hackney-writer at the head of the law.

The more extensive and universal the business may be, with less difficulty is every thing, to a stripling, rendered dark, mysterious, and unintelligible. Provided a youth, in circumstanced, proves one of strong parts and an inquisitive turn, he will probably, upon the general ballance of the books, be attentive to the general profits, from a principle of curiosity only: yet he may only view those in the gross; how, and in what manner those profits arose, or whether they are true or false, is easily obscured under some intermediate account to that of profit and loss; a matter easily practised, to blind the eyes of one unacquainted with the niceties of accountantship en parties doubles *.

* Many have formed fictitious SETTS of ACCOUNTS, in order to deceive the public, and those who have been taken into partnership by such villains; of which I have been informed we have a late instance in a certain BANKRUPT of the city of London: others keep DOUBLE SETTS of BOOKS, to answer double purposes.

Let the transactions of a counting-house, therefore, be as important in particular, as infinite in diversity; let those transactions be judiciously conducted, and methodically adjusted, according to the nicest arts of mercantile skill; yet, if a youth is not furnished with pre-requisite knowledge to enable him to make the best advantage of what he sees transacted, he cannot be much the wiser for being placed in a counting-house of universal business. All that is transacted may be no more to him than a regular confusion, who is disqualified to view the connection of the whole, with an eye of understanding. Without being thoroughly knowing and expert in mercantile calculations and accountantship, and duly initiated into the arcana mercatorum * * * * *, what advantage can a young gentleman receive?

Every common sailor who takes a share in the toil, will hardly be presumed fit for command. Being placed in the center of practical business, and taking some inferior part in it's transactions, is far from being sufficient to qualify a young gentleman to hold the rudder of large concerns hereafter. The mechanic artizan and manufacturer, it is true, may be insensibly disciplined to perform works of the hands with wonderful dexterity: even children, we know, may be trained to do extraordinary things that way, by reiteration of one and the same work. In like manner may the mechanical merchant be bred; but where so general a knowledge, such variety of accomplishments, so clear a head, and so much real judgment and address are absolutely necessary, no man, acquainted with the world, can imagine, that being bred in a parrot-like manner should, at this time of day, enable the young merchant to excel in the arts of commerce.

214

We are not insensible there have been some gentlemen, who, destitute of all previous requisite mercantile instruction, have, from very trifling beginnings, struck into foreign commerce; and, by the uncommon strength of their natural abilities, prompted by great industry, and favoured by a series of fortunate events, have acquired great estates. Such as these we have known; and we have known likewise, that where this hath been done, without clandestine and dishonourable measures, those gentlemen have been of capacity and application as singular as their good fortune: they have indeed been persons rather to be admired than imitated. But traders, who, without their superlative talents, have been doing enough to follow such examples, if for a time they have happened to shine in the commercial world, it has been like those meteors in the natural; which, after furnishing matter of astonishment for a while, have soon destroyed themselves, and involved in their ruin all who have been unhappy enough to be within the sphere of their influence.

Though we have thus taken the freedom to signify our disapprobation of the usual methods of bringing up our young British merchants in general, yet we are sensible, very sensible, that too many youth, as well among merchants as other ranks of men of business, reap little advantage by the happy opportunities they sometimes enjoy, of excelling in their peculiar province. The best examples and instruction, the most interesting incitements to attention and assiduity, make little impression on the desultory and inconsiderate. The distinguished figure in trade some young gentlemen make, in comparison to others, sufficiently discriminates the superior benefits they have received from those counting-houses, wherein they have been happily bred.

But what advantage can such expect to receive, that are unhappy enough to fall into the hands of those who are capable, yet not inclined; or of those who are incapable, though well inclined, to do them justice? Instead of a constant succession of merchants, eminent for their skill and ingenuity, may we not rather expect to see a daily declension? And may not the kingdom be thus left destitute of a competent number to prosecute it's foreign traffic, either with that emolument to themselves, or that benefit to the state it will admit of? Under such melancholy circumstances, it will be matter of no great admiration to hear woeful complaints and lamentations on the decay and badness of trade, when the defect and imperfection may manifestly lie in traders themselves.

Without expatiating on a matter so apparent to every one, who will give himself the liberty candidly and impartially to weigh and consider it, we shall only observe, That nothing seems more wanted than a proper place, or well regulated institution for mercantile education; where the theory and practice of trade might be taught, as near as could be at the same time, and a general knowledge of commerce, and it's practical arts communicated, as the first step towards engaging in any particular branch of it.

And, as the reduction of the interest of money will have a tendency to induce many persons of mature years to strike into trade, as well as a greater number of young people to be trained up for it, in order to settle either at home or abroad: as the loveners of interest will certainly increase the number of British traders in Europe, and, it is to be hoped, the trade of the nation proportionably: and, as all other countries are increasing their trade and traders likewise, it follows, that the skill, address, and ingenuity of our British merchants, cannot, at present, be too great. Whereas, when the trade of our own nation, as well as that of others, was in very few hands in comparison to what it is now, and the interest of money double and treble what it is at present: when these were the circumstances of public affairs, and the benefits of trading between the Exchange and the Exchequer were extraordinary, as well as the profits on trade in general, numbers acquired very great estates, without any great accomplishments. This great change in the state of our affairs, pointing out the reasonableness and necessity of the proposed institution, it is humbly presumed, that it will prove as acceptable to all wise and good men, as the same is zealously intended for the public benefit and utility.

The General PLAN Delineated.

Of the several particulars to be taught in the proposed COLLEGE.

It is proposed to take no young gentleman into this mercantile seminary, under fifteen years of age; nor any but such

who are qualified in school-arithmetic, and masters of a tolerable current hand-writing [*].

> [*] It is my intention, some time or other, to draw up a plan for the education of the British merchant from his infancy, as preparatory to his admission into a college of this kind.

A thorough knowledge and expertness in mercantile computations being previously necessary to all other accomplishments, it is proposed to go through every distinct course relative thereunto; and that in so intelligible and scientific a manner, as the rationale of every thing may very clearly appear [*]. For as, from the whole of this design, we have in view the gradual exercise and improvement of the understanding, and insensibly strengthening the judgment, so nothing, it is conceived, will be more naturally conducive thereunto, than demonstrating the reason and foundation of all rules given in the courses of our mercantile calculations; skill in figures being founded in reason [†], facility of operation in reiterated practice: which the professors should not be wanting duly to promote.

> [*] See our article MATHEMATICS.
> [†] See our article ARITHMETIC.

Knowledge in the foreign exchanges being very essential to the qualification of the merchant, this subject should be treated in all it's various lights.

That a clear idea may be formed of our intention with regard to this particular, it may be necessary to observe:

1. That the most concise and practical methods of converting the sterling money of England into the monies of exchange and of account of all places throughout Europe be demonstrated, according to the direct courses of exchange established for those purposes, and vice versâ.

2. The methods of converting sterling money into those of all other places of commerce, wherewith England has no direct established courses of exchange, but is under the necessity of making use of the intermediate exchange of other places: together with the nature of the agios, and the manner of turning their bank monies into current, and the reverse.

3. The manner of calculating all the foreign monies throughout Europe into those of every other distinct country, either by direct or intermediate exchange; which makes a much greater variety of cases than those, who are not thoroughly acquainted with this extensive subject, can imagine.

4. The art of arbitrating [*] the prices of exchange throughout all Europe [†].

> [*] Les arbitrages, en matière de change, ne sont autre chose qu'en présentément d'un avantage considérable qu'on commettant doit recevoir d'une remise ou d'une traite faite pour un lieu préférablement à une autre.
> Le pair, ou l'égalité des monnaies courantes, ou le pair des places, qui est le point le plus délicat, le plus essentiel, & le plus inconnu du commerce de change; & de banque, se prend en deux manières.
> La première est au pair, qui suppose un juste rapport & une valeur exacte de la monnaie d'un pais avec celle d'un autre, comme quand 1 rixdale de 50 sols, monnaie courante de Hollande, ou d'Amsterdam, est comptée en égale valeur de 1 ♥ (a) de 60 sols Tournois de France, ou de 54 deniers, ou pence, ou 4½ chelings d'Angleterre, & ainsi des autres places.
>
> sans cette considération, on ne peut pas directe la perte ou le porte qu'on fait sur change, on fait les marchandises étrangères; car comme il y a un pair & égalité des monnaies à des poids du monde, il est aussi nécessaire qu'il y ait un pair & égalité des monnaies; autrement on se regarderoit le sauveroit ce qu'il fault, si à le prix qu'on fait demanderoit d'une chose, soit en change, soit en marchandise, seroit haut ou bas.
> La seconde espèce d'égalité entre les places, est celle du prix courant du change, par laquelle on entend seulement cette proportion réglée d'une place avec une autre place, par la connaissance d'une ou de plusieurs comparées entr'elles. Quelques-uns pourront dire que la connaissance du profit & de la perte qu'on fait, sur des lettres de change, dépend du retour des sommes à leur principe, & que le pair est une spéculation inutile. On peut répondre à cela que, à la connaissance du profit; & de la perte qu'on fait sur les lettres de change, dépend du retour des sommes à leur principe, & du lieu d'où elles sont sorties, on ne peut pas dire le même chose de celles, qui ne retournent point, soit qu'elles soient employées, & consumées dans le pais même, soit pour achat de marchandises, soit pour pension, ou pour des affaires particulières.
> D'ailleurs, s'il eut nécessaire d'attendre ce retour, pour savoir le profit qui le fait sur une lettre de change, & en

cette connoiffance dépendit de l'avenir, il faudroit conclure que dans le tems que l'on donne ou que l'on prend de l'argent à change, on ne le fauroit pas, & s'il on ne le favoit pas, ce feroit négocier fans connoiffance de caufe & au hazard, puis qu'on ignoreroit le profit ou la perte qu'on y feroit. *Idem.*

(a) Le lecteur est averti que cet ouvrage ainsi été fait lorfque l'Ecu de France au valoit que fix fols Tournois, est ben droit en pair aux le modelle de Hollande & 9c fols. Mais les monnoyes de France ont changé fouvent depuis, & font fujettes à des variations continuelles; ainfi au lieu de marquer la valeur d'écu de France dans la préfente année 1751, on le fuppofe toûjours de l'ancienne valeur de fix fols Tournois ; à quoi on fera attention. *Traité Général du Commerce, par Samuel Ricard d'Amfterdam.*

† See our articles ARBITRATION OF EXCHANGES, EXCHANGE, ENGLAND, HOLLAND, HAMBURGH, and fuch other heads to which from these we refer.

This is a fubject of great delicacy, not only in point of computation, but in point of application to the purpofes of drawing and remitting money, and negociating bills of exchange throughout Europe, to the beft advantage at all times. And what that advantage is, can never be known to any, except thofe who are fkilled in this important and myfterious branch.

Thofe merchants or negociators of foreign monies by exchange, who may be only acquainted with a few places, whofe exchanges they are capable of arbitrating, cannot be judges of the profits to be made by other places: and therefore, for want of an univerfal knowledge herein, we will prefume to fay, that daily opportunities, of no inconfiderable benefit, efcape notice.

Although the inftability of the exchange is juftly enough compared to the wind, yet that inftability is the very caufe of the profit to be made thereby: and for this plain reafon, becaufe it is fcarce ever poffible, that the courfes of exchange between feveral nations fhould ebb and flow in an equality of proportion.

And whoever trades as a merchant, that is to fay, as an exporter and importer in Europe, muft of neceffity have to do with bills of exchange, and with drawing or remitting: and, if fo, he fhould by no means be unacquainted with thofe art of making the beft advantages by fo doing; but this is not poffible to be done, without being thoroughly fkilled in their arbitration, to a demonftrative exactnefs.

The more general the trade of a merchant is, the more univerfal fhould his knowledge in this particular be. And thofe who may have views in dealing largely by exchange, will certainly find their account beyond expectation, in being fundamentally grounded in this fubject; for a trader of a good general foreign correfpondence may, by this means, gain more by dint of credit and fkill, than others, unacquainted herewith, can do, perhaps, by dint of hard money [*].

[*] See our articles ARBITRATION OF EXCHANGES, HOLLAND, HAMBURGH.

A knowledge alfo of the intrinfic value of foreign coin, or fpecie [*], fhould go hand in hand with the knowledge of exchange †; the profit arifing upon the exportation or importation thereof, from one foreign country to another, being grounded on the due confideration of both. To which fhould be added, the nature of dealing in bullion gold and filver to the beft advantage; the various calculations neceffary to that end, and the methods pointed out that are proper to be taken, in order to prevent impofition in regard thereunto ‡.

‡ That a more lively idea may be obtained of dealing in foreign fpecie to the beft advantage, we would recommend the collection of the feveral coins current throughout Europe, with the feveral ftandards affined thereunto, for the ufe of the college.

† See the article COINS.

‡ See the articles ASSAY, AQUA FORTIS, AQUA REGIA, BULLION GOLD and SILVER, FLUX, MINEOUGY, METALLURGY, MINEROLOGY, ORES, QUANTATION, REFINING SILVER, TESTING.

That the young merchant may not be deficient in whatever has affinity with exchanges, there fhould be compiled a fuccinct collection of the effential cuftoms and ufages of Britifh and foreign merchants relating to bills of exchange, together with the principal law-cafes that have been determined in the courts of judicature in England and Scotland, and foreign countries [*], which, with other occafional admonitions, may not a little contribute to prevent his being unwarily drawn into litigious broils; than which, nothing is lefs compatible with a life of traffic.

[*] See the article BILLS of EXCHANGE.

From the knowledge of thefe particulars, the collegian fhould be led to the comparifon of foreign weights and meafures, and the methods of converting thofe of one country into thofe of any other [*].

[*] See ENGLAND, HAMBURGH, HOLLAND, MEASURES, WEIGHTS.

It is unneceffary to obferve further upon this head, than that there is no poffibility of underftanding foreign invoices [*], and accounts of fales, without being capable to reduce the ftandard weights and meafures, as well as the monies of foreign countries, the one into the other. Nor without it can any previous computation be made, whether exportation or importation of merchandize, between nation and nation, will or will not turn to advantage.

[*] See INVOICE, and ACCOUNT of SALES.

Exportation and importation of domeftic and foreign commodities leading to the bufinefs of the cuftom-houfe, the calculation of the duties, fubfidies, drawbacks, and bounties, becomes a qualification not the leaft neceffary in an undertaking of this nature; as it is below the dignity of the merchant to fee wholly with the eyes of others, in what fo nearly concerns his own intereft [*].

[*] See our TABLE SHEETS of the cuftom-houfe duties, alfo the articles CUSTOMS, DUTIES, and our INDEX for whatever relates thereunto.

In regard to points of this nature, all due attention fhould be given to the tariffs, duties, impofts, and other charges, which are laid upon the Britifh produce and manufacture in foreign countries; and to inculcate, at the fame time, the prudential neceffity of obtaining fuch fatisfactory knowledge, by pro forma accounts of fales from foreign parts, before engagements are precipitately entered into [*].

[*] See ACCOUNT of SALES, TARIFFS, TREATIES of COMMERCE.

To thofe who have not been early exercifed in numbers, and are not become expert in their operation, this variety of calculations may appear fomething laborious. So it would be, if the method of inftruction is not fo peculiarly contrived as to render the whole rather an entertainment, than any thing like a difagreeable drudgery.

The minds of young perfons are not to be touched by abftracted ideas; they have need of agreeable and familiar images; they cannot reafon, or be brought to delight in bufinefs, without being pleafurably trained to them; and what is of the greateft moment muft be rendered lovely, and reprefented under fenfible and beautiful forms.

Yet what depends upon practice and exercife, can only be obtained by practice and exercife, though the rules and principles of that practice fhould be ever fo well comprehended. ' I wifh, fays a wife man [*], that Paluel or Pompey, the two ' famous dancing-mafters of his time, could have taught us ' to dance and cut capers by only feeing them do it, without ' ftirring from our places, as fome pedants pretend to inform ' the underftanding, without ever fetting it to work; or that ' we could learn to ride, handle a pike, touch a lute, or fing, ' without the trouble of practice; or as thefe attempt to ' make us judge and fpeak well, without exercifing us in ' judging and fpeaking †.'

[*] Montaigne.

† The great Mr Locke fpeaks to the fame purpofe. We are born with faculties and powers, fays he, capable of almoft any thing; fuch, at leaft, as would carry us farther than can eafily be imagined: but it is only the exercife of thefe powers which gives us ability and fkill in any thing, and leads us towards perfection.—A middle-aged ploughman will fcarce ever be brought to the carriage and language of a gentleman, though his body be as well proportioned, and his joints as fupple, and his natural parts not any way inferior. The legs of a dancing-mafter, and the fingers of a mufician, fall as it were naturally, without thought or pains, into admirable and regular motions. Bid them change their parts, and they will in vain endeavour to produce like motions in the members not ufed to them; and it will require length of time, and long practice, to attain but fome degree of a like ability. What incredible and aftonifhing actions do we find rope-dancers and tumblers bring their bodies to! Not but that fundry, in almoft all manual arts, are as wonderful; but I name thofe which the world takes notice of for fuch, becaufe, on that very account, they give mo-

216

any to fee them. All thefe admired notions, beyond the reach, and almoft the conception of unpractifed fpeftators, are nothing but the mere effects of ufe and induftry in ... which bodies have nothing peculiar in them than thofe of the unexand bodies on. ——As it is in the body, fo it is in the mind; practice makes it what it is, &c. Locke's conduct of the Underftanding, folio, page 375.

That the juvenile mind may not be difagreeably wearied with too continued an attachment to the fame thing, the conftitution of the college fhould be fo modell'd as to have interludes, by tranfition to matters of a lighter kind, which do not require that feverity of attention, yet to fuch chiefly as have a clofe connection with practical bufinefs, in a real life of trade. Amongft thefe we look upon a facility in writing a plain, ftrong, fenfible letter of bufinefs upon all occafions. As trade can only be carried on by an epiftolary correfpondence, a good mercantile ftile may, perhaps, be as neceffary a part in the education of the merchant as any thing elfe. Thoufands, in foreign trade, correfpond for many years without ever feeing one another; but they can bee the intelligent man of bufinefs as thoroughly by his letters as by his converfation; and fometimes better indeed; for many may get the light knack of prating, who are not able to write a correct and pertinent letter of bufinefs.

Letters of trade, wrote with judgment, and language fuitable to the fubject, beget refpect and confidence. We have heard a worthy and ingenuous merchant declare, That his being capable of correfponding in a manner fomething fuperior to the generality, was the means of getting him a very good eftate, from a very fmall beginning; this talent having brought him very large commiffion bufinefs, a branch always defired, not only as it brings a fecure profit, but as it proves the means of gaining the young merchant, efpecially, experience at the rifque of others.

They muft have little knowledge of language who can imagine, that the mere tranfcription of other perfons letters, with precipitation, for the fake of copies only, will ever qualify a young gentleman, with a fmall fhare of literature, to carry on a judicious correfpondence himfelf *. Nothing can effectually do this, but being properly put on the exercife of his own genius, and, from time to time, having his ftile corrected, with fuitable admonition.

* Yet this is the only method taken to inftruct them herein; which muft be the reafon why fo few write grammatically or intelligibly; which I could fhew by fome thoufands of merchants letters in my poffeffion.

Though it is not neceffary that the merchant fhould be a perfon of great learning, yet it is abfolutely neceffary he fhould be capable of writing grammatically, otherwife his fentiments are liable to be miftaken, which will be attended with confequences either injurious to himfelf or his correfpondents. And young gentlemen of this clafs muft certainly ftand in need of fome affiftance in this refpect, unlefs they can be fuppofed to have a miraculous advantage over other perfons, and to obtain a facility to indite with brevity, fulnefs, and perfpicuity, by inftinct or infpiration.

Having arrived at a tolerable maftery in ftile, as well as computation, the fcene fhould be difcreti mall; diverfified; variety in applications of the mind being as occafionally requifite, as variety in diet to the body. To this end, the young merchant fhould be gradually initiated into a knowledge of the grand books.

That this part of his erudition may be rendered rather familiar and pleafurable than otherwife, we judge it neceffary to commence with communicating a knowledge of every diftinct auxiliary to the principal books, and of the form of every kind of voucher, and of every fort of inftrument practifed among merchants for their mutual fecurity: fuch as BILLS of LADING, CHARTER-PARTIES, POLICIES of INSURANCE, and the like *.

* See thefe feveral articles.

We would not be underftood to mean the giving only a fuperficial view of thofe kind of writings and inftruments, but to inculcate the nature, legality, and utility of them; and, at the fame time, to enforce the neceffity of fuch writings and inftruments being ftrongly and intelligibly drawn, to prevent ftrife and litigations: as alfo fhewing that, without fuch legal vouchers, the grand books are of no authority, either in cafes of arbitration, or in the face of courts of judicature; thefe being no more than an artificial index to the original vouchers and teftimonials.

From thefe inftructions, fo given as to make a proper impreffion, the next ftep fhould be to proceed, in a natural progreffion, to explain fyftematically the axioms and rational maxims and principles whereupon the whole art of accountantfhip, as practifed by the moft fkilful merchants, according to the method of double-entry, is grounded. At the fame time, the fuperlative excellency of this art, in comparifon to all others that have been adopted to anfwer the like purpofes, fhould be amply illuftrated, by appofite examples; as it always exhibits the true reprefentation of a merchant's affairs:

and, provided the books are duly pofted up, this excellent method is preventive of all deftructive confequences, which attend irregularity and confufion in a trader's accounts *.

* This method of inftruction is widely different from the ordinary one that is practifed.

It is not neceffary, indeed, that a merchant engaged in large concerns fhould keep his own books, as he may probably employ his time to far greater advantage; but it is indifpenfably neceffary that he fhould be capable of doing fo: how is it poffible, otherwife, that he fhould be able to judge when they are kept as they ought to be? Nor can he be capable of fo infpecting them as to be duly acquainted with the ftate of his own affairs *.

* There are many who have book-keepers, that are not judges whether their accounts are kept as they ought to be or not, according to the nature of their tranfactions. Is it at all extraordinary that fuch fhould be unfuccefsful?

It is an unbecoming meannefs, not to fay a confummate folly, in any man, whofe fortune is daily at ftake, to depend upon others to give him what they pleafe for the ftate of his affairs. It is juftly proverbial among the Dutch, That the man who fails did not underftand to keep his accounts: and it may be truly faid, a merchant without that fkill is in as bad a fituation as the mariner on the wide ocean, without chart or compafs whereby to direct his courfe.

This inimitable method of accounts, being founded on the principles of reafon, will prove a kind of practical logic to young people, when it is rationally and methodically communicated, not mechanically, and by rules depending on the memory only; which latter does not merit the name of inftruction at all. And even rules, and the principles of reafon whereon they are grounded, being ever fo well underftood, yet, without the due application and exercife of thofe rules and principles to ufeful purpofes, they are little better than a dead weight to the memory, and a clog to the underftanding: whereas, when thefe rules and principles are duly applied, and made habitual, by being reduced to practice in matters of ufe, they are a whet to the genius, and ftrengthen the intellectual faculties *.

* The common way of inftruction of this clafs of people is by mere rules, without any reafon or demonftration given of thofe rules; which is a mere mechanical and parrot-like way of teaching; whereas, were young people habituated to know the reafon of every rule they go by, in the courfe of their education, it would infenfibly lead them to pry into the reafon of every thing elfe; which would prove of no little aid to their underftandings in general.

In order to apply thefe rules and principles of reafoning to accounts, a concife introductory fyftem fhould be formed, and that exemplified by tranfactions foreign and domeftic, drawn from real bufinefs. And, that the young merchant may be completely grounded herein, he fhould be afterwards exercifed in ftating the real occurrences of fome of the greateft and moft univerfal merchants, from their original books.

Nor will fuch original books of accounts be of ufe only to ground a young gentleman to the utmoft perfection in the art of accountantfhip, but will, at the fame time, familiarife to him fo great a variety of interefting tranfactions in foreign trade, conducted with judgment and addrefs, that will qualify him to launch into commerce with great advantage *.

* To this end, I would propofe that the college fhould be fupplied with a great variety of complete fetts of the real accounts of many diftinguifhed and eminent merchants deceafed; they being of no other ufe to executors after being a few years in their poffeffion, there would be no great difficulty to obtain a great variety of thefe. If this feminary was furnifhed with the genuine accounts and letters relating thereto of the following merchants (a), who trod the Royal Exchange with fupreme credit and dignity, the unexperienced might receive great benefit and advantage, by having

judicious lectures read upon the same. For, by having the transactions of persons of great experience and discernment before us, and their motives nakedly laid open, as appears by their genuine mercantile letters, no one will doubt but great knowledge may be thereby obtained for the conduct of young people: to know only the several ways of trading of the skilful and prosperous, is of no little utility; but to be let into the motives of their measures, and the address whereby their many hazardous adventures have been conducted, is of no less benefit to the young trader than the genuine history of great statesmen and commanders are to those who shall aim at following their examples.

(a) The accounts we mean, are such as those of a Louvreure, St Timpey and Seignouret, Daniel Arthur, Bradey and Smith, Tourton and Gauger, William Henry Cornelisson, Coppins, Sir David Easter, Sir Peter Meyer, Sir Theodore Janssen, Sir John Williams, Sir Randolph Knype, Sir Peter Deland, Samuel Sheppard, Sir Francis Eyles, James Milner, ——— Olmius, Sir Samuel Clarke, Sir Alexander Cairns, Henry Cairns, Deborah Dunt, widow, Longuet and sons, Sir Henry Furnese, Sir James Bateman, Sir James Dollyffe, Sir William Chapman, Samuel Holden, and many of the other distinguished merchants of the city of London, and other parts of the kingdom, as well as of the British factories in foreign ports, and numbers of others who are now living in the highest credit.

About twenty years since, some mercantile accounts of no little consequence fell into my hands to audit and [...] between the late Samuel Holden, Esq; governor of the Bank of England, and some considerable merchants of Russia. In the examination of these accounts, it was necessary for me to consult the course of correspondence for many years back; and I must confess it not only gave me great satisfaction as well as advantage, from the perusal of Mr Holden's letters in particular, but they very [...] with great sagacity: Cleave himself, perhaps, had he been bred a merchant, could not have formed a mercantile epistle more laconic, elegant, and perspicuous; whereas those of many of his correspondents were as mean and unintelligible as their business was injudiciously conducted.

Thus rationally introduced into this method of accounts, in all it's ordinary forms, as practised by the most ingenious and experienced, our young traders should afterwards be instructed so to contract their accounts, as to have much less writing than is commonly used in most counting-houses. The auxiliary books should not only be contrived in a method far more concise than usual, but other parts of their accounts kept in a much shorter manner than is generally practised, and yet without the least deviation from the spirit and essence of this incomparable art.

The usefulness of the abridgment proposed, in this respect, will consist in keeping the books always duly posted up; without which it is impossible the merchant should, at all times, be so thoroughly acquainted with his affairs as he ought. But those who are not complete masters of this art, although they may perfectly understand the common methods, yet have so much writing therein, and thereby find it so laborious, that they frequently practise less accurate methods of accountantship, only to save so much writing; which is too often attended with no little disorder and confusion in their affairs.

That every advantage may be reaped which this art of accountantship will admit of, the student should be put also into the method of keeping, with very little trouble, an abstract of the state of his affairs, within the compass of a pocket-ledger, as a constant check and remembrancer for the due government of his concern.

That no point of practice in any counting-house whatever may be concealed, the usual methods of making out accounts of sales, invoices [*], &c. should be laid open, together with the nature of all intermediate accounts, which are made use of in order to answer such purposes as may be thought necessary by the more skilful.

* Though many of these arts are not strictly just and honourable, yet the young merchant should not be ignorant of them, lest he should be liable to daily imposition by others.

Method and regularity being the life of a trader's affairs in general, the same should not be neglected in every circumstance relating thereunto. Thus the due arrangement and methodizing of the original vouchers of his transactions, for immediate reference, should be duly inculcated and exemplified. As the grand books are of no authority without them [*], the one ought to be as regularly disposed as the other, in the way they will admit of. Neglects of this kind, either by misplacing or losing those testimonials, being productive of great perplexity and vexation in public business, order and regularity in all things cannot too early be made habitual.

* Much deceit and knavery have been practised by subtle bankrupts and others, by forging formal waste-books, journals and ledgers, &c. seemingly very regularly kept, &c. which have too often passed for genuine, because the several vouchers have not been duly scrutinised into from whence those accounts have been formed.—This is what should be strictly examined into by the commissioners of bankrupts, and council in their pleadings, &c. and by those who enter into partnerships, &c.

Moreover, the trader, whose whole fortune, or more, is frequently embarked in business, and whose anxiety is often sufficiently engaged for the event of his enterprizes, should be accustomed, from his youth, to treasure up all knowledge relative to his profession; more especially so, since it frequently admits of a variety of occurrences, no less singular than interesting. It will, therefore, hardly be thought unnecessary to familiarize him to keep a well-contrived alphabetical register of all such essential occurrences, as may be requisite for him to have recourse to throughout the whole of his life. For it is little to the reputation of the trader to be obliged to ask information of others, in important transactions which relate to himself; and in such too, probably, as either passed through the counting-house where he was bred, or, perhaps, his own; yet, for want of a proper memento, he may sometimes commit such egregious mistakes, as may prove an injury to his estate, as well as blemish to his character.

The next business should be to furnish the young merchant with some knowledge relating to the funds and stocks of this kingdom; negociation of that sort, on the account of foreigners, and others, having multiplied with the increase of the national debt.

We would not be understood to mean the knowledge of the stock-jobber only, but such a knowledge of the funds, in their foundation on the public credit, and how they are affected ab extra, as well as ab intra, so as to distinguish the real from the fictitious causes of the fluctuation of their prices. However mankind may have been misled, and interested at times, yet doubtless there are such chances, whereby an observing person may make a very good judgment when there is money to be got or lost, by this our standing lottery [*].

* There is so great variety of artifices practised at certain conjunctures, to raise and fall stocks, for the private interest of jobbers, and those who are in the secret of public affairs and great companies, that they would take me up a volume to display in their proper colours. See the articles Bubbles, Stocks, Stock-jobbing.

Provided this should be no otherwise serviceable than to prevent a rash and indiscreet dabbling in stock-jobbing, it may prove the saving, though it should not the improving of a fortune. The young trader may hereby receive information enough upon this head, to enable him to give such seasonable advice to correspondents, as may be the means of gaining him no inconsiderable commissions in that shape, though his own fortune should not admit of his occasionally trading in the stocks for himself.

In the course of this mercantile progress, the next step necessary should seem to be to give the young merchant a general survey of the trade and commerce of the world [*].

* See the several nations of the world throughout the Dictionary, and their principal provinces, countries, duchies, &c. for commerce.

However unnecessary some may imagine this general knowledge of trade, who look not beyond the circle of their particular branch, yet we cannot help thinking such knowledge may prove of no little advantage to the trader of genius: for it is the nature of foreign commerce to be variable and fluctuating; that branch which shall afford considerable profit at one time, may be scarce worth engaging in at another; by reason the greater the advantage is, the greater is the confluence of traders into that branch in particular: multitudes thus striking into one and the same trade, foreign markets are glutted, and the British, as well as other produce and manufactures, become a drug.

Other causes likewise conspire to this. All nations are now convinced that trade is the best source of wealth and of power: wherefore some are daily attempting either to supply themselves with what they took from others, or other nations are attempting to obtain a share in their supply.

But whoever considers in what manner the more skilful merchant prosecutes his trade, will hardly disallow the necessity of a pretty general knowledge therein. As, 1. Our national produce and manufacture being more than our consumption,

218

a part is exported ; and, in return, foreign goods, or bullion, or both, are brought home. 2. Selling the goods exported at one port, and loading there to sell at another, whereby a larger profit is made than if the goods exported had been carried directly thither. 3. Bringing away the produce and manufactures of other countries, from whence and when they are cheap, to supply countries when and where the same sell dear. 4. Bringing home the produce of other countries, and exporting the same in manufactures. 5. Freighting and hiring out shipping to various parts of the world.

The merchant, by thus knowing how the several parts of the world are connected with each other in their mutual intercourse of commerce, how the redundancies of this country supply the deficiencies of that, will be capable of foreseeing when any ill consequences threaten either that branch of traffic in which he is particularly concerned, or the trade of his country in general. It will open to his view by what means several branches have been acquired; how some have been stagnated and lost; and what measures may be taken by the government, in concert with the practical merchant, to revive them, or supply the mischief, by opening new channels of commerce.

It is too little knowledge of trade, not too much, that will make the merchant rashly adventurous and projecting, upon weak and groundless foundations. A person, knowing in more branches than one, will of course embrace that which is the more suitable to his fortune, and the least hazardous. As many have been undone by rashly grasping at a greater share of business than they had either capital or ability to manage; so, on the other hand, many have been ruined by an unaccountable attachment to one branch, when common prudence cried aloud for their relinquishing a ruinous trade, and striking into the prosperous.

This part of the institution, therefore, it is presumed, may prove a sovereign preservative against each extreme of imprudence; our intention hereby being to prevent precipitate engagements, and too projecting a turn on the one hand, as likewise too contracted a view, and pusillanimity on the other.

It is not by the merchant as by the particular mechanic or artisan. The potter cannot easily strike into the business of the shipwright, any more than the latter can into that of the watch-maker or the weaver, &c. This is not parallel in regard to merchant and merchant: for the exporter of woollen goods can as easily export tin or lead, or hard-ware, &c. and have his returns by exchange, in dollars of Leghorn, or ducats of Venice, as well as in dollars of Spain, or mallreis or moidures of Portugal, &c. Or cannot the merchant who last woollen goods to Spain or to Italy, send another species of woollen goods to Russia, and have his returns in rubles, Russia hemp, linnen, rhubarb, or pot-ash, &c. as easily as in Spanish dollars, wines, and raisins? In fine, the imports and exports to and from his own nation to all others, together with a knowledge of their monies, weights and measures, duties, imposts, and all customary charges, ought to be familiar to the accomplished merchant; that, upon the declension of any particular branch of national trade, he may apply himself to the more advantageous for the time being.

Or, even if the national trade in general should undergo a temporary declension, yet the trade of the world will afford the true-bred merchant eternal opportunities of advantage: such a one will find no difficulty to trade in various branches, from one foreign nation to another, as it were independent of his own, whilst all the profits are brought home, and center within himself.

We are not unaware it may be objected, that a merchant cannot have that universal knowledge in the qualities of commodities, necessary for variety of foreign markets, &c. and, therefore, cannot so easily turn himself from one branch of foreign trade to another. To which it may be replied: were merchants obliged to depend wholly upon their own judgment herein, there would be some weight in the objection. But this is not the case. For the reputation of manufacturers and warehouse-men, and other dealers, in their negociations with merchants, is not only at stake in one respect, but they can safely depend upon well-experienced brokers and packers in others, to prevent impositions of this nature: so that there is not that necessity for the merchant to have so deep a knowledge in the qualities of goods in general, as if the case was otherwise. However, this matter should by no means be disregarded in a collegiate establishment; a mercantile museum, or repository, being indispensably necessary to such a design, which should be furnished with samples * of the unperishable staple commodities and produce of the principal trading parts of the world.

* To these should be joined labels, describing the distinguishable characteristics of their several qualities, according to the degrees of comparison: this will accustom a young person to form some judgment in the qualities of those commodities wherein he may be hereafter induced to trade. If this expedient should have no other effect than to make a proper impression, that a merchant himself should not be wholly regardless of the qualities of those commodities wherein he may happen to deal, it may answer a very good purpose, but can prove no way detrimental: he may chuse whether he will regard any but those he may occasionally traffic in, and such he cannot be too well acquainted with. See the articles MANUFACTURES, MECHANICS, MUSEUM.

Very far from raising an uncontroulable adventurous spirit, in causelesly rambling from one branch of trade to another, on the contrary, every measure should be used to check it, by throwing in such a weight of prudential knowledge as will ballast the most towering and extravagant disposition of that kind.

In view to which, the tutors should not be wanting to instil the necessity of guarding against casualties and injurious events, in every shape, so far as the extent of human foresight may be presumed to go in the train of business. Thus with regard to exportation for proper, or company account, the necessity of pro-forma accounts should be duly inforced, before adventures are undertaken; as also the prudence of buying at best hand, and judiciously dividing the hazard, by not trusting too large a capital upon one bottom, or in one hand; not to trade beyond themselves, or leave their concerns too much to others; of prudentially insuring, not only from the danger of the seas, but from the danger of bad debts in foreign parts. For young people should be admonished rather to be contented with smaller profits, than not to allow the usual extra-commission, for a good correspondent to remain the middle man upon those occasions, persons of experience well knowing the measures too often taken by factors, provided they have not this extra-allowance.

These, and all other such-like measures, should be duly regarded by the instructors; since not only the improvement, but the security of the merchant's fortune, in trading in the capacity of a principal for his own account, so greatly depends. And although, by pursuing measures so circumspect, our young merchant's profits, at first setting out for himself, may be less than those of more bold adventurers, yet he will much sooner grow rich than those who make too much haste to become so.

Acting likewise in the capacity of a factor does not require less precaution: for a just and honourable regard, had, in the way of trade, to the interest of others, seldom proves detrimental to our own. Whether this is not one, and even the most effectual means to increase commission-business, we leave those to judge who act as principals themselves. As trading in this shape is the most beneficial and lucrative, so it is not the least delicate to conduct: to the best advantage. In respect to a matter of this importance to the young merchant, the best advice should be inculcated. To which end, those measures should be pointed out that have been successfully taken by the more judicious to gain commissions.

No employment requiring a more ready use of the principal modern languages than the mercatorial, a collegial institution would be judged materially deficient, if destitute of professors to train up those students properly therein: wherefore, for whatever branch of trade the young merchant may be intended, he should, through the course of this education, be able to obtain either a knowledge of the French language, or the Italian, the Spanish, the Portuguese, or even the Dutch, High or Low; and, indeed, a facility in writing of several, or all of them, is necessary for the general merchant: for, although some may think that the French alone, from it's universality *, sufficient, yet many foreigners will rather prefer a British correspondent, who writes his native language well, than that of him who only writes the French or the English.

* It has proved no mean stroke of the French policy to make their language so universal as they have done. Among their system of arts for the propagation of their commerce, there is no one, perhaps, that has more tended to render it universal than this, however some may slightly think of it. Where there is one book in the English language read throughout the world, there are doubtless many thousands of the French; and such is the vanity of that nation (n), that they are superlatively modest in decrying most others, in order to render their own the more superb in the eyes of strangers. The best of every thing is scarce any where to be found but in

France; and they as arbitrarily govern the fashions of the world, in what shall be eat, drank, and wore, in other nations, as they are governed at home? Are not also the furniture, buildings, and even the pleasures of the reft of mankind, in a great measure, settled by this grand regulator of modes and fashions? How far this, with the univerfality of their language, has contributed to univerfalize their commerce, I am afraid has never been sufficiently confidered in this kingdom. This is apparent from many parts of our work.

(a) See Mr Addifon's Freeholder, No. 50. and bishop Sprett's Anfwer to that diftingenuous Frenchman Su Liere.

What renders this the more necessary is, that such who are pretty general traders, and not capable themselves of writing in the modern languages, as their affairs may require, are under the daily necessity of applying to those who make it their business to translate for them, and write answers to their foreign letters. Now, besides the meannefs and expence of such a practice, do not such merchants run the hazard of having the arcana of their business betrayed, and themselves therein fupplanted? Nor are hired tranflators themselves always able to give the genuine fenfe of a letter, or to write a pertinent anfwer, with the proper turn of phrafe. How injurious a practice of this kind may frequently prove, we leave those to confider whom it may concern. Moreover,

When a merchant has eftablifhed his credit among the trading world for worth, honour, and punctuality, there is no end of his correfpondence. It is the common practice among merchants of honour, all over the world, to make mutual tenders of their fervices upon any natural occafion that offers, which is taken cordial and refpectful; and, if they meet with a correfpondent who writes their language well, and takes their fenfe clearly, it is frequently inftrumental to produce profitable negociations that, perhaps, might never have been the cafe, if the agreeable correfponding language had been wanting.

The moft capital houfes of mercantile trade throughout Europe being generally compofed of feveral partners, for the greater fatisfaction of foreign correfpondents, it is cuftomary for the one or the other of thofe partners to travel into foreign countries, in order to make the better judgment of the credit and fortune of their correfpondents, cement ties of commercial friendfhip with others, and extend their traffic in general. Where fuch travelling correfpondents meet with traders who fpeak their own language with propriety, it fhould feem to have a tendency to promote more harmony than is cultivated with thofe who do not; in the fame manner as we obferve ftrangers, who think alike, and between whom there is a fimilitude of manners, fhall, at firft fight, contract permanent and beneficial friendfhips.

As foreign merchants refort to England with this intent, fo the Englifh frequently take the tour into foreign countries. But, to go without language, he may almoft as well be deaf as dumb: he ftands but an indifferent chance to cultivate advantageous friendfhips, and promote the honour and intereft of the houfe wherein he is concerned. Few foreigners fpeak Englifh, which makes it the more neceffary for the Englifh to fpeak and write the language of foreigners with whom they do or are likely to correfpond.

That a knowledge of geography is peculiarly neceffary to the merchant, need not be urged; and that fome fkill in navigation is likewife requifite, cannot be lefs obvious, feeing they have conftant concerns with mafters of fhips and infurance, &c.

That the merchant fhould make fome farther advance than this into the mathematical literature, will hardly be difputed, when we take a comprehenfive view of the nature of his employment; for, although we fuppofe him to be an expert practical arithmetician, yet, methinks, he fhould not be mechanically fo only: he fhould be habituated from his infancy to know the reafon of all rules by which he works [fee ARITHMETIC] for then he will apply his fkill in figures pertinently to whatever occurs, which otherwife is fcarce poffible; and it is better to fee with our own eyes than through the medium of others. A man, indeed, may content himfelf with the common theorems for gauging and menfuration, &c. yet to work, only by line and by rule, illy becomes fo high a character. We cannot therefore but think, that fuch a knowledge in algebra and geometry, as will lead the merchant into the rationale of every calculatory qualification for which he may have occafion, muft be of ufe to prevent deception. How far alfo fome knowledge in this fcience may be helpful to the improvement of the underftandings in general of young people of this clafs, may deferve confideration. [See

our article MATHEMATICS.] Likewife how ufefully a knowledge in fome parts of philofophy might contribute to his profperity in many branches of trade wherein he may be engaged, appears from various parts of his work. [See our INDEX] and alfo the article PHILOSOPHY.

The bufinefs of this clafs of trade s being not only under the controul of the peculiar and municipal laws of their country, but to the eftablifhed cuftoms and ufages of the me catorial, as well as many branches of the civil law, and the laws of nations and commercial treaties; it will hardly be faid, that the merchant ftands in need of no knowledge of this kind. Certain it is, if he is ignorant of the penalties to which he is liable, and the rights and privileges to which his profeffion entitle him in any refp ct, he not only runs the rifque of daily impofition, but of abfolute ruin. It is, therefore, we have, throughout the courfe of this work, pointed out moft of the laws and ufages of every kind, to which this trader is liable. [See our GENERAL CONTENTS delineated, at the beginning of the firft volume, and the GENERAL INDEX at it's conclufion, and the INDEX and CONTENTS which we fhall annex to this fecond volume.

As the public funds of this kingdom, and the great monied corporations eftablifhed in confequence thereof, are chiefly under the management and direction of the moft diftinguifhed merchants of the city of London, does it not become neceffary that they fhould be thoroughly informed in what relates to the fupport of the public credit, when the truft repofed in them is for no lefs than the property of fourfcore millions of fterling money? We do not intend, by what is here faid, to fignify the crafty fkill of ftockjobbing, we having before touched that point; we mean, that in this college fhould be taught, in a proper manner, a perfect knowledge of the public revenue in every branch thereof, all the laws relating thereto, and the feveral variations which the funds have undergone: upon the whole, here fhould be taught, fcientifically, the real principles to preferve public faith and credit, the foundation on which the p operty of the monied intereft ftands, at prefent; what meafures may be reafonably judged expedient in future, for the due fecurity of fo confiderable a proportion of the wealth of the nation, as well as what are the moft general eligible ways and means to raife the public fupplies hereafter on all emergencies, the moft for the general intereft and honour of the kingdom See the articles DEBTS [NATIONAL DEBTS], CREDIT [PUBLIC CREDIT], FUNDS, INTEREST of MONEY, and MONEY.

The ftudy of commerce, as well as that of the public funds and revenue in a national and political view, both in general, and as the feveral branches of it come occafionally under the confideration of the legiflature, or the public, by intended regulations, becomes another principal particular to be cultivated in this feminary. See the INDEX to the firft and fecond volumes.

This part of knowledge will, we apprehend, be thought of no little importance to the mercantile profperity, as it has been deemed a great merit in merchants, on public conjunctures, to have afforded fatisfaction to their fellow-citizens, in their affociations in this metropolis upon thofe interefting occafions; and the higheft honour to have given the legiflature fatisfactory accounts in matters of concernment to the traffic of the kingdom.

The memorable defeat of the French bill of commerce, in the reign of the late queen Anne, is fufficient to confirm the truth of this *.

* When Great-Britain, under the conduct of the late duke of Marlborough, had reduced France to the neceffity of fuing for peace, there were two treaties fet on foot, the one of peace, the other of commerce. But the treaty of commerce would not take effect, unlefs the parliament confented to reduce the high duties, and take off the prohibitions fo wifely laid on French commodities. As this would have deftroyed all the beft branches of our trade, and deprived many hundred thoufand of our manufacturers of their fubfiftence, it began to give an alarm: which became general enough the merchants, and traders, who knew the fatal confequences of it. Many pamphlets were publifhed, to convince our legiflature, that the preferving our looms, and the reft of Great-Britain, were of greater confequence to the nation, than gratifying our palates with French wine. This treaty, however, was to be fupported at any rate; which confidered feveral ingenious merchants of long experience, and well fkilled in trade, together with the late earl of Halifax and earl Stanhope, to ufe their utmoft endeavours to defeat it; which they effectually did, by the fatisfactory accounts thereof they laid before both houfes of parliament, and from what they publifhed from time to time, under the title of the Britifh Merchant, or Commerce preferved.

Sir Charles Coke, merchant at that time, made so clear a defence of our trade at the bar of the house of lords and commons, that he was afterwards deservedly made one of the lords commissioners of trade and plantations, and chose a member of parliament.

Sir Theodore Janssen, Bart. also, furnished many useful materials, which contributed towards the carrying that national point.

James Milner, Esq; merchant, and member of parliament, made appear, before the house of commons, the great importance of our trade to Portugal, and of the treaty of commerce which supports the same, in opposition to the French bill of commerce.

Mr Nathaniel Toriano, merchant, shewed the consequence of opening the French trade according to the proposed treaty, in so strong and so clear a light, as to convince even them who discouraged his speaking before parliament, of the destruction that must have inevitably fallen upon our country, had that treaty been rendered effectual by parliament.

Mr Joshua Gee, Mr Christopher Haynes, Mr David Martin, and several other very able and distinguished merchants, well acquainted with the interests of the trade of the nation, were extremely helpful likewise in defeating that pernicious treaty, and therefore latest posterity will have their names in honourable remembrance.

But we need go no further than our present time for instances of this kind. We have a conspicuous example before us, in one of the present representatives of this great city in parliament; who, upon all occasions, has manifested so superlative a knowledge in the general commerce of the nation, as deservedly to be distinguished with the highest honour and applause: which, one would think, should animate every young merchant to endeavour, next to his province, to excel in this kind of knowledge.

And, although every one cannot expect to be blessed with the genius of a Barnard and a Beckford, yet every merchant of distinction should be emulous to exert himself in the service of his country, in a manner so consistent with his profession. Every trader having a private interest in the promotion of the general trade, and practical traders having greater opportunities than others of knowing the true interest of the nation in that respect, it seems a duty owing to themselves, as well as their country, to turn their thoughts sometimes that way. Besides, in regard to their own particular interest, if they are not thoroughly acquainted with the political nature of that peculiar branch of knowledge, wherein they are personally concerned, how is it possible they can duly support and defend it on any great exigencies, in the eye of the legislature?

For the proper instruction of the students in each of these branches, it is supposed, that the college is provided with tutors well accomplished to act their respective parts, with all advantage to the collegians, and credit and honour to themselves.—It is supposed likewise, that the college is provided with a library of the best authors in all the modern languages, who have treated upon the several subjects before enumerated, and with a complete mathematical and philosophical apparatus for every purpose intended.

And now, if the reader will take a transient retrospect in his mind of what has been said, he will hardly scruple to grant, that merchandising, and the united qualifications necessary to form this skilful British trader, have as good a claim to the appellation of an art or a science, as most that are so honoured and distinguished should we say, that commerce is the grand support of most other arts that are solidly useful to mankind, it is no more than it deserves; and therefore it will not be thought unreasonable, that PRACTICAL TRADE, and MERCANTILE NEGOCIATIONS in general, should be reduced to as regular a method of institution, as it's inferior and dependent arts.

Of the PLAN of EXECUTION.

If the judicious reader should be candid enough to admit the preceding plan of particulars to be unexceptionable, and that there is nothing intimated therein, but what appears indispensably necessary to train up the merchant suitably to his great employment; yet it may be said, this is no great advance towards the carrying such a design to it's desireable height of perfection, in point of execution: it is far easier

to suggest the particulars requisite, than to obtain fit and capable persons for the office of instructors in an establishment of this kind. There is more difficulty attending this, perhaps, than there is in any other literary institution; for, in the distinct branches hereof were to be taught in the usual scholastic way, which is practised in public schools and other collegial seminaries, I am afraid it would frustrate the end proposed, and rather mar than forward the student in his accomplishments.

The merchant is expected to engage in trade for himself, and hazard his fortune therein, by the age of 23 or 24 at farthest many are impatient to stay so long: whereas the learned professions, as they are distinguished, give the student, upon the general, above ten years more in his application, before he is judged capable to make any tolerable figure in life; and that by subsisting only on the interest of his fortune, if he has any, but not hazarding the principal money, as the young merchant is obliged to do, before he can raise any sort of reputation in the commercial world.

This being the case, and the skilful merchant standing in need of so great variety of knowledge, in order to preserve and improve his fortune, every expedient should be devised, every art practised, that will conduce to give him the greatest fund of useful knowledge in the least time.

Without entering into a critic upon the usual methods of education in England, which, indeed, have been sufficiently exposed by learned men already; we shall only endeavour to shew in general, wherein, we apprehend, the method for accomplishment of the merchant ought to differ from that which is commonly practised, in regard to the more learned classes of the community.

The life of the merchant being a conversable one, his employment leading him to transactions even from the mechanic and manufacturer to the minister of state, his method of erudition, methinks, should be as different from that scholastic way, as his profession is from all others: the man of business has not 20 years to devote to the mere study of languages, metaphysics, and criticism, &c. Prudence directs him to apply early to those things indispensably requisite to prosperity in his employment; and what may adorn the learned professions, might spoil him for his own *.—When the merchant's accomplishments are equal to, or above his employment, and not his employment superior to his accomplishments, then he may be at liberty to aim at what advances leisure and prudence will admit, in the belles lettres and the liberal arts; but to aim at this before is acting as wisely as the peasant, who by turning star-gazer got smothered in a ditch.

> * Sir William Temple gives it as his opinion, that even the men of learning may be so overladen with learning, as to be weaker in point of judgment than if they had less.—So the merchant, if overstocked with that sort of literature which may be above or beside his province, he may be the worse merchant, though the greater scholar.—What Sir William says may deserve attention—' Who can tell, says he, whether learning may not even weaken invention, in a man that has great advantages from nature and birth; whether the weight and number of so many other men's thoughts and notions may not suppress his own, or hinder the motions and agitations of them, from which all invention arises; as heaping on wood, or too many sticks, or too close together, suppresses, and sometimes quite extinguishes a little spark that would otherwise have grown up to a noble flame. The strength of the mind, as well as of body, grows more from the warmth of exercise than of clothes; nay, too much of this foreign heat, rather makes men faint, and their constitution tender and weaker than they would be without them.'—Temple's Works, vol. i. fol. p. 158. If this observation of Sir William's should prove true, the merchant, with a share of learning suitable only to his profession, added to his conversable knowledge of the world, and the constant exercise of his own judgment in active business, may become a much wiser man, a more useful member to the community, than the profound scholar, whose understanding is drowned in the ocean of knowledge borrowed only from others.

Upon the whole, what we would mean to say is, that there should seem to be a certain pitch of literature, beyond which it is dangerous for the commercial man to advance; and really the field of knowledge, which the nature of the mercantile employment require, is not so scanty as some may be wont to think *: nor should the manner of communication of what is requisite be in the ordinary scholastic way, the merchant's time being limited, as before observed, to so few years, for the course of his erudition.

> * See our Universal Dictionary throughout, in what relates to his accomplishments.

Nor will a profound knowledge, in every mercantile branch which we have particularised, answer the end: there are, perhaps, many far more learned divines, lawyers, and physicians, who live in obscurity, than those who gain their thousands a year, and make a pompous figure in life: some study the externals, the knowledge of the world, and the craft of rising without merit, while others study only to deserve what they never arrive at.—The merchant must be the man of the world, as well as skilful in the requisites of his profession; but his being immured in a college to converse only with the dead letter, and the jargon of the schools, will render him as unfit for his profession, as Sir Isaac Newton was for a dancing-master.

Wherefore the question is, what is the best method to train up this man of business? We say he must not be deficient in some of the principal modern languages, nor should he be incapable of reading a Latin author at least, though it may not be necessary for him to be a classical critic. If he enters the college with a childish smattering of this tongue only, he should not leave it, without such a fundamental mastery, that he can improve himself therein at intervals, even in the height of his mercantile concerns.

The business of languages, especially the learned ones, as they are eminently distinguished, is made an Herculean toil, in the packhorse road of an ordinary English education; yet no nation has better helps to facilitate their acquisition.— We abound with English translations, both literal and free, of the poets as well as prosaic authors, more than sufficient to enable a person to read any of the rest; sufficient, however, to capacitate the man of business to read any he may chuse; and he has scarce ever occasion to speak or write that dead language; though why the English, as well as foreigners, should not be accustomed to speak the Latin, there can be no substantial reason given, perhaps.—The English are remarkable for writing Latin inferior to none; and why they should not speak it equally well, if trained to it, is not easy to say. Because we can never be able, say some, from the change of customs, and extraordinary difference of idiom, &c. to speak that language with a Roman elegancy, are we therefore not to attempt it at all? Would not a conversible use in this dead language, from our infancy, greatly expedite the acquisition of the modern, which have a near affinity therewith? This will hardly be gainsaid *.

* 'If a man could be got, says our great Mr Locke, who, him-
'self speaking good Latin, would always be about your
'son, talk constantly to him, and suffer him to speak or
'read nothing else (a), this would be the true genuine way,
'and that which I would propose, not only as the easiest
'and best, wherein a child might, without pains or chiding,
'get a language, which others are wont to be whipped for
'at school, six or seven years together; but also as that,
'wherein at the same time he might have his mind and
'manners formed, and he be instructed to boot in several
'sciences; such as are a good part of geography, astrono-
'my, chronology, anatomy, besides some parts of history,
'and all other parts of knowledge of things, that fall un-
'der the senses, and require little more than Memory.
'For these, if we would take the true way, our knowledge
'should begin, and in those things be laid the foundation;
'and not in the abstract notions of logics and metaphysics,
'which are fitter to amuse than inform the understanding,
'in its first setting out towards knowledge.
'When young men have had their heads employed a while
'in those abstract speculations, without finding the success
'and improvement, or that use of them which they expect-
'ed, they are apt to have mean thoughts, either of learn-
'ing or themselves; they are tempted to quit their studies
'and throw away their books, as containing nothing but
'hard words and empty sounds; or else to conclude, that,
'if there be any real knowledge in them, they themselves
'have not understanding capable of it. That this is so,
'perhaps, I could assure you upon my experience. Amongst
'other things to be learned by a young gentleman in this
'method, whilst others are only taken up with Latin and
'languages, I may also set down geometry for one, having
'known a young gentleman, bred something after this
'way, able to demonstrate several propositions in Euclid,
'before he was thirteen.'

(a). This is the method by which the celebrated Montaigne was taught Latin, and from which very probably Mr Locke might borrow the thought. What Montaigne says of himself may deserve regard:— 'No doubt but Greek and Latin are very great ornaments, and of very great use, but we buy them too dear: I will here discover one way, which also has been experimented in my own Person, by which they are to be had better cheap, and such may make use of it that will. My father, having made the most precise enquiry that any man could possibly make, amongst men of the greatest learning and judgment, of an exact method of education, was by them cautioned of the inconveniences then in use, and made to believe, that the tedious time we applied to the learning of the languages of these people who had them for nothing, was the sole cause we could not arrive to that grandeur of soul and perfection of knowledge with the ancient Greeks and Romans: I do not, however, believe that to be the only cause; but the expedient my father found out for this was, that in my minority, and before I began to speak, he committed me to the care of a German, who has since died a famous physician in France, totally ignorant of our language, but very fluent, and a great critic in Latin.

'This man, whom he had fetched out of his own country, and whom he entertained with a very great salary for this only end, had me continually in his arms: to whom there were also joined two others of the same nation, but of inferior learning, to attend me, and sometimes to relieve him, who all of them entertained me with no other language but Latin. As to the rest of his family, it was an inviolable rule, that neither himself, nor my mother, man nor maid, should speak any thing in my company, but such Latin words as every one had learnt only to gabble with me. It is not to be imagined, how great an advantage this proved to the whole family; my father and my mother, by this means learning Latin enough to understand it perfectly well, and to speak it to such a degree, as was sufficient for any necessary use; as also those of the servants did, who were most frequent with me.—To be short, we

'did Latin it at such a rate, that it overflowed to all the neighbouring villages, where there yet remain, that have obtained by custom, several Latin appellations of artisans and their tools. As for what concerns myself, I was above the years of two before I understood either French or Perigordin, any more than Arabic; and, without Art, Book, Grammar, or Precept, Whipping, or the expence of a Tear, had by that time learned to speak as pure Latin as my master himself. M. for reason, there were no grounds to give me a theme after the college fashion, they put a others in French; but in this they were of nothing to get at the word Latin, to turn it into that which was pure and good, as Nicho as Grouchi, who was a book De Comitiis Romanorum, William Guerente, who has writ a comment upon Aristotle, George Buchanan, that great Scotch poet, and Marcus Antonius Muretus who as both France and Italy have acknowledged for the best orator of his time, my masters everyone have all of them told me, that I had in my infancy that language so very ready and pat, that they were afraid to enter into discourse with me; and particularly Buchanan, whom I since saw attending the late Marshal de Briac, then told me, that he was about to write a treatise of education, the example of which he intended to take from mine, for he was then tutor to that count de Briac, who afterwards proved so valiant and brave a gentleman. As to Greek, of which I have but a smattering, my father also designed to have taught it me by a trick, but a new one, and by way of sport, tossing our declensions to and fro, after the manner of those, who by certain games, and tables and chess, learn geometry and arithmetic: for he, amongst other rules, had been advised to make me relish science and duty by an unforced will, and of my own voluntary motion, and to educate my soul in all liberty and delight, without any severity or constraint.'

Besides the practice of conversation, as recommended by Mr Locke and Montaigne, and indeed by all the learned men of other nations, the next means is translation; which, according to the learned Mr Askham *, who was preceptor to queen Elizabeth, ought to be double; that is to say, not only Latin into English, but the same English again into the original Latin, whereby learners have the classical authors to correct themselves by; which, being of the pure Roman phrase, is a far better standard for correction than the judgment of the generality of schoolmasters.

* See the Schoolmaster: or, A plain and perfect way of teaching children to understand, write, and speak the Latin tongue. By Roger Askham, Esq; preceptor to her majesty queen Elizabeth, corrected and revised, with an addition of explanatory notes, by the Rev. Mr James Upton, A. M. rector of Brimpton in Somersetshire, and late fellow of King's College in Cambridge. Printed in the year 1711, for Benjamin Tooke, at the Middle Temple Gate in Fleet-Street.—This I think is one of the best books I ever met with to help youth forward in the Latin tongue, with great care and pleasure, and which I myself have experienced.

' But, if such a man cannot be got, says Mr Locke, who speaks good Latin, and, being able to instruct your son in all these parts of knowledge, will undertake it by this method, the next best is to have him taught as near this way as may be, which is by taking some easy and pleasant book, such as Æsop's Fables, and writing the English translation (made as literal as it can be) in one line, and the Latin words which answer each of them, just over it in another. These let him read every day over and over again, till he perfectly understands the Latin; and then go on to another fable, till he be also perfect in that, not omitting what he is already perfect in, but sometimes reviewing that, to keep it in his memory. And, when he comes to write, let there be set him for copies;

which, with the exercise of his hand, will also advance him in Latin. This being a more imperfect way than by talking Latin unto him, the formation of the verbs first, and afterwards the declensions of the nouns and pronouns perfectly learned by heart, may facilitate his acquaintance with the genius and manner of the Latin tongue, which varies the signification of verbs and nouns, not as the modern languages do, by particles prefixed, but by changing the last syllables. More than this of grammar * I think he need not have, till he can read himself Sanctii Minerva, with Scioppius and Perizonius's notes.'

* The absurdity, says the late ingenious Mr Clark of Hull, in his New Latin Grammar, of teaching the Latin tongue by a grammar in Latin, is so very gross, that one would wonder how it should ever enter into the head of any person of common sense, much more how it should ever become a national practice. But common custom in most cases of import ... is so far from being the rule of right, that it is the very reverse of it, and in no case more flagrantly than this. The imposing of public prayers for the use of the people in a language they know not, as senseless and ridiculous a practice as it is, is not more so than it is to pretend to teach a language by rules writ in the very language to be learnt, and which consequently the learner cannot understand, or make any use of, till he is rendered into a language he does know; and then it is the translation only, and not the original, that is of use to him. In short, the most rude and barbarous nations upon earth cannot furnish us with any instance of a custom, that carries more of stupidity in the front of it. And therefore it is somewhat strange, that a practice so mischievous, as well as ridiculous, should not long since have had a stop put to it by law. Our legislators have almost all in their turns been considerable ...... by it; and, unless they please by their authority to prevent it, their posterity after them are like to suffer on in the same manner to the end of the world. For public custom is seldom to be conquered but by authority, especially where people are got into a wrong way, so perverse or weak are the generality of mankind. It is, therefore, very much to be wished, the legislature would take the matter under consideration, and, to save a deal of pain and plague, as well as a miserable waste of time to the youth of the nation, put an effectual stop to the senseless and barbarous custom of teaching the Latin tongue by a Latin grammar. They have highly merited of the people of Great Britain, by delivering them from a grievance of a like nature, the use of the Latin tongue, or doggerel rather under that denomination, in the practice of the law.

Another act of that nature, in pity to the poor suffering youth of the kingdom, would, I dare say, be as kindly and thankfully received, by all true lovers of their country and good letters. Whether it may be reasonable or proper for authority to impose the use of any one grammar, I shall not take upon me to determine here; but this I shall be bold to say, that it is as reasonable to forbid by law the pretence of teaching the Latin tongue by a grammar writ in Latin, as it is to forbid the use of that language in the public worship of God. Both practices are equally ridiculous, though not equally pernicious. For the thing proposed in both cases is utterly unattainable. Youth can no more learn by the help of a language they do not understand, than the people can pray to God in a language they do not understand, which every body sees to be impossible, and nonsense to pretend.—So far the ingenious Mr Clark.

In teaching of children this too, I think, is to be observed, that, in most cases where they stick, they are not to be further puzzled, by putting them upon finding it out of themselves; as by asking such questions as these, viz. which is the nominative case in the sentence they are to construe? Or demanding what aufero signifies, to lead them to the knowledge what abstulere signifies, &c. when they cannot readily tell. This wastes time only in disturbing them; for, whilst they are learning, and apply themselves with attention, they are to be kept in good humour, and every thing made easy to them, and as pleasant as possible *. Therefore, whenever they are at a stand, and are willing to go forwards, help them presently over the difficulty, without any rebuke or chiding; remembering, that, where harsher ways are taken, they are the effect only of pride and peevishness in the teacher, who expects children should instantly be masters of as much as he knows: whereas he should rather consider, that his business is to settle in them habits, not angrily to inculcate rules, which serve for little in the conduct of our lives; at least are of no use to children, who forget them as soon as given. In sciences where their reason is to be exercised, I will not deny, but this method may sometimes be varied, and difficulties proposed on purpose to excite industry, and

accustom the mind to employ its own strength and sagacity in reasoning. But yet, I guess, this is not to be done to children whilst very young, nor at their entrance upon any sort of knowledge; then every thing of itself is difficult, and the great use and skill of a teacher is to make all as easy as he can. But particularly, in learning of languages, there is the least occasion for posing of children. For languages, being to be learned by ROTE, CUSTOM, and MEMORY, are then spoken in greatest perfection, when all rules of grammar are utterly forgotten. I grant the grammar of a language is sometimes very carefully to be studied, but it is only to be studied by a grown man, when he applies himself to the understanding of any language critically, which is seldom the business of any but professed scholars. This, I think, will be agreed to, that, if a gentleman be to study any language, it ought to be that of his own country, that he may understand the language which he has constant use of, with the utmost accuracy.' See Locke of Education.

* These sentiments of Mr Locke have induced many to oblige the public with literal translations of several of the introductory classical authors, for the use of schools; and which, I doubt not, have proved extremely helpful; especially when the learners have been exercised by Mr Ascham's method of double translation, and the grammar rules have been explained at proper times, in plain English. Many teachers of the dead languages are ridiculous and pedantic enough, to act in defiance of the opinion of Mr Locke, Montaigne, Ascham, and other the most learned men in Europe, as might be easily shewn, and will not suffer youth to have all those helps for which these great men have so wisely commended: yet too many of these learned asses are obliged to make use themselves of these very auxiliaries, which they deny to children; in which a gentleman and myself once accidentally detected his son's schoolmaster at his own house.—Must not this be, with design to make the children believe, that their masters are so superlatively profound in these languages, that they stand in need of no expositor or annotator, when they really stand in need of them as much as the youths themselves? Or, must it not be with intent to lay every obstacle in the way of their improvement, that they may exert their preceptorial tyranny with less restraint? There cannot be too many helps for the acquisition of languages, both ancient and modern; and those, I am afraid, who the most strenuously oppose them, I shall always suspect, since the above accident, have the greatest occasion for them.

Monsieur Rollin, than whom few have better understood the method of training up youth in the learned languages, is of the same sentiment: 'La première question, dit-il, qui se présente, est de savoir quelle méthode il faut suivre pour enseigner la langue Latine. Il me semble qu'il présent l'on convient assez généralement que les premières règles que l'on donne pour apprendre le Latin, doivent être en Latin, parce qu'en TOUTE SCIENCE, en toute connoissance, il est naturel de passer d'une chose CONNUE & CLAIRE à une chose qui est INCONNUE & OBSCURE. Ou a senti qu'il n'étoit pas moins absurde, & moins contraire au bon sens, de donner en Latin les premiers préceptes de la langue Latine, qu'il le seroit d'en user ainsi pour le GREC, & pour toutes les LANGUES ÉTRANGÈRES.'

Those who would require greater satisfaction in relation to the method suggested for the speedy and familiar acquisition of languages, we refer them to consult not only those principal authors beforementioned, but such also who have followed the principles of those learned men, and wrote, since their time, upon the utility of the plainest and most literal translations (something in the way proposed by Mr Locke) in order to facilitate the knowledge of the Latin tongue in particular *.— And, after the student is a master of these several authors, by the constant exercise of the method of double translation, and having the grammatical rules familiarly explained to him occasionally in plain English, he will be able of himself to read with pleasure several of the other classical authors; especially those with free and elegant translations, such as those wrote by Guthrie, Melmoth, Dunster, Dr Martyn, and divers others; as also those commentators who have wrote in Latin upon the Roman classics. Upon the whole, however necessary some learned men may think it, that the youth of this nation intended for the learned professions should plod on in the old way of gaining a knowledge of the dead languages, it is to be hoped that the parents of those who are intended for merchants will think it the worst method that can be taken for them: and what is the worst method for their attainment of a knowledge in the Latin tongue, can never be the best to be followed in relation to the modern languages.—

They muft be acquired by conftant converfation with fuch who fpeak with propriety; by double tranflation, and by having the grammatical part eafily explained in their native language, from the mouth of the tutor, and not by a multitude of rules got by heart, which only ferve to burthen the memory, render learning difagreeable to youth, and retard their proficiency.—If I remember right, bifhop Sprat, in the Life of Cowley, fays, That he could never be br uglt to learn the Latin tongue by grammar rules, and yet few of the moderns have wrote that language with greater purity.

> * The firft that I remember to have appeared upon this occafion, was Mr Philips, fub-preceptor to his royal highnefs the duke. (2.) Mr Clark, of the public grammar fchool of Hull, author of two Effays on Education and fludies of A New Grammar of the Latin tongue, and Literal Tranflations of feveral of the Introductory Latin Claffics. (3.) Doctor Stirling. (4.) N. Bailey, Mr Watfon, and others.

Before we difmifs this point of language, we will take leave to make one obfervation more; which I have never met with in any of thofe authors who have wrote upon the beft methods of obtaining a knowledge of languages. The reader, however, will pleafe to take notice that what we are about to fay is only intended as a requifite addition to what has been already propofed by Mr Locke, Mr Afcham, and thofe other authors before quoted, in regard to the ufefulnefs of prepared literal tranflations, &c.

Another thing we defire the reader will pleafe to obferve, is, that we take it for granted no youth is admitted into the college before the age of 15 at leaft, and that he has been fomewhat initiated into Latin and French, and can write his native language tolerably, together with a pretty good current hand.

Now, what we would humbly fubmit to further confideration is, in relation to the moft natural method of making ufe of proper literal tranflations in the propofed college, in order to render the fpeaking and underftanding of the Latin tongue, or any of the modern languages, very eafy and familiar to the mercantile ftudent: and what we have to propofe is comprehended under the few following words:

The conftant proper ufe of a LIVING DICTIONARY, and a LIVING GRAMMAR, and proper LITERAL TRANSLATIONS.

That all literal tranflations may be made a proper ufe of, by the means of a living dictionary, it is propofed there fhall be a kind of defk, elevated to a pitch proper for the purpofe, wherein there fhall always be one perfon conftantly tranflating, with an audible voice, either Latin into Englifh, or Englifh into Latin; or French into Englifh, or Englifh into French; and the like of any other modern language to be learned; and thofe tranflations to be in as literal a manner as the different idioms of the languages will admit of, fo as to be perfectly intelligible.—At the fame time fhould be explained, viva voce, the peculiar cuftoms and antiquities of the Romans, when any thing occurs that renders the fame neceffary to the better underftanding the author which is thus publickly tranflating.

1. Let it be fuppofed, that, while fuch a conftant tranflation, during the hours of education, is going on, a profound filence is preferved, and due attention is given by the ftudents to fuch tranflation.

2. Let it be fuppofed, likewife, that one fingle day only in the fix is allotted for the explication of the rules of grammar, of any author that has been tranflated, in the fame public way, relating to the peculiar language to be acquired.

Thefe fimple exercifes being fuppofed to be fteddily purfued, in regard to any language, what may we reafonably prefume to be the confequence?

In this exercife, the reader will pleafe to obferve, that the ear and the memory of youth only are conftantly employed, with refpect to the point of double tranflation; and that the underftanding is familiarly worked upon, in order to imbibe and retain the rules of grammar, without the leaft difagreeable application or fatigue.

It is by the conftant ufe of the tongue, the faculties of hearing and the memory only, whereby mankind obtain the knowledge to fpeak, write, and underftand their native languages: and, if, in the public way of teaching any other languages, we can fall nearly upon the like meafures, is it not very reafonable to hope and expect that any other languages may be thereby acquired as familiarly and infenfibly as we do our mother tongues? That this muft be the effect of fuch exercifes, we have not only the judgment of fo great a man as Mr Locke, but the experience of a Montaigne, our great queen Elizabeth, and Madam Dacier.

By thumbing over the DEAD DICTIONARY and DEAD GRAMMAR, a youth of 15 fhall, perhaps, make fhift, with Herculean toil, and the help of his fchool-fellows, to hammer out, in a very pitiful way, thirty or forty lines of an author in a day, the greateft part of which he too often as foon forgets as learns: whereas, by means of the conftant exercife of the LIVING DICTIONARY, and the LIVING GRAMMAR, and LITERAL TRANSLATIONS, he may, with great eafe and pleafure, learn fome hundreds of lines in a day, and retain the greateft part of the words and phrafes in his memory.

Whether thefe exercifes will be attended with advantages fo fuperior to what the ordinary ones are, it may be neceffary to enter into a further eclairciffement of the plan propofed.—To which end, the reader is defired further to obferve, that

The whole college is fuppofed to confift only, or chiefly, of young ftudents who are defigned for the mercatorial employment.—That their continuance therein is propofed to be from the age of 15 to 19, and that the whole number of them fhall be divided into four or more claffes; that is, thofe of the firft year's ftanding fhould be of the firft clafs, thofe of the fecond of the next, &c.

At the firft commencement of this inftitution, the frefhmen, who enter at 15, muft be affifted, as much as poffible, by the means propofed, for the firft year, by the tutors; but, upon their enterance into the fecond year, thofe of the firft clafs may, in a great meafure, be inftructed by the meafures fuggefted, by their fellow ftudents of the fecond year's ftanding; and thofe of the fecond year's ftanding be inftructed by thofe of the third; and thofe of the third by thofe of the fourth year's ftanding; which will prove of no lefs eafe to the tutors, than benefit to themfelves.—To explain myfelf.

1. It is prefumed that thofe ftudents who enter into the fecond year have, in the way propofed, gone through two, three, or more of the introductory Latin claffical authors, befides two or three French authors * which are proper for the occafion. At the fame time, the reader is defired to obferve, that there are ftated times for their improvement in figures, and their mechanical hand-writing, and fomething of geography.

> * The plaineft profe authors we judge beft to begin with.

2. That three or four, or more, of the moft expert ftudents of the fecond clafs fhould be conftant public tranflators to thofe of the firft clafs, the tutor always attending to explain difficulties, as they occurred.—Thofe of the third clafs to thofe of the fecond, and thofe of the fourth to thofe of the third clafs, &c.

3. This will refrefh the memories again of the ftudents with the authors which they had read in their prior clafs, habituate them to a graceful pronunciation and elocution, and prove of great eafe to the lungs of the tutor, whom we cannot prefume to be capable of continuing a public tranflation feveral hours in the day; but this may be very eafily done by a requifite number of the ftudents of a fuperior clafs, in the prefence of the tutor appointed for the inftruction of the clafs.

4. By thefe fimple exercifes, fteddily and judicioufly purfued, the ftudents cannot trifle away a moment's time of the hours allotted for their inftruction, which they do when left intirely to themfelves, with the ufe only of their dead dictionary and grammar, and without any proper tranflation to affift them.

5. It is fuppofed, as before intimated, that there is a profound filence always preferved in the room of public tranflation; that is, nothing is to be heard but the continued voice of the public tranflator for the time being.—If any thing is capable of fixing the attention of youth, this method feems to bid very fair for it, becaufe it is not attended with the leaft degree of toil or perplexity, every obftacle to their advancement being agreeably removed.

6. In order to judge whether due attention hath been given by every individual to the voice of the public tranflator, it fhould be an eftablifhed rule for the tutor to caufe, every day, fuch as he may fufpect of inattention to mount the defk, and to retranflate publickly fuch a part of what has been done, perhaps, feveral times over by the appointed tranflators; and thofe who prove delinquents, and appear to be remarkably neglectful, will not only be thus ignominioufly expofed, but they fhould be punifhed, by being that day confined to fuch extraordinary exercifes, while their fellow ftudents, who have behaved well, fhould be indulged in their diverfions, and admitted to a table, for their meals, where there was fomething more delicate than at the table of fuch delinquents.—Something of this kind might be attended with very happy confequences to the youth, and of no little eafe to the refpective tutors.

We shall say no more in relation to languages.—The next points are those of FIGURES and ACCOUNTANTSHIP; and these, likewise, and such other parts of the mathematics, and, experimental philosophy, as we have touched upon; we would have taught as much in the same way as their peculiar nature will admit of; we mean, with relation to the rationale of the rules given for the practical operations of arithmetic, and the principles whereupon the art of accountantship by debtor and creditor, is founded, &c. together with proper lectures upon the mathematical and philosophic parts.—But, as the utility of the arithmetic and accountant-ship branches, in particular to the merchant, depends upon the ready and expert practice, the greatest variety of examples should not be wanting to exercise the several rules and principles thereof: yet these examples, also, we would have all performed in a public way, that the student should not have it in his power at all to trifle away his time: forthat we judge a very essential point to be guarded against throughout the whole of this institution: but this can never be effectually done, provided a public lecturer, or demonstrator, is not constantly employed in those parts, as well as in the languages, and the silence and attention of the students are, at the same time, so diligently engaged as thoroughly to comprehend whatever they are thus publickly instructed in; and are able, also, to exercise the same in those practical uses which the nature of their employment may occasionally require: yet this cannot be effectually done, unless they have great variety of practical exercise in the several and respective branches *. Wherefore,

* That the fundamental principles of every branch may be duly impressed upon the mind, they should, together with proper examples, be fairly written, at the proper times appointed for that purpose, into books, by every individual student; and they should be also taught how to keep an alphabetical common place book, wherein to register whatever they may hereafter have occasion to refer to.

The reader will please to observe, that another material and general principle, whereupon we propose the PLAN of EXECUTION to be founded, is, GREAT PRACTICE AND EXERCISE, in every branch of erudition. And, to corroborate our opinion herein, we shall again appeal to the authority of Mr Locke:

' No body is made any thing by hearing of rules, says he, or
' laying them up in his memory; practice must settle the ha-
' bit of doing, without reflecting on the rule; and you may
' as well hope to make a good painter or musician extempore,
' by a lecture, and instruction in the arts of music and paint-
' ing, as a coherent thinker, or strict reasoner, by a set of
' rules, shewing him wherein right reasoning consists.' Locke's Conduct of the Understanding, vol. iii. p. 395.

With respect to the knowledge of the laws, customs, and usages relative to the employment of a merchant, those likewise, we apprehend, should be inculcated not only by PUBLIC LECTURE, but by FAMILIAR CONVERSATIONS upon the subjects of averages, barratries, bottomrees, bankruptcies, charter-parties, demurrages, exchanges [bills of exchange] and all other the variety of occurrences that arise in the course of practical business, all which will afford a wide field for improvement in matters of real use.—In relation to the method of instruction by public lecture, that is obvious enough to every one.—But what we mean by familiar conversation, may require some explanation. To which we shall only observe, that one or two evenings in the week, after the college exercises, should be set apart for those students, who are competently advanced, to give their opinion in the English language, or any other of the moderns, in the presence of the proper professor appointed for this branch, upon any of the beforementioned subjects, or any other relating to mercantile affairs; it being supposed, that the subject has been given out some days before-hand, in order for them to consult the proper books in the college, or their own libraries, for that purpose. By this pleasing conversible exercise, the young students will be early inured to reflection, and retention of what they read, when they are under the necessity of communicating publickly

what authors they have consulted upon the occasion.—Besides, many of these points may lead to some debates; the professor may start objections, and ask their true opinions, when the subject is properly opened by him: and, by familiar interrogatories made from the chair, this will naturally draw out such answers as will shew who have, and who have not been assiduous in their applications to understand the subject from the books of authority.

The great Montaigne says, ' If I was compelled to choose, I
' should sooner, I think, consent to lose my sight than hear-
' ing and speech. The Athenians and Romans held the ex-
' ercise of familiar conference and debate in great honour in
' their academies.' Mr Locke had so high an opinion of it's
utility, as to recommend it in the following words: ' That
' there should be proposed to young gentlemen rational and
' useful questions, suited to their age and capacities, and on
' subjects not wholly unknown to them, nor out of their way;
' such as these, when they are ripe for exercises of this nature,
' they should extempore, or after a little meditation upon the
' spot, speak to, without penning of any thing: for I ask, if
' we will examine the effects of this way of learning to speak
' well, who speak best in any business, when occasion calls
' them to it, upon any debate, either those who have ac-
' customed themselves to compose and write down before-
' hand what they would say; or those, who thinking only
' on the matter, to understand that as well as they can, use
' themselves only to speak extempore. And be that shall
' judge by this, will be little apt to think that accustoming
' him to studied speeches and set compositions is the way to
' fit a young gentleman for business *.'

* Cicero, if I may be allowed once to mention such a name
in a design of this nature, somewhere speaks of C. Curio,
who had never read any books of eloquence, nor made any
historical collections, nor understood any thing of the public or private part of the law; yet was so happy in expressing
himself, as to be esteemed one of the best orators of his
time. What gained him this applause, was a clear shining
phrase, and a sudden quickness and fluency of expression,
which was acquired purely by the benefits of his private
education, being always used to a correct way of speaking
in the house wherein he was brought up.

The same exercises of constant public lectures and public conversations, we also judge to be the most naturally adapted to the attainment of the other branches enumerated in the general plan, and, therefore, we shall only further observe,
1. The reader will please to remark in general, throughout the execution of every part of the proposed plan, we would recommend a similitude and uniformity of practice, viz. the constant exercise of the faculties of hearing, speaking, and registering by writing, the fundamental principles of whatever shall be taught in the college; and this without any retardment whatever to the progress of the student, every difficulty being agreeably removed as soon as it occurs.
2. The variety of capacities among youth, it is to be feared, is commonly too little attended to in their education: methods, suitably adapted to one genius, mar, blunt, and confound another. To prevent prejudicial consequences of this kind, our plan of execution is so devised as to suit any variety of capacities and dispositions. The slower genius and milder complexion will here have the fairest play to exert itself, without that awe and perplexity which often nips it in it's tender bud. On the other hand, the strongest and most nervous capacity, the genius of the greatest sprightliness and vigour, will have every advantage to fix it's fire, and agreeably mould and fashion it to application.
Emulation in youth, like ambition in men, exciting to the most laudable endeavours, no expedient should be wanting first to raise, and afterwards to cherish and support this noble passion.
One motive of this kind will be peculiar to these young gentlemen: which is, their being made sensible how easily they may advance each other's credit and interest in the way of trade: but, without suitable qualifications to play skilfully into each other's hands, they should be convinced that they can never hope to reap such benefit by their mutual intercourse of friendships.
The experienced well know how merchants properly situated at home and abroad may promote one another. This is often done by persons bred in separate practical counting-houses in the ordinary way: but, where young people are bred up together, in the like maxims and practices, and where personal friendships are contracted from their youth, they will more naturally fall upon measures for their common advantage: especially so, when such have been properly pointed out to them in the course of their collegial erudition, and deeply impressed in their tender years.
In carrying the whole of this design into execution, the natural and ordinary practices of men of sense and genius should be made the principal guide. From art should be only borrowed such helps as will aid and assist, no way cramp and suppress, the intellectual powers and faculties; and how far those powers and faculties will carry youth, under an institution whose sole foundation is to render every acquisition as pleasing

and delightful as possible, but, perhaps, scarce even here as
by experimented [*]. In the common method of acquiring
knowledge, men been generally but intent upon the dead letter;
whereas, if the real convertible practices of matter and, people
regulated and conducted, and improved by natural and engaging arts, were made the principal transactions in every kind
of literary institution, we might, indeed, have less pedants,
but more truly useful members of the community.

* 'Un maître habile & attentif met tout en usage pour rendre
'l'etude aux jeunes gens agreable. Il prend leur ton, il
'il etudie leur goût: il consulte leur humeur, il met en
'jeu au travail: il paroit leur en laisser le choix : il ne fait
'point une régle de l'etude, il en excite quelquefois le desir
'par la refus même, & par la cessation, ou plutot par l'in-
'terruption : en un mot, il se tourne en mille formes, &
'invente mille adresses pour arriver à son but.' Rollin des
Belles Lettres. Du Gouvernement des Colléges.

'I would not, says Montaigne again, have this pupil of our's
'imprisoned and made a slave to his learning; nor would I have
'him given up to the morosity and melancholic humour of a
'sour, ill-natured pedant. I would not have his spirit cowed
'and subdued, by applying him to the rack, and tormenting
'him, as some do, fourteen or fifteen hours a day, and so
'make a pack-horse of him. Nor should I think it good,
'when, by reason of a solitary and melancholic complexion,
'he is discovered to be much addicted to books, to nourish
'that humour in him, for that renders them unfit for civil
'conversation, and diverts him from better employments.—
'The place of education, adds he, should be painted with
'the pictures of joy and gladness, Flora and the Graces, as
'the philosopher Speulippus did his ; that, where their profit
'is, they might there have their pleasure too.'
We would not have it signified, that these young gentlemen
can be expected to arrive at so great a mastery in every thing
we have suggested, as to become perfect proficients therein.
The youth of many, and the shortness of time proposed for their
continuance in the college, cannot well allow of this. But
we take upon us to say, that all who have tolerable natural
abilities can scarce avoid contracting so good a habitude of attention and application to business, as will grow up with
them throughout the whole of their lives, and, indeed, qualify them ever after to be their own instructors. ' It is not,
' as Mr Locke observes, the business of education, in respect
' to knowledge, to perfect a learner in all, or any of the sci-
' ences, but to give his mind that freedom, that disposition,
' those habits, that may enable him to attain any part of
' knowledge he shall apply himself to, or stand in need of in
' the future course of his life.'
It having been a dispute among the learned world, whether a
public or a private education is to be preferred, it may be necessary to observe, that, according to the proposed institution,
the end of both may be effectually answered at the same time:
and that not only in regard to the point of mercantile accomplishment, but in regard also to the morals of young people;
for such should be the discipline established for the conduct of
this design, that every moment of time might be properly regulated, even that portion allotted for diversions, in order to
render them innocent, at the same time that they are manly,
pleasurable, and healthful.
Some of the wisest men in all ages have been of opinion, that
there is no one living to whom nature has not given a capacity
to understand some one science, or to be better formed to excel in one employment or profession, rather than in another.
Many there are, who, to no purpose, applying to one branch
of knowledge or business, have made very great proficiency
by being turned to a different.
As many, we presume, are bred to merchandizing, or, as a
learned divine expresses himself upon a similar occasion, have
run their heads against a counting-house, who might have
done their country notable service at a plough-tail, the proposed institution will serve as a proper place of trial, in order
early to discover whether a youth has, or has not, a suitable
capacity for the merchant. This will be easily discernable in
two years time, at furthest; and, if he does not happen to be well
turned for that employment, it will not be too late for a parent
to think of some other, more agreeable to his son's natural genius and capacity: for, however common it may be, it is
never the less ridiculous, instead of adapting the studies or
profession of a youth to his genius, to act the reverse, by a-
dapting his genius to his studies or profession. To this it may
be imputed, that many formed by nature to shine in some
principal post, to be the envy of foreign nations, and admiration of posterity, and the honour and ornament of the age

in which they lived, have been utterly lost to themselves and
their country.
And so easy, familiar, and engaging, ought the manner of
exercising, and reducing to practice every branch of the plan,
that it will be scarce possible for a young person to have any
latent abilities for a merchant, and those not to appear in the
most conspicuous manner. So that our institution, considered
in this light also, cannot but prove of great public utility, it
having so happy a tendency to the saving estates, in private
families, by keeping those out of trade who are unfit for it, as
to the raising great ones, by throwing others into it with every
advantage.
The reason for proposing this regulation as well of the plan of
execution as the general one, is, that, in case there should be
occasion to call in assistants ; under the chief professors, the
method of execution may, on no account whatever, be de-
viated from by such assistants, for that would be leaving them
to a random way of instruction, without any check or controul, and suffering them to break in upon the several parts
of the institution, as regulated for the acquisition of each
branch : which would prove detrimental to the order and connection of the whole. Beside, nothing is more common than
for inferior assistants, who are capable only to act some under-
part, to have different methods of instruction, peculiar to
themselves ; and as the incapacity, or ill conduct of those assistants, may make it frequently necessary to change them,
was the method of instruction to be changed at the same time,
it would eternally bewilder the young students, and greatly
retard their progress. But, by adhering inviolably to a well-
digested plan of execution, as strict an eye will be kept over
assistants, that they steadily perform their duty, according to
the method prescribed to them, as is over the young people
themselves ; whereby it will not be in the power either of the
one or the other to trifle away their time, and neglect the
performance of what is daily expected of both [*].

* Le principal est comme l'ame, qui met tout en mouvement,
& qui préside à tout. C'est sur luy que roule le soin d'étab-
lir le bon ordre, de maintenir la discipline, de veiller en
général sur les études & sur les mœurs. Rollin des Belles
Lettres.

By this steady and uniform discipline in executing the whole,
what may appear very difficult, and even impracticable to
some, will be found quite otherwise to those who have a just
idea of the happy and extraordinary effects of order and regularity ; for those effectually preserve what the contrary absolutely destroy.
Merchants coming so early in life into the business of the
world, have not time for the attainment of what is called a
learned education. It is, therefore, our plan is so devised,
as, in a great measure, to supply that deficiency. And what
the intelligent reader will observe to be peculiar to it is, without young people who are intended for business running the
hazard of being captivated with such refined and scholastic
speculations as might not only prove detrimental, but absolutely ruinous to their way of life.
Nor is it less observable, that the utility of this institution does
not altogether consist in the proper choice of matter, but in
the manner of communication ; the method of conducting
the whole being such as will insensibly engage young minds
in the habit of close thinking, steadiness and attention, as
well as inspire them with ambition to excel in their peculiar
province. These are qualifications that cannot be set at too
high a rate ; for, while young people's minds are thus emu-
lously engaged, their morals will be more effectually preser-
ved, than by all other measures, perhaps, that could be taken
for that purpose.
The time proposed for the continuance of these young gentlemen in the college, is from 15 to 19 years of age; in which
they will be qualified to enter into any counting-house whatsoever, of the most extensive and universal trade : and there
can be no doubt but their superior qualifications will prove an
agreeable recommendation to the more skilful and ingenious
merchants, though they may be quite otherwise to those of
the opposite turn. Such a fund of pertinent knowledge will
our young merchant be furnished with, and so expert will he
be in every part of the business of the practical counting-
house, that he cannot fail to form a right judgment of every
thing he sees transacted during the time of his clerkship : nor
will it be in the power of the ignorant or the artful, in any
respect whatever, to perplex or misguide him. From having
also such principles inculcated in his youth as serve to raise an
emulation, excite industry, and fix the attention to business,
no advantages will escape his notice, through negligence or

226

want of discernment. On the contrary, he will be able to break through all obstacles to his advancement, and not only to make the most of every fortunate occurrence that falls in his way, but, if such are wanting, even to frame beneficial occasions for himself.

It may be reasonably enough presumed, that many who are already engaged, will regret their not being bred according to the proposed establishment. Such, however, may receive no little advantage, even by the perusal of these papers; at which we shall heartily rejoice. And if any of those gentlemen, after the expiration of their ordinary clerkship, should be inclined to think they might reap any benefit by this institution, they should be admitted, and treated in the most gentleman-like manner.

It is far from being the least disreputation to any gentleman to be instructed in what so nearly concerns his interest, and whereon the whole happiness of his life depends; especially so, when he has never had proper opportunities of being suitably instructed before: but it is a very deplorable situation, for the young merchant to be liable to be daily over-reached and outwitted, if not diligently reined, by correspondents more knowing than himself in the arts of negotiating business. It is most certainly, therefore, for more advisable for him, after the completion of their ordinary clerkship, to wait a year or two, if needful, for thorough qualification, before they rashly hazard their fortune. It may possibly too be as requisite for many to unlearn some things, as to acquire others, before they turn self-adventurers. Young people, eager and ambitious to make a figure in trade for themselves, may think it lost time to wait at all for their due accomplishment. This is a great mistake. Let them consider, that, to save and improve their fortunes is gaining time, but to lose them quite otherwise.

ADVERTISEMENT.

If the public should judge it necessary to introduce any other kind of accomplishment into a college of this nature, that may be easily done, provided any thing of this kind should take place: I have only intimated those qualifications that are indispensably necessary.

That the public may be apprized for whom this institution is designed, it is proper to inform them, that it is calculated chiefly for the following classes of gentlemen.

1. For the sons of merchants designed for trade, whom their parents would chuse to have brought up according to the proposed plan; their own counting-houses not admitting of their being bred in so methodical and scientific a manner.

2. For others, intended for any particular branch of merchandising whatever; as that of a Portugal, Spanish, Russia, Hamburgh merchant, &c. &c. who, after having been four years under this institution, will be qualified to enter, either at home or abroad, into any of those respective counting-houses, with all desirable benefit and advantage.

3. For such gentlemen who, having passed the usual time of their clerkship, think they may reap any advantage from this institution.

4. For the sons of American planters.

5. For the sons of such wholesale dealers whose engagements in trade, both at home and abroad, are often as extensive as those of very eminent merchants.

6. For gentlemen of maturity, who are possessed of handsome fortunes, and would gladly engage in trade as merchants for themselves, or in conjunction with others, could they be expeditiously accomplished in a genteel manner.

7. For such gentlemen who may have expectation of consulships, &c. wherein a knowledge in the practical arts, customs, and usages of merchants, is absolutely necessary.

8. For those gentlemen who have views of being settled in any of the chief branches of the public revenue, or for such who would be accomplished to supervise business they may think proper to carry on, by the means of clerks or agents, wherein a complete knowledge of figures and accountantship is requisite.

9. For gentlemen who may chuse to carry on foreign trade, by being their own supercargoes, or for such who are intended for supercargoships belonging to any of the capital trading companies.

10. For such young gentlemen of fortune, who may be expected hereafter to take a share in the government and direction of any of the great trading or monied corporations.

11. For young gentlemen intended to be called to the bar, to whom a knowledge in the practical mercantile arts and accountantship may prove beneficial, in order to enable them the better to unravel such complicated cases in mercantile accounts, as may come before them in their pleadings, relating either to the foreign or domestic transactions of merchants*.

* Litigations among traders making so large a share in the business of the bar, a student of the law cannot have too minute and comprehensive a knowledge of the practical arts of merchants, as they relate both to their foreign and domestic negotiations.

To set this matter in it's proper light would require a distinct tract. As these learned gentlemen, however, are so thoroughly sensible of this, we shall only observe, what a celebrated lawyer, who had entered deeply into the study of practical trade, says upon the subject of the exchanges; which will be found to hold good also, in regard to other the principal parts of mercantile transactions.

After having recounted the names of many of his profession, eminent for their abilities, who have written on the exchanges; and having shewn the great importance of the subject; this writer speaks in the following manner:

' This subject of the exchanges contains many very knotty points, and is held among all the lawyers to be dark, difficult, and intricate.

' 1. Because the method of exchanging, now in use, differs widely from the ancient practice.

' 2. Because controversies relating to exchanges are not so common as others, and therefore less understood.

' 3. Because of the concise abstruse terms, in which exchange-contracts are expressed, and which lawyers are quite strangers to.

' 4. Because of the daily new inventions, by which this matter has been rendered so intricate, that, besides the negociators themselves, there are very few, even among the men of literature, who understand it. And merchants have truck out so many arts in the negotiation of exchange, that they exceed the bounds of such who attempt to determine the controversies relating to them; and, indeed, the difficulties attending them are to be resolved only into the depth of mercantile skill and subtilty; so that it is no wonder, that Navar, in his tract of usury, a man of great learning, and especially conversant in subjects of this kind, confesses to have learnt the whole praxis of exchanges, of which he there treats, from the capital merchants of his city.

' Those who take depositions in cases of this kind, construe the same author, are often perplexed and confounded; wherefore persons, profoundly skilled in the practical arts of the exchanges, should be appointed to hear evidence on these occasions. Lawyers are, for the general part, wanting in the first rudiments and principles of these negociations; and are at a loss to ascertain facts, from whence judgment should proceed. Insomuch as looking the knot, whose texture they are unacquainted with, the more they labour, the firmer the tie. Since, therefore, they are so ignorant of the usages and customs which relate to merchandizing, wherein merchants themselves only are perfectly skilled, it is not to be admired, that traders in general, as I have heard many of them declare, had rather trust to their own judgment, than rest on the opinions of the ablest lawyers.' Sigismundi Scaccia Tractatus de Commerciis & Cambiis.

12. Lastly, For any young gentlemen of honour and fortune, to whom a practical knowledge of figures and mercantile accountantship may be of use, as well in their private affairs* as those which concern them in a public capacity †; as also to give them a true idea of the art of merchandizing, in order the more familiarly to initiate them into the studies of the national commerce in general. Likewise to initiate young persons of quality into a well-grounded knowledge in the PUBLIC REVENUE, the TARIFFS in relation to merchandizes in foreign nations, and TREATIES of COMMERCE, subsisting between the several states of Europe; for all these might be regularly taught in this college.

* ' Merchants accounts, says Mr Locke, though a science not likely to help a gentleman to get an estate, yet possibly there is not any thing of more use and efficacy to make him preserve the estate he has. It is seldom observed, that he who keeps an account of his income and expences, and thereby has constantly under view the course of his domestic affairs, lets them run to ruin: and I doubt not but many a man gets behind-hand before he is aware, or runs farther on, when he is once in, for want of this care, or the skill to do it. I would therefore advise all gentlemen to learn perfectly merchants accounts, and not to think it a skill that belongs not to them, because it has received it's name, and has been chiefly practised by men of traffic.'

† Besides, such is the excellency of this art, that whoever is fundamentally grounded in it's rationale, will as familiarly apply it to the accounts of the nation, as to his own personal affairs. None who are thoroughly acquainted with the extensive application of this method of account keeping, will think this is saying too much of it. See the article NATIONAL ACCOUNTS. Of what benefit this may prove to the nation, and how useful and honourable to themselves in a public capacity, need not be said.

227

The mercantile ftation, it is certain, affords as large a profpect for opulent acquifitions as any other; and eftates got by
trade have, perhaps, been far more numerous, than thofe by
any other way whatfoever. [See the article COMMERCE.]
As the relation alfo merchants ftand in to the community, is
not inferior to moft in point of importance, fo neither have
they been behind-hand with any, in their zealous attachment
to the intereft of thofe countries and princes, that have duly
protected and encouraged them in their commerce. Hiftory
furnifhes remarkable inftances of this. At prefent we fhall
take notice of a few only, which are fufficient to endear the
character of a merchant to every nation, that depends upon
foreign trade for it's fupport.
Charles the Vth, emperor of Germany, being reduced to
great diftrefs by the unhappy expedition of Tunis, experienced a powerful fuccour in money from the Fuggers, a fingle
family of merchants only, but at that time the moft opulent
and diftinguifhed traders of Auxbourgh. For the fecurity
and repayment of thofe large fums, wherewith they had fupplied the government, his imperial majefty gave them written
obligations, under his royal hand and feal.
To give a demonftration of their zeal to the intereft of their
country, and their inviolable attachment to the perfon of his
majefty, thofe merchants requefted the emperor, as he was
one day taking an airing by their houfe, to do them the
honour to regale himfelf, to which his majefty readily con-
defcended. After the collation was over, thofe merchants
defired permiffion of the emperor to burn a faggot of cinna-
mon in the hall, where the entertainment was made, not only with intent to adminifter all they could to his majefty's delight, but to give further proof of their hearty affection to
his perfon and government. Which they did, by burning
up thofe bonds of the emperor they had taken for their money
with the faggot, and fo fet fire to them before the emperor's
face.
Another inftance not lefs remarkable, is that of the memorable James Cœur, a merchant of Bourges. This gentleman alone, by the wifdom of his counfels and the certainty
of his cafh, humbled the houfe of Burgundy, fecured the
crown of France to the lawful heir Charles the VIIth, and
by him to the branches of Valois and Bourbon, who fuc-
ceeded.
The conduct of the merchants of St Malo is another example worthy attention. Thofe gentlemen being highly ex-
afperated by the demand made at the congrefs of Gertruy-
denburgh to Lewis IV, of employing his troops to compel
his grandfon Philip V, then king of Spain, to abandon the
crown, united all their profits together, which they had made
by trade in the Spanifh colonies in America, and generoufly
laid thirty-two millions in gold at the foot of the throne;
and that at a time too, when the finances of France were
totally exhaufted, by a feries of unfuccefsful events: which
fuccour, being timely applied, vigoroufly renewed the war,
and anfwered the end of that nation.
Sir Thomas Grefham, our own countryman, the founder of
a college in London, for the promotion of the liberal arts,
and of the Royal Exchange for the convenience of the traders of this metropolis, is another inftance well deferving our
notice, as it manifefts how far it is in the power of merchants, even of one private merchant, to fupport governments under the greateft emergency.
This worthy citizen of London lived in the time of king
Edward the VIth, who was confiderably indebted to the
merchants of Antwerp, for money borrowed at intereft to
fupply the exigencies of the ftate. Payment of intereft at
that time being a great incumbrance to the nation, various
expedients had been confulted by the king and his council,
to difcharge thofe debts; which, being due to foreigners,
brought great contempt upon the crown, and the public
credit of England. The meafures which had been fuggefted for repayment, were, either to transport fo much treafure out of the realm, or to remit the fame by way of exchange.
The kingdom being already greatly exhaufted of it's gold
and filver, the former was impracticable, without being
ruinous to trade; and, the exchange between England and
Antwerp being at no more than fixteen fchillings per pound
of our currency, negociating the debt by foreign bills would
have funk the exchange ftill more to our difadvantage. By
which means the exportation of our gold and filver in the
way of trade, would have been more and more augmented.
Yet for the nation to continue in debt, was ftill increafing

the evil; more efpecially fo, as the creditors were foreigners,
and the intereft fent out of the kingdom. Befide, the creditors infifted on their money, or a compliance with fuch ufu-
rious meafures, for a prolongation of time, as would have
brought fuch high indignity upon the nation, as to have dif-
abled them from borrowing more money, but upon the moft
fcandalous terms.
And yet, more money the government wanted, inftead of
being in a capacity to difcharge the old debts. Under thefe
circumftances the nation was greatly perplexed, and no meafures could be thought of to extricate the kingdom from thefe
embarraffments, till Sir Thomas undertook the affair. By
whofe great knowledge in trade and fkill in the exchanges,
he exonerated the nation from it's weighty incumbrances,
without fending any money out of the kingdom.
And, although the exchange was then at fixteen fchillings, he
fo wifely managed this negociation, that he paid off the king's
debts as they fell due, at an exchange of twenty and twenty-
two fchillings per pound. Whereby the king faved no lefs
than an hundred thoufand marks clear, by this great merchant's knowledge in the exchanges.
By thus raifing the exchange alfo fo much in favour of England, at that critical conjuncture, the price of all foreign
commodities fell proportionably [*]. Which faved the kingdom in general, and that, in a very little time, no lefs than
between three and four hundred thoufand pounds fterling
more: a round fum even at this time of day, but would now
be near four times that fum, in proportion to the different values of money.

> [*] 'Whoever defires to know the ftate of our foreign trade,
> 'or our fituation as to transactions in money with other
> 'countries, unlefs where fubfidies are paid to princes a-
> 'broad, armies or fleets maintained, or the dividends or
> 'ftate of our ftocks belonging to foreigners, may have in-
> 'fluence: unlefs in thefe cafes, the courfe of exchange in-
> 'dicates the ftate of our commerce, as truly as the pulfe
> 'does that of the human body.' Sir Ifaac Newton's Ta-
> bles of the Affairs of foreign Coins. See the articles COIN,
> BALLANCE of TRADE, EXCHANGE.
> When exchange is againft a nation, the goods exported from
> that nation are fold for fo much lefs, and goods imported
> from the other fo much dearer as the exchange is above the
> par; fo that the exchange, being once againft a nation, con-
> tributes to keep itfelf fo. The exchange with Holland be-
> ing generally againft England, in time of peace as well as
> war, affects this kingdom more than, perhaps, has been
> thoroughly weighed and confidered, as could be defired;
> for, as Amfterdam is made the center of commercial corre-
> fpondence between the feveral parts of Europe, the rate of
> exchange between us and Holland, muft proportionably af-
> fect that between us and other countries with which we have
> dealings, more efpecially with thofe we negociate bills with
> always through the medium of Holland. See the article
> HOLLAND.

Nor did the advantages to the nation from the eminent fkill
of this great Englifh merchant, terminate here only. For,
as, when the exchange was fo greatly to the difadvantage of
England, gold and filver were daily exported out of the kingdom in great plenty; fo by which raifing it, in the courfe of
his money negociations for the fervice of the ftate, he caufed
the fame to be brought back again, to the general emolument
of the whole trading intereft.
Nor did the wifdom of Sir Thomas's counfels prove only of
the higheft honour and advantage to king Edward's reign,
but to thofe of his fucceffors, queen Mary and queen Elizabeth; both of thefe princeffes having made choice of him
for the management of their money, and their mercantile
affairs. With queen Elizabeth he was in fo high efteem,
that fhe not only knighted him, a matter of very high dignity in thofe days, but honoured him in every refpect; and
came in perfon to the exchange, which he had erected for
the convenience of the merchants and honour of the city of
London, and caufed the fame to be proclaimed by heralds,
and a trumpet, the ROYAL EXCHANGE: and Sir Thomas
was afterwards honoured with the appellation of the ROYAL
MERCHANT.
Thomas Sutton, Efq; another renowned Englifh merchant,
and founder of the Charter-Houfe in London, an act of benevolence worthy of a great prince, a few years after the
death of Sir Thomas Grefham, by being the grand inftrument of getting the Spanifh bills protefted at Genoa, in 158-,
retarded, for a whole year, the failing of the Spanifh armada, defigned to enflave thefe kingdoms, which proved the
happy means of defeating the invafion.

These are some of the memorable feats performed by merchants, by private merchants only; and these, without particularizing more, are sufficient to evince the truth of what has been suggested to their eternal honour. And, although great statesmen, admirals, and generals, with the aid of the public purse, and their thousands and their ten thousands to co-operate with them, may perform great atchievements; yet we find that one family of merchants has been the support of an emperor in great distress; that another single merchant alone gave the crown to the house of Bourbon; that one was a principal cause of defeating the Spanish armada, and another the restorer of the public credit of England, and the honour of the crown, when in great contempt amongst all the princes of Europe: and may be truly said, in concert with that able minister Walingham, to have laid the foundation of all the commerce and navigation we enjoy at present.

But it is not needful to go far back for instances of the eminent services that merchants have manifested to the British empire in particular; it is recent in every one's memory, that, in the late unnatural rebellion, the support of the public credit, and, in consequence thereof, the security of the establishment of the present most august, and illustrious royal family upon the throne of these kingdoms, was owing to that glorious and ever-memorable association of the merchants and traders of the loyal city of London.

The merit of persons of distinguished character in trade cannot, in the general, be measured, but by those who are well acquainted with their trading negociations. As they pass through life without much eclat, the world is little acquainted with their important services and utility to the state; whilst the histories of men in great public capacities are transmitted to posterity with all the pomp and magnificence of representation. Yet certainly that is the more profitable admonition, which is drawn from the eminent virtues of men, who move in a sphere nearer levelled to the common reach, than that which is derived from the splendid portrait of the victories and transactions of great statesmen and commanders; which serve but for the imitation of few, and make rather for the ostentation, than the true instruction of human life. It is from the practice and example of persons of private condition, that we are more naturally taught to excel in our private capacities: and, had we the genuine histories of many eminent merchants, giving a lively idea of their rise and progress in business, and of the important service they have been to their respective communities, they would naturally incite the trading part of this nation to emulate their accomplishments: and this would prove a more effectual means to produce a race of skilful British traders, than romantic narratives a race of heroes.

Nor has the security of states and empires been only owing to the occasional zealous exertion of the wisdom and and the power of merchants, but they are in a great measure the daily and perpetual support of all trading countries. For, as a nation is at all present circumstanced, those which are so situated, as to be obliged to subsist chiefly with a themselves, and without any intercourse of commerce with others, can never be able to maintain so great a share of power, as those which carry an extended foreign traffic. Domestic trade, only shifting property from hand to hand, cannot increase the riches and power of a nation, whilst foreign trade, carrying on and really bringing in a constant influx of treasure in favour of a nation, will proportionably augment its weight and interest, and at length give it the balance of power.

Great-Britain being encompassed with powerful nations, who are earnestly bent on cultivating the arts of commerce and navigation, with the utmost stretch of their address and policy, must she not soon become a sacrifice to those neighbouring potentates, if destitute of a race of ingenuous and well accomplished merchants? For, as these are the only source of our maritime strength, she could not long continue, but by their means, that happy independent empire she is at present.

The philosopher may arrive to a high pitch of improvement in agriculture, arts, and sciences; the husbandman, the artizan, and manufacturer, may reduce this speculative knowledge to practical uses, with the greatest skill and dexterity on their part; governments may enact the wisest laws, and give all desirable encouragement for the advancement of commerce, yet what will these avail, without the penetration and sagacity of the merchant, to propagate the produce of our lands, and the labour of our artists and manufacturers into foreign countries, with advantage to the state as well as to himself?

'It is foreign trade, says a great lawyer [*], that is the main sheet anchor of us islanders; without which the genius of all our useful studies, and the which renders men famous and renowned, would make them useless and insignificant to the public. When man has fathomed the bottom of all knowledge, what is it if not reduced to practice, other than empty notion [†]? If the inhabitants of this island were learned in all the languages between the rising and setting of the sun, did know and understand the situation of all places, ports, and countries, and the nature of all merchandize and commodities, were acquainted with the order and motion of all the stars, knew how to take the latitude and longitude, and were perfectly read in the art of navigation, to what purpose would all be, if there were no foreign trade? We should have no ships to navigate to those countries, nor occasion to make use of those languages, nor to make use of those commodities; what would this island be but a place of confinement to the inhabitants, who, without it, could be but a kind of hermits, as being separated from the rest of the world: it is foreign trade that renders us rich, honourable, and great; that gives us a name and esteem in the world; that makes us masters of the treasures of other nations and countries, and begets and maintains our ships and seamen, the walls and bulwarks of our country; and, were it not for foreign trade, what would become of the revenue for customs, and what would the rents of our lands be? The customs would totally fail, and our gentlemens rents of thousands per annum would dwindle into hundreds.'

* Mollov De Jure Maritimo & Navali.

† Every step that is made in the progress of knowledge, whether it proceed from reading, observation, or experience, ought to be applied to the affairs and transactions of life; for this is, in truth, the only proper use of all kinds of study; which, without it becomes not only an useless, but a troublesome sort of pedantry, more calculated to interrupt and confound, than to serve and promote a true genius. Essay on the Education of a Nobleman, printed 1730.

Since then it is so unexceptionably apparent, that foreign traffic is our grand preservative both by sea and land, and since, as lord chancellor Bacon justly observes, MERCHANTS AND TRADERS ARE IN A STATE, WHAT THE BLOOD IS TO THE BODY, the abilities and ingenuity of this part of the community is most certainly of the last importance to the whole British empire.

From these considerations there naturally arises the idea of dignity, as inseparably annexed to the character of the merchant; he being a principal party in the security and preservation, as well as in the constant support of the kingdom: and from hence we may presume it is, that family alliances have been so frequently contracted between the gentry and the trading part of the nation. [See the article COMMERCE.]

'Nor, says the learned bishop Sprat, ought our gentry to be averse from the promoting of trade, out of any little jealousy, that thereby they shall debase themselves, and corrupt their blood: for they are to know, that traffic and commerce have given mankind a higher degree than any title of nobility, even that of civility and humanity itself. And at this time, especially above all others, they have no reason to despise trade as below them, when it has so great an influence on the very government of the world [*].'

* Vide History of the Royal Society.

There are but few who are capable of distinguishing themselves in any eminent degree, in the great leading debates of senates; much fewer of conducting fleets, armies, or the councils of princes. The talents of a Burleigh or a Colbert are very rare indeed, so are those of a Blake or a Marlborough. But every valuable capacity may make a pretty good figure in trade, by being bred with the advantage of the proposed institution. And as amongst these there will be, doubtless, different degrees of capacities, as well as of assiduity and application, the young person who shall happily have an extraordinary turn for mercantile acquirements, may become a Gresham, a Barnard, a Gore, Vansack, &c. whilst the same genius in the army, the navy, or any branch of the civil government, might have lived and died, perhaps, in obscurity.

As in these several capacities there is but one path to greatness, and few amongst a numerous gentry have opportunity or abilities to become eminent therein, many of the younger branches of our best families pass their days in an inglorious ease, quite lost to themselves, as well as to the public: whereas, if they turned their eyes to commerce, it would furnish them with a thousand means, whereby they might promote themselves, and reflect a lustre on their ancient stock.

Merchants, it is true, have no exemption from those casualties, to which the whole human species is liable; yet, in the way of trade, these are often ballanced by prosperous contingencies. When it happens otherwise, the really unfortunate scarce ever want succour in distress. Even when misfortunes have proceeded from unhappy mistakes in point of conduct, yet, where neither integrity and skill have been wanting, such rarely fail to rise again, in some reputable channel of business or other, dependent on merchants; of which there are numberless instances. For it is no undeserving encomium on the trading class of the community, to say of them, that no persons, under the heavens, shew greater humanity and generosity, towards an unfortunate, yet upright fellow-trader: which consideration is no small inducement for the younger branches of our most honourable families to engage in commerce.

Moreover, when it so falls out, that any of our noble and honourable families enjoy a numerous progeny, and the patrimonial estate is greatly diminished by fortunes to the younger, wherein lies the indignity for the elder to be privately interested with a younger brother of abilities bred to merchandizing? Might not such measures contribute to free the family inheritance from too weighty incumbrances? If the fortune of the younger does not happen to be competent, wherewith to carry on that compass of lucrative commerce that presents itself, an additional capital will enable him to do it: and the elder, having a proportion of the profits for the hazards he runs, will afford him better interest for money than he can otherwise make at present. It is the constant practice in Holland and Italy, for those of the highest honour to be interested in this manner with merchants of eminence; and in France this practice has been thought so beneficial to the state, that it has been encouraged and enforced by several royal edicts [*]. And, perhaps, this has not been a stroke of policy the least refined for the advancement of the trade and navigation of that kingdom; such measures frequently supplying private traders with as large capitals in trade as they can employ therein, and those upon terms quite easy and agreeable. Engagements of this nature are called by the French Societes en commandites [†]. See the article Anonymous.

[*] This edict is so remarkable as to deserve notice.

EDIT DU ROY,

Portant que les nobles pourront faire le commerce de mer, sans deroger à la noblesse. Donné à S. Germain en Laye, au mois d'Août 1669.

LOUIS par la grace de Dieu, roy de France & de Navarre : A tous presens & à venir. Salut ; comme le commerce & particulierement celui qui se fait par mer, est la source seconde, qui apporte l'abondance dans les etats, & la répand sur les sujets à proportion de leur industrie, & de leur travail, & qu'il n'y a point de moyens pour acquerir du bien, qui soit plus innocent, & plus legitime : aussi a-t-il toujours été en grande consideration parmi les nations les mieux police, & universellement bien reçû, comme des plus honnêtes occupations de la vie civile, &c. &c. 'A ces causes, desirant ne rien obmettre de ce qui peut d'avantage exciter nos sujets à s'engager dans le commerce, & le rendre plus florissant, & de nôtre grace speciale, pleine puissance & autorité royale, nous avons dit, & declaré, & par ces presentes signées de notre main, disons, & declarons, voulons & nous plait, que tous gentils-hommes puissent par eux ou par personnes interposées, entrer en societé, & prendre part dans les vaisseaux marchands, denrees & marchandises d'iceux, sans que pour raison de ce, ils soient censés de réputés déroger à noblesse, pourvû toutefois qu'ils ne vendent point en détail, &c. &c.

Signé LOUIS, & sur le reply par le roy, COLBERT.

This was strongly enforced again by another edict in December 1704, which is called Edit du roy, qui permet aux nobles, excepté ceux qui sont revetus de charges de magistrature, de faire commerce en gros, & qui declare quels sont les marchands à les negociants en gros.

[†] Celui qui vendra faux sachant en commandite, doit justes les pour sûr au marchand qui fait honneur de bien, & experte des manufactures, ou du commerce qu'il veut entreprendre; car c'est sur la fidelité, & sur industrie qu'il doit fonder l'esperance qu'il a de produire en les conduant son argent, &c. Parfait Negociant, Savary.

Persons of low grovelling minds, and little industry themselves, are often strangely chagrined and irritated against those who attempt any thing new in the public service, though highly commendable in itself, and the very attempt highly meritorious. With such sordid and pitiful spirits, the sha-

---

dow of novelty, in any undertaking, is condemnation sufficient. As such deserve rather pity or contempt, we shall only confront them with what that wise and public-spirited prelate, bishop Sprat [*], has again observed ; who, (speaking of the first establishment of the Royal Society of London, says, ' That, if all things which are new be destructive, all ' the several means and degrees by which mankind has risen ' to the perfection of arts were to be condemned. If so, to ' be the author of new things, be a crime, how will the first ' civilizers of men and makers of laws, and founders of governments escape? Whatever now delights us in the works ' of nature, that excels the rudeness of the first creation, is ' new. Whatever we see in cities or houses above the first ' wildness of fields, and meanness of cottages, and naked'ness of men, had it's time, when this imputation of no'velty might as well have been laid to it's charge. It is not ' therefore an offence to profess the introduction of new ' things, unless that which is introduced prove pernicious in ' itself, or cannot be brought in without the extirpation of ' others which are better.'

[*] Vide History of the Royal Society.

As nothing of this kind can be alledged against the present institution, it's novelty, with the judicious part of mankind, will render it the more praise-worthy ; it requiring greater industry, and different talents to strike out new paths to knowledge, rather than supinely to plod on in the old, when much better can be found.

And, as there appears to be a glorious spirit in the legislature to promote the trade of the kingdom to the utmost ; as his majesty himself has, by his royal speech from the throne, expressed his earnest recommendation of, and his hearty concurrence [*] with every wise measure to advance the national commerce, we may reasonably hope, this our humble attempt will meet with the approbation of all true friends to our trading interest.

[*] ' Let me earnestly recommend to you the advancement of ' our commerce, and cultivating the arts of peace, in which ' you may depend on my hearty concurrence and encou'ragement.' His Majesty's Speech, Nov. 29, 1748.

It is no great honour to the British nation, that there should be a necessity for the younger sons of our nobility and gentry to be sent to Holland and elsewhere out of the kingdom, for mercantile qualifications. But, when we have an institution within ourselves far superior to any in other countries, it will be as little credit as advantage to British youth, to go abroad for what they can have much better at home.

And, if a young gentleman is intended to settle in a counting-house abroad, or to travel before he enters into trade for himself, his having spent a few years under this institution, will far better capacitate him to reap proper advantage by either, than the crude, immethodical, and narrow way can, in which the generality are bred at present.

It is easy enough to hit blots, and to point out evils highly detrimental to the community. The many wise may discern the grievance and lament it, but the remedy generally lies deep, and in the hands of few ; and to those few is the world indebted, for the execution of all designs of public utility and happiness. Whether such is not the nature of the present, is submitted to those who are judges of it's merit and tendency.

Before I draw to the conclusion, I would desire the reader will please to suppose the following plain case, viz. that two young persons, of equal age and abilities, are placed in the respective counting-houses of their own fathers, who are merchants inferior to none for eminence, skill, and ingenuity in their profession, and both equally sollicitous that their sons should become so likewise : let it be further supposed, that the one of those young persons is bred, previously to his being taken into business under his father, a few years under the proposed institution, at the age proposed, and the other not, but is turned into his father's counting-house as raw and as ignorant as the generality really are ; I would appeal to every man of sense and impartiality, who is a judge of the usefulness of our plan, and capable of setting a due value upon a proper mercantile qualification, which of those young people is likely to become the best accomplished merchant, and so be the most prosperous in his employment ?

Could the experiment be fairly tried, is there not all imaginable reason to believe, that the one would be better qualified for business, by being a single year afterwards only in his father's counting-house, than the other would in three, or perhaps in five years? The one would be capable of making a good judgment of all the law transacted without any instruction, and thereby might naturally delight in business; while the other, for want of the like foundation, might never understand his business as he ought, and therefore take an invincible dislike to it; whereby, instead of becoming the complete merchant desired, he might, on the contrary, become only an eternal disquietude to the best of parents.

If this is not unlikely to prove the case, when a young person is bred, even under the eye of an own father, anxious for his son's welfare, what may we presume to be the consequence, when he has not the like happy opportunity of being trained up under a parent? When this is the case, is it not the most adviseable for such a young gentleman to lay the best foundation for such a young gentleman, before he enters into any merchant's counting-house whatever? For, if he falls into the hands of a man of honour and skill, of one who does not intend only to take his money, but do him justice, will not a young person so previously accomplished, as we propose, be infinitely more capable of reaping the benefit of his situation, than one destitute of those advantages?

But if, on the other hand, a young person is not so happy as to fall into such a merchant's counting-house, is it not highly prudential, that he should be secure of a good foundation before-hand, in order to make the best advantage under the worst situation?

The reader will please to observe, that this institution is intended to train up the young merchant from 15 to 19 years of age, in order the better to prepare him than he is, by being bred in the ordinary way, for admission into any merchant's practical counting-house; wherein, if we suppose him placed for three or four years more, he may be then sufficiently accomplished to hazard his estate in trade, and not before. But,

That experienced merchant Sir Francis Brewster, who lived in the reign of king William the IIId, has proposed a different way of breeding up young merchants of condition and fortune to practical commerce; which, as it seems to coincide, in some respect, with our proposed institution of a mercantile college, the reader may not be displeased with that merchant's sentiments: and, indeed, if our young merchant was first regularly trained up in the literary mercantile college we would establish, his entrance into Sir Francis's college, if well regulated for the purpose, might, perhaps, as well, if not better qualify him for practical trade, than the ordinary way of going apprentice generally does.

' I think it a mortal distemper, says Sir Francis, in trade (nor to be cured, because in the first concoction) that we have so few men of university learning conversant in true mercantile employments: if there were as much care to have men of the best heads and education in it, as there is in the law, the nation would fetch more from abroad, and spend less in law-suits at home. We have it reckoned up by the infallible author, as the glory of a city, That her merchants were princes and nobles; their business and transactions in the world with such, is more than belongs to any other set of men: would it not then be the honour of a nation, as well as profit, to have men of the best sense and learning in the foreign negoce of a kingdom? If such had been in the trade of these kingdoms, it seems reasonable to believe, we had not lost the most considerable navigating trade and employment of our seamen.

It would be an astonishing observation to men of any country but our own, to see more heads employed in Westminster-Hall to divide the gain of the nation, than there are heads on the exchange to gather it together. I have sometimes thought, that, if these kingdoms lay not under the confusion and unintelligibleness of understanding in trade, as the builders of Babel did in languages, we might, without the sin of those arrogant architects, erect such towers in trade, as might overtop the universe in that mystery.

We see how all arts and sciences have been improved in this kingdom within the compass of one century, but amongst them all the merchant's part the least: and the reason is plain, men of small learning and moderate understanding are generally put in it: for, though there are some of excellent parts and clean heads among them, yet the major part are not so polished: I speak not this to abate the respect that I shall always think is due to the profession, and all men in it, but we know it is the vanity of the nation: scarce a tradesman but if he have a son that a country schoolmaster tells him would make a scholar, because he learns his grammar well, but immediately passes the approbation of his kindred, who judge it very so hopeful a youth should be lost in trade, the university

is the only soil fit for him to be planted in.

By such disposition of the youth of our nation, many a good tradesman is lost, and poor scholars in every respect made; and, if this humour prevails in mechanics, and men of ordinary quality, much more, and with better pretensions, it affects our gentry: to be sure the eldest son is above trade, and, if the younger be of a quaint and studious temper, they are thought fit for the law, not many for the pulpit, which I confess I likewise think a mistake in our gentry; had we more of them in the clergy, we should have fewer to defend, that might be better builders of houses than of the church. But, to return to what I observe of the improvement in all the employments in the kingdom, I see none that have arrived to that vast increase as those in the law: this, perhaps, is accounted an evil, but I will not quarrel with that law rule; I hope it will be no offence to wish them among us, [the merchants] but not with their bar-gowns; they would, in my opinion, look better in a COUNTING-HOUSE than in the TEMPLE; and, had the humour of our ancestors run that way as much as it did for the law, there might have been as great an enlargement in maritime traffic and navigation, as there is now of the law: I presume none will say, that they began with equal numbers; trade had the primogeniture, and set forth with the employment of the people, before there could be work for lawyers; and I believe those of best value amongst them do not think their growth and gain contribute to either in the advantage of the nation, though without the profession there can be no securing property; but, perhaps, the numbers make more work than there would be if they were less: Hamburgh, though a place of great trade, allows but two: and, though our foreign plantations are filled with men of no better principles than they leave behind them, yet they have few among them who raise their fortunes by the law; for which no reason can be given, but that there is not a foundation and nursery for that profession to breed up men of learning and ingenuity in.

I have been the longer on this subject, because there seems to me an expedient in this matter; and that is, to make such provision for noblemen's and gentlemen's children, as may be equally reputable with the inns of court, for young gentlemen to come to from the universities, and, with less charge than their expence in seven years studying the law, become expert in trade.

To be thus managed: in each maritime city and considerable port of the kingdom, to have a COLLEGE built, in which there may be some persons of experience in trade, to teach and direct in the mystery of it, to all parts of the world: and, that they may have the practic, as well as theory, that every person entering himself into the society may be obliged to bring in a thousand pounds stock, which will make a capital, perhaps, of 20 or 30,000l. sterling, to traffic with in 30 cities, &c. in the kingdom: they to be obliged to spend five years in this society, and, at the end of that term, to receive the principal they brought, allowing the casualty of profit and loss, as it happens: going thus out, they will be entered in trade, and probably have a fund to begin with; and, by this means, trade will fall into the hands of gentlemen, persons of learning and consideration in the nation, and likewise preserve from misfortunes numbers that now miscarry in their studies of the law, through ill conversation, and having no employment.

To this project (a word now traduced to contempt, though in it's self of good signification both for peace and war) I foresee two objections that will be made against it, and they are these:

First, This will make too many merchants.

Secondly, That this will leave no room for younger brothers, that have nothing to prefer them in the world but a small sum to put them apprentice to a merchant, by which they often raise their fortunes in the world.

To the first I answer, That the evil of having too many merchants is in the numbers that are bred up from apprentices, many of which, coming into business without FUNDS, strain their credit, which to keep above water, they are forced to venture at all ways that have but a probability of success, to keep themselves in business, and then, to comply with their credit, often fell to loss, which in the end brings them to misfortune, and that begets an opinion that there are too many traders; whereas the true reason is the want of STOCK, not NUMBER of merchants.

The second objection, That this will hinder merchants from taking apprentices, is in part answered in the first, that their number prejudices trade: but there is a farther consideration in this matter, and that is, two sorts of youths stand candidates for a mercantile education, gentlemen with a capital, others of lefs quality, with none. I think it will admit of no queſtion which ſhall be preferred, and that the other may be more profitably employed for the nation and themſelves, in trades that require more labour and lefs ſtock.

But, after all I have ſaid, my wiſhes are greater than my expectation, to ſee trade thus courted in a kingdom that treats it as ſome do their wives, conſidering them no farther than to the production of a legitimate poſterity, reſerving their careſſes and delights for a miſs: ſo the humour of this age ſeems to incline, whilſt foreign commerce is neglected, and men's thoughts and deſigns run after offices and employments in the ſtate; to pay which, ſpider-like, the nation ſpins out her bowels to catch flies; and the ſmalleſt goes farther, ſuch food turns into poiſon, where it feeds men freely in their mouth; and ſuch too often ſupplant better men, or find ways to be preferred before them: to ſay this will be no offence to deſerving men; and, for others, I ſhall only deſire them to ſuſpend their reſentments until the thought paſt comes forth, and

then they will have more reaſon, becauſe it will often in my way to be more particular, when I come to ſpeak of the trade of Ireland; in which there have of late been ſuch notorious demonſtrations how ill men in offices and places of truſt may ruin and deſtroy a kingdom, as admits of no defence. I have for this the authority of both houſes of parliament, in their addreſſes to the king: and the infallible author tells us, That he who ſaith to the wicked, Thou art righteous, the people will curſe, nations ſhall abhor him.' Sir Francis Brewſter's Eſſays on Trade and Navigation, 1695.

And now it may be proper juſt to review what we may reaſonably expect to be the obvious and apparent conſequences of this inſtitution to the public, which will be chiefly comprehended under the following particulars, viz.

I. It will raiſe a noble ſpirit of emulation among our young British merchants to excel each other in the arts of merchandiſing; from whence the nation in general, as well as individuals, may reap unſpeakably more benefit and advantage by trade and navigation.

II. It will enable our young merchants the better to cope with foreigners, in all the methods of negociating mercantile buſineſs of every kind, which may prevent their being made the dupes of ſome of thoſe ſubtle traders who are very artful in drawing young people of good fortune into ſchemes of trade, which always prove beneficial to the one, but very often greatly injurious to the other.

III. It will qualify ſuch young people who may be placed at ſeveral of the Britiſh factories abroad, to promote each other's intereſt in the way of trade, in a manner not ſo generally known and underſtood, as well as the intereſt of thoſe who ſhall continue at home.

IV. It will capacitate them ſo to correſpond with foreign nations, as to obtain the moſt uſeful kind of intelligence from time to time; whereby they will the better know when and where there is money to be got, by trading between one foreign nation and another, as well as between their own and others.

V. It will qualify them either to be particular or general merchants; or particular ones generally, and general ones occaſionally; wherein conſiſts the judgment, in ſome meaſure, of the moſt ſkilful and vigilant merchant.

VI. It may have a tendency to convince the younger branches of our moſt honourable families, that the art of merchandizing does not require ſuch mean talents as ſome of them have been wont to think; but that, on the contrary, there is ſcope enough to employ the moſt capacious underſtanding, and the fineſt genius: and that foreign trade affords as large a field for profit and honour as any other employment whatever.

VII. It cannot fail to have the happieſt tendency to prevent misfortunes and bankruptcies amongſt thoſe merchants who ſhall be thus regularly bred.

VIII. It may give the young merchant ſo good a knowledge of the fundamental principles and maxims of policy, whereupon the true intereſt of the national commerce is grounded, as to render them the better capable hereafter to diſtinguiſh themſelves in the promotion of the ſame, upon all public occaſions and emergencies.

IX. It may prove of benefit and advantage to the lawyer, the gentleman, and nobleman, in the lights wherein repreſented, to paſs a year or two in this college, even after he has left any other univerſity.

1. The reader will pleaſe to obſerve, by the references we have made throughout this article, that our Dictionary of Commerce is eminently calculated for the accompliſhment of the Britiſh merchant in whatever we have pointed out as the moſt eſſentially neceſſary for him to be inſtructed in, and may prove as helpful to the profeſſors in ſuch a college, as to the ſtudents themſelves.

2. That an inſtitution of this kind will raiſe the character of the merchant to ſuch a degree of knowledge in this employment, as will render him capable of embracing or ſtriking out every kind of honourable advantage which the nature of his employment will admit of, and thereby put him above the ſcandalous arts of robbing the public revenue, or breaking to grow rich upon the ruin of his creditors: in brief, a collegial courſe of erudition will excite the younger branches of the beſt families in the kingdom, with fortunes ſuitable, to commence merchants, and, conſequently, will tend abſolutely to exclude from this reſpectable profeſſion all low-bred people, deſtitute of fortune as well as education.

3. That this inſtitution is adapted to form perſons of worth and quality in general, for the accompliſhed men of buſineſs of any kind, the better to enable them to preſerve and improve their eſtates, be they either in land, or in the public funds.

* The lord Verulam touches upon the DOCTRINE OF BUSINESS; which, notwithſtanding he has conſidered it in a light ſomething different to what that judicious reader will obſerve we mean by it, from the drift of our Dictionary; yet, having in near an affinity with what we aim at, that great man's ſentiments may well deſerve attention in this reſpect.

'1. We divide the doctrine of buſineſs, ſays lord Bacon, into the doctrine of various occaſions, and the doctrine of riſing in life. The firſt includes all the poſſible variety of affairs, and is as the commendation to common life; but the other collects and ſuggeſts ſuch things only as regard the improvement of a man's private fortune; and may, therefore, farve each perſon as a private regiſter of his affairs.

'2. No one hath hitherto treated the doctrine of buſineſs ſuitably to it's merit, to the great prejudice of the character both of learning and learned men: for from hence proceeds the miſbelief which has found it as a reproach upon men of letters, that learning and civil prudence are ſeldom found together. And, if we rightly obſerve thoſe three kinds of prudence which we lately ſaid belong to civil life, that of converſation is generally deſpiſed by men of learning as a ſervile thing, and an enemy to contemplation; and, for the government of laws, though learned men acquit themſelves well when advanced to the helm, yet this promotion happens to few of them: but, for the preſent ſubject, the prudence of buſineſs, upon which our lives principally turn, there are no books extant about it, except a few civil admonitions, collected into a little volume or two, by no means adequate to the copiouſneſs of the ſubject. But, if books were written upon this ſubject, as upon others, we doubt not that learned men, furniſhed with tolerable experience, would far excel the unlearned, furniſhed with much greater experience, and outſhoot them in their own bow (a).'

(a) 'This may be extended to civil knowledge in general, ſo as to comprehend not only politics, converſation, and buſineſs, but alſo commerce, and the particular arts of agriculture, navigation, architecture, war, trades, &c. for a man of general knowledge, ſuch as the author, or Mr Boyle, for inſtance, muſt needs be more capable of improving any particular arts or ſciences than a perſon wholly bred up to, and employed about one buſineſs only.' Shaw's note.

4. That, although a method of education, accommodated to the man of buſineſs in a manner ſo ſuperior to what is generally given him, may be attended with a greater expence, yet, it is to be hoped, that will never be an objection againſt it's public eſtabliſhment, it being intended only for ſuch people of condition and fortune who can and will chearfully afford it.

' It is the worſe ſort of huſbandry, ſays the great Mr Locke, ' for a father not even to ſtrain himſelf a little for a ſon's edu- ' cation, which, let his condition be what it will, is the beſt ' portion he can give him.

' He, as the ſame author continues, that at any rate pro- ' cures his child a good mind, well principled, tempered to ' virtue and uſefulneſs, and adorned with civility and good ' breeding, makes a better purchaſe for himſelf than if he had ' laid out the money for an addition of acres: ſpare it in toys ' and play-games, in ſilks, ribbons, and laces, and other ' uſeleſs expences, as much as you pleaſe, but be not ſparing ' in ſo neceſſary a part as this. It is not good huſbandry to ' make his fortune rich, and his mind poor; and I have of- ' ten, with great admiration, ſeen people laviſh it profuſely

' in tricking up their children in fine cloaths, lodging and
' feeding them fumptuoufly, allowing them more than
' enough of ufelefs fervants, and yet, at the fame time,
' ftarve their minds, and not take fufficient care to cover that
' which is the moft fhameful nakednefs, viz. their natural
' wrong inclinations and ignorance. This I can look on as
' no other than a facrificing to their own vanity, it fhewing
' more their pride than true care of the good of their chil-
' dren : whatfoever you employ to the advantage of your fon's
' mind, will fhew your true kindnefs, though it be to the leffen-
' ing of your eftate.   A wife and good man can hardly want
' either the opinion or reality of being great and happy ; but
' he that is foolifh or vicious can be neither great nor happy,
' whatfoever you leave him. I afk you, whether there be
' not fome men in the world whom you had rather have
' your fon be, with FIVE HUNDRED POUNDS per annum,
' than fome others you know with FIVE THOUSAND?'

Of the erecting of the propofed COLLEGE.

Do not the famous univerfities of this nation demonftrate that
there is no people in the world more liberal in their donations
towards the building of colleges for every literary kind of inftitution? And fhall we entertain an opinion that a MERCAN-
TILE COLLEGE will not one day obtain an eftablifhment in this
kingdom, which may enable the nation the better to fupport
all others? Shall we be daily very bountiful in our fubfcrip-
tions towards the erection and fupport of infirmaries and hof-
pitals, for the maintenance of the poor ; and fhall we not think
of the erection of a college, which will impower individuals the
more generoufly to contribute to the fupport of fuch laudable
charities? Is there lefs wifdom in the eftablifhment of a feminary to guard merchants againft misfortune, than to provide
a college for them after their ruin? Shall the nation never have
another GRESHAM nor a SUTTON? But, if no individual
fhould ever think of an eftablifhment of this kind, what is it
that the merchants of this kingdom are not able to do from their
own parfe? Or, why may not their application to parliament
be attended with the defirable fuccefs, if the public fhould be
lukewarm to promote this defign in another fhape? Will it be
lefs honour to the kingdom to build a college for the education
of her merchants, than a repofitory for the productions of nature and now? Is it not the induftry and ingenuity of the mer-

chants that ftamp a value upon thofe productions, and are the
great fupport of all art and fciences? Is not the merchant daily
called upon to take a fhare in the legiflative power, and why
fhall not fuch a refpectable member of the community be
trained up with advantages equal to the other principal claffes
of people in the ftate?

Advertisement.

NEW MERCANTILE INSTITUTION

Is carried on at *Waterside*, near *Hempsted* in *Hertfordshire*,

By *MALACHY POSTLETHWAYT*, and Company.

Also contiguous to the said Institution is established, a

NEW CLASSICAL ACADEMY, for the *antient* and *modern* Languages, and modern History ; and another *Academy* for the Mathematics and Philosophy.

By the Rev. JOHN STIRLING, D. D. Vicar of *Great Gaddesden* in *Hertfordshire*, and Chaplain to his Grace the Duke of *Gordon*, and proper PROFESSORS and ASSISTANTS.

The Intention of this Academical Part is as follows, *viz.*

1... To bring up young *Gentlemen*, who are designed for *Merchants*, or any of the Classes enumerated in the *Plan*, with every Advantage, proper to prepare them for the *Mercantile Institution*, before they are of Age to be admitted therein.

2. .. For other young Gentlemen of Distinction, whose Friends do not intend them for Merchants, *&c.* yet would be glad to have them initiated into the *antient* and *modern Languages*, and other branches of useful and polite Learning, according to the Method proposed in the Supplement.

N. B. It is desired to be particularly observed, that throughout this whole Design, there is a *private Tuition* united with a *public Education*, which is peculiar to this Institution.

The TERMS and CONDITIONS may be seen at large in the *Supplement*.

[Reprinted from Postlethwayt 1751, opposite title page.]

234

CHAPTER 7

THE REV. WILLIAM THOM: ANONYMOUS SCOTS

POLEMICIST AGAINST THE UNIVERSITIES

As indicated on its title page ([Thom] 1762a), the next essay was published in London in 1762 in the rhetorical form of a letter from an unspec-
ified "Society" to a lawyer identified only by the initials "J.M." Appearing later in '62 ([Thom] c,d), ostensibly written by respective individuals
not connected with the society, were "letters" in turn approving the bulk
of the position taken in The defects of an university education, and ridicul-
ing that outlook.

A 1778 source (Thom, [46]) listed the two sequels, but not Defects
itself, as pamphlets by Glasgow clergyman William Thom, only to transfer
attribution of The scheme for erecting an academy at Glasgow (pamphlet d)
to "a young Gentleman since deceased" to whose work the Rev. Mr. Thom was
"privy." In 1799 (Thom, 263-347), however, all three items appeared
within a posthumous collection of Thom's writings (Mepham to Sheldahl
1987, bibliographical information). A 1983 commentator (Dow, 18) stated
justifiably that "there is no doubt" that William Thom wrote all three
pamphlets.

The three essay letters represent a clever strategy for promoting the
author's educational views (Dow 1983). They are introduced without qualification in Defects, supposedly by a thoughtful group of Glasgow citizens.
They are then modified somewhat in Remarks upon a pamphlet concerning the
necessity of erecting an academy at Glasgow, providing a qualified

endorsement of the earlier statement that might attract broader support. Finally, the blistering attack of the Scheme on the ideas previously advanced serves only, by its absurdity, to enhance their appeal. The omission or independent attribution of the first and third essays in listing Thom's writings in 1778 implies that he was as yet unready to acknowledge the strategy. The pretense that the polemics of the last "letter" represented a serious argument obviously required the assertion of independence.

William Thom, 1710-90, was awarded a master's degree by the University of Glasgow in 1732. Three years later he was "licen[sed]" by the Church of Scotland at the presbytery, or district, level, obtaining authority to perform all clerical functions except the administration of sacraments. Thom was fully "ord[ained]" in 1748, at the direction of the churchwide Assembly,[1] following nearly two years of parishioner protest to his faculty-sponsored candidacy. The Presbyterian clergyman became well-known in his day for "eccentric sayings and sarcasms" that according to a source of that year were often still recalled in 1920 (Scott, 412).

Making special reference to contemporary Scotland, the Rev. Mr. Thom wrote widely on topics of religion, education, and agriculture, in particular (Scott 1920, 412-13; and Thom 1778, [46]). Glasgow bookseller James Duncan, the publisher of Thom's two 1762 sequels (c,d, titles) to the essay reprinted below, sold many of his sermons and other short writings (Thom 1778, [46]), perhaps having earlier printed them.

William Thom wrote "a number" of "satirical" pamphlets, besides his Scheme, that were "directed against the faculty of . . . Glasgow" (Dow 1983,

---

[1]In America, ministerial candidates of the United Presbyterian Church, up to its absorption in 1983 within the new Presbyterian Church (U.S.A.), went through the same two-stage process of licensing and ordination (Holland to Sheldahl 1988, source also of distinction between the two phases).

23, note 4). Indeed, a fourth anonymous 1762 work was <u>A defence of the</u> <u>College of G--------w, against an insidious attempt to depreciate the</u> <u>ability and taste of its professors</u> (last word italicized on title page). It concerned ([Thom] 1762b, 3-6) a formal statement by the faculty and administration at Glasgow hailing the birth of a son, the future George IV (Langford 1984, [411], 417), to King George III and his wife. The author ([Thom] 1762b, 6-14) found it highly embarrassing in both form, grammar included, and content; and so could defend the university only by speculating, against all evidence, that the statement was really a forgery rather than the product of "a learned Society" (10). Such satire could only have served his broader aim of discrediting university education in Scotland (Dow 1983, 18-19), at least (Thom 1762a, 3) for nondivinity students.

Without seriously intruding on the contents of the essay that follows, three introductory points may be noted. First, the "Academy" called for, as an alternative to university education ([Thom] 1762a, 19), would be any- thing but a narrow vocational institution, granting that it would be more '"practical"' in nature (Dow 1983, 21) than British higher education of the day. Instead, Thom (1762a, 22, 30) recommended a very broad academic cur- riculum that did not include writing, arithmetic, or bookkeeping, fields that in his opinion could be left to already existing private commercial schools.

Second, in criticizing the emphasis at the University of Glasgow on philosophical studies Thom referred by implication to the holder since 1752 of the Chair of Moral Philosophy, Professor Adam Smith (<u>D.n.b.</u> 1917, s.v. "Smith, Adam," 412). Specifically, Thom (1762a, 5) acknowledged that the chairholder was one of the best of a series of "very able Masters" who had taught moral philosophy "in a very ingenious Manner," and referred to the

237

ethical theory (6, reference to a system based on "Sympathy") developed in Smith's 1759 book <u>Theory of the moral sentiments</u> (<u>D.n.b.</u> 1917, s.v. "Smith, Adam," 413). A 1987 American symposium conducted on Smith's ethics (American Philosophical Association, Eastern Division, 439) points to continuing interest in the 1759 work. The Rev. Mr. Thom (1762a, 6) criticized Glasgow moral philosophers for generating their theories through "thin metaphysical Reasoning."

Finally, William Thom devoted two full pages (1762a, 20-21) to very favorable coverage of an existing Scots commercial college at Perth. Bookkeeping had been taught at Perth as early as 1729 (Murray 1930, 48), and in 1762 renowned accounting author John Mair was the recently appointed schoolmaster, teaching arithmetic, accounts, mathematics, and experimental philosophy (Mepham and Stone, 1977, 129). Distinguished accounting and commercial writer Robert Hamilton taught later in the century at Perth Academy (Murray 1930, 49; and Yamey 1963, 172-73), which still existed as of 1977 (Mepham and Stone, 129).

THE

D E F E C T S

OF AN

UNIVERSITY EDUCATION,

AND ITS

Unfuitablenefs to a Commercial People :

WITH

The Expediency and Neceffity of Erecting at *Glafgow*, an ACADEMY, for the Inftruction of YOUTH.

—————————

In a LETTER to *J. M.* Efq;

From a SOCIETY interefted in the Succefs of this Public-fpirited Propofal.

[By the Rev. Wm Thom, A. M., fovan]

==========

L O N D O N :

Printed for *E. Dilly*, at the *Rofe*-and-*Crown*, in the *Poultry* ; and fold by *A. Donaldfon*, at *Edinburgh* ; and *Daniel Baxter*, at *Glafgow*. M.DCC.LXII.

[Price One Shilling.]

THE

DEFECTS

OF AN

UNIVERSITY EDUCATION.

SIR,

LAST Time we were in Company with you, you was pleafed to exprefs much Surprife, " That fo few Inhabitants of " this City fend their Sons to the Uni- " verfity!" And a Friend of yours added, " That fuch of us as had got a complete " Courfe of Univerfity-Education, had gene- " nerally little more Knowledge or Tafte than " thofe who never had that Advantage."

We are fenfible that neither of you is fingular in your Opinion : Many have exprefled the fame Surprife, with lefs good Humour than you did; they have attempted to ridicule us, and feem to imagine, that our Capacities are flower, and our Underftandings duller, than thofe of other Men commonly are.

B   We

We readily acknowledge, that there is a good deal of Truth in both the Remarks. In proportion to its Populoufnefs, this City fends few Scholars to the Univerfity ; and many who have been there are hardly to be diftinguifhed from their Fellow-Citizens, who were never at a College.

And yet we hope it is not difficult to make an Apology for ourfelves, in both thefe Particulars. We will tell you what we apprehend are the Reafons that moft of us who have had an Univerfity-Education are fo little improved by it; when this is done, we imagine your Wonder will ceafe, that fo few among us chufe to fend their Sons to a Place where themfelves reaped fo little Benefit; and we beg Leave to acquaint you with a Propofal that is talked of among our Fellow-Citizens, which, if it is gone into, and properly executed, will put an end to your Surprife, and will, we hope, in a fhort time, remove the ill-grounded Reproach, " That " our Citizens are dull," as it will be an effectual and lafting Method to improve our Youth.

Candid People will prefume or allow, that it is very unlikely the Blame of our Want of Knowledge fhould lie all on one Side ; we think, that from our general Conduct and Tranfactions with the World, we have given little or no Ground to have it fufpected, that the Size of our Underftanding is inferior to that of other Men : If we have little Tafte, or Learning, the Fault may

may be in fome degree in our Teachers; the Things taught may be too abftrufe to be underftood, or fuch as muft foon be forgot, being unfuitable to us, and having no Relation to the Circumftances and Manner of Life we are afterwards to be in.

That a great Part of the Courfe of Philofophy taught at our Univerfity is of this Nature, is but too obvious : It is evident, that the Univerfities of *Scotland* in general, and particularly this of *Glafgow*, have been founded and defigned purely or chiefly for the fake of that Theology which was in vogue two or three hundred years ago, fome of the Claffes bear evident Marks of this original Defign, being either totally or in part calculated for the Difputes and Wranglings of Divines, and of little Ufe to the Lawyer or Phyfician, and ftill lefs to the Merchant or Gentleman.

Of this fort we reckon Logic and Metaphyfics, which confumed one whole Seffion at the Univerfity, and Part of another. Thefe Arts or Sciences (for it is not yet agreed which of them they are) are to the greateft Part of Students quite unintelligible ; and if they could be underftood, we cannot for our Life difcover their Ufe.

Nature has made all the chief Pleafures of Life eafy to be got; fhe has alfo made all that Knowledge, which is generally ufeful, eafy to be attained : Did Men obferve this, they would foon difcover what is the Knowledge they ought

to

to acquire and teach : But it has unluckily happened that many, who ought to have been wifer, have ever neglected that Knowledge which is obvious and ufeful, and have puzzled their Brains to get what is difficult, metaphyfical, and ufelefs : From the Difficulty they have found in acquiring it, they have concluded it muft be important, and have taken much Pleafure in conveying it to others : But, if thefe learned Gentlemen would but attend a little, they would foon fee the Unprofitablenefs of what they are accuftomed fo much to magnify. What ordinary Company, what Company of Gentlemen is it, where metaphyfical Difputes or the Logic of the Schools are ever fo much as mentioned ? Will a Gentleman, by the deepeft Skill in them, make the better Figure in the Houfe of Commons, or appear with the more Dignity at the Bar ? Will his Eloquence in the Pulpit be the more perfuafive, or will he be the better fkilled in the Animal Oeconomy ? Will Metaphyfics infpire him with Devotion, give him a higher Relifh of Virtue, or enable him to act with greater Propriety in Life ? Or will the Knowledge of them be of any advantage to the Farmer, the Architect, or the Merchant ? We apprehend that none of thefe Queftions can be anfwered in the Affirmative. And muft Acquirements that are fo confeffedly of no ufe in Life, that are never fo much as talked f in good Company, wafte a Year or two of a young Man's Time ? Is Life fo long ? Is Time of fo

2   little

little Value, that there are not enow of ufeful Studies to fill it up with ? Muft Recourfe be had to Things, which any well-bred Man would be afhamed to have it fufpected, that he had ever employed his Thoughts about?

We are very forry to fay, that if the Time fome of us attended the Univerfity, and fpent fo abfurdly in hearing crabbed Queftions and metaphyfical Jargon, had been employed in teaching us ancient and modern Hiftory, and efpecially that of our own Country, we fhould have been much more obliged to the learned Profeffors; we fhould have been much better accomplifhed, and have appeared to be fo in the Judgment of thofe with whom we converfe.

But Logic and Metaphyfics, though they appear to us to be the moft abfurd, and confumed the greateft Part of our Time to no Purpofe; yet they were not the only Things that wafted it at the Univerfity : The Difquifitions we heard about the Origin of moral Virtue, are little better remembered by us, and feem to be of little more Ufe.

We are not ignorant, that the Lectures on moral Philofophy have for many Years paft been delivered in this Univerfity by very able Mafters, and in a very ingenious Manner ; and we are informed, that this was never more the Cafe than it is at prefent : But we apprehend thefe ingenious Gentlemen have rather indulged their Bias to fome fingular Opinions of their own, than communicated much Knowledge to

even

even the moft intelligent of their Scholars. We fuppofe alfo, that as their Difputes are fo abftrufe, and their Theories about the Foundation of Morality fo different, neither can be of much Neceffity or Ufe.

One contends, that Morality is founded in the Will of God; another, in Conformity and Truth; a third, in the Fitnefs and Unfitnefs, or in the eternal and unalterable Relations or Differences of Things; a fourth, in a moral Senfe or Difcernment, fuppofed to be natural to the human Mind; another eftablifhes his Syftem on Sympathy. But, whatever Scheme the Profeffor of Morality contrives or embraces, he ufes a long Train of thin metaphyfical Reafoning to eftablifh it, and fpends a great Part of the Year in laying down Arguments for, and anfwering Objections againft, his Syftem. Arguments very pleafing, and perhaps intelligible to himfelf, as they are familiar to him, and he believes they will pleafe and improve his Pupils; but they are too fubtile to be underftood by them, and leave little or no Impreffion upon any of their Minds. Here, we imagine, there is much Time loft, and Pains mifplaced. Might not thefe nice Difquifitions about the Foundation of Morality be left out, or flightly fkimmed over, and the Students be juft as knowing, and as wife? How few of them are able to apprehend fuch Arguments, or to purfue fuch Reafoning? Might not the Time be better fpent in teaching them Morality, in explaining the Nature of the

particular

246

particular Virtues ? Would not this be more adapted to the Capacity of the Scholars, and incomparably more ufeful to them through the Whole of Life ? And might not the Profeffors eafily purfue this fimple and ufeful Method of Teaching ? Ought they not to defcend to it, inftead of torturing their Invention to eftablifh what it is little matter whether it be eftablifhed or not. There are Objects, the Nature of which may be eafily underftood, when their Origin is in vain fearched after. We fhould like better that Geographer, who defcribes exactly the Courfe and Soundings of *St. Laurence* or *Senegal* Rivers, than another who tedioufly and minutely difputes about the precife Spot where each of thefe Rivers takes its Rife. And we fhould not expect that a Merchant would thrive, who, when he came to a River's Mouth, delayed to load his Ship with the Commodities which had been brought down the River, or were produced upon its Banks, till he had firft traced the River upwards, and made himfelf fure of the Place where it began. Whatever be the Foundation of Morality, the Nature of the particular Virtues may be defcribed ; the Youth are capable of underftanding them, though perhaps not able to enter into abftrufe Inveftigations about the Origin of moral Virtue. To know what Virtue is, is ufeful to Men in every Station of Life ; but who is the better for having heard or underftood a great many fubtile Difputes about its Origin. For our Parts, we fhould not grudge, though the learned
Profeffor

Profeſſor kept theſe entirely to himſelf, or he might for his particular Comfort and Satisfaction communicate his knotty Ideas to that one of his Scholars, who has moſt Connexion with leading Men, and has the beſt Chance to be recommended to ſucceed him ; and who will either eſpouſe or think himſelf obliged to be at an immenſe Labour to deſtroy the moral Theory of his Predeceſſor.

Theſe different Theories may be amuſing to contemplative Minds ; and, for aught we know, there may be ſome Truth in each of them, and at bottom they may be leſs inconſiſtent with one another than they appear to be ; but whether they be or be not inconſiſtent ; whether any of them or none of them is true, we will be bold to ſay, that no one of them, after ſo much Time and Pains ſpent upon it, ever enabled that Scholar who underſtood it beſt to reſtrain a ſingle Paſſion, or to perform one virtuous Action. And we ſhall ſurely be thought to have kept within Bounds, while we pronounce no more concerning the above-mentioned dry Parts of Science, than one who is eſteemed a good Judge has done, with reſpect to a long and compleat Courſe of Univerſity-Education *. " It would " be hard to ſay what one Duty of Society, or " what one Office as a Citizen, a Student is " qualified to diſcharge or ſuſtain, after his cloſe " Application of ſo many Years ?"

Some

* Sheridan, on Britiſh Education.

Some of us were the Scholars of an illuſtrious Teacher of Morality, himſelf a perfect and ready Maſter of Greek and Latin. He introduced, or revived, a high Taſte for Claſſical Learning in this Place ; and, while he lived, he kept it alive. If ever a Profeſſor had the Art of communicating Knowledge, and of raiſing an Eſteem and Deſire of it in the Minds of his Scholars ; if ever one had the magical Power to inſpire the nobleſt Sentiments, and to warm the Hearts of Youth with the Admiration and Love of Virtue ; if ever one had the Art to create an Eſteem of Liberty, and an Abhorrence and Contempt of Tyranny and Tyrants, He was the Man. What pity was it, that for three or four Months a Year ſuch ſuperior Talents ſhould have been thrown away on metaphyſical and fruitleſs Diſputations ! When theſe were got over, how delightful and edifying was it to hear him ! If we did not make ſome Improvement during the few remaining Months of the Seſſion, the Fault, we acknowledge, was in ourſelves ; and perhaps our Docility was leſſened, and our Minds ſtupiſied, as we had the Year before been accuſtomed to hear Lectures, which neither deſerved nor catched our Attention. For the moral Diſputes, as that Gentleman managed them (tho', as we have hinted, ſomething really uſeful ought to have been taught inſtead of them) were not reckoned ſo inſipid as the Logical and Metaphyſical. We can yet remember, that had the Regulations of the College permitted that Students might have gone directly from

C   the

the Languages to Ethics, many in this City, who looked upon Logic and Metaphyfics as futile and unintelligible, would have fent their Children to him. In that cafe, they would have had an Advantage that was much defired; their Children would have both heard the Lectures at one hour, and have been examined upon them at another; whereas, by the Rules, except they had been firft at the Logic Clafs, they could but hear the Lectures.

But befides the Intricacy of the Things taught, there was another Caufe why moft of us imbibed but little Knowledge at the Univerfity: Our Profeffors loved Rank, and kept themfelves at a greater Diftance from their Scholars, than common School-mafters do. This hindered them from knowing our Genius, or particular Turn, and directing us to a proper Courfe of Reading. When we left the Univerfity, we were totally unacquainted with Hiftory: We had formed no Plan of moral or of natural Knowledge: Had our Teachers been at a little Pains with us, they might eafily have difcerned the Bent of our Genius, and what natural Capacity each of us had; from our Circumftances, they might have formed probable Conjectures what Bufinefs in Life we were defigned for; and they might have directed us to the Books proper to be read: We are of opinion, that the Ufefulnefs of public Teachers lies in this, as much as in delivering their Lectures, and perhaps more. By fome Pains taken in this manner, Scholars might in a few Years

attain

attain more real and diftinct Knowledge, than
without fuch Direction they are ever like to attain in their Lives. We fay this, as we have
often done, from deep-felt Experience. We were,
when young, greedy of Knowledge, and continually reading fomething or other ; but nobody
was fo kind to advife us and fet us on a right
Track. We hope we are not vain in imagin-
ing, that if our Diligence in purfuit of Knowledge had been well directed, when our Memories
were ftrong, our Thirft after Knowledge great,
and our Minds free from Cares, we might have
made fome fort of Progrefs in Literature ; but
this was not done, which we deeply regret, and
muft regret while we have Breath.

Our Teachers however profeffed to be great
Admirers of the Ancients; but they were too
proud or too lazy to imitate them. Did They
fatisfy themfelves with delivering a dry Difcourfe
on Philofophy, containing Ideas to which their
Pupils were Strangers ? Did They reckon the
Bufinefs of the Day over, when the Hour was
run ? Did They expect to convey new and cramp
Notions in fuch a hurry, into the young Mind ?
Was this all that was done by *Zeno* in the *Stoa*,
by *Plato* in the *Academy*, or by *Epicurus* in his
Gardens ? No, they did much more, they threw
afide all diftant and magifterial Airs; they put
themfelves on a Level with their Scholars, they
walked and converfed familiarly with them, they
led their Minds in an eafy and gradual manner
to the Perception of Truth ; and by converfing

C 2   and

and repeating over and over the same Point, made them thoroughly to underſtand it, and fixed it in their Memories.

If the learned Gentlemen we ſpeak of had but conſidered how little they were able to recollect of a ſet Diſcourſe, or of the beſt Sermon they ever heard, we are perſuaded their Method of Teaching would have appeared imperfect even to themſelves.

We mention but another Cauſe of our having made ſo little Progreſs; and it is this: We were ſet on too many different Branches of Knowledge at the ſame time; there was an odd Sort of E-mulation induſtriouſly excited among us; it was eſteemed honourable to attend many Claſſes; it was thought ſhameful, and a Mark of Poverty, to be at few: Moſt of the Students in the three upper Claſſes were one Hour at Latin, one at Greek, one at Mathematics, and one or two at Philoſophy, all in the ſame Day; and this Me-thod was continued through the whole Seſſion: By which means our Attention was ſo divided, and our Minds ſo diſtracted with a Jumble of different Things, that not one of them took hold of us; and it was next to impoſſible, that even thoſe of us who wiſhed and endeavoured to learn, could ſucceed. This produced a laſting bad Ef-fect: An Inclination to ramble in purſuit of Knowledge ſtuck faſt with us after we left the Univerſity. We had been taught to be fond of a Fault, into which from Lazineſs or Vanity we might naturally have fallen. We could not endure

dure Conftancy and Affiduity, we foon became weary of any one thing; and, as we had been long obliged and accuftomed to do fo, we fkipped haftily from one fort of Reading to another; an Error which we have not yet been able thoroughly to correct. It is however, manifeft, that one Thing at a time ought principally to have been inculcated; but we, who ourfelves contrive Schemes of Profit, can eafily fee for whofe Benefit the Multiplicity of private Claffes was firft fet on foot, and continues ftill to be purfued.

The Things we have flightly noticed will in fome fort account for the fmall Morfel of Knowledge moft of us brought from the Seat of Learning; and if we, in the City, have little Erudition, our College-Companions in the Country have not more: We muft, and we will affirm, that it is very rare to find a Country Gentleman bred at the fame Univerfity, who is in Tafte and in Extent of Knowledge any degree above ourfelves, tho' they have had much more Leifure to purfue Knowledge, than fuited with our active and bufy way of Life: A Prefumption, both that the Things taught were improper, and that the Method of Teaching them laboured under fome effential Defect. Nay, we muft be forgiven to fay it, the learned Profeffors feem to be convinced of all this, and to be of the fame Opinion with ourfelves. They had lately two Vacancies in the Univerfity in their own Difpofal: They looked round the Country, and confidered the Abilities of all the Clergymen

men and Students who had been educated by
themfelves ; and among fuch a great Number
they could find none, that, even in their own
Opinion, were qualified to fill them. They made
choice of a Clergyman at a great diftance, and
of a Student, who both of them had got their
Education at other Univerfities : By which Step
they reflected all the Honour they could on thefe
two worthy Men ; but at the fame time made
an open and candid Acknowledgment of the
Wretchednefs of their Plan, and of their own
Debility and ill Succefs, at begetting Knowledge
in the Minds of their Scholars ; like frigid or
impotent People, who are forced to adopt Strangers into their Family, being incapable to beget
any Children of their own.

The Faults in Education we have mentioned
have had bad Effects on all forts of People, who
refort or have reforted to the Univerfity, the
Clergy themfelves not excepted ; and we own,
they have had very bad Effects upon ourfelves.
The Things taught are abftrufe and dark ; and
it is little to be wondered at, if we brought no
Knowledge of them away with us : If any of us
brought away fome knowledge of them, it is as
little to be wondered if we foon loft it : It was
of fuch a Nature as to be eafily forgot ; it was
fo remote from common Ufe, that it could not be
remembered.

Tho' we have been at fome Pains to acquire a
little Knowledge from Books and Company, we
are fenfible that in writing this Letter we give

3   but

but too manifeſt Proofs of the Defectiveneſs of
our Education. But ſtill, we believe this was
no ways owing to our Want of natural Capacity.
Our City can boaſt that it has produced as compleat Burgeſſes, and Gentlemen of as refined and
enlarged Underſtandings, as any in the Iſland ;
that is, when they were educated or improved at
other Places.

What we have ſaid, is not with a View to depreciate an Univerſity Education, but to apolo-
giſe for ourſelves, and to remove, Sir, your Surpriſe at our little Knowledge, and that ſo few of
us ſend our Sons to the Univerſity : And by
this time, we hope, our Apology will appear to
be pretty compleat ; an Apology which we have
been forced to make. When we ſaw the Laugh
raiſed againſt our Town in almoſt every Company
of Strangers, and heard ourſelves ſo often and ſo
groundleſsly reproached for want of Taſte, we
judged it was but a piece of Juſtice to ourſelves
and our Fellow-Citizens, to open our Minds to
a Gentleman of your Diſcernment and Candour ;
and when the Cauſes of what we are blamed for
are laid open, though not near ſo fully as we
could eaſily have done, equitable Judges will
ceaſe to rally us. But if we ſhall be afterwards
reproached upon the ſame Score, we will beg
leave in our turn openly to expreſs our Surpriſe,
that it ſhould ever be expected by any Man of
ſober Senſe, that we ſhould ſend our Sons to
waſte a Year or two of their Lives in learning
Things ſo uſeleſs, abſurd, and ridiculous, as
Technical

Technical Logic and Metaphyfical Speculations are confeffed to be. We attended to them with Reluctance and Difguft; we have now hardly any Traces of them in our Minds; and can we think that our Children will be more pleafed with them, or remember them better?

The fenfible Part of Mankind will, we hope, agree with us, That Education ought to be calculated for the Times we live in; that the Aim of it fhould be to make the Youth good Men, and ufeful Subjects; to prepare them to acquit themfelves well in the particular Bufinefs they are to live by, and to make a manly and decent Figure in the Companies they may be in. We think it manifeft, that the mufty and intricate Parts of Science we have mentioned, are no ways fubfervient to any of thefe Ends.

We are generally a Commercial People; except in Matters of Commerce, our Ideas are pretty much circumfcribed. The Thoughts of great Numbers among us move in no very wide Circle, and never towards Metaphyfics. We figure not to ourfelves any very wide or noble Plan of Education, which might dignify high Life, but would be meerly imaginary and unattainable in our Circumftances: To thefe our Education muft be fuitable. The Things taught us ought to be fuch as immediately fit us for Bufinefs; or are fome way relative to our Employment, or analogous to that Range of Thought to which our Bufinefs may be fuppofed naturally to lead us; or which may adorn Converfa-

tion,

tion, and free us from the Imputation of Ignorance.

What thefe Branches of Knowledge are, it
is not difficult to fee ; practical Mathematics,
Hiftory in general, the Hiftory of our own
Country, and of thofe in the Neighbourhood
or with which we carry on Commerce, natural
Hiftory, Geography, the Hiftory of Commerce,
and practical Morality. Were there any Doubt
about the Parts of Science that are propereft to
be taught us, it might be removed, by obferving, that thofe of us who are ftudious naturally
apply to fome of the Branches we have juft
mentioned. Many in this City, without any
Advantages in their Youth, have by their own
good Senfe, and the dint of Application, made
a very confiderable Progrefs in the Knowledge
of Hiftory, Belles Lettres, and Mathematics ;
but we know none who ever turned their Heads
to ideal Entities, or to quibbling Syllogifms.
And if we had an Opportunity of fuch a Courfe
of Education, our City would foon fhew to the
World, that the Defire and Tafte of ufeful and
attainable Knowledge are as general among us
as in any other City whatfoever, that is but
equally populous.

Some eight or ten Years ago, the Principal
and Profeffors of the *Marifhal College* at *Aberdeen,* "in order to render the Study of the Sciences
more natural and progreffive, did unanimoufly
agree to depart from the old Plan, and from
that time forth to obferve a very different Order.

D   They

They continued, indeed, to teach the Claffical Learning as formerly, but inftead of Logic and Metaphyfics, they appointed that Year to be fpent in teaching Hiftory, Geography, Chronology, an Introduction to natural Hiftory; and that all the Students of that Clafs fhould attend the Leffons of the Profeffor of Mathematics: That the next Year be employed in natural Philofophy, and the Laws of Matter and Motion; in Mechanics, Hydroftatics, Pneumatics, Optics, and Aftronomy; and that the laft Year of the Courfe be allowed to the Study of the abftract Sciences, Pneumatology, Morals, Logic, or the Art of Reafoning." A confiderable Improvement in the Method of Teaching, and which does honour to the Gentlemen who appointed it.

We were very much encouraged when firft we heard that the *Marifhal College* had fo far thrown back ufelefs Things, and accommodated their Courfe to modern Times. There appeared to be fo much good Senfe in what they had done, the Alterations they had made were fo vifibly advantageous and neceffary, that we made no doubt but our Univerfity would immediately follow fo edifying an Example, and would make further Improvements upon it: But after we had waited for fome time, we were entirely damped, when upon Enquiry we were informed, that the Profeffors were not to depart a Hair-breadth from their Plan and Practice. They are, it feems, tied down either by Cuftom,

or

or by Inclination, or by Rules, to obferve a
Courfe of Teaching, a great Part of which is at
this time of Day ufelefs and abfurd, and more
efpecially fo with refpect to us.

We do affure you, Sir, that when we faw
that no Relief was to be expected from the
Univerfity, we were in diftrefs for our Children,
and felt, perhaps too ftrongly, fome Emotions
of Indignation againft the learned Profeffors,
whom we looked upon as ftubbornly tenacious
of their own antiquated Plan. We had frequent
Converfations with one another, expreffing our
Grief that this was the Cafe; and fome of us
were then pretty much inclined to provide a
proper Remedy, and to remove, at our own
Expence, the Inconveniency to which our Youth
were expofed. But, through a Multiplicity of
Bufinefs, and Want of fufficient Harmony among
ourfelves, we allowed our good Purpofes to
cool; and, with refpect to fo important a Defign,
fuffered ourfelves to relapfe into a lethargic In-
activity, for which we frankly own we do not
know what Excufe to make.

What we wifhed for and intended was, to have
in this City a School or Academy for inftructing
our Youth in that Knowledge which is proper
to give them an early Liking to Religion and
Virtue; that which will fit them for Bufinefs,
and enable them to difcharge the Duties of Life
with Honour, and appear to Advantage in the
World.

D 2   We

We were roufed from our Lethargy, when we faw the Royal Burgh of *Perth* before-hand with us, in eftablifhing fuch an Academy as we wifhed for. Senfible of the like Difadvantages we complain of, they have fet us a Pattern highly worthy of our Imitation. The Magiftrates of that Town, affifted by a worthy Clergyman in the Place, have, like Gentlemen of Tafte,. and Men of the World at the fame time, generoufly provided for the Education of Youth: An Exertion of public Spirit, for which Children and Parents will efteem and honour them at prefent, and which in time to come will be remembered as a Monument of their good Senfe and provident Care of Pofterity!

Their Aim is " to train up young People for Bufinefs and active Life; or to give fuch a practical and compendious Courfe of Education, as may in fome meafure qualify the Gentleman, the Merchant, or even the Mechanic, to act with greater Advantage in their refpective Stations: For this purpofe the Town-Council have fixed upon two Mafters, with each a Salary of 50 *l.* befides a Gratuity of two Guineas to be paid at the Entry of each Student to each Mafter for the Seffion; which is to begin every Year on the Firft of *October*, and to continue 'till the End of *May*.

One of the Mafters is to deliver, 1. A fhort Hiftory of Philofophy, and the Rife and Progrefs of Arts and Sciences. 2. A Courfe of natural Hiftory,

Hiftory, in which he gives an Idea of Botany and the Animal Œconomy. 3. A compendious View of Poetry, Rhetoric, Logic, and Moral Philofophy; and 4. A Courfe of Chronology and civil Hiftory, Antient and Modern, efpe-cially the Hiftory of *Britain*, with regard to its Conftitution, political Intereft, and Commerce.

The other Mafter is to teach, 1. Arithmetic. 2. Book-keeping. 3. A Courfe of Mathematics; and 4. A Courfe of natural Philofophy, illu-ftrated by Experiments. Each of the Mafters is to finifh his whole Courfe in two Seffions, if poffible; otherwife what remains is to be gone through, at proper Times, in a fubfequent Seffion, without any further Charge to the Student. A Writing-Mafter is to attend the Academy every Day; and a Teacher is to read the fuperior Greek and Latin Claffics one Hour every Morning, with fuch of the Students as would make further Progrefs in the Languages: Both thefe Mafters to be paid by the Students.

The Inftruments for the Experimental Part, they are to purchafe by Contribution, and have already about 200 Guineas fubfcribed for that Purpofe. Their firft Seffion begins in *October*." This is their Plan. It is, no doubt, well con-trived for that Place. It has nothing in it that can be called ufelefs or fuperfluous. Every thing to be taught has a Tendency to the End propofed; but it may be proper to vary a little from it, and to make fome Additions in an Academy here.

Writing,

Writing, Arithmetic, Book-keeping, and also some Parts of Mathematics are here taught in private Schools; History, Chronology, and most of the other Parts mentioned in the *Perth* Scheme, are hardly even attempted; the Things taught are necessary to accomplish a Merchant's Clerk; the Things hitherto neglected, would form the Merchant for extensive Business and for manly Conversation; and it is unquestionably, by teaching the historical and philosophical Things, that a School either obtains or deserves the name of an Academy.

Writing, Arithmetic, and Book keeping may be left to be taught as before; and then two Masters will, with the greater success, manage the remaining Parts.

The Province of the one will be, 1. Mathematics. 2. Geography. 3. Natural History; and 4. Natural Philosophy, illustrated by Experiments.

The Province of the other will be nearly as in the Plan of *Perth*; 1. History of Philosophy, and the Rise and Progress of Arts and Sciences. 2. A compendious View of Poetry, Rhetoric, and moral Philosophy. 3. A Course of Chronology and Civil History, Antient and Modern, especially the History of *Britain*.

The Business of the one Master will be, besides Mathematics, to teach the most entertaining and useful Parts of natural Philosophy, that of the other will be chiefly History.

We

We are perfuaded that every impartial Perfon
will fee at once the great and remarkable Utility
of fuch a Courfe of Education, and the Propriety of erecting fuch an Academy in this
Place as foon as it can be conveniently done.

The Town of *Perth*, however confiderable
in itfelf, is fmall in comparifon of this populous,
wealthy, and thriving City; the fame Encouragement that is given by them, would be a very
light Burden upon us, whether it were given
out of the Revenues of the City, or contributed
by a Number of the moft opulent Citizens:
But as a far greater Number of Students would
attend the Academy here, lefs Salary to the
Teachers might ferve the purpofe; nay, there
is great Reafon to believe, that if the Magiftrates
and principal Inhabitants will, as we hope,
countenance the Project, in a very few Years
little or no Salary at all may be neceffary.

This Plan will interfere but little with that of
the Univerfity. The Aims are quite different
and diftinct; what is defigned by the Academy
is, to train up young People for Bufinefs and
active Life; the Aim of the Univerfity is, to
make Scholars of them: And, no doubt, a
great Adept in fcholaftical Learning is ftill
to be made by fome Skill in the learned
Languages, and by a long and laborious
Courfe of Study. This we eafily difcern; the
Clergy are ordinarily the People who ftudy
longeft, and enquire deepeft into Science;
they do it, or begin to do it, at the Univerfity;

and

and when Vacancies happen in Univerfities, generally fpeaking, they can only be fupplied from the Clergy, or by fuch as have been educated to be Clergymen. But the Education we propofe is compendious, and of general Ufe; our School will not keep any Student from the Univerfity, who is intent on making a great Figure, by deep and metaphyfical Refearches: And we are fure the Profeffors are more difinterefted than to wifh any Scholar fhould confume Four or Five Years at their Colleges without being better accomplifhed for Converfation, or more prepared for the Employment by which he propofes to live.

We allow the Excellence of profeffed Scholars, and fhall leave it to Colleges to fill their Heads with Materials for Argumentation : We propofe no fuch thing; and therefore we perfuade ourfelves, that the Mafters, who love every Branch of Knowledge, will encourage our Plan, and give us their beft Advice: And we fubmit it to themfelves, if it would not be worthy the Generofity of fuch Patrons of Science to apply fome Portion of their large Revenues to begin and carry on fo ufeful and neceffary a Project.

But, though contrary to our Intention, our Plan fhould feem to interfere a little with that of the Univerfity, or threaten to keep fome Scholars from them, this ought not to difcourage us, nor to put the Profeffors into any ill Humour: Senfible that they need fuch
a Motive

a Motive to roufe them to more Activity, they
fhould for their own Honour and Ufefulnefs
wifh us Succefs : Both they and the Teachers of
the Academy will the more exert themfelves,
when they know that their Honour and their Intereft too depend upon their Activity and Diligence.

It is a vulgar Error to believe, that Teachers
of Religion different from the eftablifhed one,
are in all refpects hurtful. The Reformed have
forced the Catholics to throw afide many of their
Abfurdities, and have ftirred them up to fearch
for more Knowledge. The Diffenters in England have contributed to promote the Learning
and Sobriety of the Churchmen; and perhaps
even the Seceders in Scotland have, by their Stri&-
nefs, ftimulated fome of the Eftablifhed Clergy
to a Stri&nefs and Diligence in their Office, beyond what they might otherwife have attained.

The Mafters of an Univerfity need fuch a
Stimulus, as much as the Teachers of Religion.
When Men have got into a fettled Way of Life,
Lazinefs often gets the better of the good Purpofes they really had, when they firft entered into
it. The Senfe of Duty and the Love of Fame,
are not able to overcome the Love of Eafe. It
is the Opinion of fome intelligent Perfons, that if
the Eftablifhed Clergy, inftead of having Salaries fixed for Life, were hired from Time to
Time, we fhould get better Sermons from them
than even thofe we get at prefent. Whatever
Truth there may be in this, we are perfuaded

E   there

there is much more in the Remark, when applied to the Mafters of a College. They have
their fine Lodgings, and they have their fixed
Salaries as the Clergy have; but the Clergy have
one ftrong Motive to fpur them on, which the
Profeffors have not. There are other Clergymen
juft at hand, and if any one is very lazy and
negligent, the People will leave him; but be the
Profeffors ever fo flothful, there is no College near
to receive the Students from them. Could the
Youth be taught by others at as little Expence
to their Parents, the Profeffors would be at more
pains and beftir themfelves in a very different
manner.

We have faid thus much in general, to prevent
fome Prejudices that might have been conceived
againft our Plan, as if it were to interfere with
the Univerfity; and we have fhewn that inftead
of being hurtful to that learned Body of Men,
it will produce very falutary Effects upon them;
and, we hope, it may reafonably be prefumed,
that by the Activity of our Teachers, and the
conftant and clofe Application of their Scholars,
more real and ufeful Knowledge may be delivered and acquired in two Years, than can be in
fix or feven in the difputatious and flow Method ufual in Univerfities, where there are fo
few Hours of Teaching, and fo many of Diverfion.

It has been obferved already, that the principal
Points in view in the Education of Youth ought
to be, to form them to the Love of Religion and
Virtue,

Virtue, to render them ferviceable to the Government, ufeful to themfelves and to that Society
to which they may more immediately belong,
and agreeable in the ordinary Commerce of Life.

With refpect to forming our Youth to be
good Subjects, this Plan needs make no Provifion.
The Inhabitants of this City, and of all the
Country around, are almoft to a Man well af-
fected to the prefent Government, and, were it
neceffary, would rifk their Fortunes and their
Lives in its Support. Though we think young
People ought to be made acquainted with the
Nature of that happy Conftitution under which
we live; and this may be advantageoufly done,
in reading to them the Hiftory of our own
Country.

But Religion merits the moft ferious Attention : It is judged to be a great Defect in the
ordinary Education, that, except thofe who formally fet themfelves to the Study of Divinity,
no Care is taken to acquaint the Students with
religious Principles, or to tincture them with a
Senfe of Piety. Religion takes fafter hold of the
Mind, and has a ftronger Tendency to make
Men good and virtuous, than many feem to
imagine. It is of infinite Importance, with refpect to the other World ; and it is the moft
powerful Reftraint to preferve Youth from thofe
Vices, which they are but too ready to fall into.
Vices which are both hainous, and hinder them
from making that Figure in the World which
they are entitled to make. A Senfe of God

makes the Life fober and regular. **Parents** ought to recommend Religion to their Children, and all Teachers fhould both by Example and Inftruction fhew their Scholars, that they have a high Efteem of Religion, and a deep Senfe of its Importance to promote all the valuable Interefts of Mankind.

We have lately feen a printed Sermon upon the Caufes of the Decline of Religion, and we verily expected to find one Thing affigned as a Caufe of that Decline, which has been and continues to be much talked of, and much lamented in this Place; but which, it feems, the Author did not advert to. If he had pleafed, he might have mentioned the bad Difcipline of Colleges, and the too little Appearance of Piety in the Deportment of the Mafters; which, though perhaps not fo extenfive, is as real a Caufe of Irreligion as any he has named. It produces very difmal Effects; the Students, who afterwards apply to Divinity, are cool and indifferent in the Study of it; thofe who apply to Bufinefs, in Town or Country, bring along with them from the College a vifible Averfion to Religion; and with this pernicious Contagion they infect the unwary, who fee them or converfe with them.

The blunt Saying of a plain and honeft Citizen, fome time after public Prayers began to be difufed in the Univerfity, was quite agreeable to our Sentiments. When he was entering his Son to one of the Philofophy Claffes, ' I am in- ' different, faid he, I am indifferent about your
' nice

' nice Difputes : Teach my Son Religion and
' Morality ; teach him to govern his Paffions,
' and to love God and Men : I had rather have
' him a pious and good Man, than poffeffed of
' all the curious Philofophy you can teach him
' in feven Years.'

Religion ought to be the Ground-work of
every Courfe of Education, and the Principles
inftilled into the Minds of young People
fhould be fcriptural and found. This is certainly right, in every View. We have known fome
young Men, who were marred in their Bufinefs,
and rejected by thofe who could have advanced
them, merely becaufe they were much fufpected
of entertaining fome very loofe and unfound
Opinions.

But, to confider Religion in the loweft View,
namely, as it is a Science and a Subject of Converfation, the Youth ought certainly to be taught
it. Every Gentleman and Merchant fhould be
able to talk about the Tenets of that Religion,
which is eftablifhed in his Country. He fhould
know fomething about the Government and Difcipline of that Church of which he is a Member.

We fhould weary out your Patience, Sir, and
protract this Letter to an indecent Length, were
we to mention the Ufe of every particular
Branch of Literature propofed to be taught by
the projected Plan ; and were we to fhew how
well this Plan will anfwer the remaining Ends
of Education ; namely, to prepare young People
to be ufeful in Life and to appear as accomplifhed

plifhed Gentlemen in Converfation. We will, in a few Words, take notice of the Advantages which a Plan of this fort has, effectually to communicate the Knowledge which is propofed to be taught by it.

1. The Things to be taught are all of them capable of being learned. They are commenfurate to the Capacity of the young Mind. Logical Quiddities and metaphyfical Subtleties are totally exterminated. Hiftory, Geography, the natural Productions of a Country, the Manners of the People, the Manufactures and Commodities they trade in, may all be underftood and remembered. Thefe are Things ufeful to be known by a Commercial People. And, by the way, we beg leave to fay, That if Merchants have not dipped much into metaphyfical and moral Theories, they have by their Voyages and Travels furnifhed the World with a far more valuable Sort of Knowledge: We mean that of the Manners and Cuftoms of Men, which is certainly more entertaining, and perhaps lays a furer Foundation of Morality than any of the Cobweb Schemes which have been fo finely fpun out of the Imaginations of fanciful Men, who have all their Lives been immured within a College, and are quite deftitute of the Knowledge of the World.

2. We are almoft certain of having the ableft Teachers the Nation can afford. They will readily be left to be chofen and employed by us. A Place in an Univerfity is confidered as eafy,

1   ho-

honourable and lucrative. It is almoſt looked upon as a Sine-cure; it is not ordinarily the moſt ingenious and able for teaching that is pitched upon, but he who is connected, or whoſe Friends are connected with, and can ſerve the Men in Power: and this appears to be growing more and more in Faſhion. When a Vacancy happens we hear every one ſaying, " Who will get " this Place, who has moſt Intereſt with ſuch a " Duke or ſuch a Lord." A Man's Sufficiency is ſeldom or never mentioned; his Ability is no Recommendation of him; his total Ignorance of the Things he is to teach is no Obſtacle to his being preferred to the Office: For twenty Years paſt there are not above One or Two Inſtances where one was either preſented by the Crown, or choſen by the Faculty, merely or chiefly becauſe he was thought beſt qualified to teach the Claſs he was called to teach. If there are any who are fit to teach, by a proper Encouragement we may have them.

But the Directors of the Academy, beſides Capacity to teach, muſt have other Qualifications: They muſt be Men of a grave and reſpectable Character, who will add Weight and Importance to the Things they teach, and attract the Eſteem and Love of their Scholars. The Profeſſors in our Time, to do them Juſtice, ſeemed well enough qualified in this reſpect. Several of the Things taught by them were, as we have ſaid, abſolute Futilities; and yet even in theſe Things, from the Solemnity of the Teachers, we at that

time

time fuspected there might be fome Value in them;
or, perhaps, their Diligence in teaching conferred fome imaginary Worth on every thing
they taught. We have often obferved, that the
earneft Application of Teachers to their Bufinefs
procures them Reputation, and adds Weight to
the moft frivolous and infignificant Things that
may be delivered by them. The Men were
guilty of no Littlenefs or Folly ; they were
Men of exterior Dignity, and we could not but
pay fome Regard to every thing they faid or did.
Teachers of that fort, when the Knowledge
communicated by them is ufeful and fuitable,
do fuccefsfully recommend Knowledge and
Virtue ; and by their regular, decent, and religious Behaviour, they create a Liking of Religion
in the Hearts of their Scholars.

3. The Hours of teaching in the defigned
Academy will be more than are allotted to it
in Colleges. It is abfurd and hypocritical for
Men to give high Commendations of Science,
and to ufe fo flender Pains, and fpend fo little
Time in teaching it. Men are become fo lazy,
and the Defire of Literature is fo feeble, that
it is a Wonder if Knowledge of every fort does
not take its flight from amongft us. The
Practice of Univerfities is quite altered ; not
one Half of the Hours are employed in teaching
that were one Hundred, and not a Third of
them that were two Hundred, Years ago.
The Prefident De Mefmes fhewed a Manu-
fcript of one of his Anceftors to Mr. Rollin ;
wherein

wherein that ancient Gentleman gave an Account of his Studies at the Univerſity of Toulouſe. " In 1545, ſays he, I was ſent to Touloſe with my Preceptor and Brother to ſtudy Law, under the Direction of an old gray-haired Man, who had travelled much. We got up at Four, and having ſaid our Prayers, we began our Studies at Five, with our great Books under our Arms, and our Writing-Tables and Candleſticks in our Hands. We attended at Lectures 'till Ten without Intermiſſion ; then we went to Dinner, after having haſtily collated for one Half-hour what we had writ down. After Dinner, by way of Diverſion, we read Sophocles, or Ariſtophanes, or Euripides, and ſometimes Demoſthenes, Tully, Virgil, and Horace. At one o'Clock to our Studies again, at Five we returned Home, to repeat and turn to the Places quoted in our Books till after Six, then we ſupped and read ſomewhat in Greek and Latin*." Such Pains and Time were then beſtowed.

But in our Univerſity ſeveral of the Maſters do not teach above One Hour, and others of them but Two Hours a Day. Do they really expect to convey the Knowledge of any thing ſo haſtily, eſpecially of the dark and intricate Points they uſually teach ; and we cannot but obſerve, that they treat their Students as if they were Men and Children at the ſame time. A noble Lord made a Donation of the College

F   Garden

---

* Rollin's Belles Lettres, Vol I. Chap. ii. Art. i.

Garden to the Masters and to the Students
to walk in for their Health and Recreation.
The Students, even those who entered to the
lower Classes, it is pretended, were then Men,
and had Difcretion not to deftroy the Beauty
or Policy of the Garden. They are now very
young when they enter to thefe Claffes, and
the Mafters have deprived all the Students
of the Liberty of ftepping into the Garden,
which by the Donation they had and ftill have
a legal Title to. In another refpect they treat
the very youngeft of their Scholars as if they
were full-grown Men; they teach them an Hour
or two, and then fend them adrift; and they
are fo thoughtlefs, are fo little looked after, and
have fo much Time to play, that the Leffon
fo haftily read over to them is neglected and
immediately forgot. In the cafe of the Garden,
it argues the Superiority of the Mafters to treat
their Scholars as mere Children; in the matter
of Teaching, it contributes to their Eafe to treat
them as if they were Men.

The teaching for fo few Hours in Colleges
has a very fatal Effect upon Children: by getting
fo much Diverfion, they contract fettled Habits
of Inattention, and their Minds are fo diffipated
that it is oftentimes found impoffible to fix them;
by which means many have been ruined, and
could never afterwards, by all the Arts and
Intreaties of their Parents, be brought to apply
themfelves in earneft to any Bufinefs whatfoever.

Common

Common Senfe would dictate, that the two lower Claffes at leaft, ought to be treated as Children are in other Schools; they ought to be kept as it were under the Rod, and obliged to apply to their Bufinefs for four or five Hours a Day: and fo many Hours of Attendance at the feweft, fhall, it is propofed, be given by every Teacher in the defigned Academy.

4. Our Teachers fhall ftudy the Genius, and learn the Views of each particular Scholar, and direct them to a proper Courfe of Reading when they are at Home. We fuffered fo much ourfelves, through want of fuch Direction, that we will be at the utmoft Pains that our Children may not fuffer as we have done. The Teachers will put thofe Books into their Hands which are moft accommodated to their Genius, and relative to the Bufinefs they are defigned for. They will converfe often and familiarly with them, and twice every Week will, in an eafy Manner, enquire into the Progrefs they have made, and caufe them to make Obfervations themfelves upon what they have been reading. Poffeffed of fuch Accomplifhments as we have mentioned, they will be in no dread of being puzzled by the Queftions that may be put to them by fprightly Lads of Fourteen or Fifteen, nor under any Neceffity of concealing their Ignorance by an affected Gravity, and entrenching themfelves behind a Form.

F 2   5. To

5. To confuse or distract the Minds of the Youth by different Studies at the same Time, will be avoided with the most scrupulous Care. All possible Art will be used to make what is the immediate and principal Study of the Scholars amusing and delightful to them: The other things, that are allowed them by way of Diversion, will always have some Relation to the one thing, which is at that particular time the chief Object of their Pursuit.

These are certainly great and visible Advantages, which Scholars at the Academy will enjoy above those who attend the University.— The Things to be taught are plain and important.—The best qualified Men will teach them.—The Hours of Attendance will be more than double those that are given at the University.—The Teachers will converse familiarly with the Scholars, and direct them to a proper Course of Reading,—Confusion of Studies will be cautiously avoided, and all will be done in a clear and expressive *English* Stile.

They propose at *Perth*, no doubt for very good Reasons in their Situation, to have a Teacher of the superior Classics. We confess we do not see the Propriety or Necessity of such a Teacher in the Academy here. We think it ought to be an *English* Academy, and that the chief Design of it should be to train up young People for Business. Indeed many of our Citizens have found that their Children had less Latin when they left the Humanity-Class than when

when they entered to it ; and every Body is convinced that in the Two Years fpent at Greek and Latin in the Univerfity, a very poor Proficiency is made in comparifon of what might well be expected. But the great Evil would be beft remedied by Childrens ftaying a Year or even two Years longer at the Grammar-School ; in which Two Years they would certainly acquire more Skill in the learned Languages than they could poffibly do in Six or Seven at the Univerfity : And if the Rector can difcharge his prefent Office, and alfo teach a fuperior Clafs, we are informed he is very well qualified to do it. But if it is neceffary there be another to teach the higher Claffics along with him, a very particular Search fhould be made to find a proper Perfon ; he muft be a Man of Tafte and Imagination : it is not difficult to find one who can drudge and labour, and by the help of Grammars and Dictionaries can hammer out the Conftruction, and heavily tell his Scholars the Meaning of an Author ; thefe are Commodities not rare to be found, but fuch a one is far from anfwering to the Idea we have of a Teacher of the fuperior Claffics : He fhould be a Man of Senfe and Genius, of Spirit and Vivacity, who feels the Author's Senfe, who imagines himfelf in the Place of the Poet, and is warm with his Fire ; who difcerns, who fees and feels the Beauty of the Hiftorian's Defcription. In fhort, one who feels the very Sentiments of the Hiftorian or Poet, and transfufes them into the Minds and

Hearts

Hearts of his Pupils. We would have him at
the fame time to have Difcretion enough to pafs
over feveral Parts of Ovid, Horace, and Catullus,
which were they taught in a fpirited Manner
might be dangerous to young People. A dull
phlegmatic Teacher may feem to have fome
Advantage in this Refpect : He can read over
the whole of Horace, and not mifs a Line from
Beginning to End, without a Smile ; He can
explain and comment upon the moft licentious
Paffage without feeling himfelf, and without
exciting in his Scholars any diforderly Emotion ;
but then he feels as little and makes as little
Impreffion with refpect to any the moft beautiful
Picture or ftriking Defcription : In reading
the Paffages of a Tragedy or Epic Poem,
which fhake the human Frame and fill the
throbbing Breaft with the alternate Emotions
of Admiration, Terror, Pity, and Diftrefs, his
Heart is quite unmoved, infenfible, and callous.
Such a one can never teach to Advantage, nor excite Admiration of antient Learning in the Minds
of Youth : They weary, and think it is doing
Penance to hear him.

A Teacher of Spirit and Tafte fires his
Pupils with the Love of claffical Learning :
And though it is digreffing a little from our
principal Point, we cannot but take notice,
that fuch a Teacher would be of unfpeakable
Advantage to thofe in higher Life than we are.
If Gentlemens Sons made a competent Progrefs
in claffical Learning, and were befides inftructed

4   in

in the feveral things propofed to be taught at
the Academy, we aver they would have a far
more compleat and genteel School Education,
than has ever been publicly given in this
Country.

And fuch a Teacher of Greek and Latin
fhould be carefully fought for, on account of
thofe Students who are defigned for any of the
learned Profeffions, and efpecially of thofe who
are to be Clergymen : For as Education is fo
tedious, and is become fo expenfive, we think
that Divines may and ought to be trained up in
this Method. When they are well founded in
the Languages, they may by proper Direction
be taught as much Knowledge, and to exprefs
themfelves with as much Propriety, Precifion,
and Force, as Divines ordinarily attain, in one
third part of the Time which they would be
obliged to attend a Divinity-College : And if
they were found to be as knowing as College-
Students, we do not fee but Prefbyteries might
get over any Difficulty in Licenfing them ;
provided always their Morals be good and their
Principles orthodox. For which purpofe we
would have the Gentleman who has the Direction
of their Studies found above all Sufpicion, even
tho he fhould not be fo deep in Learning as we
could wifh.

For it would feem that in Divinity it is the
Genius or the Application of the Student, and
not the Ability of the Profeffor, that produces
the Effect. We have heard fome of our Divi-
nity-

279

nity-Profeffors much run down, and others as much applauded; but we could never fee this Difference by the Effects of their Teaching, or that thofe, who ftudied under the weak Profeffor, were a whit inferior to thofe who were the Scholars of the able one : Nor indeed do we difcern that thefe Preachers appear worfe in the Pulpit or in Company, who were never at a Divinity-College at all, feveral of whom we know and efteem.

In Things that relate to Divinity, the learned Profeffors feem to think in this manner : For three or four times, they have chofen Hebrew Profeffors, who, except the Letters, were faid to know no more of the Language ; and Church-Hiftory, though they have a Profeffor of it, has not been taught for many Years paft : It is fuppofed that one may teach Hebrew, without knowing it; and that Divines may know Church-Hiftory, without being taught it : Juft as the little or great Ability of the Divinity-Profeffor makes no Alteration upon the Scholar.

But if it is fo with refpect to Divinity and what relates to it, the Cafe is quite different with refpect to a Profeffor of Mathematics : Whether he has or has not the Art of Teaching, is manifeftly known by the great or fmall Proficiency which his Scholars make. It is impoffible that thofe who ftudy at one Univerfity fhould be generally good Mathematicians, and that thofe who ftudy at another fhould generally know nothing of the Matter, if the Profeffors

wer

were equally fkilful and diligent in teaching. The Gentleman who has long taught in, this Univerfity has unqueftionably great Ability ; but whether he has run over the Propofitions in too great a Hurry, or has employed too few Hours in teaching, it is a well-known Fact, which we are forry to mention, that he has had little Succefs in teaching : There are extremely few who have been made Mathematicians by him. We mention this becaufe if the two Mafters, under whofe Direction the Academy is propofed to be, fhall be thought to have too much to do, there may be, without any additional Expence, a Teacher of Mathematics alone. If he has only the Countenance of the Magiftrates, fuch Numbers will attend him, that he will not need a Halfpenny of Salary : And if he has the Art of Teaching (which he muft have, otherwife it were better not to have him) we may reafonably expect in a very few Years to furnifh out a Choice of able Mathematicians to the Univerfity, and fave them the Trouble of going to a great Diftance in queft of one.

The Plan, as we have fpoke of it, extends to fewer Parts of Literature than that of *Perth* ; yet we perfuade ourfelves every one muft be convinced of the Advantage and Neceffity of it ; and, if poffible, we wifh to fee it eftablifhed, or at leaft begun this very Seafon.

Many Branches of Manufactures have been introduced, and many have been pufhed as far by the Inhabitants of this City as has been done

G   by

by any in the Kingdom ; and if we fhould make
no Provifion for the Inftruction of our Youth,
when fuch Provifion is fo neceffary, we fhould
but too juftly deferve Reproach.

But from the Opulence of this City, we
cannot but indulge the Hope, that the Academy
here will be more extenfive than that which
has been agreed upon by the People of *Perth*.
We wifh the *French* Language was taught more
perfectly than has yet been done here : It has
become almoft an univerfal Language, and the
Knowledge of it is particularly ufeful to trading
People ; and efpecially, we wifh that there were
an *Englifh* Belles Lettres Education. Except to
Gentlemen, and to thofe in the learned Profeffions, the learned Languages are not neceffary.
A Man may make himfelf Mafter of an im-
menfe Variety of Knowledge without any other
Language but *Englifh* : And of how great Importance would it be, if young People were
made acquainted with the Beauties of the *Englifh*
Poets, and moft elegant Profe Writers, and
were taught fomething of Compofition in their
own Language. To know their own Language
well is of more Importance to them than even the
moft full and accurate Knowledge of Greek and
Latin : While they applied to the Study of it,
they would be taught not Words but Things,
not Stile only but to fee and feel the moft noble
Sentiments, and to exprefs themfelves with Elegance and Force.

It

It is really aftonifhing, that the Study of the national Language has been fo much neglected, and that a Courfe of Education, proper for Men of Bufinefs, entirely in *Englifh*, has never been fet on-foot : If we were not accuftomed to fee the Thing every Day practifed, it would appear abfurd to the laft Degree, that Children, who are to be put to Bufinefs as foon as their Age permits, fhould fpend Five or Six Years in learn-ing dead Languages ; Languages which it is forefeen they will immediately forget when they go from School ; and which, though they could be remembered, can never be of any ufe to them. If that Time were employed in conveying Ideas into their Minds, as they are capable to receive them, and in teaching them the *Englifh* Lan-guage, they would have more Knowledge, and they would acquire a great Facility of writing and fpeaking what they know. If they were firft taught to pronounce juftly, and were then fet to compofe little Things, and to imitate the Stile of Mr. Addifon, Dr. Swift, and fome others, the Letters of Men of Bufinefs would appear to much more Advantage than fome of them do at prefent. There would not be fo frequent Complaints that People do not write to their Friends at a Diftance : The real Caufe of which oftentimes is, that they have neither a competent Stock of Ideas, nor a fufficient Com-mand of Language. To write a Letter of News, of Friendfhip, of Thanks, or Congratulation, is above their Capacity, or is at beft a tedious

G 2   and

and difficult Task. If Children were properly instructed in their Mother-Tongue, they would not when they became Men faulter and hesitate in Speech, but would express their Meaning with Ease and Beauty.

The Taste which has been raised at *Edinburgh* by Mr. Sheridan should excite our Emulation. The Parts of Science we have mentioned before are absolutely necessary; this last is also highly useful and highly ornamental.

The Plan, Sir, which we have laid before you, is neither chimerical nor difficult to be executed; it is easy, advantageous, necessary, and not expensive; and we cannot suffer ourselves to fear but that our City will immediately agree to it, or to something like it: For our own part, we have merely studied the Honour and Advantage of our Fellow-Citizens. We desire no Commendation for having mentioned to several of them the great Advantages of such an Academy. If we are in the right, you will be able to judge by this Letter, which you are at Liberty to use as you please. There are, no doubt, others of our Citizens, who are both able to form a Plan that is more compleat, and also to forward the Execution of it: Let them have the whole Praise, but let the thing be done, and done as soon as possible.

And we think ourselves sure that it will be done, when we consider the Merit and Vigilance of the honourable Gentlemen, who are our present Magistrates. One of them is illustrious

in

in his own City, is well known at a great Diftance, and has been long refpected by thofe in the highieft Rank ; he had a College-Education, but foon faw the Impropriety and Defectivenefs of it ; and, by a Strength of Judgment, a Depth of Penetration, and Retentivenefs of Memory peculiar to himfelf, he attained a Knowledge of the Laws and Conftitution of his Country, which is feldom to be found in profeffed Lawyers. He has acquired fuch Variety of Knowledge, Moral, Hiftorical, Political and Commercial, and is fo diftinct and accurate upon every Point, that few Burgeffes or others in the Ifland can pretend to excel him. What is propofed to be taught at the Academy, is but the Rudiments of a few of thefe Parts, in each of which he is a Mafter.

We have another Gentleman in public Office, who is alfo juftly looked upon as a very extraordinary and happy Genius. His Skill in Commerce is extenfive ; his Invention of new Branches of Manufacture, fertile ; his Activity to promote them unwearied ; his Generofity and public Spirit are difcerned and honoured by feveral of the Nobility, and by many of the Gentry and Men of Tafte, who court his Company : He is poffeffed of fuch Accomplifhments in Science and Tafte, which by a quick Difcernment he faw the Value of, and acquired ; that did he not by a fingular Greatnefs of Mind acknowledge the Difadvantages of his Education, hardly any body that converfes with him would fufpect but that he had been converfant in literary Contemplations from his earlieft Youth.　　We

We have, befides, many Citizens, whofe Knowledge is extenfive, and whofe Elegance of Tafte is undifputed. The Magiftrates and they will heartily concur to promote fo ufeful a Defign. They will be convinced, that among a numerous Youth there are comparatively fpeaking but few, who in Science and Tafte can hope to fucceed as they have happily done, unlefs an early and proper Method be taken to facilitate the Acquifition of Knowledge, and to teach them the Elements of thefe Parts which are of univerfal Ufe.

For that Reafon fuch an Academy as we have given a Sketch of is fo ufeful and neceffary, that there ought to be one of them in every populous City within *Great Britain* : and certainly People will fome time or other open their Eyes, and not fuffer themfelves to be deluded by mere Sounds, nor imagine that, becaufe a Thing is called an Univerfity or Seat of Learning, that therefore it will convey every fort of ufeful Knowledge ; when they fee, or may fee fo plainly, that the Knowledge taught is unfuitable to fuch People as we are ; and, were it fuitable, no fuitable Time and Pains are employed to teach it.

And we fay one thing further, in behalf of our City, which to you may appear incredible ; and yet nothing is more true. It is the Nearnefs of the Univerfity to us, that is the Caufe of our little Knowledge, and that an Academy like that now projected did not long ago take place. We expected from time to time that the Profeffors would

would turn from intricate and ufelefs, to ufeful and plain Parts of Science, and teach them with Care and Diligence. Had it not been for this vain Imagination, we are verily perfuaded *Glaf-gow* would have fet an Example to *Perth*, in-ftead of *Perth*'s having fet one to *Glafgow*.

We have at prefent the beft Hopes, and ima-gine that we are within reach of having the Re-proach of our Want of Tafte, and that we are carelefs about the Education of our Children, en-tirely wiped away. We think ourfelves as fure as we can be of any thing that is future, that, if this Propofal is properly executed, within eight or ten Years every Stranger and every difcerning Perfon will obferve a fenfible and general Im-provement in Tafte and Knowledge among the Inhabitants of this City ; and that from thence-forth there will not be the leaft Ground for any fuch Surprife as you expreffed.

But if, after all, nothing is done, we fhall fuf-fer you and every one to rally our Citizens as you pleafe ; and as your Raillery, tho' poignant, is genteel, fo far from avoiding your Company, we will court it ; and judging ourfelves uncon-cerned, we will with Patience, perhaps with Plea-fure, hear your Burlefque without opening our Mouths.

Indeed if our City fhall relapfe into a Lethar-gy, as before ; if there be not Senfe enough to fee the Utility, or if there be not Authority, or Spi-rit, or Numbers enough to forward the Execu-tion of a Project fo neceffary and eafy, we muft

4   acknow-

acknowledge that, notwithstanding all our Partiality to ourselves and our Citizens, we should not know what to say further in our Defence. We should, we fear, be forced to confess that we betrayed some Symptoms of that Dulness, and that Carelessness about our Children, for which we have been so often blamed; or that we mistook our Childrens Interest, and esteemed a small Saving of Money to be of more Importance to them, than the ample Fortunes they might be fitted to acquire, and all the great and shining Improvements in Taste and Science, which by a proper Course of School-Education they might easily make.

But if unhappily our City shall not be rouzed to Action by the Example of *Perth*, if our principal People, being too busy and careful about other Things, shall neglect or postpone a Thing so needful, we make not the least doubt, but that other populous Towns in the Kingdom, where such an Academy may be as necessary as it is here, will act a more generous and spirited Part, and will wisely sacrifice a small Expence to form the Minds of their Children, to accomplish them for Business, and to make a Gentleman-like Figure in Conversation.

Mean time useful Arts and valuable Knowledge will flourish at *Perth*. In a Commercial Sense at least, *Perth* will be the modern *Athens* of this Country: Numbers of young Men properly educated there, will spring abroad and make a Figure in the several Trading Towns of the

the Nation, and particularly in this great City. Strangers will, by the Superiority of their Parts, acquire great Fortunes ; they will lead and conduct the Affairs of this City, and be refpected by the Nobility and Gentry, while our Sons, free-born Citizens, through want of Education, will be humble and tame under the Sway of greater Merit, and make no becoming Figure.

Thefe are Events eafily forefeen. The Example of *Perth* is not that which fhould chiefly influence us ; it is the Neceffity, the vifible Neceffity of the Education propofed. Let the *Perth* Scheme be ill contrived, let it be worfe executed ; fuppofe there be fome who, from fordid Love of Lucre, are fquinting at it with an evil Eye, and wifhing to blaft it with their noxious Breath ; fuppofe they and their Emiffaries be ftriving to get hold of this hopeful Infant, to crufh it, or to ftifle it in its Cradle ; nay fuppofe, contrary to all Probability, that its frightened and felf-interefted Enemies fhould be able with their poifoned Arrows to reach its Vitals, and to lay its Head in the Duft ; it is certainly poffible to contrive the Plan of a manly and genteel Education for Men of Bufinefs, and to fecure the Execution of it, in this Place. There are here a great Number, who have been long and deeply practifed in Commerce, who have great natural and acquired Abilities, and are poffeffed of thofe Attainments which are ufeful, and which are ornamental. Thefe Gentlemen

H   are

are well qualified to direct the Education of young People who are defigned for bufy and active Life. And we muft agree, that till this be done, our City will not make that Figure in *Great-Britain* which it is capable of making, nor appear with a Luftre in proportion to its Trade, its Wealth, and its Greatnefs.

On the difagreeable Suppofition that no Academy is fet on foot here, and to prevent, were it in their Power, the difagreeable and well-forefeen Effects of that Neglect, there are not wanting a Number of judicious Citizens who feem determined to fend their Sons to be educated at *Perth*, if they fhall be informed that the Plan agreed upon there is but as well executed as it is contrived. We hope and affure ourfelves that they will not be under the Neceffity of fending them out of our own City for that Purpofe. At any rate, you know our Mind by this Letter. We hope to be exempted from your Satire; or, if you fometimes play it off in our Company, we will confider it as not intended perfonally againft ourfelves; unwilling however, to join you in it, even tho' we fee it juft, we will beg leave to be filent.

You fee, Sir, that we pay all poffible Deference to the Univerfity. It has been long, and continues to be a loud Complaint in feveral Kingdoms of *Europe*, that the Science retailed at Univerfities is unprofitable and dangerous. Wife Men have judged, that if fuch Science has taken

4   any

any hold of young People, the wifeft Thing
they can do is to unlearn and forget it as foon
as poffible *. Perfonages of the higheft Rank
and Merit have feen Caufe to be thankful or well
fatisfied, either that they never were at an Univerfity, or that by fome favourable Accidents
they were foon removed from it †. And we
know fenfible Men among ourfelves, who judge,
that it would be much better for the Intereft of
Learning, that every Part of Science were left
to be taught by private Academies and private
Teachers; that there ought to be a total Sub-
verfion of the Univerfities of this Nation;
and that the Price of the Buildings, together with
the Revenues and Salaries, ought to be applied
to augment the Livings of the Clergy, or to pay
the National Debt. On the other hand, we
think, they fhould rather be allowed to continue
as they are. They are Monuments of Antiquity. We confider what Good they may have
done of old, when the Courfe taught by them
was fuitable to thofe remote Times. There are
valuable public Libraries in them, which it were
pity not to take care of. Our City may have
Influence to procure Places in them for the fu-
perannuated Teachers of the Academy, who, by
their affiduous and ufeful Labour will highly

H 2   merit

* Molefworth's Preface to Account of Denmark Shaftef-
bury's Characteriftics, Sully's Memoirs, Difcours fur l'Efprit.

† Henry IVth of France. See Sully's Mem. Du Maurier,
&c.

merit fuch Salaries, and fuch Eafe, in their old
Age. They are ufeful in fome Refpects, and
they may change their way of Teachmg, and become fo in more. We find our Hearts warm
towards our own Univerfity, and towards the
Mafters that taught us ; with all their Defects
we loved them, and we reverence their Memory.
We remember, with a Mixture of Regret and
Pleafure, the idle and happy Days we fpent about
the College; how we went fauntering up and down
at our Eafe, with our Gowns, the Badges of
Scholars, about us; tho' it appears to you, and
if we would, we cannot get it denied, that we
received but a poor Pittance of Inftruction.

We wifh the College to fubfift and thrive;
efto perpetua. The Crown or the Faculty may
now and then pitch upon an able Teacher
educated at our Academy, or elfewhere, whom
we would wifh our Pofterity might have the
Opportunity of being inftructed by, juft as we
at prefent have the Opportunity of the Ethic
Clafs, to which many of our Citizens will fend
their Sons, after their Courfe in our own Academy is finifhed. When they have firft learned
ufeful and neceffary Things, thofe of them who
are in eafy Circumftances, and have Genius, will
be entertained with the ingenious and amufing
Theory of fo eminent a Mafter.

If there is any Expreffion in this Letter which
may feem to convey a too diminutive Idea of U-
niverfities, we beg you will look upon it as a Pufh
made

made in neceſſary Self-defence, and aſcribe it to our Eagerneſs to ſcreen ourſelves and our Fellow-Citizens from the Point of your Raillery, and that of others, which has been often and keenly levelled againſt us. With great Reſpect we are,

S I R,

Glaſgow, Oct.
 1761.

Your moſt humble Servants.

F I N I S.

CHAPTER 8

GLASGOW SCHOOLMASTER WILLIAM GORDON

The next essay was published by William Gordon (1763, title), "of the
ACADEMY, GLASGOW," just a year after his fellow townsman William Thom had
presented his case for an alternative to university education. There is no
indication, however, that the learned private teacher of commercial subjects, whose work was of a kind generally respected by the clergyman,
intended to be responding to the earlier polemics.

Glasgow had for some time been a center of business instruction. In
1695 the Town Council had appointed an instructor of navigation, bookkeeping,
arithmetic, and writing. A half century later a teacher formerly of London
had taught reading, writing, arithmetic, and merchants' accounts at his
home, boarding some of the pupils (Murray 1930, 32).

A particularly outstanding commercial teacher was James Scruton, a London "writing master and accountant" who was invited to Glasgow in 1749 by
the '"Provost [mayor] and other gentlemen"', to teach writing, arithmetic,
and accounts (Murray 1930, 32; and Random House dictionary 1966, s.v.
"provost," def. 5). Scruton taught in the city during at least the next
thirty years, much of that time in partnership with the author of the essay
that follows, and after a lapse due to illness set up a business, mathematical, and naval school at his home in 1783 (Murray 1930, 33-36).

William Gordon is said to have been the son of Cosmo, Duke of Gordon,
by a French lady whose marriage to him was not recognized in Britain (Murray

1930, 34), a reputed lineage that is mentioned again below. By 1763, at the
latest, Gordon and James Scruton were conducting a mercantile academy in
Glasgow. They were soon joined by Alexander Jack, a writing master also
interested in bookkeeping, and Robert Dobson, previously an independent
teacher of that subject. Jack withdrew from the partnership when Dobson
died in 1771, but Gordon and Scruton continued their school at least through
'78. William Gordon later headed his own schools in Glasgow and Edinburgh,
where he died in 1793 (Murray 1930, 35-37, 36n).

   The essay reprinted below opens The universal accountant and complete
merchant, appearing in its first edition in 1763 (volume 1) and '65 (2).
In his first volume, Gordon (1763, [vii-x]) devoted some four hundred pages
to basic arithmetic and algebra, and major applications to merchant trade
(particularly currency exchange), banking, insurance, shopkeeping, and the
customhouse. The recently reprinted ([Brief 1986], 12) second volume,
credited by Yamey (1963, 172) with clear and methodical presentation, is a
still longer text on "merchantile accountantship," extending coverage to
bills of exchange and promissory notes (Pryce-Jones and Parker 1976, 10,
no. 31). A 1797 book on commercial arithmetic by American writer Chauncey
Lee included a bookkeeping chapter based on Gordon's system (Pryce-Jones and
Parker 1976, 11, no. 31; and Sheldahl 1985, 23, 34, note 88).

   In 1766 the Scots schoolmaster published The general counting-house and
man of business, a text that was "[a]lmost identical" with the second volume
of The universal accountant (Pryce-Jones and Parker 1976, 11, no. 33). Five
years later he collaborated with partner Dobson on an "admirable" new arithmetic text, bringing out a revised edition in 1775 (Pryce-Jones and Parker
1976, 13, no. 36).

William Gordon was not merely a commercial schoolmaster and author. He was proficient enough in Latin to publish in 1761 a revision of a recognized translation of Livy's history of Rome, adding historical and geographical notes; and to produce twenty-two years later a new translation of the first part of that work. Gordon advertised in 1783 that '"With such of his Boarders as have had a Grammar School education, he reads some of the best Roman authors an hour every day"', and published another translation seven years later (Murray 1930, 37, 37n, quoted). He had indeed in his educational essay (Gordon 1763, 5) advised aspiring merchants to study both Latin and Greek, as a vital base for proper written and spoken expression in English, whereas clergyman Thom (1762a, 39) had found those languages important only for "the learned professions," particularly his own.

As further evidence of his scholarship, William Gordon was engaged in 1773 to edit a new edition of a ten-volume history of Scotland published a few years earlier by British historian William Guthrie (D.n.b. 1917, s.v. "Guthrie, William (1708-1770)"; and Murray 1930, 37n). He abandoned the project early on, however, having apparently failed in an effort to secure better terms for revising the "painstaking and vigorous, but inaccurate" history (D.n.b. 1917, s.v. "Guthrie, William (1708-1770)," quoted; and Murray 1930, 37n-38n).

Finally, a prior teaching partnership by one of his associates of 1765-71 combines with Gordon's reputed noble paternal parentage to invite conjecture, however idle, of possible linkages among three schoolmasters featured in this volume. Bookkeeping teacher James Stirling, A.M., was evidently a partner of Alexander Jack's, in Glasgow, in 1763. Due to the advanced degree reference, it seems somewhat more likely that he was a 1721 University of Glasgow graduate who had worked briefly for the town than the distinguished mathematician who had taught at Thomas Watts's academy in London decades earlier (Murray 1930, 38, 38n). The mathematician, 1692-1770, had studied at both Glasgow and Oxford, but been expelled from the English university in 1715 for identification with the ill-fated Jacobite rebellion (Langford 1983, 362) of that year in favor of a second Stuart restoration. Still, it is known that he had returned to Scotland, permanently, in 1735 to become a very successful mining executive, and had later conducted a surveying project that helped form a base for eventual commercial ascendancy by Glasgow (D.n.b. 1917, s.v. "Stirling, James").

Lending some credence to the statement that William Gordon's father was Cosmo, Duke of Gordon,[1] is the dedication of his 1766 accounting text to Alexander, the contemporary duke (Murray 1930, 34n). As noted in chapter 6, Malachy Postlethwayt had in 1751 (ad opposite title, emphasis in original) advertised his short-lived school in association with a classical academy conducted by the "Chaplain to his Grace the Duke of Gordon." The chaplain was the Rev. John Stirling, D.D., "Vicar of Great Gaddesden in Hertfordshire." James Stirling the mathematician had no sons (D.n.b. 1917, s.v. "Stirling, James"), but may of course have been otherwise related to the cleric.

Two of the three Latin passages in Gordon's essay, counting the title page of the source text, are translated in appendix 3. Since it appears also in one of the selections drawn from Postlethwayt's Dictionary, the other one is rendered in appendix 2.

---

[1] It seems interesting, regarding this reference, that volume 2 of the Bibliography of bookkeeping issued in 1937 by the Institute of Chartered Accountants in England and Wales was compiled by one "Cosmo Gordon" (Thomson 1963, 202).

THE

UNIVERSAL ACCOUNTANT

AND

COMPLETE MERCHANT.

IN TWO VOLUMES.

By WILLIAM GORDON,

of the ACADEMY, GLASGOW.

VOLUME I.

Quid munus reipublicæ majus meliusve afferre poſſumus, quam
ſi juventutem bene erudiamus?   CICERO.

EDINBURGH:

Printed for the AUTHOR, and A. DONALDSON.

Sold by the ſaid A. DONALDSON at his ſhops in
EDINBURGH, and the Strand, LONDON.

MDCCLXIII.

E S S A Y

O N

The EDUCATION of a YOUNG GENTLE-MAN intended for the COUNTING-HOUSE.

IT is a truth, which the ingenious writers of all ages have acknowledged, and conftant experience has confirmed, that commerce contributes to the profperity of ftates, communities, and individuals, in proportion to the wifdom of the laws and regula-tions upon which it is eftablifhed, the privileges by which it is encouraged, and the judgment and ad-drefs wherewith it is conducted. Wife inftitutions, and well-concerted encouragements for promoting the intereft of trade, are the happy effects of good go-vernment; and fuch is the peculiar importance of an extenfive and well-regulated commerce to thefe king-doms, that it is hoped it will ever be the object of our public care. But the beft regulations and the greateft privileges will fignify little, unlefs they be rendered practical, operative, and ufeful, by the fkill and addrefs of the judicious and induftrious merchant. It is he who employs the poor, rewards the inge-nious, encourages the induftrious, interchanges the produce and manufactures of one country for thofe of another; binds, and links together in one chain of intereft, the univerfality of the human fpecies, and thus becomes a blefling to mankind, a credit to his country, a fource of affluence to all around him, his family, and himfelf. What extent of knowledge, what abilities muft it require, to fit a man for fo

Vol. I.   A   great

great and valuable purpofes? And yet it is certain, that there is not another clafs of men, in the Britifh community, who labour under greater difadvantages, in point of education, than that of the commercial profeffion.

A few years are fpent at the grammar-fchool, and perhaps a few more at the univerfity; but fo little time is allotted for the grammar-fchool ftudies, that few, very few can carry from thence the knowledge or the judgment prerequifite to univerfity-ftudies; by which means a number of years is fpent, and a confiderable expenfe laid out, to very little purpofe. Add to this, the low opinion that is generally entertained of the ufe of thofe ftudies among men of bufinefs; which, when it happens to be difcovered by their children, deftroys that emulation and ambition to excel, that ought to fupport them in the elements of learning; and, in fine, induces them to confider the whole as a formal drudgery impofed on them by cuftom, which continues only for four years.

At a certain age, not after certain acquifitions, a teacher of figures and accounts is applied to; and, in this cafe, the cheapeft market is often reckoned the beft. When the round of this teacher's form is once finifh-ed, the ftudent is then turned over to the counting-houfe; where, if he is found qualified for nothing higher, which is too often the cafe, he will be employed, during the time of his apprenticefhip, in copying letters, going meffages, and waiting on the poft-office.

The bufinefs of the counting-houfe is of fuch importance, and every moment fo precious to the mafter, that had he talents for communicating, he hath no time for attending to the inftruction of an apprentice;

prentice; who, on the other hand, hath been so little accuftomed to think, that his improvement by felf-application will be very inconfiderable. Befides, his time of life, and conftant habit of indulgence, render him more fufceptible of pleafurable impreffions, than of improvement in bufinefs; the more efpecially when he was not previoufly prepared to underftand it. Wherefore it is not at all furprifing, if many, who, having no foundation in knowledge to qualify them for the purpofes of the counting-houfe, profit little from the expenfe and the time of an apprenticefhip, and from feeing the moft extenfive bufinefs conducted with all the fkill and addrefs of the moft accomplifhed merchant. The confequence muft, no doubt, be fatal to numbers; and the public intereft, as well as private, muft fuffer greatly by every inftance of this nature. It muft indeed be acknowledged, that there have been, and ftill are gentlemen, who deftitute of all previous mercantile inftruction, without money and without friends, by the uncommon ftrength of natural abilities, fupported only by their own indefatigable induftry and application, and perhaps favoured with an extraordinary feries of fortunate events, have acquired great eftates. But fuch inftances are rare, and rather to be admired than imitated. For we have likewife feen many go through all the forms mentioned above, fet out with large capitals, though perhaps without any other mercantile accomplifhment but an adventurous fpirit, who have fhone in the commercial world, while their capitals lafted, as meteors do in the natural; but, like them, foon deftroyed themfelves, and involved in their ruin all fuch who were unhappy enough to lie within the fphere

A 2   of

of their influence *. Commerce is not a game of chance, but a science; in which he who is moſt ſkilled, bids faireſt for ſucceſs; whereas the man who ſhoots at random, and leaves the direction to fortune, may go miſerably wide of the mark. Parents ought by no means to truſt the future proſpects of their children in the world to a foundation ſo weak or uncertain; and, indeed, it is not reaſonable to expect that the moſt ſubſtantial character in the Britiſh community, can be formed from an education which is common even to the meaneſt citizen.

There never was a time when the neceſſity of a reformation in this particular was greater, or promiſed more ample rewards. —— When Britain, by the force of her arms, hath opened, in all quarters of the world, a paſſage for an unlimited commerce, which the wiſdom of her councils hath eſtabliſhed and ſecured by a glorious peace; — when unanimity formerly unknown, freedom, peace, and proſperity will give new vigour to the polite arts; — when our neighbours, the French, who have long been our rivals in commerce, will ſtrain every nerve to recover by their trade what they have loſt by the war; — when the low intereſt of money, and the extent of our dominions abroad, will induce many people of fortune to ſtrike into trade, by which means the ſtores abroad will be multiplied, and many more hands employed; — it is hoped a few thoughts on the education of a merchant, will neither be unſeaſonable nor unacceptable.

To be able to read the Engliſh language with ſome

---

* Novimus novitios quoſdam, qui cum ſe mercaturæ vix dederunt, in magnis mercimoniis ſe implicantes, rem ſuam male geſſiſſe; et profecto imperitos mercatores, multis captionibus ſuppoſitos, multorumque inſidiis expoſitos, experientia videmus. St. de mercat.

caſe

eafe and accuracy, is certainly prerequifite to every
other ftudy; and it is with pleafure that we fee daily
improvements made in this particular, Men of education have not been afhamed of late to take upon them
the direction of children in reading Englifh, which,
but a few years ago, was committed to people of very little knowledge. This is a reformation, which,
as it was very much wanted, ought to be particularly encouraged and promoted; although at the fame
time the purpofes of it fhould by no means be extended, efpecially by thofe of rank and fortune, beyond its real bounds. It is imagined by fome who
have reaped little benefit from three or four years attendance at a grammar-fchool, that the new method
of teaching Englifh, will anfwer all the purpofes intended by the ftudy of dead languages to a man of
bufinefs. But this opinion is ill founded. The ftudy
of the Englifh language is not yet carried to a proper
extent; and if it was, it would ftill fall fhort of the
purpofes of a liberal education. There is no bufinefs
whatever that requires a greater correfpondence, or a
diction more pointed and concife, than that of the
merchant; and it would require a fingular ftrength of
genius to write even correctly in the Englifh language, unlefs a foundation in the Greek and Latin
languages had been previoufly laid. The arts and
fciences, by thefe means, are laid open to us, the
moft ingenious of all ages become our companions
and acquaintances, whom we may upon all occafions
with freedom confult.

The mind muft be prepared and opened by degrees; and before we know the grammar which refpects the genius of our own language, we muft go
back to the fource for the principles of which it is
                                        compofed.

compofed. The Roman language never arrived at its greateft perfection till it called in the affiftance of the Greek; and ours would have been void of force and harmony without the aid of both. Befides, no period of life is fo apt for proper impreffions, as the years allotted for the grammar-fchool, and no leffons furnifh more excellent examples of correct writing and regular living than what are contained in the claf- fics, if they are properly attended to, and judiciouf- ly improved. It is here, where youth are furnifhed with the firft opportunity of paffing a proper judg- ment on what they read, with regard to language, thoughts, reflections, principles, and facts, without which the knowledge of words would be very in- fignificant. How apt are young people, unlefs the knowledge of true criticifm be properly laid, to admire and imitate the bright more than the folid, the marvellous more than the true, and what is ex- ternal and adventitious more than perfonal merit and good fenfe? And is it not of fome importance, that youth fhould be fet to rights in particulars fo effential? It is here where the tafte for writing and living may be in fome meafure formed, the judgment rectified, the firft principles of honour and equity inftilled, the love of virtue and abhorrence of vice excited in the mind, provided the grammar-fchool ftudies be properly di- rected, and carefully purfued. *Quare ergo liberalibus ftudiis filios erudimus? non quia virtutem dare poffunt, fed quia animum ad accipiendam virtutem præparant. Quemadmodum prima illa, ut antiqui vocabant, litera- tura, per quam pueris elementa traduntur, non docet libe- rales artes, fed mox percipiendis locum parat; fic liberales artes non perducunt animum ad virtutem, fed expediunt.*

The ftudy of rhetoric and compofition ought by no
means

means to be neglected by a young gentleman intended for the counting-room. This will give him an
opportunity of reducing to practice, what formerly
he had been only taught to relish. It will not only
teach, but accustom him to range his thoughts, arguments, and proofs in a proper order, and to clothe
them in that drefs which circumstances render most
natural. By this means he will not only be able to
read the works of the best authors with taste and propriety, but be taught to observe the elegance, just-
nefs, force, and delicacy of the turns and expref-
fions; and still more, the truth and folidity of the
thoughts. Hereby will the connection, difposition,
force, and gradation of the different proofs of a difcourfe be obvious and familiar to him, while at the
fame time he is led by degrees to fpeak and write with
that freedom and elegance, which in any other way
will be found very difficult to attain.

But to fpeak or write well, however necefary it may
be, is not the only object of mercantile inftruction.
It will be of little confequence to have the underftanding improved, if the heart be totally neglected. Man
was made by nature for fociety, but the merchant
both by nature and practice; who, if he is not qualified or not difpofed to act his part well, like a bad
performer in a concert of mufic, will deftroy the harmony, and render the whole difagreeable. Therefore to tune his mind to virtue and morality, to teach
him to blend felf-love with benevolence, to moderate
his pafttons, and to fubject all his actions to the teft of
reafon, he muft have recourfe to philofophy.

The principles of law and government ought likewife to conftitute a part of the mercantile plan of inftruction; by which we are taught to whom obedience

ence is due, for what it is paid, and in what degree it may be juftly required: more particularly in Britain, where we profefs to obey the prince according to the laws; and indeed we ourfelves are fecondary legiflators, fince we give confent, by reprefentatives, to all the laws by which we are bound, and have a right to petition the great council of the nation, when we find they are deliberating upon any act, which we think will be detrimental to the intereft of the community, with refpect to commerce, or any other privilege whatever.

When a young man hath been thus accuftomed to application, reafon, and reflection, when his tafte hath been formed and his judgment confirmed; the ftudy of thofe fciences which more immediately refpect the counting houfe, will become eafy and agreeable: but it is neceffary his teachers fhould keep up the fame fpirit and dignity in their inftructions with which his earlier ftudies were animated, otherwife the defign of the whole may be in danger of being fruftrated.

The firft care of a fcholar who is put under the tuition of a new mafter, is to obferve, to ftudy, and to found him; and it generally holds, that the proficiency of the one, and the authority of the other, are both in proportion to the judgment which the fcholar forms of his mafter's prudence and abilities; for which reafon, parents cannot be too ftrict in their inquiries concerning the temper, qualifications, and character of a mafter before they truft him with fo important a charge, as the happinefs and profperity of their children during the whole courfe of their lives muft depend upon it.

Writing, the elements of arithmetic, and the
French

French language, fhould, I think, be the firft objects
of inftruction, when a young man is fent to an academy, to be prepared for the counting-houfe; and
thefe ought to be taught at particular hours on
the fame day. It is neceffary that a young man commence the ftudy of the French language early, that
he may be able not only to tranflate, but fpeak and
write the language with eafe before he enters the
counting-houfe.

Writing is a prerequifite to every other ftep; and
therefore no time fhould be loft in making him as foon
and as much mafter of the pen as poffible. To teach
arithmetic well, which is another leading ftep, requires
more fkill and knowledge than perhaps is attended to.
It is, of all other fciences, the moft neceffary to the
mercantile profeffion; and it is not a little furprifing
that it fhould by fo many be fo fhamefully neglected.
Before arithmetic is applied to computations in bufinefs, the powers, properties, and relations of numbers fhould be particularly taught and explained. Every rule fhould be demonftrated, exemplified, and illu-
ftrated in an eafy and intelligible manner; and the
examples fo multiplied and diverfified, that the learner may be thoroughly grounded, and have a reafon
always ready for what he doth; all the various com-
pendiums, which ferve to abbreviate operations,
fhould be diftinctly fhown and demonftrated, that facility and difpatch may be equally familiar. When
he hath thus become mafter of the capital rules in
vulgar and decimal arithmetic, involution and evolution, he ought then to be introduced to geometry
and algebra, which of all other ftudies contribute
moft to invigorate the mind, to free it from prejudice, credulity, and fuperftition, and to accuftom it

Vol. I.   B   to

to attention, and to close and demonstrative reasoning.
In the course of these studies, he should be taught a
new demonstration of all his arithmetical rules ; and
the whole theory ought to be reduced to practice, in
the mensuration of surfaces and solids, heights and
distances, and in constructing the instruments he hath
occasion to use. — When practice is thus joined to
demonstration, the study of the sciences becomes easy, entertaining, and instructive : whereas, was a
young man to hear nothing else but demonstration,
he would soon be wearied of that kind of study, and
consider it as very dry and insipid : but when he sees
the use of mathematics, in laying down plans and maps
of countries, selling land by measure, ascertaining
the price of labour, and determining the quantity of
liquors for a regulation of their price and duty, he
must be convinced of their influence, and admire
their excellency.   To complete his mathematical
course, he should be made acquainted with navigation
and geography.   The first, after such a general acquaintance with the mathematics, will require no
great study : but to the last more time and reading
will be absolutely necessary.

   The solution of a few problems on the globe, and
three or four studied harangues, will come far short
of answering the design.   A teacher who considers
the extent of geography necessary to a merchant, must
see that the knowledge of the globes is no more than
the elements of what he should be instructed in.   He
must be made acquainted with the use of maps, the
situation, extent, produce, manufactures, commerce,
ports, politics, and regulations, with respect to trade,
of all the nations in the world, not only by public
lectures, but by private reading and conversation.
                                                      This

This will not be the work of a few days or a month; and thofe who allot no more time for geography, know very little of the fubject. Half an hour every day for fix months together fpent in private inftruction and examination, will perhaps be found little enough for a ftudy fo extenfive and important.

When the foundation is thus properly laid by fuch a mathematical courfe as I have been defcribing, communicated in that demonftrative and practical manner, which will join fcience with judgment, and conviction with experience; the counting houfe muft begin to open, and the *arcana mercatorum* be expofed to view. Arithmetic muft again be refumed, and the former theory reduced to practice, in all the cafes which can occur to the merchant, the banker, the cuftomhoufe, and infurance-office; to which every obfervation ought to be joined, which will ferve to il-luftrate the ufe of the different examples in that particular branch of bufinefs to which they may be appli-cable. A proper courfe of reading at this period, which might be wonderfully improved by the conver-fation of a good mafter, upon the fubjects of infurance, factorage, exchange, and fuch other branches of bu-finefs, will be of fingular ufe, not only to form the mind to bufinefs, but, when he comes to act for himfelf, to prevent many tedious and expenfive pleas, which an ignorance in the practical arts of ne-gotiating them is frequently apt to create.

To this courfe of reading, an epiftolary correfpon-dence among the ftudents themfelves might, with great propriety, be added; as it would give them the practice of folding letters in a quick and dexterous manner, accuftom them to digeft well whatever they read, and improve their diction, under the correction

B 2   of

311

of an accurate mafter, to that clear, pointed, and concife manner of writing which ought peculiarly to diftinguifh a merchant. Fictitious differences among
merchants might likewife be fubmitted to their judgment, fometimes to two in the way of arbitration, and
again to a jury of fifteen; whilft one would affume the
character of the plaintiff, and another that of the de-
fendant, and each give in fuch memorials or repre-
fentations, according to the nature of the facts con-
defcended on, as he thinks moft proper to fupport the
caufe, the patronage of which was affigned him.
Thus will youth be accuftomed to think, write, and
act like men before they come upon the real ftage of
action; and their appearance in real life, will have
nothing of that awkward and ftupid manner which is
generally obferved in young men for fome time after
they enter the counting-houfe.

When a young man hath thus attained to a proper
accuracy and difpatch in figuring, and fome idea of
the different branches of bufinefs with which every kind of computation is connected; it is time
then to introduce the young merchant to book-
keeping, which is the laft, but not the leaft important branch of education previous to the counting-
houfe. It is become a proverb in Holland, that the
man who fails did not underftand accounts. And indeed, however much a merchant, who is concerned
in an extenfive trade, may be employed in matters of
a higher nature, and upon that account be neceffita-
ted to make ufe of the affiftance of others in keeping
his books, he ought certainly to be capable of keeping them himfelf; otherwife he never can be a judge,
whether juftice is done him in that effential particular
or not; neither can he have that idea of his own bufinefs,

finefs, which is indifpenfably neceffary to the profperity of his trade.

This happy method of arranging and adjufting a
merchant's tranfactions, muft, like other fciences, be
communicated in a rational and demonftrative manner, and not mechanically by rules depending on the
memory only. The principles upon which the
fcience is founded, muft likewife be reduced to practice by proper examples in foreign and domeftic
tranfactions; fuch as, buying, felling, importing
and exporting for proper, company, and commiffion
account; drawing on, remitting to; freighting and
hiring out veffels for different parts of the world;
making infurance and underwriting; and the various
other articles that may be fuppofed to diverfify the
bufinefs of the practical counting-houfe. The nature
of all thefe tranfactions, and the manner of negotiating them, ought to be particularly explained as they
occur; the forms of invoices and bills of fales, together with the nature of all intermediate accounts,
which may be made ufe of to anfwer particular purpofes, ought to be laid open; and the forms of all
fuch writs as may be fuppofed to have been connected with the tranfactions in the wafte-book, fhould be
rendered fo familiar, that the young merchant may
be able to make them out at once without the affiftance of copies.

As the following work is intended to be a complete
courfe of mercantile computations and accountantfhip, to fay more on the method of communicating
them would be unneceffary. Only I would beg leave
to hint, that there are many things, the knowledge
of which is better inculcated by public lectures, private reading and converfation, than in the ordinary
method

method of teaching, when, perhaps, there may be two or more claſſes to direct. The national commerce in general; the trade of the place where we live; the laws, cuſtoms, and uſages relative to the buſineſs of a merchant, the penalties to which he is liable, and the privileges to which he is intitled ; the duties, im-poſts, and other charges laid upon the Britiſh pro-duce in other countries, with all the known maxims that relate to the proſperity of trade; will open a wide field for improvement in matters of real uſe to the maſter as well as the ſtudent.

When the education of a young gentleman is thus conducted, from his earlieſt years, in a manner calcu-lated to engage his mind in the love of uſeful know-ledge; to improve his underſtanding; to form his taſte, and ripen his judgment; to fix him in the ha-bit of thinking, ſteadineſs, and attention ; to promote his addreſs and penetration, and raiſe his ambition to excel in his particular province; will not the tranſi-tion to the counting-houſe be extremely eaſy and a-greeable ? His knowledge will be ſo particular, and his morals ſo ſecured, that he will be proof againſt the arts of the deceitful, the ſnares of the diſingenuous, and the temptations of the wicked. He will, in a ſhort time, be ſo expert in every part of the buſineſs of the practical counting-houſe, and be able to form ſuch a judgment of every thing he ſees tranſacted, that when he comes to act for himſelf, every advan-tage in trade will lie open to him; his knowledge, ſkill, and addreſs will carry him through all obſta-cles to his advancement; his talents will ſupply the place of a large capital ; and when the beaten track of buſineſs becomes leſs advantageous, by being in too many hands, he will ſtrike out new paths for himſelf,

314

felf, and thus bring a balance of wealth, not only to himfelf, but to the community with which he is connected, by branches of trade unknown before.

How few are there, even among parents, who perhaps have felt the lofs of a proper education in their own practice, that confider the extent of knowledge requilite to make a young gentleman appear with dignity in the commercial life? and how few are there among thofe who profefs to qualify young gentlemen for the counting-houfe, that have knowledge in any degree proportionable to their credit? The reafon is obvious: In every other article of expenfe, confidered as communities or individuals, we are generally profufe: but in that which relates to education, we are fhamefully narrow. This falfe parfimony, this miftaken frugality, prevents men of genius and education from appearing as teachers, becaufe their talents will turn out to much more account, in almoft any other profeffion whatever; and if circumftances fhould have rendered it neceffary for a man of fome abilities to turn his mind this way, he is obliged to divide his ftudies among fo many different fciences, and his time among fo many different claffes, to fecure to himfelf a bare fubfiftence, that he hath neither the leifure, the means, nor the opportunity of that reading or converfation, which is abfolutely neceffary to his practice, in inftructing youth in the moft difficult and important branch of Britifh literature. And if this is the cafe with the ableft teachers, what can be expected of thofe who became teachers, becaufe they were really qualified for nothing elfe? For the inftruction of youth in every other fcience, we have not only excellent inftitutions, but eminent mafters, whofe abilities are inquired into and appro-

ved

ved of, before they are admitted to the important
truſt : but in this caſe, great pretenſions, which are
generally taken upon the teacher's word, and low
prices for the articles of education in his ſcheme, are
credentials ſufficient to procure him buſineſs, though
neither the teacher nor the ſtudents reap much advantage from it.

The art of managing and forming the mind is perhaps of all others the moſt intricate and extraordinary,
and certainly the moſt important ; which, that it may
be ſufficiently ſtudied, ought to be properly rewarded.
It is no doubt the buſineſs of magiſtrates, to intereſt
themſelves in the education of youth, ſince they are
the nurſery of the ſtate, by whom it is renewed and
perpetuated, and upon whom the national proſperity,
as well as the national exiſtence depends. If part of
the public revenues were employed in erecting academies for training up youth to buſineſs, eſpecially in
trading cities, where every maſter ſhould have a ſala-
ry proportioned to the difficulty of his department ;
if the moſt intelligent merchants were appointed as
ſuperintendants of theſe academies, who would take
care that none ſhould be admitted as ſtudents, whoſe
proficiency in the languages, rhetoric, and philoſophy
was not previouſly inquired into, nor any ſuffered
to proſecute the ſtudies prerequiſite to the counting-houſe, whoſe genius was not in ſome meaſure
turned to act with dignity in the mercantile profeſſion ; if theſe gentlemen would inquire often into the morals and proficiency of the ſtudents, converſe
frequently with the maſters on the ſubject of trade,
and admit the ſtudents according to their ſeniority in
letters to ſuch converſations, and, in ſhort, take every
other method of encouraging both maſters and ſtudents

dents to induſtry and attention, that they might go through the tedious, the difficult taſk with alacrity and ſpirit; if parents, at the ſame time, would ſet that value upon education which they ſometimes do upon trifles, and be but as careful in having the minds of their children adorned with virtue and good ſenſe, as they are in ſetting off every thing which relates to their bodies, we would then ſee a reformation indeed. Was this to be the caſe, our youth would be long acquainted with the arts of gaining before they would learn how to ſpend money, and they would not be grown old in debauchery and riot, before they were initiated into buſineſs. Was this to be the caſe, we would ſoon ſee a ſpirit of induſtry, knowledge, humanity, and good ſenſe diffuſe itſelf among all ranks and denominations, whilſt idleneſs and folly, with all their miſchievous train, would be baniſhed the ſtreets. In one word, our teachers would be men of underſtanding, our young men would be ſenators, and our " merchants would be princes."

CHAPTER 9

THE LITERARY, MATHEMATICAL, AND COMMERCIAL SCHOOL

OF THE BROTHERS CLARKE - MATHEMATICIAN HENRY

AND BAPTIST CLERIC W(ILLIAM) AUGUSTUS

The eighth essay is a 1793 announcement for the "Literary, Mathematical and Commercial School" having recently been opened in Liverpool by brothers H[enry] and the Rev. W[illiam] Augustus Clarke, listed as coauthors ([H. Clarke] 1793, [256]). The use in two places ([258], lines 6, 13) of first-person forms suggests that the pamphlet was principally the work of head-master and career teacher Henry Clarke, author of the book to which it was appended. Further reference to W. A. Clarke, described in a passing notice (Hans 1951, 96) as a "well-known Baptist theologian," is deferred until the concluding paragraphs of this introductory writeup, permitting the use of the surname to that point to refer to his brother.

Henry Clarke was born in Salford, England in 1743, and as a boy attended the town grammar school of neighboring (Random House dictionary 1966, s.v. "Salford") Manchester (D.n.b. 1917, s.v. "Clarke, Henry," name omitted in subsequent references to entry). As related below, he was destined to spend much of his life in or near that industrial area.

A northern and western city located (Columbia encyclopedia 3d, s.v. "Manchester," entry 1) on four rivers, Manchester had been associated since the fourteenth century with woolen and linen production (Webster's geographical dictionary 1977, s.v. "Manchester," def. 11). It had in the 1600s become a "notable urban cent[er]" as a cloth-finishing town (Morrill

319

1984, 293), as a prelude to playing a dominant role in the "early industrial revolution" commencing around 1750 (Langford 1984, 374, [377, quoted, 378]). During the ten years that followed the introduction of steampowered mills in Southampton, on the southern coast, in 1779, the northern city secured lasting preeminence, as it turned out, in the processing of cotton and other textiles. In Manchester in 1789, four years after Cartwright had patented the power loom he had built there and eight years after the city's first cotton mill had opened, steam power was first applied to cotton spinning (Columbia encyclopedia 3d, s.v. "Cartwright, Edmund," "Manchester," entry 1; Gilbert 1968, 75; and Webster's geographical dictionary 1977, s.v. "Manchester," def. 11).

Manchester shared handsomely in the development in the eighteenth century of a remarkable English turnkpike system, as travel time to London by mail coach was reduced two thirds, to some twenty-eight hours (Gilbert 1968, 76; and Langford 1984, [377-79]). Although it was a physically attractive town providing enhanced living conditions, "violent industrial disputes" accompanying an economic slump marred domestic tranquility in the sixties (Langford 1984, [378], 406, quoted) in this city of Jacobite political leanings (and former Puritan stronghold) that was unrepresented in Parliament (Webster's geographical dictionary 1977, s.v. "Manchester," def. 11). Thirty years later Manchester no doubt shared in a prevailing climate of "political unrest and instability" produced by steeply rising prices and relatively stagnant wages (Wilson 1977, 138, quoted, [139]).

The distinguished grammar school attended by Henry Clarke had probably originated in a collegiate church founded in Manchester in 1420. Two early sixteenth-century endowments had yielded a successful free school patterned after St. Paul's, despite the statutory adoption of the Stanbridge Latin

320

grammar briefly (Charlton 1965, 107) a serious rival to the tradition originated there by Colet and Lily (Leach 1915, 296-98). Mathematics including
logarithms and surveying applications had been taught at Manchester since
early Restoration days, and by Clarke's time optical experimentation using
a telescope was a staple part of a rich curriculum. The school enjoyed
remarkably balanced diversity in the social backgrounds of the boys and the
occupations they would later pursue. Although the most frequent career
course was in one branch or another of industry and commerce, Clarke was
only one of a number of notable mathematicians or scientists schooled at
Manchester in the eighteenth century (Hans 1951, 39-41).

Henry Clarke's formal schooling ended when at age thirteen he became
an assistant to a Quaker schoolmaster at an academy in Leeds (D.n.b. 1917).
Six years later he moved to another school in that city, conducted by a
writing master and surveyor and his partner (Hans 1951, 95). Leeds had
been a center of wool manufacturing since the 1300s, and like Manchester
to (Gilbert 1968, 75) the south and west it had thrived as a cloth-finishing
town in the seventeenth century (Guy 1984, 189-90, 293); was located on the
border of major coal fields; and was a beneficiary of major transportation
improvements, roads (Langford 1984, [377]) and canals. By 1801 Manchester
and Leeds were Britain's second and eighth largest cities with respective
populations of 84,000 and 53,000 people, representing a sum total less than
one sixth the size of London (Gilbert 1968, 75-76).

Clarke served only briefly at the second school in Leeds before taking
a European tour on which he visited several mathematicians, among whom
Lorgna of Verona would figure prominently in a key episode of his career.
Returning to Manchester in 1765, he worked briefly (D.n.b. 1917) as a

surveyor before opening a "'Commercial and Mathematical School'" in his native Salford that he would maintain until '88 or beyond (Hans 1951, 95, quoted, 96).

In part a boarding school, the Salford academy emphasized mathematics and its applications in preparing students primarily, for trades and prof-fessions. Besides math, presumably, Clarke lectured on astronomy and other scientific subjects (D.n.b. 1917; and Hans 1951, 95). Concurrently, he taught mathematics at Manchester's grammar school, headed by the usher of his own student days; and from 1772 conducted in his own academy a night school for adults frequented by artisans or "machanics," qualifying as an educational pioneer in that area (Hans 1951, 40, 96, 158, quoted; and Random House dictionary 1966, s.v. "mechanic," synonyms).

For some years Henry Clarke was a frequent contributor to mathematical or scientific periodicals, especially the Lady's Diary, a "real channel [final 's' deleted] of scientific instruction" for a predominantly female readership somewhat resembling a contemporary (Columbia encyclopedia 3d, s.v. "almanac") almanac.[1] The Diary and other popular scientific magazines of the day sponsored contests for the solution of all manner of brainteasing problems and puzzles. Salford pupils were strongly encouraged to compete, and from 1772 to '76 eight of them were contest winners (Hans 1951, 95, 155, quoted, 156-57).

In 1783 Clarke took on the additional role of "Praelector," or lecturer, "in Mathematics and Experimental Philosophy" in a remarkable new program of

---

[1]The editor of the Lady's Diary from 1773 to 1818 was the distinguished mathematician and schoolmaster Charles Hutton, whose career was in many ways similar to Clarke's (D.n.b. 1917, s.v. "Hutton, Charles"; and Hans 1951, 156, 256, s.v. "Hutton, Charles," extensive index entry). A single-entry accounting work by Hutton that was published in the United States in 1788 is reprinted in another Foundations of Accounting volume (Sheldahl 1988), a collection supplying biographical information on writers included.

extension education associated with the Literary and Philosophical Society

of Manchester, founded two years earlier by a Warrington Academy school-

master and an associate. He is said to have served throughout the "bril-

liant" eleven-year history of the "'New College of Arts and Sciences'"

(Hans 1951, 60-61, 96, 159, quoted; and Random House dictionary 1966, s.v.

"prelector"). His move by 1792 (Hans 1951, 96) to Liverpool, thirty miles

west of Manchester (Gilbert 1968, 75; and Webster's geographical dictionary

1977, s.v. "Manchester," def. 11), probably limited his participation in

the final years, however.

In 1788 Henry Clarke unsuccessfully applied for the mastership of the

academy at Stretford (D.n.b. 1917), an industrial community four miles

southwest of Manchester (Webster's geographical dictionary 1977, s.v.

"Stretford"). He may have continued teaching at Salford for as many as four

years beyond that date, but in 1792 opened in Liverpool the "multi-lateral"

academy profiled in the essay that follows (Hans 1951, 96-97, from chapter

on "Multilateral Academies").

A seaport enjoying major contemporary dock improvements (Gilbert 1968,

75), Liverpool was a leading center of eighteenth-century trade with America

in particular, specializing first in grain and slaves and later in cotton

(Harvie 1984, 426; and Langford 1984, [377]). After teaching there for only

a few years, Clarke returned briefly to Manchester before moving in 1799 to

Bristol (D.n.b. 1917; and Hans 1951, 96), though not as president or chief

tutor at the Baptist academy (McLachlan 1931, 96-98). A southwestern river

and (via the Bristol Channel) ocean city that had emerged in the fourteenth

century as England's "second commercial metropolis," Bristol like present-

day holder of that status Liverpool was in the 1700s a major site of dock

developments and port for American trade. The town with which (Morrah 1979,

64) pioneering New World explorers including Columbus himself and, as port of origin, John Cabot had been associated had a population of 68,000 when Clarke was there (Gilbert 1968, 75-76; Griffiths 1984, 216, quoted; Langford 1984, [377]; and Webster's geographical dictionary 1977, s.v. "Bristol," def. 10, "Bristol Channel," "Liverpool," def. 4).

Ineligible as a Dissenter for an English degree, the largely self-taught Henry Clarke received an honorary Doctor of Laws (LL.D.) title from the University of Edinburgh in 1802 (D.n.b. 1917; Hans 1951, 189; and Random House dictionary 1966, s.v. "LL.D."). The same year he was appointed professor of history, geography, and experimental philosophy at the Royal Military College at Great Marlow, located on the Thames thirty miles west of London. The school was moved south of the capital to Sandhurst in 1812, and Clarke retired on a pension five years later. He died at age seventy-five in 1818, survived by a wife and 6 of his 17 children (D.n.b. 1917; and Webster's geographical dictionary 1977, [459], and s.v. "Great Marlow," "Marlow," "Sandhurst").

Clarke's writings reflect at least as much breadth as his teaching fields. He published four mathematics books and, relatedly, a mariners' handbook. Other items included an eight-volume linguistics work; a geography text representing the lone product of a planned series for the military school; three pieces of satire or "burlesque," including "'The School Candidates'," a "prosaic" reaction to the aforementioned 1788 school election at Stretford; a work of criticism relating to the Roman poet Virgil; and a shorthand text (D.n.b. 1917).

The writeup on the Liverpool academy was appended to the first volume of Tabulae linguarum, a work of "antiquated philology" (D.n.b. 1917) that (if completed) supplied tables of declension and conjugation for languages from eight general groups. Forty principal languages were included ([H. Clarke] 1793, title), along with source tongues such as Gothic, Teutonic, and Saxon (volume 2) and, in one case (vol. 3), five "collateral" languages. The first volume reported that numbers 2 and 3 were "ready for the Press" (emphasis deleted) ([H. Clarke] 1793, [254]), but the implication of the D.n.b. entry (1917) that the entire work was published, indeed in the single year 1793, has not been confirmed. The entry does report that Clarke "projected many . . . books" beyond his actual publications.

The honorary degree received from Edinburgh in 1802 may have been particularly satisfying to Henry Clarke in light of a personal and professional snub of nineteen years earlier far more visible than the Stretford turndown. In 1783 this accomplished mathematician, teacher, and scholar was rejected for appointment as a fellow of the Royal Society, based on the opposition of Sir Joseph Banks (D.n.b. 1917), the society's president for forty-two years. Noted botanist Banks had collected many previously unclassified biological specimens while accompanying Captain James Cook around the world, and the plant genus Australian honeysuckle is known as "banksia" in his memory (Columbia encyclopedia 3d, s.v. "Banks, Sir Joseph," "banksia").

A prominent supporter of Clarke's F.R.S. candidacy praised him as an "'inventor'" in mathematics (D.n.b. 1917). Royal Society secretary for many years, Samuel Horsley edited a complete edition of Newton's works and held three bishoprics, but is particularly remembered for a public debate of 1783-90 on basic Christian doctrine with Joseph Priestley, who was about to help establish the Unitarian Society (Columbia encyclopedia 3d, s.v. "Horsley, Samuel"; and D.n.b. 1917, s.v. "Priestley, Joseph," 362-63). Contrary to the implication of the D.n.b. entry (1917) for Henry Clarke, he and

Priestley never resided in Leeds at the same time. Priestley had still

been teaching in Warrington, however, midway between Manchester and Liver-

pool (Webster's geographical dictionary 1977, s.v. "Warrington"), when

Clarke had opened his academy at Salford (D.n.b. 1917, s.v. "Priestley,

Joseph," 359).[2]

Clarke's rebuff by the Royal Society may have been related to a mathe-

matical literature controversy in which he had become embroiled by trans-

lating from the Latin in 1779 a book by the Italian mathematician Lorgna on

"'the Summation of Infinite Converging Series'," adding an appendix of his

own. English mathematician John Landen, a longtime contributor to the

Ladies' Diary who had been elected F.R.S. in 1766, had responded in print

that Lorgna's methods were not original, but had been developed in one form

or another by three other writers. Landen's pamphlet had led to lengthy

printed exchanges with Clarke (1793, [255]) in both 1782 and '83 (D.n.b.

1917, quoted; and Hutton 1815, s.v. "Landen, John").

One author championed by Landen was James Stirling, the Scots mathema-

tician associated with schoolmaster Thomas Watts. One recognized mathemat-

ical series is named for Stirling, as is a formula for approximating the

factorial of a positive integer (Boyer 1968, 465)[3] that until recently was

---

[2] Priestley's yearly salary at Warrington Academy in the 1760s was 100
pounds. He also received free housing, and secured income from boarders.
The Stretford mastership sought in 1788 by Clarke, who may well have then
had a large family at home, paid 60 pounds (D.n.b. 1917, s.v. "Clarke,
Henry," "Priestley, Joseph," 359). It is not stated whether a house was
provided. Given an imminent surge in price levels, 60 pounds circa 1790
would have been no better (Wilson 1977, 138-[39]) than the 20 pounds that a
schoolmaster of 1600 would in that low-paid time have "be[en] lucky to get"
(Charlton 1965, 124, quoted, 125). In Liverpool in the nineties, Clarke
(1793, [256-57]) charged annual tuition of 5 guineas (five times the entry
fee), or 5 1/4 pounds, for an enrollment not to exceed thirty pupils, a
distinct educational bargain compared to the charges assessed in the twenties
by Thomas Watts, as covered in chapter 2.

[3] In its familiar form, $n! \approx \sqrt{2\pi n}(n/e)^n$ (Boyer 1968, 465), where e is the
base for the "natural" logarithmic system (Findeis to Sheldahl 1988). An

326

a familiar textbook citation in algebra and elementary calculus (Findeis to Sheldahl 1988; and Lang 1964, vii, 179). Abraham De Moivre, another authority discussed by John Landen, published both results the same year (1730) as Stirling, then teaching (Hans 1951, 84) at Watts's academy in London, and had shown earlier awareness of the formula (Boyer 1968, 465).

Information is considerably more scarce on W. Augustus Clarke, Henry's brother. Counting both editions of one sermon, an authoritative Baptist bibliography (Starr 1947-76, s.v. "Clarke, William Augustus") attributes to him fourteen published titles. All but one of them, directly and/or via reference to another bibliographical source, are dated from the period 1775-89. The exception, the only publication for which a library source besides the British Library (traditionally, Museum) is cited, is an 1801 hymnal (W. A. Clarke, title):

> Hymns, doctrinal and experimental, for the freeborn citizens of Zion, who know their election of God, and glory in the evangelical truths comprised in the gospel of a finished salvation.

This 196-page book of 261 hymns (words only) by Clarke is found in the Franklin Trask Library (Yount to Sheldahl 1988) at Andover Newton Theological School in Massachusetts. The Baptist cleric had issued earlier hymnals in 1782 and '88 (Starr 1947-76, s.v. "Clarke, William Augustus"), the latter of which had included "spiritual remarks" on each composition for the benefit of "precious souls" in Ireland and America as well as England (W. A. Clarke 1801, xii).

The Rev. W. A. Clarke had evidently by 1801 (x) been preaching "for upwards of forty years." Cited by Hans (1951, 96) as a "theologian," he seems in fact to have honored his Baptist heritage with substantial

---

expanded version likewise identified as "Stirling's formula" is stated as an exact equality (Lang 1964, 179, italicized heading).

skepticism, even scorn, of academic theology (W. A. Clarke 1801, xi, emphasis in original):

> I have not wrote the following composition, in order to accommodate the flying camp of unexperienced professors, who have their lamps of profession without the oil of covenant grace in their souls; none but those whose scent is changed by the grace of God, will relish the things contained therein.

Titles suggest that beyond the hymnals Clarke's published books, sermons, and other writings were mostly inspirational appeals for religious faith that would bring "A bed of sweet flowers . . . [and c]omfort for drooping and dejected souls." A 1781 sermon "on the . . . deliverance of Lord G. Gordon" (Starr 1947-76, s.v. "Clarke, William Augustus") may have related to the duchy of Gordon, cited earlier regarding Malachy Postlethwayt and William Gordon.

In 1801 W. A. Clarke (title, all capitals) was preaching at the "Lazaretto, yet Smyrna Church of God . . ., Bunhill-Row." Bunhill was the London district in which the poet Milton, completely blind, had in his last years dictated some of his greatest work (Morrah 1979, 84-86). The name "Lazaretto," literally signifying a hospital for lepers or persons with similarly "loathsome" diseases (Random House dictionary 1966, s.v. "lazaretto," def. 1), was presumably intended to promise ministry to (W. A. Clarke 1801, xi) "the vileness of our contaminated wrathful nature." Smyrna, known in the present day as Izmir, Turkey, was one of the largest and richest Roman and, later, Byzantine cities of Asia Minor. The city in which Homer may have lived had been rebuilt several centuries before becoming the site (Rev. 1:4, 2:8) of one of Asia's seven original Christian churches noted by St. John (Columbia-Viking desk encyclopedia 2d, s.v. "Smyrna"). The two names juxtaposed imply that the "consistency, beauty, and harmony, of immaculate truth" (W. A. Clarke 1801, xi) will transform "wrathful" mankind

328

In light, finally, of Henry Clarke's vigorous criticism (1793, [257-58], 261) of a narrowly classical education, it is interesting that between the two world wars "the teaching of Greek and Latin" was "still the staple," though far from the whole, of academic life at Eton, England's foremost school at its level during the first half of the twentieth century (Ollard 1982, 11, 15, quoted). It was probably such considerations that prompted Hans to state in 1951 (97) that Clarke's "criticism of the contemporary syllabus and methods of the old Grammar Schools . . . is valid even now."

TABULÆ LINGUARUM.

BEING A SET OF

TABLES,

Exhibiting at fight the DECLENSIONS of NOUNS and
CONJUGATIONS of VERBS;

WITH OTHER GRAMMATICAL REQUISITES

Effential to the Reading and Speaking of the following

LANGUAGES,

VIZ.

LATIN	GOTHIC	CELTIC or ERSE		SCLAVONIC
Spanifh	German	Armoric	Irifh	Ruffian
Portuguefe	Dutch	Bafque	Scotch	Hungarian
Italian	Danifh	Bifcayen	Welfh	Bohemian
French	Swedifh	Cornifh	Manks	Polifh
Norman	Englifh	Waidenfe	Norfe	Turkifh

HEBREW	ETHIOPIC	TARTAREAN	CHINESE
Arabic	African	Kalmuc	Japanefe
Perfic	Morifco	Ottiac	Malayan
Greek	Coptic	Nagree	Javanefe
Morean	Showiah	Bengals	Algonkin
Arabefque	Shilhæ	Hindoftan	Efquimaux

With an Explication of the Lingua Franca ; and the pretended modern Egyptian, or Cant Language.
The Whole being intended to facilitate the Acquifition of any
of thofe Languages, by having in the moft confpicuous point
of view whatever is efteemed therein effentially neceffary
to be committed to Memory. The Radical or Ancient
Languages being taken from the beft Authorities ; and the
Derivative or Modern from the Determinations of the
prefent Academies and Literary Societies of the refpective
Countries.

IN EIGHT PARTS.

PART I. Containing the LATIN, SPANISH, PORTUGUESE,
ITALIAN, FRENCH, and NORMAN.

Henry Clarke

Innumerabiles pæne funt formæ et figuræ dicendi.

LONDON:

Printed for the Author, and Sold by Mr. Murray,
No. 32, Fleet-ftreet.——1793.

[Innumerable things, nearly, are revealed by forms and figures.]

331

Respecting the other Parts of Education,—Mathematics, Astronomy, Mechanics, Optics, &c. &c. they have their utility with every one more or less. With the learned Professions they constitute an essential part of their *Humanities*. The Military and Naval Gentlemen are particularly interested t' :ein ;—the various Classes of Mechanical Artists have perpetually recourse to their Assistance ; and the Merchant or Tradesman, though he may perceive no immediate connexion between these subjects and his line of profession, yet, they must certainly tend to enlarge his Ideas, qualify him better for general Conversation, and thereby render him a far more estimable Member of Society.‡

The Importance of this Plan, H. Clarke thinks it neither requisite, nor perhaps, consistent with Delicacy on his part, to enlarge upon. The Improvement of the Pupils whom he has had under his care for many Years past in Manchester ;—the distinguishing marks of preference he meets with on every occasion in the Mathematical line, and which are frequently exhibited in the different periodical Publications ; and the honourable Testimonials lately given him by some of the first literary Men in the Kingdom, will, he flatters himself, have more weight with the Public in his Favour, than the most studied Artifice of an elaborate or insinuating Address.

‡ *There are few Sciences more intrinsically valuable than MATHEMATICS.—It is hard indeed to say to which they have more contributed, whether to the Utilities of Life, or to the sublimest parts of* SCIENCE.—*Whoever, therefore, will study Mathematics, will become not only a wiser Philosopher, but an acuter Reasoner, in all the possible Subjects, either of Science, or Deliberation.*
HARRIS.

LA PHILOSOPHIE sert à orner l'esprit d'une infinité de connoissances curieuses, ELLE sert aussi à inspirer un grand respect pour la Religion. ROLLIN.
[Philosophy seeks to enrich the meaning of an infinity of fields of intellectual curiosity; it seeks also to inspire great respect for religion.]

.

P L A N

OF THE

LITERARY, COMMERCIAL AND MATHEMATICAL SCHOOL,

MOUNT-PLEASANT (MARTINDALE-HILL)·

L I V E R P O O L.

By H. CLARKE, and the Rev. W. AUGUSTUS CLARKE.

THE Number of PUPILS is limited to thirty.

On *Mondays* and *Fridays* Leffons are given on Grammar in general, — with particular and felect Exercifes in the *Englifh, Latin, Greek, Hebrew, French* and the other modern Languages.

On *Tuefdays* the Employment is writing and Penmaking, — with a particular regard to the various forms of Bills, Promiffory Notes, Epiftolary writing, and other neceffary Mercantile precepts.

Wednefdays and *Thurfdays* are appropriated to Arithmetic, Book-keeping, and the various Branches of the Mathematics, according to each Pupil's Capacity, and his intended line of Profeffion.

And on *Saturdays* Geography and Aftronomy, exemplified by Maps, Charts, Globes, and the Orrery, are the Subjects of Education ; and for which alfo are occafionally fubftituted, Select Leffons on the moft popular Parts of Natural and Experimental Philofophy, illuftrated by a number of Experiments, with an elegant and extenfive Apparatus, newly fitted up for the purpofe.

Alfo at proper intervals, other Acquifitions are attended to, fuitable to the Genius or Inclination of the
—Scholar,

333

Scholar,—as Drawing, *natural* or *linear*; Architecture; the various modes of short-hand, &c. &c.

And for the advantage of those who are intended for Mariners, Surveyors of Land, Timber-measurers, Gaugers, &c. they occasionally go through the *practical* part of the business in the actual use of the necessary apparatus,—Quadrants, Gunter's Chains, Plain-tables, Theodolite, &c. all of which are of the most modern construction.

The Hours of attendance in the summer Season, from seven to nine, and from ten to two. In the Winter Season, from nine to twelve, and from two to five.

The Terms, Five Guineas *per ann.* Entrance one Guinea.

Without entering into any further detail of the above Plan, every person of Experience must readily conceive the Extensiveness and Utility thereof. For, with respect to our present Systems of Education, are they not universally complained of as defective in the most material point—the judicious intermixture of literary attainments with their application to the purposes in life? Have not our most eminent writers in general decried the common mode pursued in our classical schools, where a youth must spend five, six, or seven years of the most valuable part of his life in passing through the common *routine* of what are called the classics, when one fourth of the time would answer the same end, were the most direct method pursued. Every sensible man must allow that one third at least of the common school-books are mere literary fribble and bombast. Is a man's judgment better informed, or are his ideas more enlarged, because he can recite the fabulous incongruities of Ovid?—That he can describe to you the form or shape of the Roman Toga?—That he can tell you the distance to an inch from Pompey's statue that Cæsar fell when he was stabbed by the Conspirators?—That he can give you the exact height of the *Tarpeian* Rock?—

K k.
Can

334

taught the principles of Trade, as unfolded in real practice; and the causes of its progress and decline;— be expert in calculating Foreign Exchanges, so as to make the utmost advantage of their perpetual fluctuation; and lastly be made acquainted with the Produce, Manufactures, Commercial laws, and Regulations of our own, and other Maritime States. And in order to form the *Complete Man of Bufinefs*, it muft be univerfally allowed, that though profound learning, and a critical knowledge of the Dead Languages, are not abfolutely required in a Merchant or Tradefman; yet, it is indifpenfibly requifite. he fhould be capable of fpeaking and writing his native tongue with perfpicuity, eafe and correctnefs.† And if he have acquired fo much of the modern languages as to enable him to carry on a correfpondence therein, he muft certainly find his account in it; not only as giving him a greater degree of refpectability in the eye of a foreign connection, but by the advantage and fatisfaction of judging and acting for himfelf without depending folely on the affiftance and integrity of others. Letters of Trade, or Bufinefs in any department, written in a Style properly adapted to the fubject, always beget Confidence and Refpect; it is therefore prefumed that no Parent can think his Son's time mifemployed, which is fpent in the ftudy of the *Englifh* Grammar, or in that of any other country where his connexions may in all probability render it requifite,—in the frequent exercife of his Genius on various fubjects, literary, commercial, or philofophical, —and particularly in acquiring an accurate knowledge of all the forms of Mercantile Correfpondence.

† *To be well acquainted with one's* NATIVE LAN-GUAGE, *is nothing to boaft of; but not to be well acquainted with it, is a* DISGRACE. CIC. *to his Son.*
The ENGLISH LANGUAGE *undoubtedly ought to form a great part of an Englifh Gentleman's Education.* KNOX.

'Can sketch you out the plan of Pindar's house at Thebes? 'Or can inform you of the length and colour of Sappho's hair ? And yet such puerilities as these are esteemed by many to be marks of profound learning ! To descend to particular instances of this mistaken notion of learning, —A Gentleman informed me a little while ago that he had spent one whole year in committing Salluft to memory, the original of which he could now repeat *verbatim*; at the same time he seriously enquired of me —whether America did not join to Europe ! —Another was ambitious of being reputed an *original* translator of Cebes from the Greek, in the accomplishing of which he told me he had sacrificed near twelve months of his time (though there were three or four excellent translations before) ;—when he was known to be so little acquainted with that necessary branch of learning called Arithmetic as to be almost totally ignorant of the first four rules thereof !

And with regard to what may be termed a *Commercial Education*, it is well known that the common mode of teaching Arithmetic and Book-keeping is very far from effecting a sufficient preparation for the Counting-house, or for any engagement in Foreign Trade : and indeed we need not be surprised, when we consider the methods pursued, that many young Merchants and Tradesmen, even of promising talents, but without better opportunities of previous instruction, should disappoint the expectations of their friends, and be, perhaps, indebted to a series of blunders for the most valuable knowledge they ever acquire.* In order to qualify Youth for the Mercantile Profession, it is absolutely necessary, that after they are tolerably acquainted with Arithmetic Book-keeping and its Appendages, they should be

* *I consider it of very great Consequence that* PARTICULAR INSTRUCTIONS *should be adapted to Young Pe f ns, whose lives are to be spent in the engagements of* COMMERCE.   *KNOX.*

. And here we cannot help adverting to the abfurd and improper mode adopted in our Public Schools for the cultivation of Youth who are intended to fill the middle fphere of life, in mechanic trades, &c. They, almoft in general purfue one common track or plan of learning. After the firft and neceffary branches, Reading, Writing, and Arithmetic (which indeed might be acquired in half the time they ufually are) the next ftep is the Grammar of the Latin tongue, through which the poor boy fweats and labours too frequently we find to little purpofe. If he has got three or four years to fpare before he goes out to bufinefs, he perhaps gets into the *Cordery*, or *Erafmus*; or, if he reaches *Cornelius Nepos*, he is looked on as a prodigy. Now, it may be reafonably afked, for what purpofe all this time has been fpent? The vulgar notion of his becoming a better *Englifh* Scholar thereby is as fallacious as it is abfurd. And what have Mechanic trades to do with Latin, any more than a common Porter or Carman has with Logic? It may indeed complete him a pedant, but can never be of real ufe in his profeffion. On the contrary, inftead of Latin, let him be initiated in thofe branches which are immediately connected with the line he is intended for, — Menfuration, Geometry, &c. Thefe will be of advantage to him, as conftituting the very foundation of his profeffion. Befides, how often do we find boys utterly averfe to the learning of Latin, even fo far, that when it is perfifted in, as to give them an utter diftafte to all kinds of learning whatever. And at all adventures, inftead of flogging and driving a language into a boy, to whom it can be of no ufe, it is certainly a more elegible mode of education, to fubftitute fuch branches as will be of real utility to him. Accuftoming boys early to handle the compaffes, and other Drawing Utenfils, in delineating the diagrams as they proceed in Menfuration, Geometry, &c. is an agreeable entertainment to them rather than a perplexing ftudy,
and

and gradually inures them to *demonstration*,—the grand basis of all useful Discoveries. The Ancients were fully apprized of the advantages arising from this mode of education. Their time was not wholly engrossed in the investigation of *Words*, they saw the necessity of applying them to, and considering the properties of *Things* at the same time: Witness the Writings of Thales, Pythagoras, Aristotle, Euclid, Archimedes, Appolonius, Ptolomy, &c. And this famous motto of Plato set over the door of his Academy at Athens ἀδεὶς ἀγεωμέτρῃΘ εἰσίτω* is a proof of the great estimation this branch of learning was held in by the ancients.

Lest any one, however, should think from what has been here advanced, that it is wished, in any degree to depreciate or under-rate *classical* Acquisition, it will not be improper to point out more particularly our own Plan in this respect,—the great and leading principle of which is, to lay *a firm and durable foundation in Grammar*: From whence the regular Gradations (or Classes) are—1. Cordery's Colloquies, and the Latin Testament;—2. Cornelius Nepos, and Phædrus;—3. Ovid's Epistles, and Erasmus's Dialogues;—4. Ovid's Metamorphoses, Virgil, and Cæsar;—5. The Greek Testament, and Cicero's Letters;—6. Lucian, Cicero de Officiis, Homer, Demosthenes, Xenophon,—and, at the same time are read, select parts of Horace, Juvenal, Virgil, Cicero's Orations, and his golden treatises De Amicitia, and De Senectute.—These, with proper written exercises, suitable to age and capacity (none perhaps preferable to those in Clarke's Introduction for the lower Classes) constitute the essential part of the Classical line of Education; and which, by a due regulation, and strict attention, is found to effect as much in two or three years, besides allowing proper intervals for other necessary improvements, as is usually accomplished only in eight or ten, and almost at the total exclusion of every other absolutely requisite acquirement.

* *Let none but those who understand Geometry enter.*

338

CHAPTER 10

"WELL-BRED" BRITISH AND AMER-

ICAN SCHOLAR WILLIAM MILNS

In light of the war of 1775-81 that produced the United States of

America, it is only fitting to close the main body of this collection of

essays with one published by an English emigrant in the new nation. In 1794

newly arrived schoolmaster William Milns (10) issued the prospectus that

follows for an innovational school that he planned to conduct in New York.

Born in 1761 (Shipton and Mooney 1969, s.v. "Milns, William"), Milns

was the son of a London "gentleman" (Hans 1951, 108). The 1794 title page

lists him as a "member" of the University of Oxford, while two later ones

(Milns 1797a,b) identify him specifically with "St. Mary Hall." Finally

disbanded in 1902, St. Mary's Hall was one of four medieval residential

houses of instruction to survive the nineteenth century. It had from 1326

on been associated with Oriel College, founded as the House of the Blessed

Mary the Virgin in Oxford, which had ordinarily supplied its principal (Hall

and Frankl 1983, [6], 59, 65).

Implying in normal usage that his studies had begun at the unusually

late age of thirty (Hall and Frankl 1983, [6]), Hans states that Milns had

"matriculated" at St. Mary's in 1791. That dating may be in error, however,

as he says also that in the "nineties" the schoolmaster headed the "City

Commercial School" at London, endeavoring to combine "'literary with commer-

cial, mathematical and philosophical education'" (Hans 1951, 108). Milns

himself (1794, title) identified it as the City "Finishing" School.

William Milns carried out his plans to conduct a private academy, in Hans's terms, in New York. Through 1798 he was listed in annual city directories as a teacher, at 29 Gold Street (Duncan 1795, 149, and Longworth 1796, 1797, 249, and 1798, s.v. "Milns, William"; and Longworth 1799, 298, no listing under that name). He later taught in Boston, where he died at age forty in March 1801 (Drake 1872, s.v. "Milns, William"). Judging from the 1794 tract, Milns' (title, [3]-4, 12-16) American career was notable especially in regard to schooling methods and the education of women, areas that were highlighted within respectively the short and long titles.

On the second page of text in his Plan of instruction by private classes . . . , Milns (1794, 4) defines the method as "setting apart a certain portion of time for each [study], and admitting, during such time, none but the students of that class." Whether or not in his own teaching, he had observed in England "the ill effects of assembling a great number of pupils, pursuing different studies, at the same time, and in the same place" (Milns 1794, [3]-4). A similar pattern was still dominant in America at the onset of independence (Cremin 1970, 505):

> The vast majority of schools remained ungraded, and most instruction
> was therefore individual, with pupils approaching the master's desk
> or lectern seriatum and reciting orally or displaying their work for
> praise or correction.

Milns states (1794, 4) that nonclassed instruction was "unavoidable" in conventional grammar schools, by implication because economic factors required the enrollment of pupils of widely differing preparation and ability. Private classes in his sense may have been conducted nearly three centuries earlier at St. Paul's, however, after the refounding by Dean Colet (Butts 1973, 225).

More specifically documented is a case from the early 1600s. Thomas Farnaby, a recognized classics scholar who was a close friend of dramatist

340

Ben Jonson's, had returned to England following Jesuit schooling in Spain, service as a shipmate of Sir Francis Drake's, and soldiering in the Netherlands. After teaching for a time at a school in (Webster's geographical dictionary 1977, s.v. "Somersetshire") southwest England, Farnaby "built an imposing school-house" in London that in "an innovation for grammar schools" reportedly "had a separate classroom for the separate" levels of Latin study. Evidently no financial sacrifice was required, as the seventeenth-century teacher "is said to have been the first schoolmaster in England to have made a fortune" (Watson 1916, 122, 123, quoted).

Milns' coverage of female education (1794, 12-16) reveals an advanced outlook from either an English or an American standpoint. Formal education for young ladies at a secondary level was as yet generally limited in England to home tutoring, usually by family members, or private residential schooling, predominantly arising after 1750. A successful early school was formed in Manchester in 1680 for daughters of Dissenters by Mrs. Frankland (Hans 1951, 194-96), sharing the name of a contemporary dissenting schoolmaster discussed in chapter 1. Boarding school instruction was largely confined, until nearly 1800, to a variety of social and artistic "'accomplishments' and a smattering of foreign languages" (Hans 1951, 208).

The new American nation was assuredly no more advanced in this area than the mother country. Physician, medical professor, and Declaration of Independence signer (Columbia-Viking desk encyclopedia 2d, s.v. "Rush, Benjamin") Benjamin Rush (1787) had seven years before Milns' arrival recommended that girls study a substantial range of subjects in anticipation of responsibilities as mothers and supportive wives (Cremin 1980, 8, 120). He observed, for example, that bookkeeping skill would enable women to help their husbands in certain occupations, and assist them in serving as executrixes should they survive their spouses (Rush 1787, 9). Even this level of enlightenment was unusual (Cremin 1980, 120), as illustrated by the viewpoint taken by a noted patron of education. Thomas Jefferson favored teaching girls "dancing, drawing, music, household economy, and French literature," as well as "alerting them to the danger of novels" (Cremin 1980, 113-14).

In terms of the positive slant taken toward female education, Milns' 1794 school announcement had a most appropriate publisher. Samuel Loudon (Milns 1794, title) was a native Scotsman who had opened a New York bookstore in the early '70s, added circulating library services to the operation at the beginning of 1774, and introduced a weekly newspaper championing the American patriot cause two years later. In advertising a new library catalog late in '74, Loudon expressed pleasure in advising '"all such connoisseurs"' as had questioned female intelligence and interest in reading that '"the ladies [we]re his best customers, and [had] shew[n] a becoming delicacy of taste in their choice of books"' (Keep 1909, 108-11, quoting 109). The same year he reprinted a two-volume Essay on the character, manners, and genius of women in different ages, a newly published version of a French work by Antoine Léonard Thomas (Bristol 1970, s.v. "B3772"; Evans 1903-55, s.v. "1774 AD: Thomas, Antoine Léonard"; and Shipton and Mooney 1969, s.v. "Loudon, Samuel"). On the British invasion of New York, Samuel Loudon moved up the Hudson (Webster's geographical dictionary 1977, s.v. "Beacon," "Fishkill Landing") to Fishkill in September 1776, resuming his operations in the city after the war, beginning in '83 (Keep 1909, 111, 111n-12n; and Kobre 1944, 137).

While in New York, William Milns was also a playwright, songwriter, and book author and editor. He wrote three comedies or farces that were presented locally, and as a lyricist supplied music for at least two of them, partially in collaboration with music composer James Hewitt, who printed and sold some of the pieces (Drake 1872, s.v. "Milns, William"; Evans 1903-55, s.v. "1797, 1798 AD: Milns, William"; and Shipton and Mooney 1969, s.v. "Hewitt, James," "Milns, William"). All in a bustle; or, the new house was written for the opening of the city's "New Theatre" (Evans 1903-55, s.v. "34111"), depicted in the frontispiece of the 1797 volume (Longwood) containing the year's New York directory. A musical composition by Milns and Hewitt for Flash in the pan was distributed in Boston, Philadelphia, and Baltimore as well as New York (Drake 1872, s.v. "Milns, William"; Evans 1903-55, s.v. "34114," "34115"; and Shipton and Mooney 1969, s.v. "Milns, William," next-to-last entry, assessing the Boston publication reported in Evans's first entry as a "ghost" based on seller advertising). Finally, the five-act farce The comet; or, he would be a philospher (Evans 1903-55, s.v. "32482") was later reconstituted as The comet; or, he would be an astronomer, a two-act play published in Baltimore some years after Milns' death, both under his name (in the form "Miln") and without attribution (Shaw and Shoemaker 1958-83, s.v. "1817: Miln, William").

In 1797 William Milns brought out three ample books, printing two of them himself in engraved editions, at the address cited earlier, as The Columbian library[,] containing a classical selection of British literature. Each volume was also issued separately from the series, the second one in the following year, when it was presented as the largest collection yet published of English fable (Evans 1903-55, s.v. "32480," "34112"; and Shipton and Mooney 1969, s.v. "The Columbian Library . . . "). Since the other book was of a different kind, volume 2 represented the only product of an original plan, evidently, to issue a seven-volume collection of British literature (Evans 1903-55; s.v. "30798," listing a 1796 Connecticut edition dismissed as a "ghost" by Shipton and Mooney 1969, s.v. "Milns, William," entry 3, erroneously citing no. 32479 from the Evans series rather than no. 32480).

Volume 1 of The Columbian library was an American edition of The well-bred scholar . . . (Milns 1797b), a text on composition and oratory that had by implication (Milns 1794, [2]) originated in England. The first part (Milns 1797b, 1-98) systematically covered English composition, including letter writing, the literary genre of fable, and the preparation of "themes" in sixteen subject areas. Some 175 pages were then devoted to oratory, particularly "demonstrative" (105-225) and "deliberative" (225-63) eloquence. Milns closed (1979b, 273-83, quoting 279) with a brief discussion of the study of French, Italian, Latin, and Greek, supplying extensive reading lists in keeping with the conviction that languages should be learned through immersion in their literatures rather than through "a detail of rules."

Milns promised (1797b, 284) at the end of the work to address "the other parts of useful learning," or, "Commercial, Mathematical, and Philo-sophical Accomplishments" (emphasis deleted), after guaging response to The well-bred scholar itself. Like the New York edition of that book, the commercial work appeared in 1797. The American accountant, or, a complete system of practical arithmetic . . . (Milns 1797a) was a 320-page treatise on commercial arithmetic "particularly adapted to the AMERICAN and BRITISH COMMERCE" (title). Preceded by a major work of 1793 by pioneer American accounting writer (Sheldahl 1985, 1-4, 24-28) Thomas Sarjeant, it was one of three arithmetic books of 1797 that were adapted to the U.S. federal systems of money and measurement (Noyes 1797; and Sheldahl 1985, 21-23).

344

One of the 1797 volumes was almost identical to Milns' work in its primary title, The American accomptant . . . by Chauncey Lee, and counting a chapter on bookkeeping was nearly as lengthy (Sheldahl 1985, 23, 46, s.v. "Lee, Chauncey"). In 1985 (Sheldahl, 23) it was stated that the relatively short book by James Noyes (1797), 1778-99 (Shipton and Mooney 1969, s.v. "Noyes, James"), "may have been based upon Miln[s'] text." That assertion is withdrawn in response to closer comparison between the two works, and Milns' own ready concession (1797a, [v]) that only following normal practice in the arithmetic literature, as represented, he had himself borrowed freely from other writers, often verbatim. Among many source authors cited were Martin Clare, the subject of chapter 3, and Thomas Dilworth and Charles Hutton, referred to in chapters 4 and 9.

His early death prevented William Milns from contributing the anticipated mathematical and philosophical works. In Boston he published only a short handwriting manual, A set of round hand copies for the use of schools (Milns [1798]). His English publications had included Penman's repository, Geographical running-hand copies, and A set of text copies (Milns 1794, title, [2], short titles), and a New York edition of the first item may have appeared in 1797 (Evans 1903-55, s.v. "32481"; and Shipton and Mooney 1969, s.v. "[Penman's Repository. Text, Round and Running Hand Copies . . .]"). Milns' advocacy (1794, 9) of a "RUNNING-HAND" method "in preference to the formal set hands usually taught" is duly noted in the essay that follows, but the relationship of A set of round hand copies to the earlier penmanship titles has not been determined.

The copy of the Boston publication (Milns [1798]) that belongs to the Library Company of Philadelphia was sold, already, "second hand" in 1798 (Bristol 1970, s.v. "B7258"). That date is nonetheless imputed to the booklet, based on Milns' listing in the New York directory through that year and his extensive New York publication record of 1797-98. A set of round hand copies opened (Milns [1798], 2-4]) with three pages showing the alphabet, both upper and lower case, in cursive form; the same content in printed form, with an italicized line of numerals in the center; and selected letters in Gothic script. The remaining dozen pages ([5-16]) each contained two short adages or maxims in very elegant handwriting, for example ([11]) "Nature and art should be united" and "Obstinate men are generally fools."

Also in Boston, serving in this case as publisher as well, Milns' engraver for the handwriting manual ([1798], title) brought out almost concurrently A set of round hand copies (full title) by J. Weedon ([1797], title). Both Evans (1903-55, s.v. "1797,AD: Weedon, J.") and Shipton and Mooney (1969, s.v. "Weedon, J.") impute the date 1797 to this booklet. It was identical to Milns' tract ([1798]) both in length and, except for reversal of the first and third pages of text (Weedon [1797, 2, 4]), format. The dozen pages of handwritten sentences ([5-16]) differed in specific content throughout, however. On the page corresponding to the citation from Milns, for example, Weedon wrote ([11]) "Never envy another's prosperity" and "Opinion too often serves for reason." With both publication dates imputed, and earlier penmanship writings by William Milns unavailable for present coverage, it seems idle to comment further at this remove on the two versions of the Boston manual.

J. Weedon was described on the title page ([1797]) as "WM: Brentford." The abbreviation was presumably for "Writing Master" (Morris to Sheldahl 1988). The other reference was apparently to Brentford, England, a town dating back to Anglo-Saxon times that today is part of a London borough (Webster's geographical dictionary 1977, s.v. "Brentford and Chiswick,"

"London," def. 4). Limited inquiry including reference to Jackson and Adams's Atlas of American history (1978, especially 36-37, 46, 50, 58, 77-78) has revealed no New England "Brentford," and the professional designation appears to have been primarily British. It is tempting, if (before consulting Boston directories of the day) premature, to conjecture that Weedon was an emigrant in the opposite direction from Milns. There is documentation, in any case, that shortly before the American Revolution, circa 1768-72, there was a newsboy from Salem, Massachusetts named Job Weeden (Shipton and Mooney 1969, s.v. "Weeden, Job"; and Webster's geographical dictionary 1977, s.v. "Essex," def. 4, "Salem," def. 5).

William Milns, finally, was one of ten thousand men and women listed in a biographical dictionary of 1872 (Drake, title, quoted, and s.v. "Milns, William") for prominent connection with the "Arts, Scices, Literature, Politics, or History" (emphasis deleted) of North America.

N.º 7.

PLAN OF INSTRUCTION

BY

PRIVATE CLASSES;

PRINCIPALLY INTENDED FOR THOSE WHO WISH TO GIVE THE

FINISHING POLISH TO THEIR EDUCATION:

INCLUDING SOME REMARKS ON THE

CULTIVATION OF THE FEMALE MIND.

———

By *WILLIAM MILNS*,
MEMBER OF THE UNIVERSITY OF OXFORD:
AUTHOR OF THE WELL-BRED SCHOLAR; PENMAN's REPOSITORY;
GEOGRAPHICAL RUNNING-HAND COPIES; &c. &c. LATE
MASTER OF THE CITY FINISHING SCHOOL, LONDON.

———

Quo semel est imbuta recens, servabit odorem
Testa diu . . . .   HORACE.

———

- - - - - - - - - In vain,
Without fair culture's kind parental aid,
Without enlivening suns and genial show'rs,
And shelter from the blast;—in vain we hope
The tender plant can rear its blooming head,
Or yield the harvest promis'd in its spring.
                                            AKENSIDE.

Further particulars may be known of the Author at his private apartments, No. 98 Maiden Lane; where his Literary Works and Manuscript Penmanship may be seen. His Publications and Plans may likewise be had of the following Booksellers: Mr. ALLEN, Pearl-street; Mr. WAYLAND, Water-street; Mr. LOUDON, do.

◄◄◄◄◄◄◄◄◄◄◄◄◄◄◄◄◄◄◄◄◄◄◄◄◄◄◄►►►►►►►►►►►►►►►►►►►►►►

NEW-YORK:
Printed by SAMUEL LOUDON & SON, No. 82, Water-street.—1794.

LATELY PUBLISHED,

IN ONE LARGE VOLUME OCTAVO,

THE

WELL-BRED SCHOLAR;

OR

PRACTICAL ESSAYS

ON THE BEST METHODS OF IMPROVING THE TASTE AND
ASSISTING THE EXERTIONS OF YOUTH IN THEIR
LITERARY PURSUITS.

———

BY WILLIAM MILNS,
MEMBER OF THE UNIVERSITY OF OXFORD, AUTHOR OF THE
PENMAN'S REPOSITORY, &c.

———

LIKEWISE JUST PUBLISHED,

A Set of Geographical Running-Hand Copies,

WRITTEN IN A STYLE PECULIARLY CALCULATED TO
UNITE ELEGANCE AND EXPEDITION.

———

ALSO,

A SET OF TEXT COPIES,

AND SOME CURIOUS SPECIMENS OF ORNAMENTAL PENMANSHIP,
BY THE SAME AUTHOR.

———

May be had of the beforementioned BOOKSELLERS.

350

PLAN of INSTRUCTION

BY

PRIVATE CLASSES.

THE advantages refulting from a liberal education are fo numerous, fo obvious, and fo univerfally acknowledged, that it would be equally ufelefs and pedantic to enumerate them here. But though there is no diverfity of opinion as to the necefity and beneficial effects of cultivating the youthful mind, yet, the greatest literary characters have differed widely both as to the branches of education particularly effential, as well as to the most fuccefsful methods of inculcating inftruction. Without entering into a comparative review of the various fpeculations of the literati, the fubfcriber deems it fufficient briefly to state thofe ideas which have occurred to him during a strict inveftigation of the fubject, and which have fince been corrected and confirmed by experience. The Grammar Schools, which were inftituted in England above two centuries ago, feem to be the models of the best feminaries of the prefent day. The fyftem of education then purfued was well enough adapted to that age; but it is by no means adequate to give the necefary polifh to a modern education. At the time of their inftitution the views of men were more confined; commerce was but little underftood; and Latin and Greek alone were cultivated as being the only vehicles of fcience. But the progrefs of knowledge fince, the boundlefs extenfion of trade, and the multiplied wants of focial intercourfe, have necefarily enlarged the circle of ftudy, and affigned to objects, not then thought of, a fuperior degree of importance. It feems to be the rational wifh of the prefent day to unite utility with elegance; and to give the polifh of refined learning to the necefary qualifications for active and commercial life. Thefe ideas have been repeatedly prefed upon the attention of the fubfcriber, whofe whole life has been devoted to literary purfuits, and whofe fweeteft pleafures have been derived from the inftruction of youth. But he has feen, and regretted,

351

the ill effects of affembling a great number of pupils, purfuing different ftudies, at the fame time, and in the fame place. He does not prefume to impute any blame to the mafters on this account, as the evil is unavoidable in fchools conducted on the common plan ; and is perhaps chiefly owing to the fmall encouragement offered to the conductors of fuch feminaries, who are compelled to make up by numbers the deficiency in price. But as there may be fome who would wifh thefe inconveniencies removed, he fubmits to the confideration and patronage of the judicious the plan of teaching by private claffes ; fetting apart a certain portion of time for each, and admitting, during fuch time, none but the ftudents of that clafs : By this regulation all confufion will be avoided, the pupils time not wafted, the feveral difadvantages of private and public inftruction obviated and all their advantages combined ; and that at a moderate expence compared with the neceffary charge of private and feparate inftruction. To thofe, therefore, who are defirous of encouraging fuch an undertaking thefe pages are particularly addreffed, in which the fubfcriber will endeavour to explain, as briefly as poffible, his own idea on the fubject, and then fubjoin a flight fketch of his plan, which he hopes to render as extenfive and univerfal as the nature of it will admit.

ENGLISH GRAMMAR, a Courfe of ENGLISH READING, COMPOSITION, and ORATORY.

IT fhould feem very eafy to convince any man of the importance of learning to fpeak and write his native tongue with propriety ; yet we find no part of education more neglected ; and that too in a country, whofe language, independent of its copioufnefs and beauty, is diffufed through fuch a vaft extent of territory in different parts of the globe. Englifh Grammar will therefore be made a particular object of attention, that the pupil may be guarded againft the folly and difgrace of leaving the moft neceffary of all attainments to chance or inftinct.

As nothing can be beautiful but what is juft, correctnefs fhould always precede elegance, and Grammar is, of confequence, made an introduction to the higher excellencies of ftyle ; but without a knowledge of the rules of compofition, Grammar would be of little ufe. Composition is not only the moft elegant, but the moft ufeful vehicle in the literary world ;—without it, Poetry, Hiftory, and Science would be unknown, and the arts would die with the inventors of them ; nor is it lefs valuable in focial and commercial life ; it is the faithful and facred medium through which the reciprocal exchange of fentiment is effected between diftant friends ; and there is nothing, perhaps, upon which the character of a merchant fo much depends as on the langhage of his letters : he is known to many of his correfpondents by no other means ; and he muft appear to very great difadvantage, if he cannot convey his fentiments with clearnefs and precifion. The pupils in this clafs, will be regularly taught to write effays, letters, themes and other exercifes of compofition ; efpecially fuch as relate to the concerns of real life, and the natural incidents of foreign and domeftic trade.

To excel in compofition, it is abfolutely neceffary that the memory be furnifhed with a competent ftock of proper materials ; the fubfcriber therefore will lead his pupil through a courfe of reading both in poetry and profe ; pointing out to them what books they fhould confult and wherein their chief excellencies and defects confift. Without this precaution, fetting a boy to compofe would be as ufelefs and tyrannical an impofition as that of the Egyptian Defpot who infifted on the Ifraelites making brick without ftraw. During this courfe of reading, the pupil will be accuftomed to felect and to commit to memory fome of the moft efteemed paffages from our beft Englifh authors, which he will be taught to recite in a manly, graceful and energetic manner. By this practice his memory will be eafily and amply ftored with the richeft treafures of his native language ; he will infenfibly acquire a fluency of expreffion, and fhake off that awkward diffidence which often renders ufelefs the poffeffion of the fineft abilities.

Some people are of opinion that it is unneceffary for a youth, ftudying the Greek and Latin Claffics, to beftow any time on a particular application to the Englifh Language, as a proficiency in the one, they contend, will neceffarily produce excellence in the other. We might, with equal propriety, affert that to ftudy Hebrew would be the readieft way to acquire a tafte for Latin compofition. Thofe who fall into this error make no diftinction between the knowledge of words and the ftructure of fentences. The ftudy of Greek and Latin, or indeed of any foreign language, will furnifh a copia verborum not fo eafily obtained in any other way ; the reafon is obvious : In tranflating from an unknown tongue, every word is a guide which leads the pupil to fearch the dictionary for a correfponding *Englifh* word ; thus, the memory becomes gradually, and as it were infenfibly, ftored

353

with a valuable affortment of the materials of fpeech : this feems
to be the only *folid* advantage that boys generally derive from the
ftudy of Latin and Greek ; but this it muft be confeffed is fufficiently great to recommend and enforce a continuation of the
practice : Perhaps, indeed, the time which thofe pupils who are
intended for a commercial life fpend on the Greek Language, in
which they make fo little proficiency, might be employed to more
advantage in the ftudy of the French, which is become, not only
a fafhionable, but almoft a neceffary accomplifhment, to perfons
of all diftinctions, in every part of the globe. It will not be
amifs to anticipate here fome objections which may perhaps be
ftarted againft the foregoing obfervation s on claffical learning.
It may be faid that the Latin and Greek languages are juftly
efteemed very important parts of polite literature : that they
contain fome of the fineft models of poetry and eloquence, and
many of the nobleft productions of genius : that they tend to
refine the tafte, harmonize the imagination, and advance the
dignity of human nature : that, therefore, thefe are additional
advantages, equally brilliant and folid, and which ought to enforce a particular attention to thofe elegant purfuits. Thefe en-
comiums are juft, and the objections fpecious ; and if they did
not imply, what never happens to be the cafe, a perfect knowledge of the languages, they would be unanfwerable. Before
any one can tafte the beauties of the antient orators and poets,
he muft be well acquainted, not only with the languages in
which they wrote, but with the fubjects of which they treated ;
and unfortunately for boys, the very plan of their education during the courfe of their claffical reading at fchool, keeps them
equally deficient in both thefe particulars : they ftudy Greek
and Latin books not for the fake of the ideas contained in them,
but for the purpofe of learning the languages ; and their attention
being wholly engroffed in fearching for words, and refolving the
grammatical conftruction, it would be abfurd to expect that they
fhould pay much, if any, attention to the fentiments or fubject :
this holds equally good with the hiftorians, as with the orators
and poets of antiquity. No one can read a book with profit and
pleafure, who is ftopt at every turn by words which he don't underftand, and by phrafes which he cannot unravel : fuch difficulties embarrafs the mind, break the thread of the narration,
tire the ftudent, and render fuch attempts at once ufelefs and
difgufting. Let us not therefore hope to accomplifh at one time,
and by the fame means, two things effentially different, and requiring methods diametrically oppofite. Thefe obfervations
may perhaps be rendered more ftriking by tracing the general
courfe of a fchool education, examining the ufual extent of a
boy's capacity, confidering the time he can fpare for his ftudies,

and paying due attention to his future prospects in life. It was a very just remark of that learned grammarian Claude Lancelot, author of the Portroyal, Latin and Greek Grammars, that " Languages, if we would possess them with any degree of perfection, are only learnt by *assiduity* and *long practice*." Both these united are absolutely necessary, even to an adult anxious for his own improvement ; how much *longer practice* will therefore be necessary for a boy, whose attention is always wandering, whose judgment is naturally weak, and whose assiduity is by no means remarkable.

If a boy begins to learn the antient classics early, and at the same time be made to study with attention his own language, and the other essential parts of a good English education, they will mutually assist each other ; and perhaps no better plan of instruction can be proposed : but, if he should spend the whole, or even the chief part of his time at Latin and Greek to the neglect of the more necessary attainments of a course of English reading, Composition, Oratory, Geography, History, and the French Language ; instead of reaping those advantages which the fond hopes of his anxious parent had led him to expect, he will find, too late, that he has neglected to lay in a store of information and delight, which would be useful to him at every turn, enable him to read with advantage, think with perspicuity, cloath his thoughts with elegant language, and express himself with energy and grace : and that, in lieu of these advantages he has only gained a smattering of two dead languages, which he never will have occasion to use, whose beauties he cannot hope to relish, and which he will probably soon forget. Let us for a moment quit argument and appeal to facts. The numerous criticisms on such writers as Atterbury, Johnson, Pope, Addison and Swift, are sufficient evidences that the most famous English authors have been found deficient, either in grammatical accuracy, purity of style, or elegance of diction, and often indeed in all. But to come still nearer home, how common is it to hear professional men, distinguished for their classical knowledge, deliver their sentiments in dry, inanimate, incorrect and uninteresting language ; and how few do we find in public assemblies, or even in the senate, capable of delivering their opinions at all. These are instances in the compass of every man's observation, and certainly deserve our very serious attention. Where do the deficiencies arise ? Evidently from a neglect in the English department. Seven years are thought necessary to initiate a youth into the mysteries of a profession or trade ; nearly as much time is bestowed in learning the rudiments of Latin and Greek ; and, strange to tell, hardly any time is allowed for the most necessary of all attainments, a thorough knowledge of his native language, a tafte for the elegant compofitions to be found in it, and an early acquaintance with the Englifh circle of polite literature and fcience.

To fuch parents who intend putting their fons to bufinefs at the age of 14 or 15, the above confiderations are of effential confequence, provided they wifh to fee them fill with dignity the refpectable ftations of commercial life. Thofe indeed, who have time to finifh their education at college, may have an opportunity to make good, in fome meafure, thefe deficiencies: but even in that cafe, if the pupil when he entered college, could read, write, and fpeak his own language with propriety, perfpicuity and elegance, and if his mind was properly ftored with a general affortment of ideas, well arranged, and ready for ufe on every occafion, would he not reap tenfold advantages from the profeffional lectures? and would not the profeffors themfelves communicate the fame inftruction with more eafe and pleafure in half the time?—To conclude this article, the length of which it is hoped the importance of the fubject will excufe, let the pupil, whatever may be his other purfuits, make the ftudy of his own language and of the many excellent productions written in it, the primary object of his concern; and let him make every other ftudy fubfervient to his improvement in this. Such a courfe of education will by degrees imprefs on his mind a juft perception of their beauties and excellencies, give him an early tafte for polite literature, and fecure his cheerful compliance with that excellent precept of Horace,

" Nocturna verfate manu, verfate diurnâ.
Thus beautifully imitated by Boileau:
" Que leurs tendres écrits; par les graces dictés,
" Ne quittent point vos mains, jours et nuits feuilletés."

How far the fubfcriber is competent to affift youth in fuch a courfe of ftudy he leaves to others to determine. Born and educated in that metropolis where the Englifh language is fpoken in its utmoft purity and elegance, and having finifhed his ftudies in an Univerfity famed for polite literature, he derives no merit from fpeaking it without any mixture of provincial founds or foreign dialects. His views in life having led him to avail himfelf of every opportunity to improve thefe valuable though in part accidental advantages, he has embraced every opportunity to examine and compare the ftyle and manner of the beft Englifh orators and readers, whether in parliament, at the bar, from the pulpit, or on the ftage.*

* He refers thofe, who may wifh to be further informed refpecting his opinions on the fubject of Education, to a book which he has lately pub-

WRITING, ARITHMETIC, and MERCHANTS ACCOUNTS.

TO expatiate on the utility of the art of writing would be impertinent ; from the ftatefman to the peafant all feel its influence, and acknowledge its ufe ; fome have indeed difputed whether excellence in the execution be a defirable acquifition. The fubfcriber has always been of opinion that it is neceffary to do *well* what it is neceffary to do at all ; and when he addreffes himfelf to the Merchant and the Trader, he knows all argument is fuperfluous ; but furely the gentleman and the fcholar will admit, that many a beautiful idea has been loft, becaufe the pen has not been fo ready as the head ; and many tedious volumes of criticifm and explanatory notes would have been unneceffary, if authors had ftudied to write legibly. The great fuccefs the fubfcriber has experienced in his mode of teaching this art ; the many fine writers to be found among his pupils ; and the general and decided partiality of his friends in favour of his RUNNING-HAND, peculiarly calculated to. unite EXPEDITION with ELEGANCE, and acquired with much eafe in a fhort time, determine him to perfevere in the fame plan in preference to the formal fet hands ufually taught. He is ambitious that his pupils fhould fit down in the counting houfe or ftudy, and write, with eafe and expedition, as beautifully as if they had the ufual fchool affiftance under the infpection of the mafter.

The fcience of numbers is the Mathematician's corner ftone, the Mariner's guide in the pathlefs ocean, and the philofopher's clue through the mazes of fcience. It is yet more, it is the grand foundation on which commerce erects her ftately creft ; collecting, as in a focus, the riches of the world, and diftributing impartially thofe riches to the induftrious. No wonder therefore it fhould be held in high eftimation in every flourifhing commercial city. It will be the fubfcriber's grand object to make his pupils thoroughly acquainted with the rationale of this fcience ; to teach them the fhort and concife methods ufed by the moft experienced in real bufinefs ; to make them complete mafters of the calculation of foreign exchanges, and the caufes of their fluctuation ; to explain to them the origin and nature of the public funds ; and to make them expert at every fpecies of calculation.

lifhed on that fubject, entitled the " Well bred Scholar, or Practical Effays on the beft methods of improving the tafte, and affifting the exertions of youth in their literary purfuits."

B

The elegant method of keeping Merchants accounts by double entry, commonly called the Italian method of Book-keeping, will be taught on such a plan as will enable the pupil to understand clearly the reasons on which this most useful invention is founded; and the examples given him, for his practice, will be such as allude immediately to the transactions of real business, so that he may be fully prepared to enter upon the management of any set of books, let the concerns be ever so extensive.

GEOGRAPHY, the Use of the GLOBES, and HISTORY.

THESE branches of useful science are so closely entwined, and have so near and so necessary a connection, as not to be separated without injury to the learner. Of what service would the minutest inspection of maps be, or the most accurate knowledge of the divisions of the globe, if we did not extend our enquiries to their natural produce, their commodities, the extent of their commerce, the manners and customs of their inhabitants, and the causes of their progress and decline? Geography gives us a comprehensive survey of the present state of the world; and History exhibits to our view a striking picture of past ages, delineated with a masterly pencil. To these objects the attention of youth cannot be too strongly directed; and while the pupil is tracing with eager curiosity, the rise and fall of other empires, he cannot but feel himself more immediately and more deeply interested in the revolutions of his native country. To assist in the geographical part, the subscriber has brought with him from England a very choice pair of modern globes, maps, charts, &c.

NAVIGATION and MATHEMATICS.

THOSE who are desirous of learning the art of Navigation, will have an opportunity of doing it upon true mathematical principles. The subscriber has not only been long accustomed to the theory but has taken the opportunity of his late voyage across the Atlantic to perfect himself in the practical part. The newest and most approved methods of determining the longitude by the distance of the moon from the sun or a fixed star; how to find the latitude when a meridian altitude cannot be obtained; the best way to ascertain the variation either by an amplitude or azimuth, and every other help to a sea journal, will be clearly shewn from examples actually performed at sea. The Navigator will likewise be directed how to choose his instruments, by what criteria he may judge of their excellence, and how to correct them by every possible mode of adjustment so that he may allow for their errors, if faulty, and thereby be able to depend on his observations. Those who have an inclination may at the same time be taught any other branch either of speculative or practical mathematics.

SHORT-HAND.

THIS is a very useful accomplishment : it enables us to trace the ideas of the speaker as fast as he can utter them, and is a secret, yet faithful, remembrancer of our own private transactions : The subscriber will willingly assist any pupil wishing to learn so useful an art,

FRENCH,

THE delicacy and vivacity of the French Language has long made it a necessary part of education to all who move in the circles of fashion. The many elegant and masterly productions on polite literature, and the sciences, written in that language, and the successful endeavours of the French Academicians, to fix upon it the stamp of grammatical accuracy, have made it an object of importance to the learned in every part of the globe; but independent of these, it has the still higher recommendation of COMMERCIAL utility ; it is one of the strong ties, cementing the interest, and improving the friendship of both nations. We are experimentally convinced, that a knowledge of their language has led us to an acquaintance, not only with their manners and customs, but with their real views ; and we no longer see them through the distorting medium of partial, or, which is the same thing, political information. The subscriber has tasted the pleasures and advantages resulting from so valuable an acquisition ; he cannot, therefore, recommend it too earnestly ; nor will his utmost exertions be wanting to render his recommendation effectual. He likewise means to avail himself of the assistance of some foreigner in this class, that the pupils may have the additional advantage of catching the true accent from the lips of a native ; while he will himself more particularly attend to the purity of their translations and exercises into the English

Language, and to the pointing out the differences of their grammatical conftruction and idiomatical phrafes.

◆》》 《《◆·》》 《《◆·》》 《《◆·》》 《《◆·》》 《《◆ 》》

LATIN and GREEK.

IT may perhaps be expected that in fuch a general review of the different parts of education, fome rules ought to be given to fhorten the way towards a more fpeedy attainment of the Latin and Greek. It has been already remarked that they are only to be learned by perfeverance and application, and as the beforementioned departments are fufficient *to* occupy the whole of one perfon's time, the fubfcriber means to confine his attention to them; If the plan of private claffes fhould not meet the wifhes of the public, he may then inᵗ all probability propofe a more general one, calling to his aid fuch affiftance as would enable him to include a complete courfe of education. Claffics would then naturally claim a fhare of his attention; and he would endeavour to propofe and adopt fuch methods as might give them every poffible advantage without fuffering them to interfere with other neceffary purfuits.

◆》》 《《◆·》》 《《◆·》》 《《◆·》》 《《◆·》》 《《◆·》》 《《

CONCLUSION,

CONTAINING SOME REMARKS ON THE PROPER OBJECTS OF

FEMALE EDUCATION.

" Delightful tafk! to rear the tender thought,
" To teach the young idea how to fhoot,
" To pour the frefh inftruction o'er the mind,
" To breathe the enliv'ning fpirit, and to fix
" The gen'rous purpofe in the glowing breaft."
                                    THOMSON,

IT has been matter of amazement, that while great ftrefs is laid upon the improvement of a boy's time, the education of young Ladies fhould be fo much neglected. This neglect, cannot arife from any contempt either of their perfons or abilities, as it is univerfally allowed that chiefly to an intercourfe with the Fair Sex, is to be afcribed that gentility and politenefs only obfervable in polifhed countries; and that, in point of intellectual acutenefs, the female mind often exhibits ftrong marks even of fupériority. The neglect then muft arife from an idea that their views in life render fuch attainments fuperfluous ; and that a few external accomplifhments are fufficient to enable them to fill even the moft genteel ftations of domeftic life with refpectability. Such reafonings are but forry compliments to the Ladies, and will, upon inveftigation, be found equally trifling and ungenerous. If indeed, the only views of men or women were, to rife early, labour hard, and fcrape money together, regarding that as the only blefling of life, a very trifling education would ferve for either. But are there no pleafures of an intellectual nature ? No enjoyments arifing folely from a reciprocal exchange of fimilar fentiments ? No delights. beyond what ignorance or pertnefs can conceive ? Surely to the virtuous and the wife, fuch reflections as thefe are worthy confideration. As to the ufual hackneyed arguments againft femaleimprovement, they are either cruel or ridiculous. To keep a young lady in ignorance, left fhe fhould make an improper ufe of her knowledge, is tyrannical ; the fame reafons might debar her the ufe of knives and fciffars, becaufe it is poffible fhe may hurt herfelf with them. To fay that the cultivation of the female mind renders it unfit to attend to the duties of domeftic life, is ridiculous : for, if that were true, even the elements of learning, as reading and writing, would be not only ufelefs but dangerous ; and the moft ignorant and vulgar woman would be the beft wife and fondeft mother. But, fay fome, " look at the generality of young girls who are fond of reading, and you will find them neglecting every thing elfe, and ftuffing their heads continually with novels and fuch like trafh." Such a conduct is, no doubt, improper, and dangerous in the extreme : but, it only proves the neglect and neceffity of proper cultivation. Such a mind is like a luxuriant foil over-run with weeds ; it will not remain barren, and the only way to prevent noxious fprouts is to plant in it fomething valuable. If you would reap joy in Autumn and enjoy the *fruits of it* in winter, you muft fow inftruction in fpring, and prune its luxuries in fummer.

" Infant reafon grows apace
" And calls for the kind hand of an affiduous care."

" All this may be very fine," fays the ignorant or the felfifh man, " but give me a wife that will look after her children, fee that the baker and butcher don't cheat me, and make a good pudding ; and fhe has knowledge enough for one." It may be fo ; every man to his tafte ; yet, there are others, who, when the buftle of the day is over, would find a pleafure in a little rational family converfation by their fire fide : and if their wives and daughters fhould happen to know that the ftars are not made out of old moons, that the globe is not flat like a bowling green,

that Conftantinople is not in England, and that there once lived
fuch men as Addifon, Pope, and Shakefpere : Such hufbands
or fathers might neverthelefs be fatisfied that a little knowledge
in things of this nature, did not make the puddings lefs palatable,
nor the domeftic concerns lefs regular. "Would you then," it
may be afked, "have a young lady go through the fame courfe of
ftudy as a boy?" By no means : that would be as abfurd as a total
neglect. It is as ridiculous and reprehenfible to fee a lady affect-
ing the airs of a pedant, as it is diftreffing and difgufting to fee
her ignorant and forward. The means fhould always be proportioned to the end propofed ; and as their occupations in life
are different, fo ought to be their plans of inftruction.

This is not the proper place to make any remarks on thofe
parts of female education, which come more immediately under
the infpection of a Governefs ; nor indeed on the more fhowy
accomplifhments, fuch as Drawing, Dancing, Mufic, &c. The
fubfcriber will, therefore, confine himfelf to thofe which appear
to him not only the moft ufeful, but indifpenfably neceffary,
and to which he means to confine his attention in the propofed
plan.

READING and ENGLISH GRAMMAR.

AS Englifh and Grammar are undertaken to be taught even
in the loweft fchools, it fhould feem unneceffary to touch
upon them here. And if the art of reading confifted merely
in gabbling over a few verfes in the bible, or a paragraph in the
newfpaper, it would in this place have been unnoticed. In order to read well, great attention muft be paid to diftinctnefs
and propriety ; the ftops and paufes muft be carefully obferved, not only to diftinguifh them, but to explain why they are
introduced. Without thefe precautions it is impoffible to underftand what we read ourfelves, or pleafe others in the recital
of it. As to Englifh Grammar, the ufual methods of learning
its rules by heart, from a printed book, is of very little ufe. It
is in the practical application of Grammar that we muft look
for its advantages. A young lady may have learnt that an adjective marks the quality of a fubftantive, and that a verb de-
notes action, without being able to point out the adjective or
verb in a fentence, or even underftanding what fuch phrafes
mean. One hour's exercife of the judgment in examining the
words of a fentence, and pointing out their dependance upon
one another, will be of more real advantage, than fix months
fpent in committing dry and technical rules to the memory. The

one method is eafy and pleafant, and will be purfued as an amufement ; the other is difficult and difgufting, and always hated as a tafk.

⬤⬤⬤⬤⬤⬤⬤⬤⬤⬤⬤⬤⬤⬤

WRITING and ACCOUNTS.

THE particular advantages attending thefe neceffary accomplifhments are too obvious to need any comment : it feems only neceffary, therefore, to remark, that while young ladies are employed in thefe attainments, great care fhould be taken that they do not acquire bad habits ; fuch as, leaning againft the table, fitting awry, and holding the pen aukwardly—fuch habits being not only ungraceful, but fome of them prejudicial to health ; and when once acquired, with great difficulty removed. Neatnefs and elegance fhould likewife characterize whatever is the offspring of female induftry ; a carelefs manner and flovenly performances fhould be particularly guarded againft as exceedingly difgraceful to a young lady, who fhould imprint on her mind that excellent precept of one of our poets.
" All fhould be *fair* that lovely woman does."

⬤⬤⬤⬤⬤⬤⬤⬤⬤⬤⬤⬤⬤⬤

GEOGRAPHY, HISTORY, and the Ufe of the GLOBES.

THE utility of thefe branches has been already inveftigated, and the remarks before infifted on are equally applicable to young ladies as to boys ; unlefs, indeed, we adopt the abfurd and tyrannical idea that it is not the part of a woman to join in converfation or underftand the purport of it. Here, it may be again obferved, that the method of burdening the memory with a great number of hard names learnt by heart from a printed book, is a difgufting and ufelefs tafk. More real information may be acquired in one leffon by fearching the places on a globe or map, tracing the courfes of the rivers, obferving the relative fituations of the countries, and examining the nature and properties of the foil, than by a year's labour of the memory in any other way. The principal parts of the hiftory of each country fhould be infifted on, at the fame time that we examine their geographical fituation : thus they will mutually affift each other, and the ftudy will become profitable and pleafant, inftead of ufelefs and difgufting. The practical problems on the Globes will be likewife a very amufing recreation, and the method of finding the time of the rifing and fetting of the fun, moon and ftars—how to know the time of day at any other part of the world—why the day is of different length in different places, and longer in summer than in winter—how to diftinguifh the ftars from the planets, in what they differ, and by what means eafily to know them ; with a great variety of other rational and entertaining enquiries, may be eafily acquired without any labour of the mind, or burden of the memory. The want of method in teaching is the only obftacle that impedes the eafy and pleafant attainment of thefe ufeful and intereffing ftudies.

FRENCH.

IT will be only neceffary to add to what has been already advanced on this fubject ; that particular attention will be paid to point out to the ladies in this clafs the difference in the grammatical conftruction and idiom of the two languages, fo as to make them a mutual help to each other ; and as the fubfcriber intends to avail himfelf of the affiftance of a foreigner, the pupils cannot fail eafily and fpeedily to acquire the true accent and pronunciation.

The Ladies will be divided into Claffes, and attended in the Morning.

The Gentlemen will be likewife divided into Claffes, and attended in the Afternoon.

There will be an Evening Clafs for fuch Gentlemen as cannot attend in the day.

N. B. Il enfeigne l'Anglois aux Etrangers.

The terms and time, with every other particular, may be known of the Subfcriber at his apartments, No. 98, Maiden-Lane, which he has fitted up for the reception of his pupils. He will remove to a commodious Houfe, which he has taken in a central fituation, as foon as he can obtain poffeffion.

AN ESSAY FROM THE DISSENTING ACADEMY AT WARRING-
TON: PRIESTLEY'S TRACT, ORIGINATING IN 1765, ON
"Liberal Education for Civil and Active Life"

Joseph Priestley's essay on liberal education appeared in print seven
times between 1765 and 1826. First published (Priestley [1803, 439]-40,
original preface) with a syllabus of the Warrington Academy history lectures and an educational commentary, it accompanied the lectures when they
were finally published, in Birmingham, in 1788, and continued to appear in
editions or printings of 1793, 1803, from Philadelphia, and 1826. The following reprint is drawn from the American edition by way of the 1826 volume
(D.n.b. 1917, s.v. "Priestley, Joseph," 369; and Priestley [1803, 4]).

Having earlier been closely associated scientifically with Benjamin
Franklin, Priestley had followed his three sons to the United States in 1794,
and settled in a river town of (Webster's geographical dictionary 1977, s.v.
"Northumberland," def. 3) east central Pennsylvania, Northumberland. He
disliked Philadelphia, the national capital in the '90s, and turned down a
chemistry chair at the University of Pennsylvania. Priestley became good
friends with Thomas Jefferson, who as vice-president and president corresponded with him on proper education for a republic, and "sometimes dreamed
of luring better neighbors, including Priestley, to his part of Virginia"
for mutual intellectual stimulation. The Englishman corresponded less regularly with political adversary John Adams. Joseph Priestley died in Northumberland in 1804 (Cremin 1980, 108-9; D.n.b. 1917, s.v. "Priestley, Joseph,"
364-65, 371-72; Huxley 1874, 12-13; and Perry 1984, 142-44, quoting 143).

THE

𝔗heological and 𝔐iscellaneous

WORKS

OF

JOSEPH PRIESTLEY, LL.D. F.R.S. &c.

WITH

NOTES, BY THE *EDITOR.*

———◆———

VOLUME XXIV.

CONTAINING

LECTURES ON HISTORY AND GENERAL POLICY;

TO WHICH IS PREFIXED,

AN ESSAY ON A COURSE OF LIBERAL EDUCATION
FOR CIVIL AND ACTIVE LIFE;

AND AN

ADDITIONAL LECTURE ON THE CONSTITUTION OF THE
UNITED STATES.

GEORGE SMALLFIELD, PRINTER, HACKNEY.

LECTURES

ON

HISTORY AND GENERAL POLICY;

TO WHICH IS PREFIXED,

AN ESSAY ON A COURSE OF LIBERAL EDUCATION
FOR CIVIL AND ACTIVE LIFE:

AND AN

𝔄𝔡𝔡𝔦𝔱𝔦𝔬𝔫𝔞𝔩 𝔏𝔢𝔠𝔱𝔲𝔯𝔢

ON

THE CONSTITUTION OF THE UNITED STATES.

———————

THE WHOLE CORRECTED, IMPROVED, AND ENLARGED.

———————

——————— JUVAT EXHAUSTOS ITERARE LABORES,
ET SULCATA MEIS PERCURRERE LITORA REMIS.
BUCHANANI FRANCISCANUS.

———◆———

[*Philadelphia*, 1803.]

AN ESSAY

ON A COURSE OF

LIBERAL EDUCATION FOR CIVIL AND ACTIVE LIFE.

FIRST PUBLISHED IN 1765.*

———◆———

It seems to be a defect in our present system of public education, that a proper course of studies is not provided for gentlemen who are designed to fill the principal stations of *active life*, distinct from those which are adapted to the *learned professions*. We have hardly any medium between an education for the counting-house, consisting of writing, arithmetic, and merchants' accounts, and a method of institution in the abstract sciences: so that we have nothing liberal that is worth the attention of *gentlemen* whose views neither of these two opposite plans may suit.

Formerly, none but the clergy were thought to have any occasion for learning. It was natural, therefore, that the whole plan of education, from the grammar-school to the finishing at the university, should be calculated for their use. If a few other persons, who were not designed for holy orders, offered themselves for education, it could not be expected that a course of studies should be provided for them only. And indeed, as all those persons who superintended the business of education were of the clerical order, and had themselves been taught nothing but the rhetoric, logic, and school-divinity, or civil law, which comprised the whole compass of human learning for several centuries, it could not be expected that they should entertain larger or more liberal views of education; and still less, that they should strike out a course of study for the use of men who were universally thought to have no need of study; and of whom few were so sensible of their own wants as to desire any such advantage.

Besides, in those days, the great ends of human society seem to have been but little understood. Men of the greatest

* For the *Preface*, then prefixed, see Appendix, No. I.

371

rank, fortune, and influence, and who took the lead in all the affairs of state, had no idea of the great objects of wise and extensive policy; and therefore could never apprehend that any fund of knowledge was requisite for the most eminent stations in the community. Few persons imagined what were the true sources of wealth, power, and happiness, in a nation. Commerce was little understood, or even attended to; and so slight was the connexion of the different nations of Europe, that general politics were very contracted. And thus, men's views being narrow, little previous furniture of mind was requisite to conduct them.

The consequence of all this was, that the advances which were made to a more perfect and improved state of society were very slow; and the present happier state of things was brought about, rather by an accidental concurrence of circumstances, than by any efforts of human wisdom and foresight. We see the hand of Divine Providence in those revolutions which have gradually given a happier turn to affairs, while men have been the passive and blind instruments of their own felicity.

But the situation of things at present is vastly different from what it was two or three centuries ago. The objects of human attention are prodigiously multiplied; the connexions of states are extended; a reflection upon our present advantages, and the steps by which we have arrived to the degree of power and happiness we now enjoy, has shewn us the true sources of them; and so thoroughly awakened are all the states of Europe to a sense of their true interests, that we are convinced, the same supine inattention with which affairs were formerly conducted, is no longer safe; and that, without superior degrees of wisdom and vigour in political measures, every thing we have hitherto gained will infallibly be lost, and be quickly transferred to our more intelligent and vigilant neighbours. In this critical posture of affairs, more lights and superior industry are requisite, both to ministers of state, and to all persons who have any influence in schemes of public and national advantage; and consequently a different and a better furniture of mind is requisite to be brought into the business of life.

This is certainly a call upon us to examine the state of *education* in this country, and to consider how those years are employed which men pass previous to their entering into the world: for upon this, their future behaviour and success must in a great measure depend. A transition which is not easy can never be made with advantage; and therefore it is certainly our wisdom to contrive, that the studies of youth should tend to fit them for the business of manhood; and that the objects of their attention and turn of thinking in younger life, should not be too remote from the destined employment of their riper years. If this be not attended to, they must necessarily be mere novices upon entering the great world, be almost unavoidably embarrassed in their conduct, and, after all the time and expense bestowed upon their education, be indebted to a series of blunders for the most useful knowledge they will ever acquire.

In what manner soever those gentlemen who are not of any learned profession, but who in other capacities have rendered the most important services to their country, came by that knowledge which made them capable of it, I appeal to themselves, whether any considerable share of it was acquired till after they had finished their studies at the university. So remote is the general course of study at places of the most liberal education among us from the business of *civil life*, that many gentlemen, who have had the most liberal education their country could afford, have looked upon the real advantage of such an education as very problematical, and have either wholly dispensed with it in their own children, or, if they have sent their sons through the usual circle of the schools, it has been chiefly through the influence of custom and fashion, or with a view to their forming connexions which might be useful to them in future life. This appears by the little solicitude they shew about their sons being grounded in those sciences, in which they themselves might possibly have been considerable proficients, when they applied to them; but which, from their being foreign to the business of life in which they were afterwards engaged, they have now wholly forgotten.

Indeed, the severe and proper discipline of a grammar-school is become a common topic of ridicule; and few young gentlemen, except those who are designed for some of the learned professions, are made to submit to the rigours of it. And it is manifest, that when no foundation is laid in a grammatical knowledge of the learned languages (which, in a large or public school, cannot be done without very strict discipline, and a severe application on the part both of the master and scholar), youth can be but ill qualified to receive any advantage from an university education. Young gentlemen themselves so frequently hear the learning which is taught in schools and universities ridiculed, that they often make themselves easy with giving a very superficial attention to it, concluding from the turn of conversation in the company they generally fall into, and which they expect to keep, that a few years will confound all distinction of learned and unlearned, and make it impossible to be known whether a man had improved his time at the university, or not.

These evils certainly call for redress ; and let a person be reckoned a projector, a visionary, or whatever anybody pleases, that man is a friend of his country who observes and endeavours to supply any defects in the methods of educating youth.   A well-meaning and a sensible man may be mistaken, but a good intention, especially if it be not wholly unaccompanied with good sense, ought to be exempted from censure.   What has occured to me upon this subject I shall, without any further apology, propose to my fellow-citizens and fellow-tutors, hoping that it will meet with a candid reception.   It is true, I can boast no long or extensive experience in the business of education, but I have not been a mere spectator in this scene ; which I hope may exempt me from the ridicule and contempt which have almost ever fallen upon the schemes of those persons who have written only from their closets ; and, without any experience, have rashly attempted to handle this subject, in which, of all others, experiments only ought to guide theory, upon which hardly any thing worth attending to can be advanced *à priori ;* and where the greatest geniuses, for want of experience, have been the greatest visionaries, laying schemes the least capable of being reduced to practice, or the most absurd if they *had* been put in practice.*

Let it be remembered, that the difficulty under present consideration is, how to fill up with advantage those years which immediately precede a young gentleman's engaging in those higher spheres of active life in which he is destined to move.   Within the departments of *active life,* I suppose to be comprehended all those stations in which a man's conduct will considerably affect the liberty and the property of his countrymen, and the riches, the strength, and the security of his country : the first and most important ranks

---

* Since this was written, which is nearly forty years ago, few persons have had more to do in the business of education than myself; and what I then planned in theory, has been carried into execution by myself and others, with, I believe, universal approbation. *(P.)*

of which are filled by gentlemen of large property, who have themselves the greatest interest in the fate of their country, and who are within the influence of an honourable ambition to appear in the character of magistrates and legislators in the state, or of standing near the helm of affairs, and guiding the secret springs of government.

The profession of law, also, certainly comes within the above description of civil and active life, if a man hope to be any thing more than a practising attorney ; the profession of arms too, if a gentleman have any expectation of arriving at the higher ranks of military preferment : and the business of merchandise, if we look beyond the servile drudgery of the warehouse or counting-house. Divines and physicians I consider to be interested in this subject only as gentlemen and general scholars, or as persons who converse and have influence with gentlemen engaged in active life, without any particular view to their respective professions.

That the parents and friends of young gentlemen destined to act in any of these important spheres, may not think a liberal education unnecessary to them, and that the young gentlemen themselves may enter with spirit into the enlarged views of their friends and tutors, I would humbly propose some new articles of academical instruction, such as have a nearer and more evident connexion with the business of active life, and which may therefore bid fairer to engage the attention, and rouse the thinking powers of young gentlemen of an active genius. The subjects I would recommend are CIVIL HISTORY, and more especially the important objects of CIVIL POLICY ; such as the theory of laws, government, manufactures, commerce, naval force, &c., with whatever may be demonstrated from history to have contributed to the flourishing state of nations, to rendering a people happy and populous at home, and formidable abroad ; together with those articles of previous information without which it is impossible to understand the nature, connexions, and mutual influences, of those great objects.

To give a clearer idea of the subjects I would propose to the study of youth at places of public and liberal education, I have subjoined plans of three distinct courses of lectures, which, I apprehend, may be subservient to this design, divided into such portions as, experience has taught me, may be conveniently discussed in familiar lectures of an hour each.*

The first course is on the STUDY OF HISTORY in general, and in its most extensive sense. It will be seen to consist of such articles as tend to enable a young gentleman to read history with understanding, and to reap the most valuable fruits of that engaging study. I shall not go over the particulars of the course in this place ; let the syllabus speak for itself. Let it only be observed, that my view was, not merely to make history intelligible to persons who may choose to read it for their amusement, but principally to facilitate its subserviency to the highest uses to which it can be applied ; to contribute to its forming the able statesman, and the intelligent and useful citizen. It is true that this is comprising a great deal more than the title of the course will suggest. But under the head of *Objects of attention to a reader of history*, it was found convenient to discuss the principal of those subjects which every gentleman of a liberal education is expected to understand, though they do not generally fall under any division of the sciences in a course of academical education ; and yet, without a competent knowledge of these subjects, no person can be qualified to serve his country except in the lowest capacities.

This course of lectures, it is also presumed, will be found to contain a comprehensive system of that kind of knowledge which is peculiarly requisite to gentlemen who intend to *travel*. For, since the great objects of attention to a reader of history, and to a gentleman upon his travels, are evidently the same, it must be of equal service to them both, to have their importance and mutual influences pointed out to them.

It will likewise be evident to any person who inspects this syllabus, that the subject of COMMERCE has by no means been overlooked. And it is hoped that when those gentlemen who are intended to serve themselves and their country in the respectable character of merchants, have heard the great maxims of commerce discussed in a scientifical and connected manner, as they deserve, they will not

---

* These *Syllabuses* are not now annexed to this *Essay*, as they were at its first publication. That relating to the " Lectures on History" will of course be contained in this work; and the publication of the two others was rendered unnecessary for the reasons already given in the Preface. *(P.)* For the " Plans of Lectures on the History of England, and on the Constitution and Laws of England," see *Appendix*, Nos. II., III.

easily be influenced by notions adopted in a random and hasty manner, and from superficial views of things, whereby they might otherwise be induced to enter into measures seemingly gainful at present, but in the end prejudicial to their country, and to themselves and their posterity, as members of it.

The next course of lectures, the plan of which is briefly delineated, is upon the HISTORY OF ENGLAND, and is designed to be an exemplification of the manner of studying history recommended in the former course, in which the great uses of it are shewn, and the actual progress of every important object of attention distinctly marked, from the earliest accounts of the island to the present time.

To make young gentlemen still more thoroughly acquainted with their own country, a third course of lectures (in connexion with the two others) is subjoined, viz. on its PRESENT CONSTITUTION AND LAWS. But the particular uses of these two courses of lectures need not be pointed out here, as they are sufficiently explained in the introductory addresses prefixed to each of them.

That an acquaintance with the subjects of these lectures is calculated to form the statesman, the military commander, the lawyer, the merchant, and the accomplished country gentleman, cannot be disputed. The principal objection that may be made to this scheme, is the introduction of these subjects into academies, and submitting them to the examination of youth, of the age at which they are usually sent to such places of education. It will be said by some, that these subjects are too deep and too intricate for their tender age and weak intellects; and that, after all, it can be no more than an outline of these great branches of knowledge that can be communicated to youth.

To prevent being misunderstood, let it be observed, that I would not propose that this course of studies should be entered upon by a young gentleman till he be sixteen or seventeen years of age, or at least, and only in some particular cases, fifteen years; at which time of life, it is well known to all persons concerned in the education of youth, that their faculties have attained a considerable degree of ripeness, and that, by proper address, they are as capable of entering into any subject of speculation as they ever will be. What is there in any of the subjects mentioned above, which requires more acuteness or comprehension, than algebra, geometry, logic, or metaphysics; to which students are generally made to apply about the same age?

377

And if it be only an outline of political and commercial knowledge, &c., that can be acquired in the method I propose, let it be observed that it is nothing more than the rudiments of any science which can be taught in a place of education. The master of science is a character of which nothing more than the outline is ever drawn at an academy or the university. It is never finished but by assiduous and long-continued application afterwards. And supposing that only the first rudiments, the grand, plain and leading maxims of policy, with respect to arts, arms, commerce, &c., be communicated to a young gentleman, if they be such maxims as he is really destined to pursue in life, is it not better that he have some knowledge of them communicated early, and at a time when it is likely to make the deepest and most lasting impression, than to be thrown into the practice without any regular theory at all? It is freely acknowledged, that the man of business is not to be finished at an academy, any more than the man of science. This character is not the child of instruction and theory only; but, on the other hand, neither is it the mere offspring of practice without instruction. And certainly, if a knowledge of these subjects be of any use, the earlier they are attended to (after a person is capable of attending to them to any purpose), and the more regular is the method in which they are taught, the greater chance there is for their being thoroughly understood.

When subjects which have a connexion are explained in a regular system, every article is placed where the most light is reflected upon it from the neighbouring subjects. The plainest things are discussed in the first place, and are made to serve as axioms, and the foundation of those which are treated of afterwards. Without this regular method of studying the elements of any science, it seems impossible ever to gain a clear and comprehensive view of it. But after a regular institution, any particular part of a plan of instruction may be enlarged at any time with ease, and without confusion. With how much more ease and distinctness would a person be able to deliver himself upon any subject of policy or commerce, who had had every thing belonging to it explained to him in its proper connexion, than another person of equal abilities who should only have considered the subject in a random manner, reading any treatise that might happen to fall in his way, or adopting his maxims from the company he might accidentally keep, and, consequently, liable to be imposed upon by the

interested views with which men very often both write and
speak. For these are subjects on which almost every writer
or speaker is to be suspected ; so much has party and interest to do with every thing relating to them.

Since, however, these subjects do enter into all sensible
conversation, especially with gentlemen engaged in civil
life, it is a circumstance extremely favourable to the study
of them, that conversation will come greatly in aid of the
lectures the young gentlemen hear upon them. It cannot
fail to rouse their attention, and increase their application
to their studies, when they hear the subjects of them discussed by their fathers and the elder part of their friends
and acquaintance, for whose understanding and turn of thinking they have conceived a great esteem. They will listen
with greater attention to grave and judicious persons, and
become much more fond of their company, when they are
able to understand their conversation, and to enter occasionally into it ; when they can say that such a sentiment or
fact was advanced in their lectures, and that one of their
fellow-pupils or themselves made such a remark upon it.
It is no wonder that many young gentlemen give but little
attention to their present studies, when they find that the
subjects of them are never discussed in any sensible conversations to which they are ever admitted. If studying
these subjects only serve to give the generality of young
gentlemen a taste for conversing upon them, and qualify
them to appear to tolerable advantage in such conversations,
the variety of lights in which they are viewed upon those
occasions cannot fail to make them more generally understood ; and the better these subjects are understood by the
bulk of the nation, the more probable it is that the nation
will be benefited by such knowledge.

If I were asked what branches of knowledge a young
gentleman should in my judgment be master of before he
can study this course with advantage, I would answer, that
a knowledge of the learned languages is not absolutely necessary, but is very desirable ; especially such an insight into
Latin as may enable a person to read the easier classics, and
supersede the use of a dictionary, with respect to those
more difficult English words which are derived from the
Latin. The student of this course should understand French
very well ; he should also be a pretty good accountant, be
acquainted with the more useful branches of practical mathematics ; and, if possible, have some knowledge of algebra

and geometry, which ought to be indispensable in every plan of liberal education.

Some will be ready to object to these studies, that a turn for speculation unfits men for business. I answer, that nothing is more true, if those speculations be foreign to their employment. It is readily acknowledged, that a turn for poetry and the belles lettres might hurt a tradesman; that the study of natural philosophy might interfere with the practice of the law, and metaphysics and the abstract sciences with the duty of a soldier. But it can never be said that a counsellor can be unfitted for his practice by a taste for the study of the law, or that a commander would be the worse soldier for studying books written on the art of war; nor can it be supposed that a merchant would do less business, or to worse purpose, for having acquired a fondness for such writers as have best explained the principles of trade and commerce, and for being qualified to read them with understanding and judgment.

It must be allowed, that the mechanical parts of any employment will be best performed by persons who have no knowledge or idea of any thing beyond the mere practice. When a man's faculties are wholly employed upon one single thing, it is more probable that he will make himself completely master of it; and, having no further or higher views, he will more contentedly and more cheerfully give his whole time to his proper object. But no man who can afford the expense of a liberal education, enters upon any business with a view to spend his whole life in the mere mechanical part of it, and in performing a task imposed on him. A man of spirit will laudably aspire to be a master in his turn; when he must be directed by his own lights, and when he will find himself miserably bewildered, if he have acquired no more knowledge than was sufficient for him while he followed the direction of others. Besides, in the case of merchandise, if one branch fail, there is no resource but in more extensive knowledge. A man who has been used to go only in one beaten track, and who has had no idea given him of any other, for fear of his being tempted to leave it, will be wholly at a loss when it happens that that track can be no longer used; while a person who has a general idea of the whole course of the country may be able to strike out another and perhaps a better road than the former.

I am aware of a different kind of objection, from another quarter, which it behoves me not to overlook. The advocates for the old plan of education, and who dislike innovations in the number or the distribution of the sciences in which lectures are given, may object to the admission of these studies, as in danger of attracting the attention of those students who are designed for the learned professions, and thereby interfering too much with that which has been found, by the experience of generations, to be the best for scholars, the proper subjects of which are sufficient to fill up all their time, without these supernumerary articles. I answer, that the subjects of these lectures are by no means necessary articles of a mere scholastic education ; but that they are such as scholars ought to have some acquaintance with, and that without some acquaintance with them, they must on many occasions appear to great disadvantage in the present state of knowledge.

Time was when scholars might, with a good grace, disclaim all pretensions to any branch of knowledge, but what was taught in the universities. Perhaps they would be the more revered by the vulgar on account of such ignorance, as an argument of their being more abstracted from the world. Few books were written but by critics and antiquaries for the use of men like themselves. The literati of those days had comparatively little free intercourse but among themselves ; the learned world and the common world being much more distinct from one another than they are now. Scholars by profession read, wrote, and conversed in no language but the Roman. They would have been ashamed to have expressed themselves in bad Latin, but not in the least of being guilty of any impropriety in the use of their mother tongue, which they considered as belonging only to the vulgar.

But those times of revived antiquity have had their use, and are now no more. We are obliged to the learned labours of our forefathers for searching into all the remains of antiquity, and illustrating valuable ancient authors ; but their maxims of life will not suit the world as it is at present. The politeness of the times has brought the learned and the unlearned into more familiar intercourse than they had before. They find themselves obliged to converse upon the same topics. The subjects of modern history, policy, arts, manufactures, commerce, &c., are the general topics of all sensible conversation. Every thing is said in our own tongue ; little is even written in a foreign or dead language ; and every British author is studious of writing with propriety in his native English. Criticism, which was formerly the great business of a scholar's life, is now become the amusement of a leisure hour, and this but to a few; so that a hundredth part of the time which was for merly given to criticism and antiquities, is enough in this age to gain a man the character of a profound scholar. The topics of sensible conversation are likewise the favourite subjects of all the capital writings of the present age, which are read with equal avidity by gentlemen, merchants, lawyers, physicians, and divines.

Now, when the course of reading, thinking, and conversation, even among scholars, is become so very different from what it was, is it not reasonable that the plan of even scholastic education should in some measure vary with it? The necessity of the thing has already in many instances forced a change, and the same increasing necessity will either force a greater and more general change, or we must not be surprised to find our schools, academies, and universities deserted, as wholly unfit to qualify men to appear with advantage in the present age.

In many private schools and academies, we find several things taught now, which were never made the subjects of systematical instruction in former times; and in those of our universities, in which it is the interest of the tutors to make their lectures of real use to their pupils, and where lectures are not mere matters of form, the professors find the necessity of delivering themselves in English. And the evident propriety of the thing must necessarily make this practice more general, notwithstanding the most superstitious regard to established customs.

But let the professors conduct themselves by what maxims they please, the students will of course be influenced by the taste of the company they keep in the world at large, to which young gentlemen in this age have an earlier admission than they had formerly. How can it be expected that the present set of students for divinity should apply to the study of the dead languages with the assiduity of their fathers and grandfathers, when they find so many of the uses of those languages no longer subsisting? What can they think it will avail them to make the purity of the Latin style their principal study, for several years of the most improvable part of their life, when they are sensible that they shall have little more occasion for it than other gentlemen, or than persons in common life, when they have left the university? And how can it be otherwise, but that their private reading and studies should sometimes be different from the course of their public instructions, when the favourite authors of the public, the merits of whom they hear discussed in every company, even by their tutors themselves, write upon quite different subjects?

In such a state of things, the advantage of a regular, systematical instruction in those subjects which are treated of in books that in fact engage the attention of all the world, the learned least of all excepted, and which enter into all conversations, where it is worth a man's while to bear a part, or to make a figure, cannot be doubted. And I am of opinion that these studies may be conducted in such a manner as will interfere very little with a sufficiently close application to others. Students in medicine and divinity may be admitted to these studies later than those for whose real use in life they are principally intended; not till they be sufficiently grounded in the classics, have studied logic, oratory, and criticism, or any thing else that may be deemed useful, previous to those studies which are peculiar to their respective professions; and even then, these new studies may be made a matter of amusement, rather than an article of business.

With respect to divines, it ought moreover to be considered, that the same revolutions in the state of knowledge, which call their attention to these new studies, have, in a great measure, furnished them with *time* for their application to them, by releasing them from several subjects, the study of which was formerly the great business of divines, and engrossed almost their whole time. And though new subjects have been started within the province of divinity, it does not appear to me that they require so much time and application as was usually given to those other studies, the use of which is now superseded. I mean principally school divinity, and the canon law; not to mention logic and metaphysics, which were formerly a more intricate business, and took up much more time than they do now.

Let a person but look over the table of contents to the works of Thomas Aquinas,* which were read, studied, or commented upon, by all divines a few centuries ago; and he will be convinced that it must have required both more acuteness to comprehend the subjects of them, and more time to study and digest them in any tolerable manner, than it would require to become exceedingly well versed in all the branches of knowledge I would now recommend.

* See some account of their subjects, Vol. III. p. 365; V. pp. 171, 172.

c 2

The canon law was not less complex than both the common and statute law of England; and every clergyman of eminence was under a necessity of understanding, not only the general principles and theory of that system, but even the minutiæ of the practice. Good sense and a free access to the Scriptures have at length (assisted perhaps by an aversion to abstract speculations) thrown down the whole fabric of school divinity, and the rise of the civil above the ecclesiastical power in this realm, has reduced the theory and practice of the English canon law within very narrow bounds. And as to the little that now remains in use, very few clergymen need trouble themselves about it. In this country a knowledge of the *canon law* cannot be said to be of any use, and that of the *civil law* of the Romans can only be interesting to curious and speculative persons, having no connexion with any laws in the United States.

It is acknowledged that the attention of students in theology, and other learned professions, is much engaged by mathematical and philosophical studies which have been cultivated of late years. I rejoice in so valuable an accession to human science, and would be far from shortening the time that is given to them in places of liberal education. I rather wish there were more room for those studies in such places, and better provision for teaching them. But notwithstanding this, there is room enough for a small portion of time and attention to be given to the subjects I would here recommend; and it is not much of either that I would plead for in the case of gentlemen intended for the learned professions.

The method in which those lectures may be taught to the most advantage, I apprehend to be the following; and experience has in some measure formed my judgment in this case.

Let the lecturer have a pretty full text before him, digested with care, containing not only a method of discoursing upon the subjects, but also all the principal *arguments* he adduces, and all the leading *facts* he makes use of to support his hypothesis. Let this text be the subject of a regular, but familiar discourse, not exceeding an hour at a time, with a class not exceeding twenty or thirty. Let the lecturer give his pupils all encouragement to enter occasionally into the conversation, by proposing queries, or making any objections or remarks that may occur to them. Let all the students have an opportunity of perusing this text, if not of copying it, in the intervals between the lectures, and let near half of the time for lecturing be spent in receiving from the students a minute account of the particulars of the preceding lecture, and in explaining any difficulties they might have met with in it, in order that no subject be quitted till the tutor be morally certain that his pupils thoroughly understand it.

Upon every subject of importance, let the tutor make references to the principal authors who have treated of it; and if the subject be a controverted one, let him refer to books written on both sides of the question. Of these references let the tutor occasionally require an account, and sometimes a written abstract. Lastly, let the tutor select a proper number of the most important questions that can arise from the subject of the lectures, and let them be proposed to the students as exercises, to be treated in the form of orations, theses, or dissertations, as he shall think fit. Moreover, if he judge it convenient, let him appoint rewards to those who shall handle the subject in the most judicious manner.

Young gentlemen designed for the learned professions need not be put upon these exercises, or reading all the authors referred to. It may be sufficient for them to attend the lectures as they are delivered. And as I would not advise that the lectures be given with shorter intervals between them than three days, they cannot interfere much with their application to their proper studies.

I think I could assign very satisfactory reasons for each of the directions I have laid down above; but I flatter myself they will suggest themselves, if not upon the bare perusal, at least upon any attempt to reduce them to practice. I shall only take notice of an objection that may be made to one particular article in this method.

Some may object to the encouragement I would give the students to propose objections at the time of lecturing. This custom, they may say, will tend to interrupt the course of the lecture, and promote a spirit of impertinence and conceit in young persons. I answer, that every inconvenience of this kind may be obviated by the *manner* in which a tutor delivers himself in lecturing. A proper mixture of dignity and freedom (which are so far from being incompatible, that they mutually set off one another) will prevent or repress all impertinent and unseasonable remarks, at the same time that it will encourage those which are modest and pertinent.

But suppose a lecturer should not be able immediately to give a satisfactory answer to an objection that might be started by a sensible student. He must be conscious of his having made very ridiculous pretensions, and having given himself improper airs, if it give him any pain to tell his class that he will reconsider a subject, or even to acknowledge himself mistaken. It depends wholly upon a tutor's general disposition, and his usual manner of address, whether he lose or gain ground in the esteem of his pupils by such a declaration. Every tutor ought to have considered the subjects on which he gives lectures with attention, but no man can be expected to be infallible. For my own part, I would not forego the pleasure and advantage which accrue both to my pupils and to myself, from this method, together with the opportunity it gives me of improving my lectures, by means of the many useful hints which are often started in this familiar way of discoursing upon a subject, for any inconvenience I have yet found to attend it, or that I can imagine may possibly attend it.

I cannot help flattering myself that were the studies I have here recommended generally introduced into places of liberal education, the consequence might be happy for this country in some future period. Many of the political evils, under which this and every country in the world labour, are not owing to any want of a love for our country, but to an ignorance of its real constitution and interests. Besides, the very circumstance of giving that attention which I would recommend to its constitution and interests, would unavoidably beget a love and affection for them, and might perhaps contribute more to produce, propagate, and inflame a spirit of patriotism, than any other circumstance. And certainly if there be the most distant prospect of this valuable end being gained by an application to these studies, it cannot fail to recommend them to every true lover of his country, in an age in which the minds of so many are blinded and misled by a spirit of faction; and, what is more alarming, when a taste for luxury and expense is so high, that there is reason to fear it may, in many cases, be superior to all other regards; and when in many breasts it already apparently threatens the utter extinction of a spirit of patriotism.

What was it that made the Greeks, the Romans in early ages, and other nations of antiquity, such obstinate patriots, that they had even no idea of any obligation superior to a regard for their country; but that the constant wars they were obliged to maintain with the neighbouring nations, kept the idea of their country perpetually in view, and always opposed to that of other nations? It is the same circumstance that gives our common soldiers and seamen more of the genuine spirit of patriotism than is felt by any other order of men in the community, notwithstanding they have the least interest in it. Now the course of instruction I would introduce would bring the idea of our country more early into the minds of British youth, and habituate them to a constant and close attention to it. And why should not the practice of thinking, reading, conversing, and writing, about the interest of our country, answer the same purpose with the moderns, that fighting for it did among the ancients?

It is a circumstance of particular consequence, that this enthusiastic love for our country would by this means be imbibed by persons of fortune, rank, and influence, in whom it might be effectual to the most important purposes; who might have it in their power, not only to wish well to their country, but to render it the greatest real services. Such men would not only, as is the case with private soldiers or seamen, be able to employ the force of a single arm in its defence, but might animate the hearts and engage the hands of thousands in its cause. Of what unspeakable advantage might be one minister of state, one military commander, or even a single member of parliament, who thoroughly understood the interests of his country, and who postponed every other interest and consideration to it!

This is not teaching politics to low mechanics and manufacturers, or encouraging the study of it among persons with whom it could be of no service to their country, and often a real detriment to themselves; though we may see in those persons how possible it is for the public passions to swallow up all the private ones, when the objects of them are kept frequently in view, and are much dwelt upon in the mind. The same zeal that is the subject of ridicule in persons of no weight or influence in the state, would be most glorious and happy for their country in a more advantageous situation.*

Some may perhaps object to these studies, as giving too much encouragement to that turn for politics which they may think is already immoderate in the lower and middle ranks of men among us. But must not political knowledge be communicated to those to whom it may be of real use, because a fondness for the study may extend beyond its proper

* During the sixty years since this paragraph was written, "mechanics and manufacturers," whom my author had, certainly, no intention to depreciate, have been more and more disposed to claim, as, thanks to general education, they have become more and more prepared worthily to employ, their "influence in the state."

bounds, and be caught by some persons who had better remain ignorant of it? Besides, it ought to be considered, that how ridiculous soever some may make themselves by pretensions to politics, a true friend of liberty will be cautious how he discourages a fondness for that kind of knowledge which has ever been the favourite subject of writing and conversation in all free states. Only tyrants and the friends of arbitrary power have ever taken umbrage at a turn for political knowledge, and political discourses, among even the lowest of the people. Men will study and converse about what they are interested in, especially if they have any influence; and though the ass in the fable was in no concern who was his master, since he could but carry his usual load; and though the subjects of a despotic monarch need not trouble themselves about political disputes and intrigues, which never terminate in a change of measures, but only of men; yet, in a free country, where even private persons have much at stake, every man is nearly interested in the conduct of his superiors, and cannot be an unconcerned spectator of what is transacted by them. With respect to influence, the sentiments of the lowest vulgar in England are not wholly insignificant, and a wise minister will ever pay some attention to them.

It is our wisdom, therefore, to provide that all persons, who have any influence in political measures, be well instructed in the great and leading principles of wise policy. This is certainly an object of the greatest importance. Inconveniences ever attend a general application to any kind of knowledge, and, no doubt, will attend this. But they are inconveniences which a friend to liberty need be under no apprehensions about.

What is said in this essay to recommend the study of the principles of general policy to Englishmen, is much more applicable to Americans, as every individual has much more influence in public measures. In fact, the greatest attention is actually given to them by almost all persons in the United States. It is therefore the more necessary that they be well instructed in the true principles of government and general policy, that they may be the better qualified to give their votes on public occasions with real judgment, and without prejudice, to which members of free states are peculiarly liable; every competitor for power having an interest in biassing others in favour of himself and his peculiar principles.

I may possibly promise myself too much, from the general introduction of the studies I have recommended in this essay, into places of liberal education; but a little enthusiasm is always excusable in persons who propose and recommend useful innovations. I have endeavoured to represent the state of education in this view as clearly and as fully as I have been able; and I desire my proposals for emendations to have no more weight than the fairest representation will give them in the minds of the cool and the unbiassed.

APPENDIX 2

TRANSLATIONS OF THE FRENCH (OR LATIN) PAS-
SAGES IN POSTLETHWAYT'S ENTRY, FROM CHAP-
TER 6, "The British Mercantile College"

Note. All translations except the first one (Latin) are from French.
Page references are to Postlethwayt's Dictionary (1751-55), vol. 2.
Professor Patti Mills of Indiana State University provided very helpful
advice concerning the French passages, and assisted by her colleague
Professor James Loyd translated the Latin item.

Page 218

We have known certain newcomers, who when they have just given themselves over to trade, involve themselves in big transactions and conduct
their affairs badly. And indeed we see in practice inexperienced merchants
subjected to numerous lawsuits and insidious plots. Let merchants keep an
account of their business and not spare the pen. Stracca. On commerce,
par. 2, p. 357.

Page 218

Traders are ignorant who enter the field without instruction, having
not served their apprenticeship with qualified merchants who have all the
qualities necessary for doing business. It is impossible for a trader to
succeed in his enterprises if he does not know his profession perfectly.
Perfect merchant by Savary.

Page 220

Arbitrages, in the matter of exchange, are nothing but an expectation
of a considerable benefit that a principal ought to receive from a remit-
tance or draft made for one place in preference to another.

391

Par, or equality in current moneys, or par of exchange, is the point most delicate, most essential, and most independent in regard to the commerce of exchange and of banking, itself taking two forms.

The first is at par, which assumes a fair relation and an exact value of the money of one country with that of another, as when one rixdale of 50 sols, in current money of Holland, or Amsterdam, is counted as equal in value to one unit of 60 sols Tournois [minted at Tours] of France or of 54 pennies, or pence, or 4 1/2 shillings of England, and so on for other places.[a] Without this knowledge, one cannot know the profit or loss made on exchanges, or on foreign merchandise; for as there are a par and equality of the weights and measures of the world, it is necessary also that there be a par and equality of the moneys; otherwise a merchant would neither know what he was doing, nor if the price demanded of him for something were to change, whether the merchandise were expensive or cheap.

The second kind of equality between places is based on market exchange prices, by which is meant simply that ratio required of one place with another for recognition of one price or of several prices compared among themselves. Some might say that recognition of profit and loss made on bills of exchange depends upon return of the sums to their source, and that par is a useless speculation. To this one may respond that, if recognition of the profit and loss made on bills of exchange depends on return of the sums to their source, and on the locality from whence they came, the same things cannot be said of those that are not returned at all, either those

---

[a]The reader is advised that this work was written when the French ecu was valued at only 60 sols Tournois, its being at par with the Dutch rixdale of 60 sols. But the moneys have changed often since then, and been subject to continual variation; thus instead of indicating the value of the ecu of France in the present year 1731, one may always assume the ancient value of 60 sols Tournois; to which we will return. General facts of commerce, by Samuel Ricard of Amsterdam.

that may be used or consumed in the same country, or for the purchase of merchandise, or for annuities, or for special transactions.

In any event, if it were necessary to wait for this return in order to know the profit made on a bill of exchange, so that such knowledge depended on the future, one would have to conclude that at the time a person gives or takes money in exchange, he might not know of it (the profit); and if he does not know, this constitutes trading without knowledge of reason and risk, since one would be ignorant of the profit or loss he might have made.

Page 227

"The first question," he says, "that presents itself is what method should be followed in teaching the Latin tongue. It seems to me that at present people rather generally agree that the first rules to be given in teaching Latin should be stated in French, because in every science, in every field of knowledge, it is natural to move from a thing known and clear to a thing that is unknown and obscure. They have felt that it would be no less absurd, and no less contrary to good sense, to give the fundamental precepts of the Latin language in Latin, than it would be to use them for Greek, and for all foreign languages."

Page 229

"A skillful and attentive schoolmaster puts all his resources into use in order to make study agreeable to young people. He seizes their time; he notes their preferences; he considers their temperament; he mingles play with work; he seems to let them choose between the two; he does not impose a rule of study; he sometimes excites desire for study by refusing it, and by stopping, or rather interrupting, it; in a word, he turns himself into

a thousand shapes, and contrives a thousand skills, in order to achieve
his goal." Rollin of belles-lettres. <u>Of the government of colleges.</u>

<u>Page 233</u>

EDICT OF THE KING, Providing that nobles may conduct commerce at sea,
without prejudice to their nobility. Rendered at S. Germaine in Laye, in
the month of August, 1669.

LOUIS by the grace of God, king of France and of Navarre: To all present and still to come, greetings: As trade, and particularly that which is
conducted by sea, is the second source that brings abundance to nations, and
that repays subjects in proportion to their industry and their work, and of
which there is no means more legitimate or unobjectionable for acquiring
goods; so it has always been highly esteemed among the most civilized
nations, and recognized universally as one of the most honest occupations
of civic life, etc., etc. For these reasons, desiring in no way to obstruct
anything that may positively motivate our subjects to engage themselves in
trade, and render it more flourishing, and worthy of our own special grace,
full power and royal authority, we have said and declared, and by these
presentments signed by our hand do say and declare, and resolve with pleasure, that any gentlemen may themselves or through intermediaries enter into
partnership, and take part in commercial, commodities, and merchandise shipping without prejudice on that basis to their nobility, provided always
that they not sell at retail, etc., etc. Signed LOUIS, and for reply by
the king, COLBERT.

This was strongly enforced again by another edict in December 1701,
which is called "Edict of the king, which permits nobles, except those who
have assumed charge of the magistracy, to conduct wholesale trade, and
declares who are the wholesale merchants and traders."

394

[Note to prior passage of regular text.] +Those who wish to become limited joint-stockholders should seek out a merchant who is a man of quality and is capable of the manufacturing or trade that he wishes to undertake; for it is upon his fidelity and industry that he should found the hope that he can profit by entrusting his money to him, etc. <u>Perfect merchant</u>, Savary.

Addition - <u>Title page</u>, vol. 2 (first sentence is from Latin)

Set forth most clearly.

I think I have rendered service to commerce, in having made it known as a science in a nation that had long attached to it only a mechanical purpose, and in which the idea of the noble has not always been truly joined to that of the useful. The political world and mankind generally will assign commerce an honorable place amidst the other sciences, and the commercial profession will be [recognized as] noble, when those who are distinguished from other persons by their range or genius speak out in its favor. <u>Elements of commerce.</u>

APPENDIX 3

TRANSLATIONS OF THE LATIN PASSAGES
FROM GORDON'S TITLE PAGE AND ESSAY

Note. Professor Patti Mills generously supplied the following translations. Page references are Gordon's 1763 volume.

Title page

What greater or better civic duty can we assist, than if we should educate our youth well? Cicero.

Page 4n. Passage from Stracca translated as first item in appendix 2.

Page 6

Why therefore do we instruct children by means of the liberal studies? Not because they can impart virtue, but because they prepare the spirit to accept virtue. Just as the ancients called "literatura" that by which the basic principles of education were imparted to children, one does not teach the liberal arts, but soon prepares a place for learning. Thus, the liberal arts do not lead the spirit to virtue, but prepare it.

REFERENCE LIST[1]

Abelson, Paul. 1906. The seven liberal arts: A study in medieval culture. [New York]: Teachers College, Columbia University; reprint, New York: Russell & Russell, 1965.

Agnew, L. R. C. 1970. Scottish medical education. In O'Malley 1970b, 251-61.

Alcuin [also known as Albinus]. [C. 786]. Alcuin on St. Peter's School, York, 732-786. In Leach 1911, 11-17, odd nos. (Latin text, 10-16, even nos.).

——. 796. Ex-schoolmaster Alcuin recommends Eanbald II, Archbishop of York, to separate the grammar, song and writing schools. In Leach 1911, 19.

Alfred, King [of Wessex (the dominant English kingdom)]. [C. 893]. State of education in England in 871 and c. 893. In Leach 1911, 23, 25.

American Philosophical Association, Eastern Division: Eighty-fourth annual meeting. 1987. Proceedings and Addresses of the American Philosophical Association 61 (November):[411]-45.

Axtell, James L. 1968. The educational writings of John Locke: A critical edition with introduction and notes. Cambridge: Cambridge University Press.

Bede ["The Venerable" B.]. [731]. The ecclesiastical history of the English people (or The history of the English church and nation). Text of Colgrave and Mynors 1969. (Familiar date not bracketed in citations.)

---

[1]When more than four locations are listed by a publisher, only the first one is cited, with et al.' Several reprint editions are cited under both editor(s) and author, to facilitate separate reference to text and to introduction, notes, or commentary. An "editor" who is not expressly identified as such on the title page is shown (in brackets) in that capacity only if editorial content is minor in relation to total size of the volume. Anthologized sources are cited (at least first) by editors' titles, and page numbers uniformly are shown for the reprints only, to permit their use with original dates in textual citations. Page numbers are given for the English translations, only, of items that appear within Leach's 1911 collection, by way of juxtaposed pages, in both Latin and English. Titles have been conformed to a standard format, applied flexibly regarding (in particular) the initial capitalization of subtitles, so that numerous stylistic variations are not shown.

Bidwell, John, to Terry K. Sheldahl. 1988. May 12, 18, both by telephone. Reference/Acquisitions Librarian, William Andrews Clark Memorial Library, University of California at Los Angeles.

Black, Robert C. III. 1966. The younger John Winthrop. New York and London: Columbia University Press.

Blair, John. 1984. The Anglo-Saxon period (c. 440-1066). In Morgan 1984, [52]-103.

Blair, Peter Hunter. 1962. An introduction to Anglo-Saxon England. Cambridge: Cambridge University Press.

Boyer, Carl B. 1968. A history of mathematics. New York, London, and Sydney: John Wiley & Sons.

Brand, Paul. 1987. Courtroom and schoolroom: The education of lawyers in England prior to 1400. Historical Research 60 (June):[147]-65. Formerly The Bulletin of the Historical Research Society.

[Brief, Richard P., ed]. [1986]. "Accounting Thought and Practice Through the Years": A 46-volume series of major books in the history of accounting, including 25 titles published here for the first time. Catalog for series edited by Brief. New York: Garland Publishing.

Brinsley, John. 1622. A consolation for our grammar schooles; or, a faithful and most comfortable incouragement, for laying of a sure foundation of all good learning in our schooles . . .. London: Richard Field for Thomas Man; reprint, under the basic title, New York: Scholars' Facsimilies & Reprints, 1943. Intro. and bibliographical note by Thomas Clark Pollock; microfiche ed. of reprint, Gottlieb, Miller, and Page 1970-78, no. 11306.

_____. 1627. Ludus literarius; or, the grammar schoole; Shewing how to proceede from the first entrance into learning, to the highest perfection required in the grammar schooles . . .. [2d ed]. London: Felix Kyngston for John Bellamie; reprint, under title (unpunctuated) through "schoole," Liverpool: Liverpool University Press, and London: Constable & Co., 1917. Ed., with intro. and bibliographical notes, by E. T. Campagnac; microfiche ed. of reprint, Gottlieb, Miller, and Page 1970-78, no. 11022.

Bristol, Roger P. 1970. Supplement to Charles Evans'[s] "American Bibliography." Charlottesville: University Press of Virginia, for Bibliographical Society of America and Bibliographical Society of University of Virginia.

Butts, R. Freeman. 1973. The education of the West: A formative chapter in the history of civilization. New York et al.: McGraw-Hill Book Co.

Canonical duty of bishops to maintain schools. 826. In Leach 1911, 21, 23.

Charlton, Kenneth. 1965. Education in Renaissance England. London: Routledge & Kegan Paul, and Toronto: University of Toronto Press.

Cheney, Edward Potts. [1904]. European background of American history, 1300-1600. [New York: Harper & Bros.]; reprint, Glucester, Mass.: Peter Smith, 1976.

Clare, M[artin]. 1758. Youth's introduction to trade and business. Containing . . . . 8th ed. London: For Fuller, Dod, Ward, Baldwin, Crowder, Davey and Law, and Woodgate. Preface, iv-vi, reprinted in chapter 3.

[Clarke, Henry]. 1793. Tabulae linguarum. Being a set of tables exhibiting the declensions of nouns and conjugations of verbs . . . Vol. 1. London: For the author. Appended announcement by H. and W. A. Clarke, [256-62], reprinted in chapter 9.

Clarke, W[illiam] A[ugustus]. 1801. Hymns, doctrinal and experimental, for the freeborn citizens of Zion, who know their election of God . . . . London: W. Justins.

Cohen, Sheldon S. 1974. A history of colonial education; 1607-1776. New York, London, Sydney, and Toronto: John Wiley & Sons.

Cohen, Sol, ed. 1974. Education in the United States: A documentary history. 5 vols. New York: Random House.

Cole, Arthur H. 1946. "An essay on the proper method for forming the man of business," 1716. Introduction, 1-11, followed by Watts 1716a. Boston: Baker Library, Harvard University Graduate School of Business Administration. Kress Library of Business and Economics, no. 4.

Colet, John. C. 1518a. Colet's articles of admission to St. Paul's School. In Sol Cohen 1974, 1:155-56.

_____. C. 1518b. Colet's statutes of St. Paul's School. In Sol Cohen 1974, 1:151-55.

Colgrave, Bertram, and R. A. B. Mynors, eds. 1969. Bede's ecclesiastical history. Oxford: Clarendon Press. A new translation, by Colgrave, of Bede [731], juxtaposing the English rendition, page by page, with the Latin text. With editors' introduction and notes. Oxford Medieval Texts, ed. V. H. Galbraith, Mynors, and C. N. L. Brooke.

The Columbia encyclopedia. 3d ed. 1963.

The Columbia-Viking desk encyclopedia. 2d ed. 1960. Used to supplement an incomplete copy of preceding source.

Coote, Edmund. 1596. The English schoole-maister. Teaching all his scholers, of what age soever, the most easie, short, and perfect order of distinct reading, and true writing our English tongue . . . . London: Widow Orwin for Ralph Jackson and Robert Dexter (or Dextar); reprint, as The English schoole-maister, 1596, Menston, England: Scolar Press, 1968. A Scolar Press Facsimile; microfiche ed. of reprint, Gottlieb, Miller, and Page 1970-78, no. 11307.

Council of 994 (?). 994?. In Leach 1911, 37.

Cremin, Lawrence A. 1970. American education: The colonial experience, 1607-1783. New York: Harper & Row Publishers, Harper Torchbooks ed.

_____. 1980. American education: The national experience, 1783-1876. New York: Harper & Row, Publishers.

The dictionary of national biography (D.n.b.). 1917. 22 vols. London: Geoffrey Cumberledge for Oxford University Press; reprints, in slightly revised format, 1921-22, 1937-38, 1949-50.

Dilworth, Thomas. 1768. The young book-keeper's assistant: Shewing him, in the most plain and easy manner, the Italian way of stating debtor and creditor . . .. 5th ed. London: H. Kent.

Dow, Louis A. 1983. An early proposal for a school of business. Alabama Business & Economics Journal 6 (January):17-24.

Drake, Francis S. 1872. Dictionary of American biography, including men [and women] of the time . . .. Boston: James R. Osgood and Co.

Duncan, William. 1795. The New-York directory and register, for the year 1795. Illustrated . . . New-York: T. and J. Swords for the author (or compiler); microprint, Shipton 1955-83, no. 28598.

Dunton, John. 1818. The life and errors of John Dunton, citizen of London . . .. 2 vols. [Ed. "J.B.N.," as prefatory "Memoir" is signed]; reprint, New York: Burt Franklin, 1969. Main body of work first published (presumably in London) by S. Malthus, 1705.

Eliot, Charles W. 1884. What is a liberal education?. Century Magazine 28 (June). In Early reform in higher education, ed. David N. Portman, 23-46. Chicago: Nelson-Hall Co., 1972. Professional Technical Series.

Elyot, Sir Thomas. 1531. Thomas Elyot on the education of a gentleman. In Sol Cohen 1974, 1:156-63.

Evans, Charles. 1903-55. The American bibliography of Charles Evans: A chronological dictionary of all books, pamphlets, and periodical publications printed in the United States from . . . 1639 . . . [through] 1800. 13 vols. [Chicago], vols. 1-12, and [Worcester, Mass.]: American Antiquarian Society, vol. 13; reprint, New York: Peter Smith, 1941-42, vols. 1-12, and [Gloucester, Mass.]: Peter Smith, 1962, vol. 13. The final volume was compiled by Clifford K. Shipton, who expanded the basic title from "American bibliography," and substituted "1800" for "1820" in recognition that Evans's planned scale of coverage required a second massive project, to be undertaken by Shaw and Shoemaker (1958-83).

Findeis, John, to Terry K. Sheldahl. 1988. May 11, in his office. Mathematics faculty, Armstrong State College, Savannah, Ga.

Fletcher, William Younger. 1902. English book collectors. Ed. Alfred Pollard (assumed to relate to original edition); reprint, New York: Burt Franklin, 1969. Bibliography and Reference Series, no. 209.

Fraser, Elspet. 1938. Some sources of Postlethwayt's Dictionary. Economic

History 3 (February):[25]-32. Emphasis supplied in title, per text.

Garraty, John A., and Peter Gay. 1972. _The Columbia history of the world_. New York: Harper & Row, Publishers; reprint, as _The university history of the world_, Poole, [England]: New Orchard Editions, 1985. Printed by Pitman Press, Bath.

Gilbert, Martin. 1968. _British history atlas_. Cartography by Arthur Banks. London: Weidenfeld and Nicolson; reprint, as _Atlas of British history_, [New York]: Dorset Press, div. of Marboro Books, 1985.

Gilbert, [Sir] Humphrey. C. 1570. Humphrey Gilbert's plan for Queen Elizabeth's Academy. In Sol Cohen 1974, 1:171-75.

Gillingham, John. 1984. The early Middle Ages (1066-1290). In Morgan 1984, 104-65.

Goldsmiths'-Kress Library of Economic Literature: A consolidated guide to segment 1 of the microfilm collection. 1976-87. 7 vols. Woodbridge, Conn. and (vols. 5-7 only) Reading, England: Research Publications.

Gordon, William. 1763. _The universal accountant and complete merchant_. In two volumes. Vol. 1 Edinburgh: For the author and A. Donaldson. Introductory essay, 1-17, reprinted in chapter 8.

Gottlieb, Jean S., Miller, Michael I., and Page, Joseph L., eds. 1970-78. _The Microbook Library of English Literature_. A microfiche collection, titles 10001-40193. Chicago: Library Resources Inc., an Encyclopedia Britannica Co. Original editor-in-chief was Herman C. Bernick.

Gras, N. S. B. 1928. An old-time type of merchant. _Bulletin of the Business Historical Society_ 2 (May):1-2.

Griffiths, Ralph A. 1984. _The later Middle Ages (1290-1485)_. In Morgan 1984, [166]-222.

Grun, Bernard. 1979 (renewal of 1975 copyright). _The timetables of history: A horizontal linkage of people and events_. New, updated ed. New York: Simon and Shuster; Touchstone Books ed., 1982. Based on _Kulturfahrplan_ by Werner Stein.

Guy, John. 1984. The Tudor age (1485-1603). In Morgan 1984, [223]-85.

Hall, Michael (text), and Ernest Frankl (photographs). 1982. _Cambridge_. Englewood Cliffs, N.J.: Prentice-Hall.

_____. 1983 (renewal of 1982 copyright). _Oxford_. 3d ed. Englewood-Cliffs, N.J.: Prentice-Hall.

Hans, Nicholas. 1951. _New trends in education in the eighteenth century_. London: Routledge & Kegan Paul. International Library of Sociology and Social Reconstruction, ed. W. J. H. Sprott (founded by Karl Mannheim).

_____. 1958. _Comparative education: A study of educational factors and traditions_. 3d ed. London: Routledge & Kegan Paul. Same series.

Harvie, Christopher. 1984. Revolution and the rule of law (1789-1851). In Morgan 1984, [419]-62.

Haskins, Charles Homer. 1927. The Renaissance of the Twelfth Century. Cambridge: Harvard University Press.

Heer, Friedrich. 1962. An open society. Selection from The medieval world by Heer, trans. Janet Sondheimer. [London]: Weidenfeld and (?) Nicholson. In Young 1969, 16-24.

Henry [VI], King of England and [ostensibly] France. 1440. Foundation charter [of Eton College] of 11 Oct. 1440. In Leach 1911, 405-11, odd nos. Part of "Foundations of Eton College, 1440-6," 405-15, odd nos.

[Herwood, Herman, ed]. 1938. The Herwood Library of Accountancy: A catalog of books printed between 1494 and 1900 in the Herwood Library . . . . New York: Herwood & Herwood; reprint, New York: Arno Press, 1980. Dimensions of Accounting Theory and Practice, ed. Richard P. Brief.

Holland, the Rev. Ellen, to Terry K. Sheldahl. 1988. March 25, by telephone. Interim Associate Pastor, First Presbyterian Church, Savannah, Ga.

Hollander, Stanley C. 1953. Malachy Postlethwayt's British Mercantile College, 1755. The Accounting Review 28 (July):434-38.

Hoyt, Robert S. 1966. Europe in the Middle Ages. 2d ed. New York, Chicago, San Francisco, and Atlanta: Harcourt, Brace & World.

Hutton, Charles. 1815. Philosophical and mathematical dictionary: . . . Mathematics, astronomy, and philosophy, both natural and experimental . . . . 2 vols. New ed. London: For the author and numerous booksellers.

Huxley, Thomas. 1874. Joseph Priestley. In Science and education, by Huxley, [9]-39. Introduction by Charles Winick. New York: Citadel Press, 1964. Science Classics Library, ed. Dagobert D. Runes and Thomas Kiernan.

Jackson, Kenneth T., ed., and James Truslow Adams, ed.-in-chief, orig. edition. 1978. Atlas of American history. Rev. ed. New York: Charles Scribner's Sons.

Johnson, E[dgar] A[ugustus] J[erome]. 1937. Predecessors of Adam Smith: The growth of British economic thought. London: P. S. King & Son, and Orchard House, Westminster, and New York: Prentice-Hall.

Junge, Ewald. 1984. World coin encyclopedia. New York: William Morrow and Co.

The jurisdiction of the grammar-schoolmaster, chancellor of Cambridge University, and archdeacon of Ely, defined. 1276. In Leach 1911, 203-9, odd nos.

Keep, Austin Baxter. 1909. The library in colonial New York; reprint, New York: Burt Franklin (Lenox Hill), 1970. Research & Source Works Series, no. 638.

Kobre, Sidney. 1944. The development of the colonial newspaper. [New York?: For the author (inferred from copyright page)]; reprint, Gloucester, Mass.: Peter Smith, 1960.

Koyre, Alexandre. 1965. Newtonian studies. [Cambridge: Harvard University Press]; reprint, Chicago: University of Chicago Press, Phoenix Books, 1968.

Landreth, Harry. 1976. History of economic theory: Scope, method, and content. Boston et al.: Houghton Mifflin Co.

Lang, Serge. 1964. A first course in calculus. Reading, Mass.: Addison-Wesley Publishing Co., and Don Mills, Ontario: Addison-Wesley (Canada).

Langer, William, comp. and ed. 1972. An encyclopedia of world history: Ancient, medieval, and modern, chronologically arranged. Boston: Houghton Mifflin Co.

Langford, Paul. 1984. The eighteenth century (1688-1789). In Morgan 1984, [352]-418.

The Lateran Council orders every cathedral to provide free schools for the clerks of the church and poor. 1179. In Leach 1911, 123.

Leach, Arthur F. 1915. The schools of medieval England. [London: Methuen & Co.]; reprint, New York: Barnes & Noble, and London: Methuen & Co., 1969.

Leach, Arthur F.[, ed]. 1911. Educational charters and documents, 598 to 1909. Cambridge: Cambridge University Press.

Leclercq, Jean. 1961. Monastic culture as a link with antiquity. Selections from The love of learning and the desire for God by Leclercq, trans. Catharine Misrahi. New York: Fordham University Press. In Young 1969, 41-50.

Lee, Patricia-Ann. 1970. Some English academies: An experiment in the education of Renaissance gentlemen. History of Education Quarterly 10 (Fall):273-85.

List of deaths for the year 1759. 1759. The Gentleman's Magazine. 29: 293-94.

Lobban, R. D. 1976. Doctors. London: B. T. Brasford. Past-into-Present series.

Locke, John. 1705. Some thoughts concerning education. 5th ed. London: For A. and J. Churchill; reprint, Axtel] 1968, [109]-325, editor's "Collation," 326-38.

Longworth, David. 1796. The New-York directory. In The American almanack, New-York register, and city directory, for the twenty-first year of American independence, containing most things useful for a work of this kind ..., by Longworth, [125]-332. New-York: T. and J. Swords for the author (or compiler), 1796; microprint, Shipton 1955-83, no. 30701.

Longworth, David. 1797. Longworth's American almanack, New-York register, and city directory, for the twenty-second year of American independence . . .. New-York: T. and J. Swords for the author; microprint, Shipton 1955-83, no. 32386.

_____. 1798. The New-York directory. In Longworth's American alma-nack, New-York register, and city directory, for the twenty-third year of American independence . . ., by Longworth, [87-305]. New-York: T. and J. Swords for the author ("publisher"), 1798; microprint, Shipton 1955-83, no. 34012.

_____. 1799. Longworth's New-York directory. In Longworth's American almanack, New-York register, and city directory, for the twenty-fourth year of American independence, by Longworth, [147]-396. New-York: John C. Totten and Co., 1799; microprint, Shipton 1955-83, no. 35740.

Lunt, W. E. 1957. History of England. 4th ed. New York, Evanston, [Ill.], and London: Harper & Row, Publishers. Harper's Historical Series, ed. Guy Stanton Ford.

Malynes, Gerard. 1656. Consuetudo, vel lex mercatoria, or the ancient law-merchant. London: William Hunt.

Martin, John. 1854. Bibliographical catalogue of privately printed books. 2d ed. [England]; reprint, New York: Burt Franklin, 1970. Bibliography and Reference Series, no. 357.

McConnell, James. 1985. English public schools. New York and London: W. E. Norton & Co.

McLachlan, H. 1931. English education under the Test Acts, being the his-tory of the non-conformist academies, 1662-1820. Manchester: Manchester University Press. Publications of the University of Manchester no. 113, Historical Series no. 59.

McMickle, Peter L., and Richard G. Vangermeersch. 1987. The Origins of a great profession. Memphis, Tenn.: Academy of Accounting Historians. Entry cited was contributed by R. Andrew Landrum.

Mepham, M[ichael] J[ames], to Terry K. Sheldahl. 1987. February 6. Dean, Faculty of Economic and Social Studies, Heriot-Watt University, Edinburgh. (On leave.)

Mepham, M[ichael] J[ames], and Williard E. Stone. 1977. John Mair, M.A.: Author of the first classic bookkeeping series. Accounting and Business Research. No. 26, Spring, 128-34.

Milns, William. 1794. Plan of instruction by private classes . . .. New-York: Samuel Loudon & Son; microprint, Shipton 1955-83, no. 47115. Reprinted in chapter 10.

_____. 1797a. The American accountant, or, a complete system of prac-tical arithmetic. Containing . . .. New-York: J. S. Mott for Milns; microprint, Shipton 1955-83, no. 32479.

Milns, William. 1797b. <u>The well-bred scholar, or practical essays on the best methods of improving the taste, and assisting the exertions of youth in their literary pursuits</u>. 2d ed. (unengraved). New-York: Literary Printing Office (namely, By the author); microprint, Shipton 1955-83, no. 32480.

_____. [1798]. <u>A set of round hand copies for the use of schools</u>. Boston: John West; microprint, Shipton 1955-83, no. 45781.

Milton, John. John Milton describes a complete education. 1644. In Sol Cohen 1974, 1:182-87. (From Milton's <u>Tractate on education</u>. 1673 edition reprinted in volume 3 of <u>The Harvard Classics</u>, ed. Charles W. Eliot, [233]-47. New York: P. F. Collier & Son, 1909, 1937.)

Morgan, Kenneth O., ed. 1984. <u>The Oxford illustrated history of England</u>. Oxford and New York: Oxford University Press. Paperback ed., 1986, 1987.

Morrah, Patrick. 1979. <u>Restoration England</u>. London: Constable.

Morrill, John. 1984. The Stuarts (1603-1688). In Morgan 1984, [286]-351.

Morris, Susan D., to Terry K. Sheldahl. 1987. March 23. Reference Department, University of Georgia Libraries.

_____. 1988. July 8, by telephone.

M[u]lcaster, Richard. 1581. <u>Positions: Wherein those primitive circ[u]mstances be examined, which are necessarie for the training [u]p of children, either for skill in their booke, or health in their bodies</u>. London: Thomas Vautrollier; reprint, as <u>Positions:</u>, New York: Longmans, Green, and Co., 1888. Biographical appendix by Robert Hebert Quick; microfiche ed. of reprint, Gottlieb, Miller, and Page 1970-78, no. 10543.

Munro, Dana Carleton. 1908. The Renaissance of the Twelfth Century. <u>Annual report of the American Historical Association for the year 1906</u>. In Young 1969, 6-9, in edited form as "A period of new life."

Murray, David. 1930. <u>Chapters in the history of bookkeeping, accountancy, & commercial arithmetic</u>. Glasgow: Jackson, Wylie & Co., for University of Glasgow; reprint, New York: Arno Press, 1978. The Development of Contemporary Accounting Thought, ed. Richard P. Brief. (Copy used was reproduced from from original edition by Duopage Process, in U.S.A.)

Note. 1968. In Coote 1596, reprint, opposite copyright page.

Noyes, James. 1797. <u>The federal arithmetic; or, a compendium of the most useful rules of that science adapted to the currency of the United States for the use of schools and private persons</u>. Exeter, [N.H.]: Henry Ranlet for the author; microprint, Shipton 1955-83, no. 32605.

Ollard, Richard. 1982. <u>An English education: A perspective of Eton</u>. London: Collins.

O'Malley, C. D. 1970a. Medical education during the Renaissance. In O'Malley 1970b, 89-102.

O'Malley, C. D., ed. 1970b. The history of medical education. Berkeley, Los Angeles, and London: University of California Press. UCLA Forum in Medical Sciences, no. 12.

Oxford curriculum in 1267. 1267 (from title). In Leach 1911, 191, 193, 195.

Park, Carolyn, to Terry K. Sheldahl. 1988. April 28, May 13. Collections Manager, Historical Society of Pennsylvania.

Perry, Lewis. 1984. Intellectual life in America. New York, London, Toronto, and Sydney: Franklin Watts.

Pollock, Thomas Clark. 1943. Introduction for Brinsley 1622, reprint, iii-viii; Bibliographical note, ix.

[Postlethwayt, Malachy], a merchant of London. [C. 1730]. The accomplish'd merchant. [London: By or for the author]. Reprinted in chapter 5.

Postlethwayt, Malachy. 1751. The merchant's public counting-house: or, New mercantile institution: Wherein is shown, the necessity of young merchants being bred to trade with greater advantages than they usually are . . . . [2d ed]. London: For John and Paul Knapton.

_____. 1751-55. The universal dictionary of trade and commerce . . . . 2 vols. London: For John and Paul Knapton. Selected entries reprinted in chapter 6, "The British Mercantile College," 2:218-36, in particular.

Poynter, F. N. L. 1970. Medical education in England since 1600. In O'Malley 1970b, 235-49.

Priestley, Joseph. [1803]. Lectures on history and general policy; To which is prefixed, an essay on a course of liberal education for civil and active life . . . . [Philadelphia]; reprint, vol. 24 of The theological and miscellaneous works of Joseph Priestley . . ., ed. [J. T. Rutt]. [London]: G. Smallfield, Hackney, [for Tegg, Milliken, and Griffen and Co., 1826]. "Prefixed" essay, [7]-25, reprinted in appendix 1.

Pryce-Jones, Janet, comp., and R[obert] H. Parker, annotation. 1976. Accounting in Scotland: A historical bibliography. 2d ed. Edinburgh: Institute of Chartered Accountants of Scotland; reprint, New York and London: Garland Publishing, 1984. Accounting History and the Development of a Profession, ed. Richard P. Brief.

Quick, Robert Hebert. 1888. Appendix. Richard Mulcaster. M[u]lcaster 1581, reprint, [299]-309.

The Random House dictionary of the English language. The unabridged edition. 1966.

Redlich, Fritz. 1970. The earliest English attempt at theoretical training for business: A bibliographical note. History of Political Economy 2 (Spring):[199]-204.

The refoundation of Canterbury Cathedral and Grammar School. 1541. In
    Sol Cohen 1974, 1:164.

Reigner, Charles B. [1958]. Beginnings of the business school. Baltimore
    Chicago: H. M. Rowe Company.

Richardson, H. G. 1941. Business training at medieval Oxford. The Amer-
    ican Historical Review 46 (January):259-80.

Rush, Benjamin. 1787. Thoughts upon female education, accommodated to the
    present state of society, manners and government, in the United States of
    America . . .. Philadelphia: Prichard & Hall; microprint, Shipton 1955-
    83, no. 20691.

Schools at the Council of Westminster. 1200. In Leach 1911, 139, 141.

Scott, Hew. 1920. Fasti Ecclesiae. The succession of ministers in the
    Church of Scotland from the Reformation. New ed. Vol. 3, Synod of
    Glasgow and Ayr. Edinburgh: Oliver and Boyd.

Seybolt, Robert Francis. 1925. Source studies in American colonial edu-
    cation: The private school. Urbana: University of Illinois. Bureau of
    Educational Research, College of Education, University of Illinois,
    Bulletin no. 28.

Shaw, Ralph R., and Richard H. Shoemaker, comps. 1958-83. American bibli-
    ography: A preliminary checklist, 1801 to 1819. 23 vols. New York
    (vols. [1-19]), or Metuchen, N.J. and London ([20-23]): Scarecrow Press.
    Vols. [1-19] supply the yearly listings, while nos. [20-23] include three
    index volumes. The final volume was prepared by Frances P. Newton.

Sheldahl, Terry K. 1985. America's earliest recorded text in accounting:
    Sarjeant's 1789 book. The Accounting Historians Journal 12 (Fall):1-42.

Sheldahl, Terry K, ed. 1988. Accounting literature in the United States
    before Mitchell and Jones (1796): Contributions by four British writers,
    in American editions, and two pioneer local authors. New York and London:
    Garland Publishing. Foundations of Accounting, ed. Richard P. Brief.

Shipton, Clifford K., ed. 1955-83. Early American Imprints. Series 1,
    1639-1800. Microprint collection, titles 1-49,197 (with occasional omis-
    sions). New York: Readex Microprint Corp., and Worcester, Mass.: Amer-
    ican Antiquarian Society. Includes reissue of titles. Production after
    1974 appears to have concerned correction and refinement.

Shipton, Clifford K., and James E. Mooney. 1969. National index of Ameri-
    can imprints through 1800: The short-title Evans. 2 vols. [Worcester,
    Mass.]: American Antiquarian Society, and [New York?]: Barre Publishers.

Sjoblom, Jorme, to Terry K. Sheldahl. 1988. May 23, by telephone. Refer-
    ence Librarian in Special Collections, University of Baltimore.

Southern, Richard W. 1961. Latin culture becomes widespread. Selection from The making of the Middle Ages by Southern. New Haven: Yale University Press. In Young 1969, 25-40.

_____. 1987. The change role of universities in medieval Europe. Historical Research 60 (June):[133]-46.

Starr, Edward C., ed. 1947-76. A Baptist bibliography: Being a register of books printed by and about Baptists, including works written against the Baptists. 25 vols. Philadelphia: Judson Press (vol. 1), and Rochester, N.Y.: American Baptist Historical Society (vol. 25).

Statutes of the Westminster School. 1560. In Sol Cohen 1974, 1:165-71.

Stephens, M. D., and G. W. Roderick. 1977. Education and the dissenting academies. History Today 27 (January):47-54.

Talbot, C. H. 1970. Medical Education in the Middle Ages. In O'Malley 1970b, 73-87.

[Thom, William]. 1762a. The defects of an university education, and its unsuitableness to a commercial people . . .. London: For E. Dilly. Reprinted in chapter 7.

_____. 1762b. A defence of the College of G--------w, against an insidious attempt to depreciate the ability and taste of its professors. [Glasgow: For James Duncan, Jr. (apparently)].

_____. 1762c. Remarks upon a pamphlet concerning the necessity of erecting an academy at Glasgow. In a letter to the authors. Glasgow: For James Duncan, Jr.

_____. 1762d. The scheme, for erecting an academy at Glasgow, set forth in its own proper colours. In a letter . . .. Glasgow: For James Duncan, Jr.

Thom, William. 1778. The revolt of the ten tribes. A sermon . . .. Glasgow: Robert Chapman and Alexander Duncan for James Duncan[, Jr].

_____. 1799. The works of the Rev. William Thom - late minister of Govan. Glasgow: For James Dymock.

Thomson, Hugh W. 1963. Bibliography: Books on accounting in English, 1543-1800. In Accounting in England and Scotland: 1543-1800, double entry in exposition and practice, by B[asil] S. Yamey, H[arold] C. Edey, and Thomson, 202-26. London: Sweet & Maxwell, 1963; reprint, New York and London: Garland Publishing, 1982. Accountancy in Transition, ed. Richard P. Brief.

Tompson, Richard S. 1971. The English grammar school curriculum in the 18th century: A reappraisal. British Journal of Educational Studies 19 (February):32-39.

University of London Library. 1970-83. Catalogue of the Goldsmiths'
Library of Economic Literature. 4 vols. Cambridge: Cambridge University
Press (vols. 1-2), and [London?]: Athlone Press (3-4).

[Walker, Obadiah]. 1673. Of education, especially of young gentlemen. In
two parts. [2d ed]. Oxford: at the Theater; reprint, as Of education,
1673, Menston, England: The Scolar Press, 1970. A Scolar Press Facsimile.

Watson, Foster. 1916. The old grammar schools. [Cambridge: Cambridge
University Press]; reprint, New York: August M. Kelley Publishers, 1969.
Reprints of Economic Classics.

Watts, Thomas. 1716a. An essay on the proper method for forming the man
of business; in a letter, &c. London: For Strahan, Taylor, Clements,
Nutt, and Morphew; microfilm, Woodbridge, Conn.: Research Publications,
n.d. Goldsmiths'-Kress Library of Economic Literature, segment 1, reel
313.

_____. 1716b. An essay on the proper method for forming the man of
business . . .. London: For Strahan, Taylor, Clements, Nutt, and Morphew; reprint, edited, in Cole 1946, [13]-28. Reprinted in chapter 2.

Webster, William. 1718. An attempt towards rendering the education of
youth more easy and effectual, especially with regard to their studies at
the writing-school. London: H. Heere for C. King, A. Bettesworth, and
J. Roberts; reprinted in Webster 1719, appendix.

_____. 1719. An essay on book-keeping, according to the true Italian
method of debtor and creditor, by double entry . . .. London: H. Meere
for C. King, A. Bettesworth, W. Means, and E. Symon.

_____. 1722. Arithmetic in epitome: or, A compendium of all its
rules, both vulgar and decimal. In two parts . . .. 3d ed. London:
Meere for King and Bettesworth.

_____. 1726. An essay on book-keeping . . .. 3d ed. London: For
King and Bettesworth. Component essay, [73]-88, reprinted in chapter 4.

_____. 1734. An essay on book-keeping . . .. Dublin: George Grierson.

_____. 1735. An essay on book-keeping . . .. 5th ed. London: For
Bettesworth, C. Hitch, and D. Brown.

Webster's new geographical dictionary. 1977. Springfield, Mass.: G. & C.
Merriam Co. "A Merriam-Webster."

Weedon, J. [1797]. A set of round hand copies. Boston: S[amuel] Hill
(also engraver); microprint, Shipton 1955-83, no. 33188.

Wells, M[urray] C. 1978. Accounting for common costs. [Urbana]: Board
of Trustees, University of Illinois. Center for International Education
and Research in Accounting, monograph no. 10.

[William of Wykeham]. 1382. Foundation deed of Winchester College. 20
October 1382. In Leach 1911, 321-29, odd nos.

Wilson, Charles. 1977. The British Isles. In An introduction to the sources of European economic history, 1500-1800, ed. Wilson and Geoffrey Parker, 115-54. Ithaca, N.Y.: Cornell University Press, 1977. World Economic History, ed. Wilson. Sec. 5.10, 142-51, contributed by Bruce Lenman.

Yamey, B[asil] S. 1963. A survey of books on accounting in English, 1543-1800. In Accounting in England and Scotland . . ., as cited above (Thomson 1963), 155-201.

Yntema, James, to Terry K. Sheldahl. 1988. May 23, by telephone. Operations Supervisor of Special Collections, University of Chicago Library.

Young, Charles R., ed. 1969. [New York]: Holt, Rinehart & Winston; reprint, Huntington, N.Y.: Robert E. Krieger Publishing Co., 1977.

Yount, Diana, to Terry K. Sheldahl. 1988. May 5, 10, latter by telephone. Associate Director, Franklin Trask Library, Andover Newton Theological School.